10

D0457119

The Germans, the Allies, the Partisans, and the Pope, September 1943–June 1944

ROBERT KATZ

THE BATTLE FOR ROME

SIMON & SCHUSTER

NEW YORK   LONDON   TORONTO   SYDNEY   SINGAPORE

SIMON & SCHUSTER
Rockefeller Center
1230 Avenue of the Americas
New York, NY 10020

For information about special discounts for bulk purchases,
please contact Simon & Schuster Special Sales at
1-800-456-6798 or business@simonandschuster.com

Maps copyright Jeff Ward

Designed by Karolina Harris

Manufactured in the United States of America

1   3   5   7   9   10   8   6   4   2

Library of Congress Cataloging-in-Publication Data
is available.

ISBN 0-7432-1642-3

To Beverly, once more, with love

Ed io a chi dedicarrò il mio Candelaio? A chi, o gran destino, ti piace ch'io intitoli il mio bel paranimfo, il mio bon corifeo? . . . A Sua Sanità? A Sua Maestà Cesarea? no. A Sua Serenità? no. A Sua Altezza, Signoria illustrissima e reverendissima? non, no. Per mia fé, non è prencipe o cardinale, re, imperadore o papa che mi levarrà questa candela di mano, in questo sollennissimo offertorio. A voi tocca, a voi si dona . . . voi, coltivatrice del campo dell'animo mio, [a voi] che, con acqua divina, che dal fonte del vostro spirto deriva, m'abbeveraste l'intelletto. . . . Però, qualunque sii il punto di questa sera ch'aspetto . . . godete, dunque, e, si possete, state sana, ed amate chi v'ama.*

— GIORDANO BRUNO, *CANDELAIO*, 1582

---

* To whom shall I dedicate my *Candelaio* [Candlemaker]? In whose name would it please you were I to present this play, by which I hope to procure his or her favors? To whom shall I give this candle of mine . . . ? To His Holiness? no. To His Imperial Majesty? no. To His Highness, the Seigniory of the most illustrious and most reverend lords? no, no, no. By my faith, no prince, no cardinal, king, emperor, or pope shall ever hold this candle in his hand. 'Tis yours alone, and upon you I do bestow it; you, who cultivate the gardens of my mind . . . you, from whence the celestial waters of the fountain of your spirit slake my thirst for truth. . . . So, whatever may be the worth of this evening's entertainment . . . enjoy this play of mine, and, if you can, stay well, and love, everlastingly, the one who loves you.

ACKNOWLEDGMENTS

I wish to thank the following people who contributed to the realization of this book in one way or another, and often in more ways than one: Anna Baldinotti, Greg Bradsher, Richard Breitman, Agostino Cardelli, Mauro Clementi, Saskia Cornes, Marika Cuccaro, Ian Drury, Vincenzo Frustaci, Wayne Furman, Annabella Gioia, Massimiliano Griner, David Hapgood, Antonino Intelisano, Alan Katz, Howard Katz, Jonathan Katz, Ninfa Colasanto Katz, Stephen Katz, Lutz Klinkhammer, Johanna Li, Gemma Luzzi, Susan Colgan Matson, Giuseppe Mogavero, Margaret Mushinski Ochs, Oscar Ochs, Massimo Palazzeschi, Antonio Parisella, Daniela Petracco, Michael Phayer, Augusto Pompeo, Alessandro Portelli, Alex Rosenberg, Carole Rosenberg, Margherita Ruggiero, Elvira Sabatini Paladini, Dario Scatolini, Francesco Sinatti, Michael Sissons, Judd Tully, Romina Zamponi, Annalisa Zanuttini, Susan Zuccotti.

I thank these institutions as well: Archivio Centrale dello Stato, Archivio di Stato di Roma, Archivio Storico Capitolino, Biblioteca della Camera dei Deputati, Biblioteca Nazionale Centrale Vittorio Emanuele II, Biblioteca di Storia Moderna e Contemporanea, Centro Documentazione of *Il Messaggero*, Istituto Romano per la Storia d'Italia dal Fascismo alla Resistenza, Museo Storico della Liberazione di Roma (all of the above in Rome), Biblioteca Comunale di Pergine Valdarno, the New York Public Library and the Frederick Lewis Allen Memorial Room, and the National Archives and Records Administration, Washington, D.C.

Peter Matson, my friend and agent since book one, had the idea for this one. Bob Bender at Simon & Schuster had the special fondness for the story that made the telling possible, and soon afterward, I discovered that same rare quality in Ion Trewin of Weidenfeld & Nicolson in the U.K. I would like to record an additional note of gratitude to all of them.

I also owe years of thank-yous to the two extraordinary men who played quite different but nonetheless major roles in the Rome of those days, and at war's end never stopped resisting tyranny and oppression. Both of them are flourishing even now in their ninth decade. I thank Rosario Bentivegna and Peter Tompkins. Finally, feeling certain that no future retelling of Rome's wartime ordeal can be complete without recollecting the remarkable exploits of Carla Capponi—she died while contributing to this book—I conclude these words of gratitude in remembrance of the life she led.

CONTENTS

SPRING

CAST OF CHARACTERS

THE OCCUPIERS

The SS

Lieutenant Colonel Herbert Kappler, brilliant sleuth–turned–chief of the Gestapo in Rome.

Polizeiführer General Karl Wolff, head of the SS in Italy.

Colonel Eugen Dollmann, Wolff's erudite protégé, roving liaison between the highest echelons of the SS (beginning with Himmler) and the Fascist hierarchy, the Roman aristocracy, and the Vatican.

Captain Erich Priebke, Kappler's closest aide, sometime second-in-command; police bureaucrat–turned–counterintelligence torturer.

Captain Theodor Dannecker, "Jewish expert," on a mission from Berlin.

Major Hellmuth Dobbrick, martinet police battalion commander who refused to obey an order said to be the will of the Führer himself.

The Wehrmacht

Field Marshal Albert Kesselring, Supreme Commander, southern front, known as "Smiling Albert."

General Rainer Stahel, razor-blade salesman–turned–Commandant of Rome.

Lieutenant General Kurt Mälzer, Stahel's successor, gourmand, alcoholic, self-styled "King of Rome."

General Eberhard von Mackensen, Commander, Fourteenth Army, scion of a Prussian family of the military elite.

The Diplomats

Baron Ernst von Weizsäcker, German Ambassador to the Holy See, a former second-in-command in the Foreign Office, new to Rome, with a secret, unauthorized peace plan of his own.

Albrecht von Kessel, Weizsäcker's closest aide, a vocal anti-Nazi in the private salons of friends.

Consul Eitel Friedrich Möllhausen, acting head of the German embassy in Rome, the youngest chief of a Nazi diplomatic mission, a nonmember of the Nazi Party, with a penchant for aiding Jews.

Gerhard Gumprecht, middle-ranking diplomat in an apolitical post, destined to a historic role in averting a crisis in German-Vatican relations.

THE FASCISTS

Pietro Caruso, Questore (Rome's Chief of Police), a bungler and a lout who rightly feared retribution.

Pietro Koch, head of the Special Police Unit (the Koch Gang), ex–Italian army officer of German origin. The twenty-five-year-old self-proclaimed "doctor" and adventurer formed and led an anti-Partisan police formation that rivaled the Gestapo in truth-through-torture techniques.

Franco Argentino (also known as Walter Di Franco), a mercenary double-agent, with links to the American OSS but who had cast his lot with the more-to-his-liking Koch Gang.

Guido Buffarini-Guidi, Minister of Interior, the "most hated man in Italy," according to the Duce, "even more hated than me."

THE VATICAN

Pope Pius XII, Roman-born Eugenio Pacelli.

Cardinal Luigi Maglione, Secretary of State, believed by the OSS to be the Vatican's only high-level pro-American.

Monsignor Giovanni Battista Montini, Undersecretary for Ordinary Affairs and the future Pope Paul VI.

Monsignor Domenico Tardini, Undersecretary for Extraordinary Affairs.

Monsignor Alberto Giovannetti, an official in the Secretariat of State.

Father Pankratius Pfeiffer (Padre Pancrazio), Abbot-General of the Order of Salvatorians and Pius's liaison to the German occupiers; a Bavarian with boyhood memories shared by several of the chiefs of the occupation.

Bishop Alois Hudal, pro-Nazi rector of the German church of Rome and sometime papal emissary to the occupiers. Too pro-Nazi to be accepted in the Vatican's inner circles, but a useful intermediary on occasion.

Monsignor Mario Nasalli Rocca, Pius's liaison to Regina Coeli prison.

Count Giuseppe Dalla Torre, director and chief editor of the Vatican newspaper *L'Osservatore Romano*; he wrote what the Holy Father thought—but not at one of the most crucial moments of the period.

THE ROMAN RESISTANCE

THE PARTISANS OF GAP CENTRAL
(PATRIOTIC ACTION GROUPS — GAPPISTI)

Rosario "Sasà" Bentivegna (code-named Paolo), 22, medical student.

Carla Capponi (Elena), 25, chemical laboratory worker.

Marisa Musu (Rosa), 19, university student in chemistry.

Mario Fiorentini (Giovanni), 25, university student in mathematics.

Lucia Ottobrini (Maria), 20, government clerk (wife of Giovanni).

Carlo Salinari (Spartaco), assistant professor of literature, Commander of Gap Central.

Franco Calamandrei (Cola), law school graduate, Vice Commander of Gap Central.

Pasquale Balsamo (Pasquale), university student.

Maria Teresa Regard (Piera), 20, journalist.

Duilio Grigioni (Duilio), old-time anarchist, concierge of the apartment building that harbored Gappisti in a secret part of its basement.

Raoul Falcioni (Raoul), Roman taxi driver, twice the age of most of the others, but no less audacious.

Guglielmo Blasi (Guglielmo), idealized and somewhat idolized true member of the working class, but not as true as thought.

THE MILITARY COUNCIL OF THE CLN
(NATIONAL LIBERATION COMMITTEE)

Riccardo Bauer, representing the Action Party.

Sandro Pertini, representing the Socialist Party; future President of Italy.

Giuliano Vassalli, Pertini's deputy and Matteotti Brigade commander.

Giorgio Amendola, representing the Communist Party; son of a nationally famous early opponent of Mussolini, the Liberal Party's Giovanni Amendola.

Ivanoe Bonomi, head of the CLN, a pre-Mussolini prime minister; master politician and rare survivor of the regime, with his anti-Fascist, democratic credentials uncompromised.

THE CLANDESTINE MILITARY FRONT (PRO-MONARCHIST)

Colonel Giuseppe Cordero Lanza di Montezemolo, a patriot and royalist seeking accord with the CLN.

General Simone Simoni, another authentic patriot in an organization filled with opportunists.

Lieutenant Colonel Giovanni Frignani, the captain who physically arrested Mussolini on orders from the King.

THE ALLIES

General Harold Alexander, Deputy Allied Commander, Mediterranean Theater.

Lieutenant General Mark Wayne Clark, Commander, United States Fifth Army, Eisenhower's choice to be the first warrior since the sixth-century Byzantine general Belisarius to succeed where Hannibal failed: in effecting the conquest of Rome from the south—a mission-turned-obsession for Clark.

Major General Geoffrey T. Keyes, Commander, II Corps, Fifth Army.

Major General John P. Lucas, Commander, VI Corps, Fifth Army, leader of the invasion at Anzio, where his long career as a sound but cautious commander ended in bitterness and acrimony.

Major General Lucian K. Truscott, General Lucas's replacement.

Brigadier General Robert T. Frederick, Commander, First Special Service Force, the creator of America's first elite corps, the U.S.-Canadian Take No Prisoners "Devil's Brigade."

Harold H. Tittmann, Jr., United States Chargé d'Affaires to the Holy See.

Sir D'Arcy Osborne, British Minister to the Holy See.

General William "Wild Bill" Donovan, founder of America's first intelligence agency, the Office of Strategic Services (OSS), forerunner of the CIA.

THE OSS SPIES IN ROME

Peter Tompkins, twenty-four-year-old American intelligence agent and Chief of the mission in Rome, operating in the guise of a Fascist aristocrat; handpicked by Donovan.

Maurizio Giglio (Cervo), Allied double agent—serving as a lieutenant in the Rome police and secretly running the OSS's Radio Vittoria, a valuable intelligence link between Peter Tompkins and the Fifth Army.

Franco Malfatti, head of the Socialist Party's information service, the "eyes and ears" of Tompkins's spy network—a vast array of volunteers gathering intelligence from every corner of Rome and the nearby countryside.

Captain André Bourgoin, a French national and former intelligence agent of the Deuxième Bureau, now working for the OSS, running agents with dubious credentials.

Clemente Menicanti (Coniglio), ex–Fascist military intelligence agent recruited by Captain Bourgoin, a ruthless rival of Tompkins with his own political agenda.

Enrico Sorrentino, another OSS-recruited Italian intelligence operative, who pitted himself against both Menicanti and Tompkins.

Arrigo Paladini, an Italian OSS agent who like Giglio and Malfatti sided with Tompkins.

THE ROMANS

THE JEWISH COMMUNITY

Ugo Foà, President of the Rome community, World War I hero, President of the veterans organization and a judge appointed by the Fascist regime, but like all Jews ostracized professionally and socially under the 1938 anti-Jewish legislation.

Dante Almansi, President of the national Union of Italian Jewish Communities and Mussolini's Vice Chief of the national police until the Fascist turnabout against Jews.

Israel Zolli, Rome's Chief Rabbi, a naturalized Italian from the pale of eastern European Jewry, born in 1881, the year of the great pogroms, who had the terror of imminent doom in his blood.

Renzo Levi, President of DELASEM, an organization that assisted Italian Jews emigrating from Fascist Italy either by choice or by expulsion.

Settimio Sorani, DELASEM's chief executive, the Roman Jew most knowledgeable (along with Levi) about the details of the ongoing Holocaust—considered preposterous by Foà and Almansi.

Settimia Spizzichino, born in the Roman ghetto, the only woman to survive the mass roundup and deportation to Auschwitz of the Jews of Rome.

THE DIARISTS

Mother Mary Saint Luke ("Jane Scrivener"), well-placed and remarkably astute American nun working in the Vatican Information Bureau. Her true identity remained undisclosed until 1981.

M. de Wyss, Swiss journalist and long-time correspondent in Rome with a wide range of sources.

Carlo Trabucco, Roman journalist, of the anti-Fascist political center, unemployable but hardly idle.

THE ARISTOCRATS

Princess Enza Pignatelli Aragona Cortes, whose years of friendship with the Pope prepared her for a unique role as a messenger of hope.

Marchesa Fulvia Ripa di Meana, also a long-term friend of the Pope, who enlisted him to her one-woman battle to rescue her cousin, the Resistance leader Montezemolo, from the torture chamber of the Gestapo.

Princess Virginia Agnelli, glittering eminence behind the most secret papal audience of the occupation.

MAPS

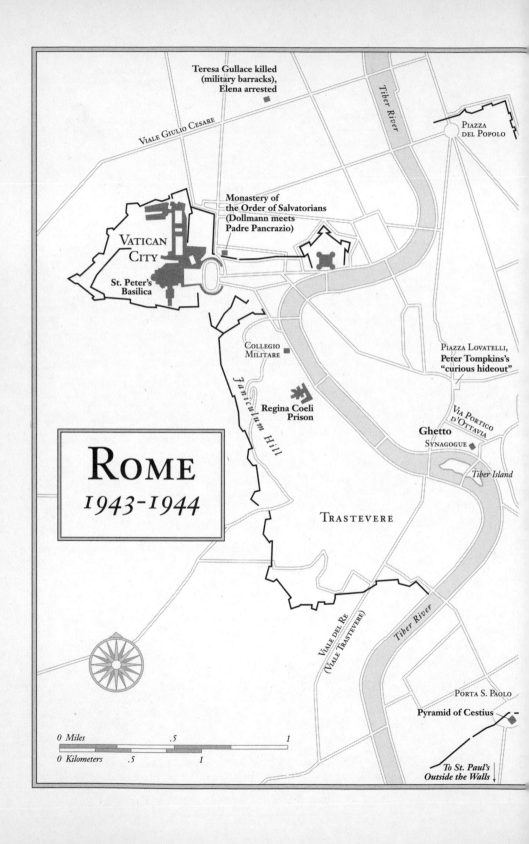

Teresa Gullace killed
(military barracks),
Elena arrested

VIALE GIULIO CESARE

Tiber River

PIAZZA
DEL POPOLO

Monastery of
the Order of Salvatorians
(Dollmann meets
Padre Pancrazio)

VATICAN
CITY

St. Peter's
Basilica

COLLEGIO
MILITARE

PIAZZA LOVATELLI,
Peter Tompkins's
"curious hideout"

Janiculum Hill

Regina Coeli
Prison

VIA PORTICO
D'OTTAVIA

Ghetto
SYNAGOGUE

Tiber Island

ROME
1943-1944

TRASTEVERE

VIALE DEL RE
(VIALE TRASTEVERE)

Tiber River

PORTA S. PAOLO

Pyramid of Cestius

*To St. Paul's
Outside the Walls* ↓

0 Miles   .5   1

0 Kilometers   .5   1

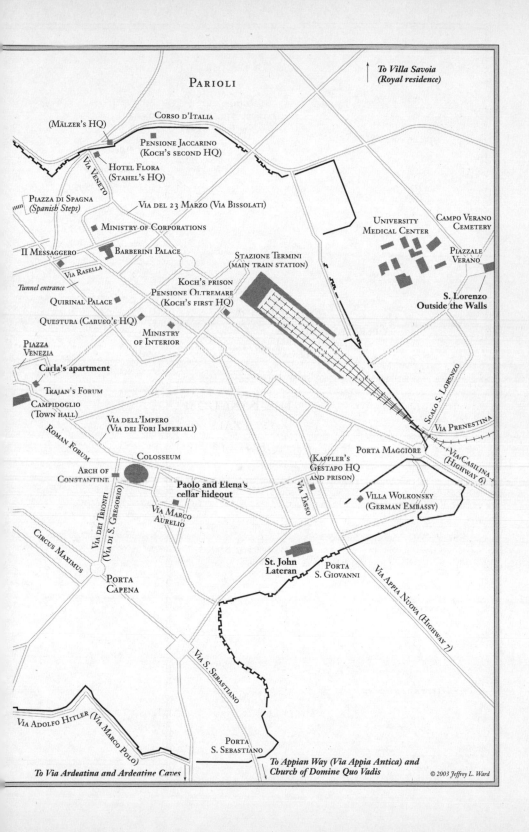

PARIOLI

To *Villa Savoia*
(Royal residence)

Corso d'Italia

(Mälzer's HQ)

Pensione Jaccarino
(Koch's second HQ)

Via Veneto

Hotel Flora
(Stahel's HQ)

University
Medical Center

Campo Verano
Cemetery

Piazza di Spagna
(Spanish Steps)

Via del 23 Marzo (Via Bissolati)

Ministry of Corporations

Piazzale
Verano

Il Messaggero

Barberini Palace

Stazione Termini
(main train station)

S. Lorenzo
Outside the Walls

Via Rasella

Koch's prison
Pensione Oltremare
(Koch's first HQ)

Tunnel entrance

Quirinal Palace

Questura (Caruso's HQ)

Ministry
of Interior

Scalo S. Lorenzo

Piazza
Venezia

Carla's apartment

Via Prenestina

Trajan's Forum

Via Casilina
(Highway 6)

Campidoglio
(Town hall)

Via dell'Impero
(Via dei Fori Imperiali)

Porta Maggiore

Roman Forum

Colosseum

(Kappler's
Gestapo HQ
and prison)

Arch of
Constantine

**Paolo and Elena's
cellar hideout**

Via Tasso

Villa Wolkonsky
(German Embassy)

Via Marco
Aurelio

Via dei Trionfi
(Via di S. Gregorio)

Circus Maximus

St. John
Lateran

Porta
S. Giovanni

Via Appia Nuova (Highway 7)

Porta
Capena

Via S. Sebastiano

Via Adolfo Hitler (Via Marco Polo)

Porta
S. Sebastiano

To Via Ardeatina and Ardeatine Caves

*To Appian Way (Via Appia Antica) and
Church of Domine Quo Vadis*

© 2003 Jeffrey L. Ward

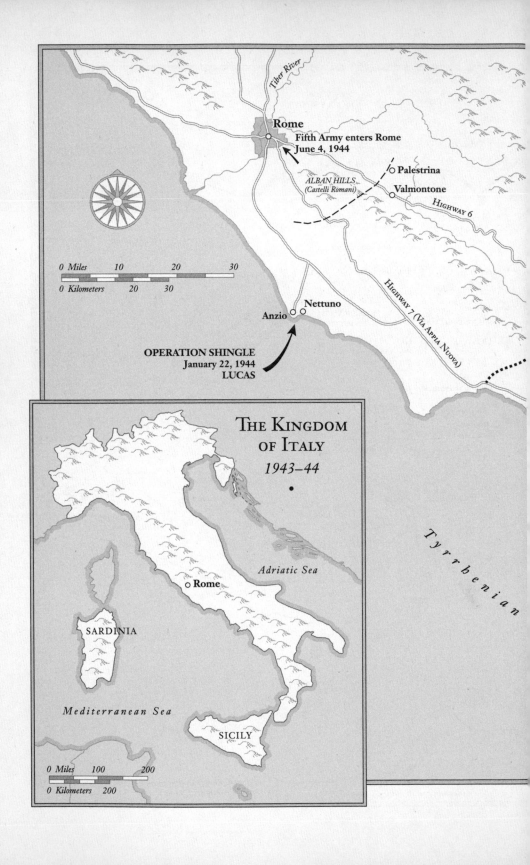

Tiber River

Rome
Fifth Army enters Rome
June 4, 1944

○ **Palestrina**

ALBAN HILLS
(Castelli Romani)

Valmontone

Highway 6

Anzio ○ ○ **Nettuno**

OPERATION SHINGLE
January 22, 1944
LUCAS

Highway 7 (Via Appia Nuova)

0 *Miles*   10   20   30
0 *Kilometers*   20   30

THE KINGDOM
OF ITALY
1943–44

Adriatic Sea

○ **Rome**

Tyrrhenian

SARDINIA

Mediterranean Sea

SICILY

0 *Miles*   100   200
0 *Kilometers*   200

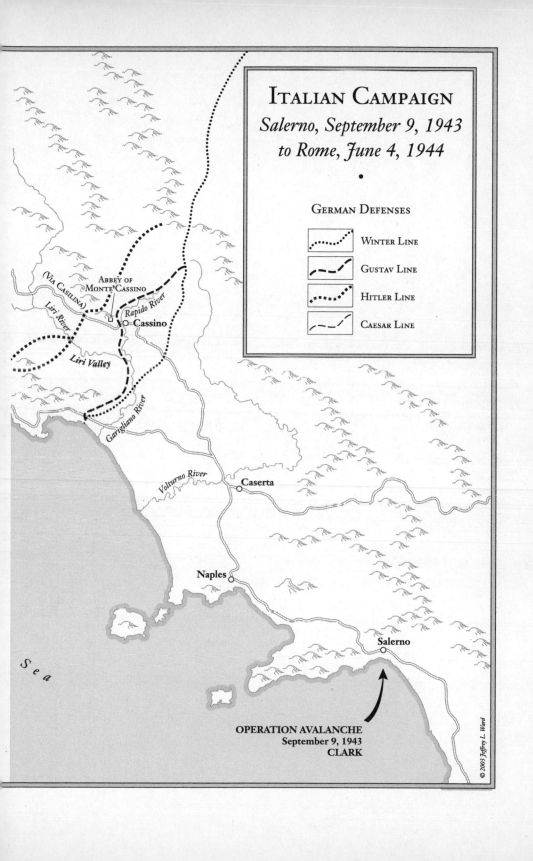

ITALIAN CAMPAIGN

Salerno, September 9, 1943
to Rome, June 4, 1944

•

GERMAN DEFENSES

Winter Line

Gustav Line

Hitler Line

Caesar Line

(Via Casilina)

ABBEY OF
MONTE CASSINO

Rapido River

Liri River

Cassino

Liri Valley

Garigliano River

Volturno River

Caserta

Naples

Salerno

S e a

OPERATION AVALANCHE
September 9, 1943
CLARK

© 2003 Jeffrey L. Ward

PREFACE:
OPEN CITY

To describe the emotions of the mind and the crowd of ideas that arise on entering this "mistress of the world" is impossible. All is confusion and agitation. The eye moves rapidly from side to side, eager to grasp every object, but continually diverted by some new scene; all is wonder.

— *Washington Irving, who arrived in Rome in 1805*

ROME today is centuries of history piled one atop another. Move about this eternal city, as they call it, and like it or not you roil the dust of time. Turn any corner, catch a play of amber light, listen not to the din that surrounds you but to what the stones have to say, and you've opened the pages of a robust tale.

On a shining spring day while writing this book, I walked down the Via Rasella. It is a short, narrow, and, considering how central it is, relatively quiet street. It descends from the Barberini Palace on a slope of the Quirinal, one of the seven hills of classical Rome. As an icon of a singular event of the 270-day German occupation of Rome during World War II, the Via Rasella has haunted three generations of Romans and has helped shape the very character of the present-day city. "When people hear me say that I live on Via Rasella," someone nearing sixty who is a lifelong resident said recently, ". . . they hear 'Via Rasella' and they say, 'Oh, where that thing happened . . .' 'What thing?' I say—I make *them* say it first. 'You mean you live there and you don't know what happened?' they say. 'Oh, I know, all right,' I say, 'and where do you think my father is?' "[1] The "thing" that happened in Via Rasella was an attack of unprecedented proportions carried out by the Roman Resistance against the occupation forces. It was a clash that led to

Rome's Ardeatine Caves massacre, a pivotal episode in World War II in
Italy. The Via Rasella is the place where the disparate worlds of nearly all the
characters in this story collide.

I know the Via Rasella probably as well as any visitor, but I was drawn there
again that day. I wanted to visit the street as one might call on an aging, lifelong friend. I feared it had suffered physically in all the refurbishing that took
place prior to the Holy Year 2000. Rome, behind a seemingly endless screen
of scaffolding, had scrubbed itself to the bone in preparation, sandblasting
into oblivion the grime, in some cases, of two thousand years, bathing its incomparable beauty in a sea of sienna and ocher paint. It looked stunning when
it came out for the Jubilee, but by now Romans were beginning to miss not
the grime but the truth-telling texture of plain old wear and tear.

Decades earlier, I had written of the signs that were still visible twenty
years after the Via Rasella attack—mostly bullet-riddled building facades.
There were ugly pockmarks in the stucco, with no commemorative plaque
or other indication of how they got there. That only added to the mystique
when you discovered what they were and understood what they represented. Now well over a half-century had gone by, and though I had seen
those bullet holes many times in the interim, I wondered how they had fared
in the big spruce-up.

The nature of the street had changed considerably, even in my time. As
Italy had grown to become one of the world's leading economic powers, Via
Rasella, like all of Rome's *centro storico*, or "historic center," had gentrified.
What used to be a block that housed families rich and poor, aristocrats
shoulder to shoulder with the *popolani*, had become well-to-do, single, professional, chic. The first difference that caught my eye were the computer-
generated notices slapped on the walls. "The residents of Via Rasella," the
signs proclaimed with rather charmless sarcasm, "thank their kind dog owners for the expressions of thoughtfulness they leave on the street every day."
The walls themselves were freshly painted and I despaired. But farther down
the street, where the Via del Boccaccio intersects, a building that had escaped the ubiquitous makeover displayed the very same spray of bullet holes
that I had first noticed so long before. Some days later I learned that permission for the owners of that building and others to fill and cover the holes had
been denied by the Belle Arti, the fine-arts authority that looks after the per-
manence of the nation's historical treasures. Some owners cheated, I know,
just as some Romans have long sought to still the voice of the Via Rasella,
but on a few buildings that violence frozen in time was undisturbed. I was reassured. Ghosts never sleep.

I T W A S the boldest and largest Resistance assault, unequaled by the Partisan movements in any other of the German-occupied European capitals. At 3:45 on the afternoon of March 23, 1944, a heavily armed column of 156 SS police marching through Rome was attacked in the Via Rasella by ten Partisans, nine men and one woman, most of them students in their twenties. The target, the 11th Company of the 3rd Bozen SS Battalion, was a new, anti-Partisan police formation. The Partisan strike force was made up of members of the central unit of GAP (Gruppi di Azione Patriottica, "Patriotic Action Groups"), the military arm of the clandestine Communist Party.

As the police column proceeded up the street, one of the Partisans, in the guise of a municipal street cleaner, lit the fuse of a homemade bomb concealed in his trash can and walked away. Some fifty seconds later, twenty-four men were blown apart in an earthshaking explosion. Other Partisans engaged the dazed rear guard with grenades and gunfire, and as nine more SS men, and two hapless civilians, lay dead or dying, they disappeared into the hideaways of the Roman underground.

Notified at his headquarters in East Prussia within minutes of the attack, Hitler shrieked for revenge, demanding a reprisal that would "make the world tremble."[2] His bile alone set in motion a hastily assembled killing machine in Rome that would overcome even internal opposition from the occupiers themselves. The next day, 335 men and teenaged boys—a near-perfect cross section of the male half of Rome, not one of them even remotely connected to the attack—were seized from various parts of the city, trucked to an abandoned labyrinth of caves in Via Ardeatina, near the Christian catacombs of ancient Rome, and slain in groups of five. It was the first wartime atrocity and one of the worst perpetrated on Italian soil.

The Via Rasella attack had been timed to coincide with twenty-fifth anniversary celebrations of the founding of Fascism to signal that the end of the long nightmare was near. It was designed to represent a dramatic escalation of the Partisan movement's battle for Rome and to galvanize the population for a general uprising. But other powers in Rome had differing designs on the Eternal City. The Resistance was the bane not only of the occupiers but also of the Vatican and to some extent the Allies. None of them, like the Resistance itself, was free of dissension and intrigue. No one, with few exceptions, wished to harm Rome. Good intentions, to repeat the proverb, paved this hell.

The dramatic story of Rome under the German occupation (September 8, 1943–June 4, 1944) remains largely untold, particularly outside of Italy. No English-language work on the subject has appeared in the last twenty years, leaving untapped a wealth of significant primary material that has since become available. Between 2000 and 2002 the CIA released the so-called crown jewels of America's wartime intelligence—hundreds of thousands of long-classified documents of its predecessor agency, the Office of Strategic Services (OSS). The declassified diplomatic papers of the Vatican archives relating specifically to the occupation of Rome have barely been skimmed, likewise those of the Italian archives; similarly under-reported—and entirely unpublished—is the mass of material generated in the mid-90s by the two Rome trials of former SS officer Erich Priebke, as well as documents from trials in the late 70s and 80s, including my own.[3] Thus, earlier books about the occupation did not have the benefit of the now nearly complete and nuanced big picture.

Consider that big picture.

On the evening of September 8, 1943, General Dwight D. Eisenhower, Supreme Commander of the Allied forces in the Mediterranean, went on the air and stunned the world, and Rome most of all, by announcing the signed capitulation of Italy—the first of the Axis powers to surrender unconditionally. What happened over the next few hours still astonishes more than half a century later:

- *For the Allies:* Timed to Eisenhower's announcement was the launch of World War II's first full-scale invasion of the European mainland. Landings on the shores of Salerno, south of Naples—and later Anzio—initiated Churchill's "soft-underbelly" strategy of penetrating what would prove to be an imaginary weakness in Hitler's "Fortress Europe." They would lead to one of the bloodiest military campaigns in U.S. history, not to speak of the devastation of Italy.

- *For the Germans:* Hitler regarded the Italian defection—which had followed the arrest of Mussolini some weeks earlier—as an act of treachery that had to be punished draconically. His Supreme Commander in the south, Field Marshal Albert Kesselring, was momentarily caught off guard, however, by the September 8 surrender, and began a tactical retreat from the capital. But when Kesselring learned that the Allied landings, which he had expected to take place just north of Rome, were actually happening 160 miles to the south, he made a lightning-quick decision to turn back and seize Rome. His task was greatly facilitated by one of the most craven acts in Italian history, the predawn flight from the capital by the King and his new government, abandoning the city and leaving no one in charge. Courageous but ragtag opposition to Kesselring's onslaught by the disoriented Italian army and some civilians was quickly crushed, leaving the Germans as the masters of Rome. But at the same time this opposition breathed life into a strategy whose time had come: armed resistance.

- *For the Vatican:* Vatican City was ringed with Wehrmacht troops, its lifeline to the outside world dependent on Hitler's whim (part of which included a threat to kidnap the Pope). Until now Pope Pius XII had labored assiduously to be seen by both the Western Allies and Germany as an authentic neutral. In this way he hoped to spare Rome from the havoc of war and to play a decisive role as a peacemaker. He was convinced that Stalin's Russia was a greater evil than Hitler's Germany, and he had been hoping to broker a general rapprochement between the Western Allies and Germany to contain if not roll back godless Communism. Moreover, that strategy of "neutrality" lay behind his already controversial policy of silence in the face of the Holocaust. Now, in occupied Rome, the most crucial test of that silence was at hand. He had not protested the distant slaughter of Europe's Jews, but should the Nazis lay the terror at his front door, could he still ignore it?
- *For the Italians:* An ignoble war fought abroad that was nominally over was now about to come home with a vengeance. Rome would awake that morning of the first day to find itself a prisoner of the Third Reich. Yet the Allies were heading its way, and the vision of Rome as eternal, somehow shielded from the "excesses" the Germans had visited upon the other cities of Europe, seemed intact. Before long, however, that vision would shatter.

In the days leading up to Italy's surrender, the government that had deposed Mussolini had declared Rome an "Open City"—a demilitarized zone—thus hoping by this measure to preserve its countless wonders from the ruins of war. Reaffirmed but not respected by the German occupiers or the Allies, this Open City proclamation would from the outset be a sham. In a matter of weeks Rome would become a mockery of an open city, a city whose walls would shake under the roar of German military traffic to the front and the thunder of Allied bombs. It would swell to nearly twice its usual size, hosting, but ever more frugally, a million refugees from the countryside. Rome would be a city of spies, double agents, informers, torturers, fugitives, hunted Jews, and hungry people.

A resistance movement would arise in this atmosphere, only to become sundered by internal crises. The six anti-Fascist parties in Rome, awakened from a forced hibernation of twenty years, would form a timid, clandestine union, but only the new generation of young men and women, the Partisans, would prove capable of striking militarily against the German occupiers. They would create an armed, insurrectional threat within Rome, hoping to discourage the Germans from attempting to hold the city. The overriding danger—indeed, Hitler's plan should the Allies try to take Rome—was a fierce engagement in street-by-street combat. For a city with its nerves worn thin and desperately short on food, such warfare would bring calamity, ruin, and a tremendous loss of civilian lives. It could even mean the destruction of everything treasured and beautiful about Rome.

This Open City was thus a tinderbox of four conflicting parties, each incompatible with the others: the Allies, trying to capture Rome as their first shining prize of war but discovering impregnable opposition instead; the Germans, trying to throw the intruders back into the sea, holding Rome hostage and using it rapaciously as a staging ground and a supply line to the front; the Pope, trying to bring the West and the Germans to terms to save the world from "Communism" and to save Rome and Vatican City from physical destruction; and, finally, the Partisans, trying to redeem Italy's honor by making Rome untenable for the occupiers.

What a change this was from the start of that summer of 1943.

SUMMER

BIMONTHLY REPORT (MAY–JUNE) OF THE QUESTORE (POLICE CHIEF)
OF ROME, JUNE 28, 1943

ACTIVITIES OF THE CLERGY AND CATHOLIC ORGANIZATIONS. The clergy continues to
maintain an attitude of cooperation with the Government . . . praying for the triumph of
the Italian armed forces and Christianity. Nevertheless, there are a few [priests] who have
made inappropriate comments . . . a certain orientation aimed at forming a so-called
Christian-Communist party has been noted. Adherents of the movement have been
detained and an investigation is under way. . . .

ACTIVITIES OF JEWS AND EFFECTS OF THE RACIAL LAWS. The Jews have apparently
abstained from politically suspect activities. Nevertheless, within their circles a conviction
is continuously gaining ground that the Axis powers cannot win the war and that with the
victory of the Anglo-Saxon armies the Jews will reacquire their lost rights. . . .

ACTIVITIES OF SUBVERSIVES AND ANTI-FASCISTS. During the period under review, police
measures have been adopted against [102] persons responsible for offending the DUCE,
subversive activity, suspicion of espionage, profiteering, incitement, defeatism and other
behavior out of step with the present political moment. . . .

PUBLIC MORALE IN RELATION TO THE PRESENT SITUATION. The morale of the people in the course of these two months has remained quite low. The unfortunate outcome of the Tunisian campaign, as expected, profoundly upset the spirit of the populace, and no one hides concern for the grave peril that threatens the very soil of the Patria. [*Dorer:21*]

The news reported in the press and on the radio yesterday evening that Rome has been declared an open city has evoked expressions of enthusiasm among the citizenry. At the Savoia Theater in Via Bergamo, where a performance of the opera *Madama Butterfly* was in progress, the news was given by an unidentified person in the audience, who held up a newspaper, eliciting a jubilant response throughout the auditorium. Some spectators in the front rows went up on the stage to celebrate the event with the performers, while others, who mistook its meaning, cried long live peace. The orchestra at the request of the audience played the first part of the Royal March. The performance then continued where it had left off.—*Telegram dispatched by the Questore of Rome, August 15, 1943 [Dorer: 103]*

ONE

TWENTY ANGELS OVER ROME

Rosario Bentivegna, nicknamed Sasà (pronounced saZAH), was a twenty-one-year-old third-year medical student, that summer of 1943. On the hot, sticky morning of July 19, he had just completed an all-night tour of duty in the outpatient clinic of the university hospital and was crossing the courtyard, heading for his bicycle, when the air-raid sirens began to wail.

Like most Romans, he paid them little heed. Although Fascist Italy had been at war alongside Hitler's Germany for the past three years, this was still Rome, the pride of civilization. Other great cities and much of the rest of Europe lay in shambles, millions dead, but Rome remained in all its splendor, its best (and virtually only) air defense the spiritual and physical presence of the Pope. Here in the Holy Father's long shadow, the sirens had had but one practical meaning: enemy aircraft were passing overhead, making for less-favored regions far away. Somewhere, bombs would fall soon enough; distant, unfortunate people would die, but Sasà was on his way to a rendezvous with his latest girlfriend, a young Austrian actress whom he had met at fencing practice. He had one foot on the pedal of his bike when the first "stick"—eight 500-pound bombs—fell from *Lucky Lady*, the American B-17 leading a mighty armada of Flying Fortresses and B-24 Liberators that were blackening the skies of Rome. The bomb bays were opening not "somewhere" but directly overhead.

Until now, Sasà had led a charmed life. Born in Rome, he was from a propertied, upper-middle-class family—part of which had fought with

Garibaldi in Risorgimento times and part with his great nemesis, Pius IX, the last pope to rule an earthly realm, the sovereign Papal States of central Italy. As a student of medicine, Sasà had been exempt from military service until the past February, and after only three months of service in the medical corps in Rome, he was given the choice of continuing his university studies as a civilian or being shipped to the front. The front meant North Africa, the Balkans, or worst of all Russia, where by then more than 200,000 Italians had been killed in action and nearly a million taken prisoner. Irking his Fascist superiors, he chose Rome.

Sasà was an anti-Fascist—a decision made at the age of fifteen when he had barely outgrown the uniform of the paramilitary Fascist boys' organization Balilla. His recollection of how it happened is an epiphany of a coming of age in a certain time and place:

> "Tell me, Sasà, are you a Fascist?" It was my friend Luciano Vella, who was just a little older than I, who asked me that point blank. We were walking on a beach in Santa Severa near Rome on a warm night in the summer of 1937. The question put that way shook me. . . . At school we always talked about the greatness of the Patria and how that was owed exclusively to the greatness and the goodness of the Duce. I loved my country and so I couldn't be against the man who everyone agreed had made it great. Yet I certainly did not approve of the gross dishonesty of the Fascist hierarchy, the vulgarity of its rituals, the fear people had of speaking their minds freely. . . . All these things ran through my mind as we walked, and I remained at odds with myself for a long time before answering Luciano's blunt question. He too waited in silence. Was I a Fascist? Finally, I managed to say, "I think so." But deep inside I knew that my answer wasn't what I meant and there was a distant voice echoing within saying that I had somehow misunderstood the meaning of greatness and that all the talk of conquest and empire, of destiny and the "fateful hills of Rome,"[1] had held sway in an impressionable boy's mind. And when I tried to counter Luciano's arguments about all the things we saw happening around us being corrupt and unconscionable by saying, yes, it was true, but that it was not the fault of Mussolini but of his unfaithful followers, it was easy for him to prove to me that I was not a Fascist.[2]

The mounting evils of the regime, once bared in one's conscience, grew easier and easier to despise if not oppose. Fascism was the very fabric of Italian life. Fascists, some of them swaggering like the Duce himself, all of them driven by a Big-Brotherdom to conform, were to be found, though not in Sasà's immediate family, among his cousins, family friends and neighbors, his teachers and his classmates. His first unguarded expression of anti-Fascism occurred in the spring of 1940. Mussolini was firing up public opinion in favor of Italy joining Hitler's war. Sasà was a high-school senior then, and the headmaster closed the school one day, sending the students into the streets to demonstrate support for the Duce. Militant Fascist youths surrounded the building to prevent anyone from entering. But Sasà and another student fought their way inside and took their places in the deserted classrooms. Caught sitting alone at his desk, he was challenged by a teacher, "Hey, you, why aren't you demonstrating?" To which he replied, "What do you think I'm doing, sir?"[3] He was interrogated by Fascist watchdogs for five hours. A year later he was arrested among a group of anti-Fascist students who had occupied Rome University. Some of his fellow students were sent off to an internal exile called *confino*, but these were Fascism's new-generation rebels, and to a large extent tolerated as such. One of Sasà's closest friends, he too a self-defined anti-Fascist, was the son of Mussolini's chief of the secret police, OVRA, and it was that high official who saved Sasà from a similar punishment, with a stern warning not to frequent "bad company."[4]

Rome, though it still glittered that morning of July 19, had become a city of gloom. Fascist rule, bled almost dry by the war, was sick and at that moment more feeble than most of the world knew. The situation had taken a sharp turn for the worse only ten days earlier. The Allies had landed in Sicily on July 10, meeting scarce opposition, and the Mediterranean island appeared to shrink to a mere stepping-stone to mainland Europe. Fascism had boasted that without its consent not even a swallow could fly over Rome. But now American and British air power controlled the Italian skies, flying with impunity over Rome, launching leaflets that taunted the Romans ("Today we choose to drop pamphlets even though we now can choose to drop bombs"), goading them to come to their senses and "separate your destiny from the men of the regime."[5]

The regime, more than retreat from braggadocio, had shown a measure of its greatest fear on the evening of July 18, the last Sunday of a Rome about to disappear. People had flocked to the beaches to escape afternoon temperatures in the nineties, but that evening, a radio address by the National Secretary of the Fascist Party, Carlo Scorza, sought to disabuse the people of the notion of escape of any kind. Mussolini's Italy was in shark-filled waters. It was do or die:

> If the enemy were to be victorious what fate would await us? The Nation would be torn apart, the people reduced to a breed of servants, most of [them] under the crack of the Russian whip. The ablest would be shipped off to work in the mines of the Urals or the steppes, while the less fit would be consigned to cultivate flowers for English ladies or hand-paint ceramics for their baronets. Our pillaged museums, pacified schools, silent arsenals, ports emptied of our fleet, factories stilled, abandoned fields, would bear witness for centuries of the curse of our dead. Only our hotels—crowded with rowdy and rednecked American and British tourists—would speak to the world of how the heirs of the Seigniory, the Risorgimento, the Vittorio Veneto became the consummate cosmopolitan waiters and chambermaids, a dependency forged by our apathy. And, I would add, all that would be taken as perfectly natural by the English.
>
> Resist, resist, resist! Now or never.[6]

The first bomb to hit the university grounds ripped through Clinical Medicine, the building Sasà had left just moments before. The second tore into the nearby Institute of Hygiene. A third struck Orthopedics. There were hundreds of explosions all around him, thick, gnarled columns of black smoke rising in every direction. Wave after wave of Allied bombers (270 in all) was pulverizing the southeast corner of Rome from an altitude of "twenty angels"—U.S. Army Air Corps parlance for 20,000 feet, unreachable by Italian artillery. The target was the railway marshaling yards in the San Lorenzo district, which lay adjacent to the university medical school complex. An Allied reconnaissance damage-assessment report, filed later that day, would declare the mission a completely successful surgical strike with "no damage . . . observed in the city itself other than to a few buildings in the immediate vicinity of the Lorenzo Yards."[7] The "immediate vicinity," however, was one of the most populous residential areas of the city, and in and around those "few buildings" more than a thousand Romans would die, with thousands more injured.[8]

As the bombing continued, Sasà raced back to the hospital in a rain of shattered glass and other debris. Along with other students, he helped nurses and doctors move the patients on gurneys and stretchers to basement shelters. Even before the wards and corridors had been emptied they began to fill again with the arrival of the wounded and dying, hundreds of hemorrhaging bomb-trauma victims, men, women, and children, children who shortly before were playing on the streets of working-class San Lorenzo. Every room became an emergency room, every bed an operating table.

"We students," Sasà would later recall, "had never done anything more than provide superficial medication—and none of us had seen war—but now we underwent a baptism by fire. At first all we did was clean the wounds for treatment by the doctors, but the number of injured was soon overwhelming and we had to begin to do surgery ourselves, ligating arteries, removing shrapnel and glass, stitching together, when not discarding, flesh and limb. Within a short while we were working up to our ankles in rubble, torn clothing, and blood. We worked through that day and night, and on through the next. Only at sundown of the second day did I leave, bicycling through the completely leveled streets of San Lorenzo. It was a turning point in my life. I had seen the most hideous side of a lost war: the slaughter of the innocents. I wept as I slowly pedaled home. I felt something well within me that I had never felt before, an anger against those who had brought my country and my city to ruin—and a burning passion to make them pay."[9]

THE 262nd man to occupy the Chair of Saint Peter, Pope Pius XII, watched the bombing of Rome through small binoculars. Eugenio Pacelli, the first Roman-born pope in more than two hundred years, stood at the east-wing windows of the Vatican's Apostolic Palace in stony silence and utter horror. Death and destruction were falling from the blue skies across the Tiber, seemingly no more than an outstretched arm away. Few people loved Rome and all that it meant to Christendom more than he. At his side were his Secretary of State, Cardinal Luigi Maglione, and one of his closest deputies, Monsignor Giovanni Battista Montini, the future Pope Paul VI. Bombs were bursting not only on the rail yards, the buildings of San Lorenzo, and the university, but also, in the words that would be composed by the poet Ungaretti, they were "killing the dead," pummeling and unearthing the neighboring main cemetery of Rome, Campo Verano, defacing, for one, the Pacelli family tomb, where the Pope's parents and his brother lay interred. Pius could not have known that detail yet, but he and his aides were painfully aware of witnessing a significant failure of Vatican diplomacy.

He had been pope for more than four years now, a papacy beset almost from the start by the perils and vicissitudes of world war. Vatican City, a sov-

ereign state by treaty but a 108.7-acre enclave of the Fascist capital, had become encircled by and physically dependent in almost every way, down to its
lighting and plumbing, on a country spiraling toward ruin. On the very day
that Mussolini declared war against Great Britain and France, the idea of
Rome as an open city was conceived by the Pope. Cardinal Secretary of
State Maglione asked the British ambassador to the Holy See, D'Arcy Osborne, to obtain a commitment that the Royal Air Force would not bomb
Rome. London, itself under the German blitz of rockets and bombs, agreed
only that it would do its best to avoid damaging Vatican City, but suspicion
lingered that the Pope's efforts to spare Rome from attack were also aimed at
making the Vatican useful to its Fascist protectors. The matter worsened
when the English city of Coventry and its fourteenth-century Saint
Michael's Cathedral were bombed by the Luftwaffe. Pius, on the grounds of
Vatican neutrality, refused a British request to protest, though he continued
without surcease to press for open-city status. "The more I think of it," Osborne confided to his diary late in 1942, "the more I am revolted by Hitler's
massacre of the Jewish race on the one hand, and, on the other, the Vatican's
apparently exclusive preoccupation with the . . . possibilities of the bom-
bardments of Rome."[10]

This skewed diplomacy redoubled with America's entry into the war. The
Axis defeats at El Alamein and Stalingrad made it appear likely that the Allied armies would beat Nazism and Fascism back into the very soil from
which they had sprung. It was then that papal concern for the safety of Vatican City became an overriding issue, if not an obsession. Between March
and the end of June 1943, a diplomatic offensive by the Vatican implored
Washington to consider the dire consequences of bombing Rome. It harped
on a one-note theme: that "Vatican City itself would have little chance of escaping damage," that there was a "grave danger to Vatican City," that it
would be extremely difficult "to guarantee the security of the Vatican itself."
The search for any tack that might effect a change of heart grew more and
more peculiar. According to a telegram to the State Department from the
U.S. representative in the Vatican, Harold Tittmann, the Pope feared that
"Allied bombardment of Rome might provoke popular uprising against
diplomats residing in Vatican City. . . ." The people of Rome, Tittmann had
been told with what was by then a cliché, regarded the Vatican as a "nest of
spies." The Holy See would not be able to give Tittmann and the other
diplomats in the Vatican "adequate protection if such an uprising occurred."
Tittmann replied, somewhat undiplomatically, that "if in the opinion of the
Allies war could be shortened and thousands of lives saved by bombing

Rome they would not be deterred therefrom out of consideration for safety of a few diplomats."[11]

The prospect of an assault by the Romans on the diplomatic corps was not one of Pius's main concerns that July afternoon. When the all-clear sounded and he was brought news of the extent of the damage, which included a direct hit on the medieval basilica San Lorenzo Outside the Walls, he decided to leave the confines of the Vatican for the first time since the war and visit the afflicted quarter—overruling Montini's security cautions about waiting until morning by shouting, it is said, "At once! At once!"[12]

At 5:20 P.M., a black Mercedes, flying the black and yellow papal pennants on its front fenders, exited Vatican City and tore across Rome. Traveling without an escort and accompanied only by Montini and their driver, the Pope reached the arched entranceway to the cemetery in a matter of minutes. He stepped out of the car—an unmistakable presence in his white soutane and skullcap—and was immediately surrounded by a huge crowd crying, "Holiness! Holiness! Peace! Peace!" and "Long live the Pope!" He lifted his head and threw out his arms as if to embrace them all. The unforgettable moment was captured by an anonymous photographer (see photo section).

Soldiers and policemen already at the scene formed a protective cordon. Pius, with Montini bucking the press of flesh to keep at his side, walked to the bomb-stricken basilica named for the third-century martyr. The Pope fell to his knees not far from the bodies of the dead dragged from the rubble, aligned and covered with newspapers. "Out of the deep have I called unto Thee, O Lord," he intoned, to which the faithful responded, "I am the resurrection and the life . . ." Off to one side, Montini stood handing out banknotes to survivors.

Someone who was there remembered the scene a half-century later:

I saw a group of people in the ruins of the piazza in front of the basilica and I rushed over there because I thought that some Fascist Party chieftain, some government bigwig, maybe even Mussolini himself, had come there. I picked up a rock and I said to myself, "I'm going to crack his skull open." My wife and my daughter were buried under the rubble in Via dei Marrucini [two blocks away]; I'd been running around like a madman trying to find somebody to help me dig. You'd have needed a whole work gang but nobody had yet arrived. Other people in the same fix as I was were running with me, shouting, "Murderers!" because they thought it was a party big shot too. But some guy turned to me and said, "Calm down! It's the Pope!" It was the Pope all right, and we all broke up in tears. My wife and my daughter, I never got them out. They died there.[13]

As soon as he returned to the Vatican, Pius protested the bombing, venting his indignation in a letter to President Franklin Roosevelt. When the Allies had landed in Sicily, the American president had written to him, saying that "the soldiers of the United Nations [the Allies] have come to rid Italy of Fascism and all its unhappy symbols." But now, Pius replied, he had had "to witness the harrowing scene of death leaping from the skies and stalking pitilessly through unsuspecting homes striking down women and children." His own eyes had seen "the gaping ruins of that ancient and priceless papal Basilica of San Lorenzo. . . ." As for liberating Italy of Fascist oppression, the Pope was "above any armed conflict between nations." Rome could not be attacked "without inflicting an incomparable loss on the patrimony of Religion and Civilization."[14]

The Allied position, however, was as clear and constant as ever. Eternal City or not, Rome was the seat of government of an Axis capital, the site of not only Fascist but Nazi military objectives and enemy armed forces, both Italian and German, and as such it would remain a potential target. When some days after Pius's latest letter to Roosevelt, Tittmann remarked to Maglione that it was regrettable that the Pope "did not raise his voice clearly in some such manner as this when civilians and cultural monuments of other countries were being bombed by Germans in the early stages of the war," he learned of a more temporal reason for the Pope's displeasure. Tittmann reported to Washington that Pius had been "desperately hoping that Rome would not be bombed during the war since it would have meant so much to his prestige afterward if it could be said that city had been spared out of respect for the Holy Father."[15] Whatever his priorities, Pius, the bishop of Rome, was more resolved than ever to exercise his powers on behalf of his beloved city.

———————

THE GERMANOPHOBIC king and latter-day emperor of Italy, Victor Emmanuel III, had also watched the bombing of Rome through binoculars, powerful Italian Navy binoculars befitting the First Marshal of the Empire. The planes had flown over Villa Savoia, the royal residence, which was little more than a mile from the San Lorenzo target. He stood on a terrace, counting B-17s and B-24s, deeply impressed not only by their numbers but by their unchallenged mastery of the skies. The Queen was alarmed. "Look!" cried the King, "look how they're flying in formation. It's like a parade. Perfect formation!" From time to time, puffs of smoke from anti-aircraft artillery fire revealed how sparse those weapons were and how far below the twenty-angel mark most of them could reach. "Not even one fighter in the air," said the King. "Where are our boys? What happened to them?" [16] Victor Emmanuel had been one of the staunchest believers in the Pope's presence rendering Rome immune from attack, but the monarch was no fool. He knew that the Savoia 81 bombers and the poison gas dropped on malnourished Abyssinia to gain a puny empire had been bought on credit and that Italy was broke.

That same afternoon, shortly after the Pope's visit, the seventy-three-year-old King also went to San Lorenzo. Legend abounds in Rome of how he and his entourage were greeted in a hail of rocks hurled by scornful crowds and how when his aide-de-camp General Paolo Puntoni, like Monsignor Montini, began to pass out money, people cried to the King, "We don't want your charity! We want peace!" Puntoni's own version of the King's reception is not completely contradictory. "The people are mute, hostile," he wrote in his diary. "We go through tears and icy silence. . . . The Sovereign is stricken by this state of affairs." [17] He was stricken too when he went to inspect nearby Ciampino aerodrome, a vital military installation. Gutted and pitted with craters, aircraft and hangars destroyed, Ciampino was still burning, but worse, all but abandoned. [18] The base commander, when he was found, justified this under the phrase "preventive decentralization," but the old-soldier King knew desertion when he saw it.

The bombing of Rome may not have been the precise moment in which Victor Emmanuel decided to abandon Mussolini, but it tipped the balance. Since the beginning of the year, but decidedly more so in the last few months, the King, however skittishly, had been hatching a palace plot to overthrow the Duce and disengage Italy from hated Germany. It was only a matter of choosing the "right moment," he had told Puntoni back in March. "An error in timing," he said, "could be fatal." [19] What he meant by fatal was not to Italy but to his dynasty, the House of Savoy. For more than nine centuries the oldest reigning house in Europe had ruled one or another dominion, and had grown at last into an empire, but not before it had maneuvered itself onto the precipice of demise. The Savoyard king-emperor who stood on that brink had ushered in and harbored Fascism for twenty years to the misfortune of the people of his kingdom. For now, he still held his own destiny in his hands.

The plans to bring down the Duce were all in place. They had been deftly constructed by the minister of the royal household, a Genoese duke and master of intrigue named Pietro d'Acquarone. The King had held himself strategically aloof from the plotters, positioned to repudiate them should they fail. That was accepted Savoyard style. Victor Emmanuel's greatest fear was the presence of Hitler's army in Italy—the strike force of a potential countercoup. He knew he could expect no mercy from the Führer whose abiding abomination he had long before incurred. Yet until the evening following the bombing, he had nourished the hope of a negotiated separation from the Axis and an exit from the war with Hitler's blessing. It was not an outlandish idea. Italy had become a military and economic liability to Germany, and withdrawal from their mutual commitments would, it could be argued, benefit Berlin at least as much as Rome.

Indeed, Mussolini had promised to make that very case at a summit meeting with Hitler in northern Italy, held the day of the bombing. On short notice from the Führer, he had piloted himself in a white flying suit to the Venetian hill town of Feltre in the morning, along with his military and political advisers. They had pleaded with him to seize the opportunity and attempt to win Hitler over to the notion of an amicable divorce. Among the Italians in his company was Armed Forces Chief of Staff General Vittorio Ambrosio (a key conspirator in the royal plot), who had all but threatened him, demanding that he get them out of the conflict within fifteen days. Mussolini, suffering an "intense agony of spirit," he would later say, was not in disagreement with his aides but was immobilized by the thought of speaking to Hitler about quitting.[20] He could, in fact, barely muster a few feckless words during the daylong meeting, only once gaining a fleeting nod of sympathy from Hitler when he read a message handed to him that while they spoke Rome was under massive bombardment.

"He is mad, I tell you, mad," Chief of Staff Ambrosio erupted when he learned that Mussolini, after taking leave of the Führer, admitted he never once mentioned Italy exiting the war, and the General, on their return to Rome that evening, went straight to the King and reported. It was then that Victor Emmanuel, according to Ambrosio, took "the decision to liquidate Mussolini."[21] The date was set: Sunday, July 25.

THE HANDWRITING on the wall appeared the morning after the raid, the 20th. On a bombed-out building at the head of the Via Casalina, near the rail yards, someone had scrawled in Romanesco dialect, "Better the Americans on top of your head than Mussolini between your balls" (*"Meio l'ameri-cani su la capoccia che Mussolini tra li coioni"*). The Fascist press and radio had immediately begun to rail against the enemy incursion, but few Romans blamed the Allies, and some Italians were even perversely gladdened. A report by an OVRA secret service agent that landed on the Duce's desk on the 22nd spoke of public opinion, particularly in already-bombed Milan, "being elated." "I was in a public place when the news broke," wrote the informant, "and it was received with smug satisfaction. Many people commented that finally the high-and-mighty of Rome got a taste of what it's like in person." [22]

On that same day, Mussolini visited San Lorenzo, but in the dead of night and virtually incognito. Survivors were still searching in the rubble for signs of missing loved ones. Fourteen-year-old Arnaldo Bordoni, a barber's apprentice, was sitting on a pile of rocks with his grandparents and a cousin who was looking for her mother and sister, when he saw the Duce's car arrive. It stopped in front of a public urinal in the piazza, at almost midnight:

> I remember it like it was now [Bordoni recalled long afterward]. He was riding in an Aprilia 1500, with a slanting hood and whitewall tires. I didn't recognize him at first because I'd never seen him in person, but my grandmother had. I saw this gentleman get out of the car, wearing a jacket and a black hat and he came toward us with two or three others. . . . My grandmother got up and lunged at him in a rage and she fell over, seized by a kind of apoplexy; you can understand, here she was looking for two of her daughters, buried under all this rubble, and surely dead. Mussolini began to weep and I choked up, too. I lowered my head and after a moment or two I felt him caressing my hair. Then he turned and gestured to [one of his men] to hand him some money, but after looking through his pockets, [he] shook his head that he had nothing on him. So they all turned and got back into the Aprilia. But Mussolini, before going, glanced back at us two or three times. When I'd felt him caress me, I'd looked up at him and I saw two huge tears in his eyes, and it pained me. Even after all we had suffered, it pained me. [23]

"The people are with me," Mussolini said at lunch with his wife, Donna Rachele, on Sunday the 25th. He had seen as much at San Lorenzo, he said. He had a five o'clock appointment with the King, and Donna Rachele was pleading with him not to go. She had a premonition, she said. The King was about to betray him. That was nonsense, he said. The King was his friend. [24]

Over the past twenty-four hours, there had been a sharp twist in the conspiracy to oust the Duce. Acting more or less independently of the royal plot, a group of Fascist hierarchs, as the leaders had come to be called, had induced Mussolini to agree to hold a meeting of the Grand Council, once the supreme body of the Fascist Party and state but functionless and impotent since 1939. A resolution was to be offered, ostensibly to reinvigorate the state institutions, though its true aim was to win a no-confidence vote in the Duce and so force the King's hand. The Saturday-night meeting provided high backroom drama, with several members packing guns and grenades, since no one could predict the outcome. After nearly ten hours of rancor and recrimination, but no fireworks, it ended somewhat inconclusively. The no-confidence vote was carried nineteen to seven, yet Mussolini continued to regard the council as merely an advisory body. However, he rejected the admonitions of his loyalists to immediately arrest the dissenters. For days, rumors of a plot had reached him from various quarters. One of them, borne by Party Secretary Scorza, spoke of a decision to arrest him, at which Mussolini had scoffed, "Don't write detective stories."[25] Now, he would simply wipe the grand council slate clean. Whatever confidence had been withdrawn, he believed, would be restored by Victor Emmanuel. "I have never had friends," he had told the council, "but the King is my friend."[26]

FOR MORE than a thousand weeks the King had received Mussolini in audience at the Quirinal Palace every Monday and Thursday. In the early days, when Fascism was stylish and in its heyday; when Winston Churchill opined of Mussolini, "If I were Italian, I am sure that I would have been with you entirely from the beginning. . . ."; when Lady Chamberlain exclaimed, "What a man! I have lost my heart!" and Pope Pius XI called him "the man sent from Providence"; in those days, the Duce would repair to the royal palace in derby and tails, presenting his heroically jutting chin high on a detachable white collar. He wore the white gloves, cuffs, and spats and the mirror shine on his shoes religiously then until power and a growing disdain for the monarch allowed him to relax this rigorous attire, with the quip, "By now there are only three of us still wearing it: me and Laurel and Hardy." Nevertheless the rest of the routine had remained unvaried. He would enter the royal presence with a perfect deep bow, follow the lead of Victor Emmanuel's extended soft white hand, sit at the King's right, and when beckoned, speak in hushed tones, then, upon leaving, bow once more and back away. He had done as much only last Thursday and was to do so again on Monday, but now the grand council matter had to be disposed of and he had asked that the audience be held informally at the royal residence that Sunday afternoon.

A task force of fifty trusted Carabinieri was hiding in the bushes of the royal gardens when Mussolini's sedan passed through the gates of Villa Savoia at five o'clock. The Duce suspected nothing. His escort, three cars full of Fascist police and other aides, remained on the grounds, led to wait in places where they could, if needed, be more easily overcome. The King was on the doorstep when Mussolini got out of his car. He greeted his guest warmly and showed him inside. Mussolini wore his gray-green first marshal's uniform but it did little to shore up his courage. The Sovereign and the Duce withdrew to a corner study. Mussolini later said that the King told him that he was the most hated man in Italy and "you have only one friend left . . . me." The King said that Mussolini sagged and murmured, "Then this is my complete collapse." Each man said the other was trembling.[27]

The King's aide General Puntoni, standing outside the study with an ear pressed to the door, was the only other "witness." He heard little more than a garble, his sovereign saying, "I'm sorry, I'm sorry," then chairs moving and footsteps coming toward him. When they emerged, the King said something about the weather being hot and Mussolini agreed and moved toward his car. It had already been removed, but before he could raise any question a captain in the Carabinieri came up to him and said he had been charged by the King to protect him. He directed him toward a waiting ambulance. When the Duce demurred, he looked up and saw that he was more or less surrounded. He got into the back of the ambulance, which immediately set off at high speed, careening through the quiet Sunday afternoon streets of northeast Rome. He was the King's prisoner.

SASÀ had stayed home all that day studying for upcoming exams in general pathology. Somehow, he recalls, he sensed that this was not an ordinary Sunday. There was tension in the muggy air, heavy with rumors of a deep malaise at the heart of the regime. His stepfather, a prominent physician and professor of medicine, came home that evening having heard intimations of the Grand Council's no-confidence vote, and it was all they could do to await the state-controlled nightly news. In spite of rigid Fascist censorship, one learned to read between the lines. The broadcast would be followed by Radio London, usually jammed but not very efficiently. At 10:45, the news hour, the family was gathered around the radio, only to be greeted by maddening minutes of dead silence, a portentous departure from the norm. Finally the announcer began: "His majesty the king and emperor . . ." and Sasà knew that what was coming was news of momentous change. The phrase "*His* majesty the king . . ." had been used, not the formulation he had grown up on, "*the* majesty of the king . . ." The speaker had uttered the accursed third-person, *Lei* form of speech, which Mussolini had expelled from the language of Dante in one of the many absurd manifestations of Fascist thought control on a par with the ban on shaking hands and with diktats to wear straw hats. Yes, it was over. *His* majesty had accepted the Duce's resignation; a new government had been appointed under Savoyard loyalist *His* Excellency Army Marshal Pietro Badoglio.

Sasà leaped to his feet. It took a moment to sink in. Badoglio himself had come on the air to declare that he had been empowered to head a military government and that "the war continues," but that was not the part that sank in. Everyone in Sasà's family was overwhelmed with glee and embracing one another. He ran to the telephone, called the first person who came to mind. She was an ex-classmate, a Jew expelled from school under the racial laws. She took the news as a joke in bad taste, but at last understood it was true and erupted in tears. Bouncing back and forth from the phone to his parents, Sasà suddenly drew back one of the mandatory blackout curtains, stepped out onto a balcony and witnessed an unusual phenomenon:

> The city was pitch black, but then a light went on in another apartment whose curtain had been undrawn and the window thrown open. Then another light, and another, as little by little people came to stand at their windows and all of Rome began to light up. In that moment, nobody was afraid of any bombing, or of the Fascists, or of our "powerful ally," Germany. We were afraid no more. Not of anything. People who until now had walked with their heads bowed, were standing tall in the light by their windows. After a while, from a window in the building across from mine, a raucous voice wracked with emotion pierced the night: "Long live freedom!" I will never forget that resounding cry erupting from the bottom of one man's soul. Others responded with similar shouts and Romans everywhere began to take to the streets, drunk with joy.[28]

A foreign journalist, a Swiss woman named de Wyss who kept a wartime diary of Rome—a rare and precious document, considering the limited number of nonbelligerent-country observers in the capital at the time[29]— describes the street scene on that night:

Hearing the news, people rushed into the streets just as they were: in night-gowns, night-shirts, pyjamas, some in trousers and bare above the waist, some in slippers, some barefoot, all howling, yelling, screaming. Dishevelled, gaping, panting, they laughed and wept and threw themselves into each other's arms. They shouted "*Abbasso Mussolini*" and "*Evviva Garibaldi*"! ["Down with Mussolini" and "Long live Garibaldi"] (Why?) They hurled down the Duce's pictures and trampled and spat on them.

An old woman who lost her husband in a Fascist prison and two sons in Abyssinia and Sicily, came running, carrying Mussolini's portrait over her head, and shrieking: "That's all I have, that's all I have." She then smashed it on the pavement and stamped on it, reaching in her joy the point of hysteria. . . .

The publishing office of *Il Tevere* (a rabidly Fascist newspaper) was set on fire. People danced round clapping their hands. The police and Carabinieri looked on, grinning. They didn't interfere at all. . . .

Sasà was on the street all night. Sometime past midnight he drifted into the Piazza Venezia, beneath the very windows of Mussolini's world-famous balcony and the site of his most imposing appearances before roaring multitudes. Now it was at least as full, undoubtedly with many of the same people. Almost immediately, outsiders would begin to mock the Romans for having first cheered then jeered their Duce, but Sasà saw no contradiction. He himself had been there as an enthusiastic Fascist youth, but the war had changed him, and Italy as well.

Journalist de Wyss made her way to the Vatican:

About 2 A.M. crowds gathered in St. Peter's Square, shouting, "*Evviva il Papa!*" probably under the impression that now, if ever, the Pope would be able to mediate peace. . . . All Italians I talked to this night were dead sure of Badoglio's words: "The war continues," had been only a face-saver. "We shall have peace in no time," they insisted.

I often heard anti-German shouts. . . . Many times, on seeing Germans, they shouted: "Out with the foreigners," and the Huns generally retreated. But I also saw them applauding a bonfire of Fascist insignia.

About 5 A.M. I was dead tired and went to bed. People continued to shout, scream and laugh. Through the mists of sleep I still heard the "*Abasso Mussolini*" and the laughter of joy.

The euphoria continued well into the next day.

ANOTHER foreign eyewitness, but far from neutral was forty-three-year-old SS Colonel Eugen Dollmann, who had been living in the capital for many years, lately under the auspices of Reichsführer Heinrich Himmler as his personal representative. When he had heard the news of Mussolini's fall, he drove at once to the German embassy in the sumptuous Villa Wolkonsky, not very far from bombed-out San Lorenzo—"to await," he said, "the inevitable Fascist countermeasures."

Dollmann would have an important role to play in the coming months in Rome. When in 2000, many years after his death, the CIA would declassify its Office of Strategic Services (OSS) files, a long-held suspicion would be confirmed, that he had gone on seamlessly at war's end to serve as a source for Allied intelligence. The assessment of Dollmann's character, drawn by his British interrogator over a two-month period, July–August 1945, is a keen portrait of the man:

> Source, who is unusually vivacious for a German, is extremely intelligent and alert of mind. He is vain and without a great deal of principle but has a sense of form that would probably prevent his sinking to the depths of cruelty and cowardice of many of his colleagues. He is essentially a bon viveur, fond of women and luxury, but not a drunkard or a profligate. Is witty and is an excellent raconteur. He undoubtedly used the SS as a means to a pleasant easy existence without ever believing in National Socialism. It is thought that he has told the truth on all matters discussed with him, but that there are no doubt unsuspected chapters in his career that do not redound entirely to his credit. Reliability: Good.[30]

In the twenty-four hours prior to the Duce's downfall, Dollmann was probably the only Nazi in Rome—or Berlin—who had sensed its imminence, but he was no wiser than his compatriots in foretelling how utterly faithless Mussolini's followers would be. At the embassy, Berlin and Hitler's headquarters were working the phone lines, ordering that the countercoup be supported, the Duce rescued, and the King's new government overthrown at any cost. Along with the ambassador and his wife, Dollmann waited in vain for Fascist retaliation. "A small crowd did assemble outside the gates," he later said, "not to reinstate Benito Mussolini with our assistance, but to hurl cries of derision at the Fascists who sought refuge in the embassy."

At last, one prominent hierarch arrived, Roberto Farinacci. He had to be plucked from the crowd at the gates but had suffered no more than a few bruises and a tear in his jacket. Dollmann, who considered Farinacci "the boldest and most determined Fascist of all," had envisaged him as leading Mussolini's elite corps, the M Division, to restore the regime, but Farinacci wanted nothing more than safe passage to Germany and a change of clothes. Changes in clothing and disguises had been a topic of conversation all evening. There were reports from the headquarters of the German command post in nearby Frascati that Fascists were gathering there, too, seeking to be dispatched from Italy in German uniforms. "Just at that moment," Dollmann writes when speaking of Farinacci asking to be sent to Berlin dressed as a German airman, "the ambassadress appeared on the stairs leading to her private apartments and asked me if our friends needed any women's clothes. If so, she would be glad to oblige. My involuntary guffaw incurred universal displeasure, but the momentary vision of Farinacci leading the doughty lads of the M Division back to Rome dressed as a woman was too much for me."[31]

Farinacci was accommodated but treated with contempt, particularly when Badoglio telephoned the ambassador to extend his assurances that the war would indeed continue on the side of the Nazi ally. It was then that the fears of the Germans in Rome subsided, but Hitler could not for one moment be fooled. Immediately on receiving the news, he summoned his generals, denounced Badoglio as his "most bitter enemy," and gave a memorable snap judgment of the state of the alliance:

> Undoubtedly in their treachery they will proclaim that they will remain loyal to us, but that is treachery. Of course they won't remain loyal. . . . Although that so-and-so declared immediately that the war would be continued, that won't make any difference. They have to say that, but it remains treason. We'll play the same game while preparing everything to take over the whole crew with one stroke, to capture all that riffraff.[32]

His first impulse was to "drive into Rome with a special detail to arrest the whole government, the King and the whole bunch right away. . . . Right into a plane and off with them," he cried. Suspecting the Pope of complicity in the overthrow, Hitler targeted the Vatican—and the diplomatic corps—as well. "I'd go straight into the Vatican," he railed. "Do you think the Vatican impresses me? I couldn't care less. . . . We'll clear out that gang of swine. . . . Then we'll apologize for it afterward."[33]

In a matter of hours, however, after considering the military and political realities, the Führer restrained his savage instincts without abandoning his determination to exact revenge. Playing the "same game" as the new Italian government, he secured the Alpine passes to guarantee access to Italy and began moving twelve new divisions down the peninsula. The planned response to the expected betrayal would be the occupation of Rome, the rescue of Mussolini, and the restoration of Fascist rule.

LIKE the Germans and, incidentally, the Vatican, the Allies were taken by surprise by the coup d'état in Rome. In retrospect—with Fascism falling only six days after the San Lorenzo bombing and only two weeks after the landing in Sicily—it would seem that Washington and London had had a master plan for knocking Italy out of the war. Early in 1943 and flush with battlefield victories, the Allies had demanded nothing less than unconditional surrender from the Axis powers, but now it seemed no one was quite sure what that meant in practice and the Allies were unprepared to state the terms of any armistice, so desperately and fearfully desired by the new government in Rome. Thus the "game" of dare and deceit became a threesome.

The King's government took the initiative, launching a secret peace offensive aimed at winning something more palatable than unconditional surrender. The Allies were less than open-armed in their reception. They decided to put maximum military and political pressure on the Badoglio government. Rome played its horror-story card. Badoglio's first peace emissary was dispatched with great stealth to Lisbon, where he met with the British ambassador on August 4. According to Churchill's report to Roosevelt of what the ambassador had been told, Italy, after Mussolini, "had turned Red overnight." Twenty years of Fascism had wiped out the middle class. There was no one left between the King with his supporters and rampant Bolshevism. "If we bomb Rome again," Churchill related, "there will be a popular rising."[34]

The Allied response was to bomb Rome again.[35] There was no uprising, but Badoglio continued to trot out the Bolshevik bogey. While this policy did test the resolve of the unconditional surrender stance, it forced Rome into the foolhardy position of favoring, even fostering, the movement of German reinforcements into Italy, insofar as it "proved" Badoglio's loyalty to Hitler and provided an incentive to the Allies to offer terms.

The Allies had to figure what to do next. The war against Hitler had brought together the military might of one of the largest coalitions in history. What was called "the Allies"—and more formally the "United Nations"—was also a hodgepodge of diverse cultures with conflicting interests. In Italy alone, the Allies included the U.S. Fifth Army, the British Eighth Army, the Free Poles (2nd Polish Corps), the Free French (Corps Expéditionnaire Français), the 1st Canadian Corps, the New Zealand Corps, and a supporting cast of Brazilians, Moroccans, South Africans, and others. Commander in Chief of all these ground forces was General Sir Harold Alexander, a brooding, unassuming Briton, chosen for his military prowess, of course, but hardly the type to rein in celebrity generals such as the Eighth Army's Bernard Law Montgomery or Bernard Freyberg of New Zealand from doing as they damned pleased.

Thus what had been gained in firepower would be compromised by lack of a unified long-term vision—a failing that Kesselring would learn to exploit to great advantage. Meanwhile, Allied strategists finally devised their next move. Code-named Operation Avalanche, it was a compromise between the British desire to maintain a strong presence in the Mediterranean and the American wish to make a beeline for the Führer's jugular, straight across the English Channel, nonstop to Berlin. Avalanche, to be timed with the inevitable Italian surrender, was to be an amphibious landing on the shores of Salerno, south of Naples, on a bet that the Germans, fearing the complex logistics of fighting a war too deep in the peninsula, would turn around and withdraw to northern Italy. A worse bet would never be made, at least in this theater of operations, and a contemporary entry in Montgomery's diary makes plain that these were warriors of the wagering kind:

> Before we embark on major operations on the mainland of Europe [he wrote on September 5] we must have a master plan and know how we propose to develop these operations. I have not been told of any master plan and I must therefore assume that there was none.[36]

NOT EVERYONE in Rome was addled by wishful thinking. Although the Badoglio government instituted martial law and other repressive measures that in some cases were in excess of those of Fascist times, it did accede to the demands of public opinion to release Mussolini's political prisoners (and interned Jews). This buttressed the ranks of committed anti-Fascists, of which there had always been scattered groupings even in the darkest days. Many of them gravitated around seventy-year-old Ivanoe Bonomi, who had been head of a democratic government prior to Mussolini's seizure of absolute power. Bonomi had survived the dictatorship with his anti-Fascism uncompromised and had remained in the circles of the royal family. Back in June he had been among those who counseled the King to arrest Mussolini, though a second piece of advice—to break unequivocally with the Axis while the Italian armed forces far outnumbered the enemy within the gates—was fatefully ignored. In the last days of July, the groupings of anti-Fascists around Bonomi formed the Committee of Opposition to Badoglio[37] and by mid-August they were denouncing the government's failure to make peace while permitting the German military buildup in Italy—and, consequently, they demanded that weapons be distributed to the people of Rome in case of a Nazi attack.

THE POLITICAL ferment in Rome seethed most among the new generation of anti-Fascists. On the morning after the fall of Fascism, Sasà put aside his medical studies and went in search of political action. Like many of his fellow students at the university, he had come to think of himself as a follower of Leon Trotsky, the bête noire of Stalin and Stalinist Communism. Now, however, along with many of his friends, he sought contact with the pro-Soviet Italian Communist Party (PCI). Although a mere cadre in terms of membership—the Rome-area branch claimed but 500 adherents, many of them, it admitted, "of questionable ideological and political outlook"[38]— the party had endured the Fascist period by going underground. Its founder, Antonio Gramsci, had died in a Fascist prison, hundreds had spent years in *confino*, and its present leader, Palmiro Togliatti, had been in exile since 1927, but the party was still considered the most organized political grouping. The astonishing victory over Hitler's armies at Stalingrad and the Red Army's steady advance westward had altered the course of the war, and in Rome that summer it was buoying the fortunes of the PCI. The party saw its task as unifying the inchoate left in a peace movement. Nevertheless, Sasà, when he declared his Trotskyite leanings, was taken in with some reluctance and left to earn the party's trust by commitment and deed.

By the beginning of September, the Communists, under the umbrella of the Committee of Opposition, had joined with two other parties of the left—the liberal Action Party (Partito d'Azione) and the newly formed amalgamation of socialists, the Italian Socialist Party of Proletarian Unity (Partito Socialista Italiano di Unità Proletaria), led by Pietro Nenni—in establishing a military council. With a promise of weapons from Army General Carboni, the Committee of Opposition was to fight side by side with the Italian armed forces in the event of a German attempt to seize Rome.

Hitler had not backed away from his initial plan to rescue Mussolini and occupy Rome—now formalized as Operation Axis—but his overall war strategy, in the event of Badoglio's defection, made him willing to abandon southern Italy and draw a line of defense even north of Rome, if absolutely necessary. This of course heightened the allure of Rome's capture.

The same was true for the Allies. Endless importunings of the King's envoys could not budge Allied insistence on unconditional surrender, and an ultimatum had been issued that would expire at midnight September 1. But Eisenhower was eager to conclude the negotiations. The enormous psychological value of the first defeat of an Axis power aside, the military implications of increasing German might in Italy placed the Allied Italian campaign in continually greater jeopardy. Surrender or no surrender, the invasion of the Italian mainland had been set, the landings to take place in early September on the beaches of Salerno, just below Naples and some 160 miles south of Rome.

To calm the terror of the King and his government at being taken prisoner by Hitler, Eisenhower authorized dropping the American 82nd Airborne Division on Rome at the time of the Salerno landings to assist the Italian forces in maintaining control of the capital. This proved to be just enough to allay the King's fears, at least temporarily, and the surrender, signed in a Sicilian orange grove on September 3, was to be made public by both parties in conjunction with the invasion, set now for September 8.

SUCH was the state of affairs when on September 7, U.S. General Maxwell Taylor, second in command of the 82nd Airborne, went on a mission behind enemy lines to assess the feasibility of the air drop to secure Rome. Disguised as downed airmen and prisoners of the Italians, Taylor and his aide, Colonel William Gardiner, were spirited into the capital and received by Badoglio at his villa at about 1 A.M. on the 8th. To their confounding surprise, they were told by their host that the King's government had changed its mind. The German military buildup in and around the capital had now reached the point where the air drop would be insufficient, Badoglio claimed. The armistice, the landings on the beaches of mainland Italy, and the airborne invasion of Rome—all scheduled for later that same day—would therefore have to be postponed.

Alerted immediately, Eisenhower radioed back an unequivocal no-postponement along with a threat to expose the full record of this sordid behavior and abandon all the King's men, King included, to certain disgrace, possibly worse. Taylor had already pulled the 82nd Airborne off the runway while the paratroopers were waiting to take off, and now Eisenhower agreed to abort. Victor Emmanuel, Badoglio, and Badoglio's government were still rifling through their political pantries trying to find a palatable option, when at 6:30 P.M., as scheduled, Eisenhower went on the air and declared that Italy "has surrendered unconditionally . . . effective this instant."

Rejecting counsel that he should issue a denial, the King adjourned the last meeting of his life in Rome. Badoglio, after a delay of more than an hour, took to EIAR, Radio Rome: "To all the forces on land, at sea and in the air," he began in a tired voice that would be recorded and repeated at brief intervals to a startled nation, "the Italian government . . . recognizing the overwhelming power of the enemy . . . has requested an armistice from General Eisenhower. . . . This request has been granted. The Italian forces will, therefore, cease all acts of hostility against the Anglo-American forces wherever they may be met. They will, however, oppose attacks from any other quarter."[39]

THE ONLY other quarter that mattered at this moment were the German forces under Field Marshal Albert Kesselring, Commander in Chief of the entire southern front. Early that afternoon, the site of his command post in the Roman hill town Frascati had been bombed by the Allies. Frascati and much of the surrounding area of the Castelli Romani, or Alban Hills, had been laid to ruin—150 German soldiers and hundreds of civilians reported killed—but Kesselring had crawled out of the wreckage of his headquarters unharmed. At fifty-eight, he had spent much of his adult life under fire, as an artillery captain in World War I then rising rapidly when Hitler came to power, commanding the Luftflotte during the blitz against Britain and the razing of Rotterdam. In Italy, he would gain worldwide fame for his nickname, "Smiling Albert."

Kesselring and his officers had correctly interpreted the raid as a prelude to an Allied landing, but when official word of the Italian surrender reached him at about seven that evening, he, like all of the Germans, was taken by complete surprise. He immediately issued the code-word *Achse*, or "Axis," to go on the offensive against the Italians. They had, he said charging his armies, "committed the basest treachery . . . behind our backs. We Germans must continue to fight . . . for the salvation of Europe and Italy. No mercy must be shown to the traitors. Heil Hitler!"[40]

Still, he was uncertain whether to risk an attempt to capture Rome. An armistice implied close coordination between the Allies and the Italians, and

Kesselring grew convinced that the enemy would land near Rome to protect the government and thus assure that the surrender terms would be honored.

His first concerns were to secure the paths of retreat from Rome and the south and to regroup and link up with the German forces in northern Italy. Hitler's headquarters agreed that the desire for Rome might have to be discarded and, on instruction from Berlin, the ambassador to the King's government, Rudolf Rahn, asked that a train be put at his disposal to evacuate German diplomatic, military, and civilian personnel. The Italians, to be sure, were eager to oblige.

Kesselring's sense that all hope of taking Rome for the Führer had to be eschewed was reinforced when SS Colonel Dollmann reported to Frascati that same evening. Dollmann had come from the embassy, where the Reich's ambassador was burning documents and "pale-faced diplomats of every rank scurried to and fro," ignoring him, he assumed, "because they were afraid I would demand a seat in the special train . . ." He told Kesselring that one of his intelligence sources had informed him of General Taylor's appearance in Rome. Nothing more was known, he said, but Kesselring and his officers were quick to read the presence of such a senior paratroop commander as a portent of an airborne landing in conjunction with one from the sea. Should this occur, he told Dollmann, all was lost.[41]

Sometime during the post-midnight hours, however, when Kesselring had locked in his lines of retreat, he began to reconsider taking Rome. There were no signs of an Allied landing or airborne invasion beyond Salerno, and the Italian forces, though they still outnumbered the Germans, were acting erratically, putting up disoriented resistance and in some cases disbanding. Kesselring did not know it at the time, but the Italian military plan for the defense of Rome, code-named Memoria 44, had not yet been issued—and never would. It had lost its way in a numbing miasma of fear and confusion from the King down. For his part, Kesselring began an encirclement maneuver, one by one cutting off the eighteen roads to Rome.

THE KING and Badoglio—the Commander in Chief and the head of his military government—were ensconced with their families in the Ministry of War. At 4:30 A.M. on the 9th, while the King and Queen slept in their clothes as a preparedness measure, Army Chief of Staff Mario Roatta reported to Badoglio that the Germans were changing course. Early delight that the Germans were withdrawing had been premature. Now the Germans were sealing off the city with the apparent intention of moving in. All roads were in their hands, Roatta said, with one exception, the Via Tiburtina—the east-ward passage of the ancient Romans across the Apennine Mountains to the Adriatic Sea. If anyone had thoughts of leaving Rome, the moment was clearly at hand and fleeting. As for the Chief of Staff, his own thought was that it was a good idea "not to expose the King and the Government to the risk of capture." Roatta would later admit to having added, "Gentlemen, if the Germans get their hands on us, they will shoot us all. And why should we let them shoot us?"[42] The irony that they would have to depart from the rubble of San Lorenzo, where the Tiburtina road begins, seems not to have been noted.

Badoglio, for one, worried instead whether the "public would compre-hend the need for my departure or would they give it an outright infamous interpretation?" The answer, as it had to, came quickly:

> My internal struggle did not last very long. . . . Every personal consid-eration had to be put aside. What remained supreme were the interests only of the Patria. I declared that of course I approved of General Roatta's proposal, and that I had decided to abandon Rome, taking the Tiburtina.[43]

At the time, he put it more concisely. "I'm going," he said.

Someone had to wake the King. Briefed on the military situation, the Commander in Chief was thrown into a moral dilemma. It lasted about as long as Badoglio's, though. "Much and lively resistance," he later jotted, blaming Badoglio. "Badoglio's behavior and decision rendered departure necessary." Aide-de-camp Puntoni, as ever, backed him up: The King, he wrote in his diary, "adheres reluctantly to abandon Rome. His intention is to guarantee the continuity of the government's action in cooperation with the Allies and to prevent that the Eternal City suffer the horrors of war."[44]

No one was given the order to defend Rome. No one was left in com-mand. Fourteen of the sixteen ministers of the government were not even informed of the departure. This was not an earnest institutional retreat to a more advantageous venue. This was a panicked flight to safety.

While Rome slept, twenty-two men and women gathered in the ministry courtyard in the predawn darkness, the King carrying a cheap fiberboard suitcase, the Queen and their son, heir-to-the-throne Prince Humbert, at his side. As the party piled into seven black cars to strike eastward to the res-cuing sea, Prince Humbert, who for twenty-seven days after the war would be the last King of Italy, murmured repeatedly, "My God, what a scene!"[45]

TWO

THE PYRAMID

CARLA Capponi awoke at dawn. A spirited young woman with sparkling green eyes, she lived with her mother and younger brother in a sprawling apartment overlooking Trajan's Forum in the heart of imperial Rome. After hearing Badoglio's surrender speech, she was up late with her mother, both women wondering what next, watching flashes of artillery fire light the southwestern sky. "My God," her mother had exclaimed, "they're getting nearer and nearer. If it keeps up they'll be fighting street-by-street."

They had slept fitfully and at about 6 A.M. on September 9 were back at their open windows, hearing gunfire now coming from the south. There were voices on the street below and they saw a group of men, civilians with rifles slung over their shoulders. The men looked up at the figures in the open window, beckoning them to come and join them. The Germans were approaching the city, said the men, and they were on their way to help the army stop them.

Carla turned to her mother. "I'm going!"

"Are you crazy? They want men. What can a woman do?"

She would soon find out, she said. She threw on rough clothing, rushed downstairs and fell in with the group. They walked south along the embankment of the Tiber, picking up several more volunteers on the way, men bearing hunting rifles and two others with pistols tucked in their belts. When they reached the Porta San Paolo gateway of the Aurelian Wall, they halted at the Pyramid of Cestius, the ancient tomb said to be one of the last things seen by Saint Paul when led to his execution on the Ostian Way. Two Italian tanks were standing at the pyramid; clusters of soldiers passed by and several other tanks were positioned in the clearing. The man who was leading Carla's group finally took note of her and asked if she were looking for somebody, a relative or a boyfriend, among the soldiers.

"No," she replied sharply, "I'm looking to make myself useful."

"Good for you! But do you realize that in a little while there's going to be fighting around here?"

"That's why I came."

He acknowledged her resolve and introduced himself as a member of the Action Party. Carla, blurting the first thought that came to mind, said, "I'm a Communist."

"Ah," said the man with some amusement, "a young Pasionara!"[1]

FAR FROM being a member of the party, twenty-four-year-old Carla had never met a Communist until after Mussolini's fall. Born in Rome on the edge of Vatican City, descended from the same family as Virginia Woolf and of Viennese Jewish, Polish, and much Italian stock, Carla had lived her girlhood comfortably sheltered from the wretched Fascist experience, or so it seemed. When she was ten, the family moved into the building by Trajan's Forum and she and her sister grew into adolescence in a playground of the Roman gods. As she would remember many years later:

> The Palatine Hill became our archeological garden, where we were free to wander in our reveries among those sunken marble ruins of the columns and porticoes by the paving-stones of the Roman Forum. It was almost as if we alone had discovered the traditional burial place of Romulus when, digging one day in a patch of earth by the Basilica Aemilia, perhaps where the shops of the money changers were, we found some Roman coins, small, stained coins almost obliterated by the scorch marks of fire and the devastation of the centuries.[2]

Her political awakening began on a summer day in 1933 when her silently anti-Fascist father slapped her face on learning that she had taken part in a swimming meet sponsored by the regime. It was the only time he ever struck her and, as such, a defining moment; it opened her thirteen-year-old eyes to her father's inner pain, a silence that was eating away at his self-esteem. He was a mining engineer who worked in the state civil service and had had the rare courage not to enroll in the Fascist Party. But when he dared to refuse a membership awarded by the Duce for commendable service in World War I, that was his undoing. He was sent to work far from Rome in the endless search for coal and oil and soon died in a mine accident, bequeathing to his loved ones his anti-Fascism, but little else. From then on—it was wartime 1940—the family struggled, Carla's mother giving private language lessons to the children of the Fascist rich, Carla herself giving up her formal studies to work as a secretary in a chemical laboratory.

Their biggest financial burden was the rent on the spacious and highly desirable apartment at Trajan's Forum, but the apartment would pay them back in kind. It lay directly across from Mussolini's Palazzo Venezia balcony not a hundred yards away and, though the building was under constant police surveillance, Carla's windows became a quiet corner from which to contemplate how a single bullet might topple the whole noxious regime. In the months ahead the apartment would grow into a refuge for people on the run. That started the day after the Duce's arrest when a school friend asked Carla if she and her group of Catholic activists could meet at her place. Carla and her mother agreed and they began to welcome others. One of them was a high-school literature teacher named Gioacchino Gesmundo:

One day in August [Carla remembers], Gesmundo showed up unexpectedly and asked me to host a meeting that had to be held in strictest secrecy. He led me to understand that for security reasons it would be better if I were not introduced to the participants nor overhear what they had to say. "You play your piano [in the living room]," he said, "and we'll meet in the dining room." They arrived one by one and I let them in on a password given to me by Gesmundo. I didn't know any of them. . . . An hour and a half later, when I had played all of Chopin's nocturnes, they began to slip out. Gesmundo stayed behind for a while. He told me that the meeting had been called to discuss a special edition of [the Communist Party's clandestine newspaper] l'Unità, which was due to come out in a few days. He again asked me to keep it all secret, and that was the beginning of my underground political life, which now would widen like the ripples of a pebble thrown in water.

Along the roads to Rome, individual formations of the Italian Army, in spite of having to conduct operations in a void, were holding back the advance of the Germans and in some instances beating them into tactical retreat. The general confusion extended to Kesselring's forces as well. The Field Marshal and his officers were still incredulous that the Allies would not somehow land near Rome and the Italian military alone was numerically superior to the Germans by a factor of three to one. At this point, the morning and the afternoon of the 9th, Kesselring was seeking some kind of truce but had yet to find anyone with the power and the willingness to negotiate.

The fighting was heaviest south of the pyramid on the Via Ostiense, the Ostian Way. The first shot in the defense of Rome had been fired the night before, at about ten o'clock on September 8, when a unit of German paratroopers tried to cross the Magliana bridge over the Tiber to make for the Via Ostiense. The battle between the paratroopers and the Grenadiers of Sardinia and other formations was still going on in the morning, with heavy casualties on both sides. One Italian officer in the Grenadiers, a Lieutenant Colonel D'Ambrosio, had already entered the annals of the nascent Italian resistance when his German counterpart had demanded surrender. Replying in both German and Italian, he is said to have declared, "The Grenadiers of Sardinia do not know the meaning of the word 'surrender' "—to which the Germans pulled back under fire.[3]

Carla's group had continued down the Ostian Way, uniting with other groups of civilians. In the piazza in front of the Basilica of Saint Paul Outside the Walls a hospital tent had been set up to receive the wounded, but the long row of soldiers, whom Carla at first thought wounded, were all dead. She heard several bursts of machine gun fire and cries to take cover. The Germans were approaching.

ALTHOUGH Army General Carboni had fulfilled his promise to deliver arms to the people, the weapons proved to be vastly inadequate. Some two thousand civilians—armed one way or another—would fight alongside the army, which was also short on firepower, soldiers bearing the still-standard 91 rifle first issued in 1891. Sasà and his comrades had gone in search of weapons all that morning. "We had heard that the 81st Infantry was distributing arms to the people in Viale Giulio Cesare, but when we got there we were told to come back tomorrow, and when we put up a fight a certain Captain Borgia ordered his men to fire at us." They ran for cover, later joining in demonstrations demanding weapons to combat the German advance. "As for me," he says, "I never even got a knife."[4]

CARLA, unarmed as well, had returned to the pyramid and had joined other women volunteers in succoring the injured and carrying food and water to the soldiers and the armed civilians, among them several boys. The sounds of distant cannon and machine-gun fire were unending and as night fell the only lights around the pyramid pulsed from the tips of lit cigarettes.

By then, Kesselring had found his would-be negotiator in the commanding officer of the Centauro Division, which had not yet taken part in the fighting and was judged by its leader to be unreliable. He was General Carlo Calvi di Bergolo, a count of the lesser nobility, who to the inconsolable displeasure of the King and Queen had married their oldest daughter—one of the most beautiful European princesses of her day. Headstrong Yolanda of Savoy, once seen by the King and Queen (and Mussolini) as a prospective bride for Edward, Prince of Wales, the heir to the British throne, had wed the count. Now, in the sorry disarray left behind by his royal father-in-law, the count, by virtue of his loveless twenty-year marriage, was perhaps the ranking authority.

Calvi had dispatched his Chief of Staff to Kesselring's headquarters that afternoon in search of an end to the hostilities. Kesselring made his best offer: the Germans would respect the Open City, withdrawing well north of the capital. The only military presence in Rome, said the Field Marshal, would be a small number of his troops to occupy the German embassy, the German telephone exchange, and EIAR, Radio Rome. In case this sounded generous, Kesselring laced it with an ultimatum. The Italians had until 4 P.M. the next day to accept; otherwise he would send 700 planes to bomb Rome into submission. He had nothing near that number of bombers, but having wiped out Rotterdam with only thirty planes, he certainly had the credibility—all the more so since Rotterdam was bombed even as the Dutch were yielding to the threat. Calvi di Bergolo, on hearing the offer, was quite uncertain of what to do next, but he did have until tomorrow.[5]

At Hitler's headquarters, possessing Rome had already been scrubbed from the Führer's wish list, with a line of defense being mapped across the Italian peninsula far north of the city. Reasons were found, at least by Goebbels, why Rome—though it would be "a fine thing if we could remain"—was no longer needed. After conferring with Hitler, he wrote in his famous diary that evening, "At Rome our flanks would be too long and too vulnerable. We would always be in danger there."[6]

Kesselring, however, grew more determined. That evening he asked Dollmann whether he should worry about the possibility of having to put down a general uprising on the part of the Romans. "On the strength of almost fifteen years' experience of the Italian mentality," the incorrigibly sardonic Dollmann said later, "I felt able to reassure him. The Romans have often demonstrated in the course of their turbulent history that they dislike rising, whether in the morning or against an enemy." He went on:

> I assured Kesselring that their reaction this time would be similar: they would merely wait with folded arms to see whose hands their city fell into, the British and Americans, with the Badoglio government trailing pitifully along in their wake, or the Germans. My assertion was greeted with smiles, but the Field Marshal himself believed me.[7]

————————

THE BATTLE at Porta San Paolo, which initiated the last stand for the defense of Rome, began the next morning, September 10, and would continue all day. The fierce combat and the heroism of an improbable band of patriots around the pyramid would recast the image of that first-century B.C. Egyptianate tomb into the birthplace of the resistance, but most of the rest of Rome awoke in ignorance of what was taking place inside and around their city.

Posters freshly slapped onto the walls and read on the radio declared Rome completely calm. "Life goes on in its usual and normal rhythm," said the poster writer. "Negotiations with the command of German troops posted in the zone are taking place for the transfer of these units north."[8] This pseudo–situation report was signed by the septuagenarian Army Marshal Enrico Caviglia, who only the day before had discovered that he was the highest-ranking officer left in Rome. He had been trying repeatedly without success to locate the King for a guiding word.[9] Now, against the backdrop of thundering artillery, he hoped to assuage an anxious population while waiting for Calvi di Bergolo's dealings to mature or for some other form of enlightenment. The Committee of Opposition had formally reconstituted itself as the Comitato di Liberazione Nazionale—National Liberation Committee (CLN)—and had issued a call for insurrection, but its voice was muted by Caviglia's reassurances to the Romans, which, along with wild rumors that the Allies were on Rome's doorstep, did nothing but sap the spirit of resistance of both the military and civilians.

Swiss journalist de Wyss noted that at 2:30 P.M. on the 10th the shelling of Rome itself had begun. "People are mad with fear and excitement, and also from lack of any reliable information. Knowing nothing, I am half crazy, too."[10]

An American nun, Mother Mary Saint Luke, who worked in the Vatican

Information Bureau and lived in a convent off the Via Veneto, had started a diary two days earlier.[11] That afternoon of the 10th, she saw the beginnings of chaos:

> Italian soldiers appeared in disorder, straggling in along the Lungo-tevere, dusty, hungry and bedraggled. But there were no officers. The men reported that their officers said: "We have no more ammunition. Do what you can for yourselves, boys," and left them. . . . The men were ready to fight the oncoming Germans, but they were not led. . . . Certainly the isolated groups engaged in the disorderly struggle knew nothing of what was happening to the others.

In some places the Germans stationed inside the city were clashing with the Italians. "Blood ran in the streets," Mother Mary wrote:

> Wherever Germans were seen they were set upon. . . . Armored cars seemed to be everywhere at the same time, some manned by Italians, some by Germans, and all of them firing. The whole thing was a mixture of riot, civil war, real war and anarchy. Shops were shut and doors were closed, but that did not prevent looting . . . not only did the Germans themselves loot, but they encouraged the bewildered populace to follow their example. Some of them took photographs of the poor creatures carrying away cheeses and parcels of pasta.[12]

FEAR had overtaken the Vatican. At noon the entrances to Saint Peter's Basilica were locked. "When, in the memory of man," asked Mother Mary, "had it been shut in the daytime?" She thought it wise, however, as a protection against a panic-stricken crowd. The gates of Vatican City itself were closed as well; the Swiss Guards carried firearms instead of medieval pikes, and the Pope's personal bodyguard was greatly reinforced. But crowd control was not the first priority. For months rumors that the Germans were preparing to seize the Vatican and kidnap the Pope had been circulating among churchmen and the diplomatic corps. On August 4, Secretary of State Cardinal Maglione had summoned all the cardinals living in Rome to discuss the threat.

He had learned from the Italian government, Maglione said, that German troops were planning to capture Rome, overrun the Vatican, and carry off the Pope to Munich. Contingency plans were drawn up and by September many of them had gone operational. Members of Maglione's staff were ordered to keep a suitcase packed, documents were stashed in unlikely places, and Pius's personal files were buried under the marble floors of the papal palace.[13] Adding to the drama was the smoke wafting in the great interiors as Allied diplomats residing in the Vatican put the files to flame. The dreaded moment seemed at hand, and according to a Vatican document,[14] the commandant of the Swiss Guards was told that it was the Pope's wish that his men offer no resistance to a German takeover of Vatican City.[15] The packed suitcases may have been dragged out, but in the meantime, Maglione asked German ambassador to the Holy See Ernst von Weizsäcker for assurances that the Vatican's extraterritorial status would be respected. Weizsäcker cabled Berlin for instructions, and while Kesselring's armies drew nearer, the Pope and the cardinals waited.

AT ABOUT 4 P.M. the defenders at the pyramid were running out of ammunition and stamina. The barricades had been demolished by German shells and flamethrowers. The civilians had been joined by the retreating Grenadiers. One man among them was a civilian and an ex-officer of the Grenadiers with combat experience. He was twenty-eight-year-old Raffaele Persichetti, now a high-school teacher of literature and a founder of the Action Party.[16] He had been under fire all day, leading the others, hauling the wounded to safety, his clothing soaked by now in their blood. They could not hold out much longer. He would be home for dinner, he had told his worried mother in a phone call made in a lull in the fighting a few minutes earlier. But he would be slain instead—one of the 597 to die defending the city from the German onslaught (414 soldiers and 183 civilians, including 27 women). Persichetti would become a powerful symbol to others. He gave his name to the street that flanks the pyramid. Someone fighting alongside him at the end recounted the final moments fifty-six years later:

> I still see that battle before my eyes: the tanks coming toward us, the Germans advancing on foot behind the armor, and our side, firing, trying to stave off collapse. . . . Raffaele Persichetti and I—we were talking to each other and shooting at the same time when I saw him knit his brow as if he had suddenly grown pensive, and then he was dead, struck down by a single round. It was over and those Grenadiers had paid the highest price. They were the first . . . and they were the last, firing with us at Porta San

Paolo . . . I led the retreat . . . then we "disappeared," protected by the
neighborhood.[17]

IT WASN'T quite over for Carla. Falling back by another route, she came
face to face with a horrifying new sight: a sixty-eight-ton "Tiger" at the head
of a column of the largest and most powerful tanks of World War II. It had
drawn to a halt at the beginning of the wide boulevard Via dei Trionfi, which
gave onto her "archaeological garden," the Palatine. The big gun in its tur-
ret was rotating toward the Arch of Constantine and the Colosseum. The
Tigers began to fire to clear the piazza. Carla ducked behind a row of olean-
der bushes that lined the way just as a retreating Italian tank was broadsided
by a Tiger and a soldier was blown out of the hatch, to hang limply over the
top. Smoke began to rise from inside and she thought, "Now it's going to
catch fire":

> The young soldier began trying to pull himself out of the tank [she re-
> called], but he was either trapped or too weak. Without thinking, I ran to
> him, aware only then that I was really quite far away. The firing continued
> all around me and as I kept running to our tank, I was struck by how small
> it was; it was one of those "sardine cans," as they were called by our own
> tank corps—which, by the way, had to be recruited from men of small
> stature. I reached the soldier and began to pull him out of the hatch. He
> was in a panic, grabbing me wildly, making it that much harder. When I fi-
> nally yanked him free, he fell on me and passed out, throwing us both to
> the ground.
>
> I dragged him behind the oleander, fearing what I had already seen
> happen at the [Via] Ostiense where the Germans were shooting all the
> wounded lying on the pavement. He was drenched in blood, most of it
> gushing from a deep gash in his leg. I tore off a piece of my dress to bind
> the wound and stop the bleeding. Germans in armored cars were arriving
> nearby and I knew that if they saw him, they'd kill him. He had regained
> consciousness but couldn't move. I had to get him out of there and I pulled
> him up on my back. He kept mumbling, asking me if we were going to a
> cemetery. "Calm down!" I cried, "I'm taking you to my house." He was in
> shock, I suppose, clinging to me for dear life. He felt light at first, and I
> began crawling behind the oleander bushes until the row ended and we
> were back on the street at the foot of the Arch of Constantine. I kept going
> but by now he'd grown too heavy for me, and I realized that it was fear

alone that had given me the strength to get this far. We were at the Temple of Venus and Rome, across from the Colosseum, when a new barrage of fire opened up, bullets and shells crisscrossing just above our heads. Somehow I stumbled on, but I couldn't help thinking that I was in the middle of a battle taking place in a museum, surrounded by all these precious monuments two thousand years old. They were shooting at the site where the ancient Romans had placed a temple to the goddess of beauty, of love and to the glory of Roman civilization.[18]

The fighting around the Colosseum was heard at the Ministry of War less than a mile away, where Marshal Caviglia and the handful of remaining generals were haggling over Kesselring's terms. Kesselring had in the meantime stiffened his demands to include the Italian armies surrendering their weapons to the Germans and disbanding. No one, not even Calvi di Bergolo, was willing to sign. When General Carboni argued that the enemy would never live up to the Open City part of the agreement, which was the only attractive feature left, Calvi di Bergolo defended Germans as honorable men, good to their word. If such was his faith in Kesselring, Carboni countered, he should take command and sign—a position seized on and seconded by everyone else. Calvi di Bergolo faltered, but the sound of German firepower in his ears helped him make up his mind.

The messenger bearing Calvi di Bergolo's reply to Kesselring did not arrive in Frascati until a half-hour after the expiration of the ultimatum, but by then all resistance was folding and Kesselring remained his usual smiling self. He tucked away the signed agreement, named Calvi di Bergolo to a powerless position of being "in command" of the Open City and, in full violation of the Open City, proceeded for the sake of his Führer to occupy Rome.[19]

THE GERMANS, Mother Mary wrote in the first pages of her diary, "in rather straggling formation, marched down Via dei Trionfi, past the Arch of Constantine and down Via del Impero to Piazza Venezia, where machine guns had been barking all afternoon. Another detachment of them came in by Porta San Giovanni . . . and I think those ancient walls remembered old unhappy far-off things, very like those of today: Guiscard's Normans wrecking that neighborhood in 1084, and Bourbon's Lutheran hordes in 1527, were after all, not so very unlike Hitler's Huns riding in on their tanks and lorries, driving the defeated Romans before them as they went."[20]

De Wyss noted that the guns fell silent abruptly at 5 P.M. "I roamed through the streets to have a look," she said, writing with some disappointment about the Romans. "People were excited and depressed in turn. They fear the Germans more than ever, which is right, I suppose. All Italians I talked to asked angrily: 'But where are the Allies? But what are the Allies doing? Why are they not coming here?' None of them asked what their own army, much more numerous here than the German, was doing." [21]

Carla saw another side. She had managed, with the help of her *portiere*, the building's concierge, to get the injured tank corpsman up the 128 steps to her apartment. She and her mother dressed his wounds and put him to bed. She then returned to a nearby street, the Via Nazionale, where the *portiere* had told her several other soldiers lay wounded. When she arrived, she saw that many of her neighbors were already there pitching in. If that would be the attitude of the ordinary Romans, she remarked to the *portiere*, "the Germans won't be here for very long." [22]

News of the capitulation spread unevenly until later that evening when EIAR began broadcasting in German and German-accented Italian. Rome was occupied.

SATURDAY MORNING September 11 began in a deathly silence, after a night of sporadic gunfire throughout the city. The German troops who had blasted their way through the portals of the Aurelian Walls had had a night on the town, painting it red with blood. This was, after all, a time of revenge, though incidents of mindless gunplay, looting, burglaries, rape, and murder would continue throughout the occupation to fill the *mattinali*, the traditional daily morning reports of Rome's police stations.

The streets were deserted until Romans began to venture out later that morning, mostly in search of a place to shop for food. Calvi di Bergolo had issued his first communiqué in his new role as the commandant of the Open City. He disclosed the terms of the accord reached with the man who had conquered Rome. The city itself, Romans learned, would be off-limits to German troops with the exception of their embassy, their telephone exchange, and the radio. By early afternoon, when this message was broadcast and appeared in the newspapers—with most people unfamiliar with the name Calvi di Bergolo—the true weight of his authority was revealed. To have made such a statement about the Germans occupying only three places, Mother Mary noted, was "just silly."

The whole city was swarming with them [she wrote that day]. They were going about in armored cars with machine guns pointed significantly at the passers-by, and on foot with revolvers and rifles—and a swaggering air. There were men from the air force, infantrymen, gunners, Afrika Korps, S.S. men and railway men too. German engine drivers had been hastily brought in because the commanders did not trust the Italian ones. And they were right, because nothing could please an Italian mechanic better than to drive his locomotive with a load of Germans behind it straight off the rails.[23]

The situation was clarified in the early evening with the appearance on the walls of the city of an edict from Kesselring—ten commandments from on high. They would be followed by one decree after another, but these ten would remain the rules for the occupation of Rome. After the war they would be distorted by fading memories or designing minds, but Kesselring's decree read:

THE GERMAN COMMANDER IN CHIEF OF THE SOUTH PROCLAIMS:
1. The Italian territory under my command is declared to be a war territory. It is subject throughout to the German Laws of War.
2. All crimes committed against the German Armed Forces will be judged according to the German Laws of War.
3. Strikes are prohibited and will be punished by a War Tribunal.
4. Organizers of strikes, saboteurs and snipers will be tried and executed by summary judgment.
5. I have decided to maintain law and order and to support the competent Italian Authorities by all means necessary to provide for the well-being of the population.
6. Italian workers who volunteer for German labor service will be treated according to German standards and paid German wages.
7. The Italian Ministers and Judicial Authorities will remain in office.
8. Rail transport, communications and postal services will begin to function immediately.
9. Until further notice, private correspondence is prohibited. Telephone conversations, which must be kept to a minimum, will be strictly monitored.
10. Italian civil authorities and organizations are responsible to me for the maintenance of public order. They will be permitted to perform their duties only if they cooperate in an exemplary manner with the

German Authorities in accordance with the German measures for
the prevention of all acts of sabotage and passive resistance.
Rome, 11 September 1943
[Signed] *Field Marshal Kesselring.*[24]

That night, for the first time in six months, the Führer went on the air,
addressing the Italians specifically. He spoke from his headquarters at Ras-
tenburg in East Prussia. He had taken an invigorating walk in the woods,
recorded his speech for immediate retransmission via Berlin, and shortly
after 8 P.M. was heard on Radio Rome. In a rare instance of no enemy inter-
ference with the air waves, his voice was unusually clear, expressive of his
elation at having captured Rome. Italy would pay dearly, he said, for having
deposed "her greatest son . . . since the fall of the ancient world" and for her
unforgivable betrayal. Now the measures to be adopted in retribution would
be "very hard."[25]

THREE

ROME FEVER

Less than twenty-four hours after Hitler's radio address, in a Rome-based operation personally supervised by the Führer, Mussolini was snatched from his secret prison and flown to the Reich.

From the day of his arrest, the Duce had been moved hither and thither in an elaborate scheme of feint and dodge to foil Nazi pursuit. From a barracks in Rome to the island of Ponza, from Ponza to the northern shores of Sardinia and finally to the heights of the mainland, Gran Sasso in the Apennines, the Italian police had managed to keep one step ahead of the relentless Germans. The prisoner appeared to accept his forced retirement with a mixture of relief and deep depression.[1] But late in August the man dogging the Duce's peregrinations hardest, thirty-six-year-old SS Major Herbert Kappler—who would play one of the most prominent roles in the occupation—pinpointed his quarry's location to a third-floor suite in a ski resort hotel on Gran Sasso.

On that Sunday afternoon of September 12, German paratroopers in eight gliders swooped down into the view from Mussolini's window, overpowered the guards, and hustled the astonished prisoner into a light plane that barely managed to take off in the thin mountain air. After a couple of days of rest and recreation, reunited with Donna Rachele in Munich, he was escorted to Hitler's bunker, where the two embraced—"a deeply moving example of fidelity among men and comrades," according to Goebbels, who found the fugitive sick and frail. Goebbels, however, was among those who saw a downside to Mussolini's return. Hitler's unshakable desire to restore the Duce to power, Goebbels believed, would inevitably place some restraints on Germany's freedom to act at its pleasure in Italy.[2]

• • •

MORE good news for Hitler flowed in hourly from the front at Salerno. Kesselring's Tenth Army was whipping the Allies and, it seemed, was on the verge of driving them back into the sea.

U.S. General Mark Clark's Fifth Army had run into serious trouble with the September 9 landing on the shores of the Gulf of Salerno. The forty-seven-year-old commander, Eisenhower's protégé and Churchill's "American Eagle," had known that his invasion force would have to head directly into the line of fire of German defenses entrenched in the hills rising over the gulf. He had fought against the choice of the landing site, wanting to come ashore somewhat north of Naples where the terrain was less favorable to the enemy, but he had been overruled by limitations imposed on the size and range of his forces. Nevertheless he had remained optimistic, counting on the psychological effect on the Germans of the announcement of Italian surrender.[3] Grabbing Naples, with its excellent port facilities, was his first objective, but the real prize of course was Rome, whose capture was expected by mid-October at the latest.

Called Operation Avalanche, the landing at Salerno was a disaster from the start. One recent study, synthesizing and amplifying the vast literature on the Italian campaign, describes the initial setbacks as the Germans unleashed every weapon they possessed against the assault troops:

> Many never made it to the beaches. Some landing craft were hit by shellfire and blew up; others exploded after hitting mines emplaced in the bay or were hit by marauding Luftwaffe fighters, which bombed and strafed the invaders in the heaviest aerial resistance ever encountered during the war in the Mediterranean. As the correct beaches were missed and the timetable disintegrated, the landings quickly turned chaotic, and troops, vehicles and supplies were landed in a haphazard, sporadic manner. Units designated to assault specific objectives never appeared.[4]

With the Germans continuing to hurl their full firepower at the invaders, Eisenhower began to lose confidence in Clark—on his first time out as commander of an invasion force. The Allies' being repulsed from mainland Europe—coming after the German capture of Rome, the rescue of Mussolini, and the prospect of a Fascist restoration—would more than offset the Italian surrender. Eisenhower feared for his own job.[5] He began to pour in reinforcements, though Kesselring, sensing a huge victory, made the same decision. By that weekend the question was whose reinforcements would get there first to tip the balance. The invasion was now a race against the clock.

While waiting for help to come, Clark moved his headquarters on shore that Sunday, and though from what he saw he contemplated reembarking the entire invasion force, he made his imposing presence felt, patrolling the front tirelessly from top to bottom, encouraging and inspiring his men to hold on. A British journalist at the beachhead was inspired as well, reporting how Clark immediately "drove off in his jeep along the dusty tracks just behind the forward trenches. He stopped and talked to hundreds of officers and men during the day; wherever he went, he noticed the fatigue of the troops and often the fatalistic air of defeat. Not many of the GIs understood the true situation and listened in wonder when the tall, gangling Army commander said: 'There mustn't be any doubt in your mind. We don't give another inch. This is it. Don't yield anything. We're here to stay.' "[6]

German reinforcements began to arrive first, resulting in a major counterattack that worsened the Allied predicament. The Germans penetrated the American lines on the afternoon of September 13—"Black Monday" it would be called at the front—overrunning a battalion of the 36th Infantry Division and threatening to encircle the Allied position. The British made little headway as well. German artillery, tank, and tank destroyer units fired continuously into the attackers, but Fifth Army resistance stiffened, and by nightfall the assault slackened.

Still, Clark knew that his reinforcements from Sicily would not arrive in time, and he called for the 82nd Airborne as the only force that could move in fast enough to make a difference. On the night of the 13th, 1,300 troops parachuted onto the beachhead to bolster the 36th Infantry.

Throughout the next day, the Germans attacked along the entire front, probing for weaknesses and breakthroughs, but to no avail. Allied heavy bombers were diverted from raids on Germany. They struck German units and supplies rolling toward the beachhead and other units in assembly areas and attack formations. Finally, Allied seaborne reinforcements were in sight, and that night another contingent of the 82nd Airborne, twice as large as the first, dropped onto the beaches and deployed. By the evening of the 14th, the crisis had passed. The Allied dead, wounded, and missing at Salerno would add up to more than 13,000 (2,149 killed), almost four times as many as the German casualties, but the Allies emerged from the blood and sand with an unshakable foothold on the road to Rome.

AMONG THOSE who had survived coming ashore in a hail of enemy fire at Salerno was a twenty-four-year-old civilian on a unique and still more dangerous mission. He was an American named Peter Tompkins. Early in the war, he had been asked to parachute into Mussolini's Italy for the purpose of espionage. He had been personally recruited a few days after Pearl Harbor by Colonel (later General) William "Wild Bill" Donovan, who was then in the process of establishing America's first spy agency (forerunner of the CIA), the OSS. Donovan, as his nickname might suggest, had a predilection for working with eccentric individualists with an appetite for adventure, but if that was why he had picked Tompkins, it was only part of the reason. Tompkins, a Harvard man and an ex–foreign correspondent, was a scion of a prominent antebellum Southern family. His parents had come to Rome in the twenties to study art, and when the family fortune vanished in the Great Depression, they had remained in Italy, awaiting better times. Although educated at boarding schools in England—courtesy of his mother's friend George Bernard Shaw[7]—young Tompkins spoke Italian like a native, and was well-connected by family friendships to the royal house and, as the godson of D'Arcy Osborne, to the Vatican. After training in North Africa, he had been scheduled to accompany the 82nd Airborne in the air drop on Rome, which of course was aborted. Instead he landed with the invasion force at Salerno, with the intent to make his way to the Eternal City, setting out with a radio operator, a refugee from Franco Spain named Juan.[8]

IN ROME, few people knew where the Allies actually were and what they were up against, though the mirage of liberators just around the corner was already in view. It was the first full week of the occupation, the last week of summer, and for everyone in Rome, a week of trying to find one's way through the drastically altered social terrain. The rescue of Mussolini, although most Romans shrugged it off, would have an immediate and powerful impact on everyday life in this city. Mussolini would never again see Rome, but apparently reenergized by contact with the Führer, he was now only days away from establishing a neo-Fascist regime in occupied Italy. To be christened the Italian Social Republic (Repubblica Sociale Italiana, RSI), it would have its capital far to the north, at Salò on Lake Garda, a Nazi stronghold—and like the regime itself—on a short leash from the Reich. To help staff the Duce's new government, Kesselring freed the top Fascist hierarchs who had sided with Mussolini in the Grand Council vote against him.

They had then been arrested by Badoglio in the coup and held in a Roman military prison. Their release would signal to the party's henchmen in hiding, lusting for vendetta, that the time was at hand to crawl out, though they would do so circumspectly until the Germans fortified their hold on the city.

The occupiers, being new in town, or at least new in their role, were perhaps busiest of all. The dozen or so ranking Germans of the occupation—the military, police, SS, Gestapo, and diplomats—who in the name of saving Rome would collectively bring it to the brink of ruin, were presently ensconced in the city's two German embassies, the Villa Wolkonsky, as the seat of the diplomatic mission to Italy, and the Villa Napoleon, headquarters for the delegation to the Vatican. To a man, they were far from the stereotypical Nazis.

In Ambassador Rahn's absence during the two-day war—as some began calling the battle for control of the city—the Villa Wolkonsky had been taken over by General Rainer Stahel, Kesselring's handpicked Stadtkommandant of Rome. The eighteenth-century villa, once a parting gift of Czar Alexander I to his mistress Princess Wolkonsky, was brimming with German troops. They were bivouacked in its English gardens, which had been cleared of their famous roving peacocks, stewed and eaten over a campfire. Stahel, who in civilian life had been a door-to-door salesman of razor blades, was demanding as an officer, up from the ranks of the Luftwaffe. An air force captain in World War I, he had gone on to build a record of accomplishments in Hitler's Wehrmacht, earning the Iron Cross with oak-leaf clusters.

Stahel had installed his command post in the embassy, but he had also opened its doors to members of the German colony temporarily stranded in Rome. When Ambassador Rahn returned early that week with his closest aide, young Consul Eitel Friedrich Möllhausen, the latter showed up for work and found the place crowded with strangers who stared at him as if he were the stranger. His office was occupied by a woman lying on a bed with her baby, her husband in the shower. "But the biggest surprise," he said later, "was in the main greenhouse. Stretched out among the flowers were the bodies of four German soldiers, paratroopers fallen in the combat in the city."[9] There was, he said, much work to do. Rahn and Stahel would go at each other in a battle for turf, but within a matter of days, the ambassador would leave as a victim of an automobile accident. Möllhausen would become the master of the house—and at the age of thirty the youngest head of a diplomatic mission in the Reich.

Eitel Friedrich Möllhausen, who had persistently refused to join the Nazi Party, had seemed destined to a lackluster career. He was born in Turkey; his mother was French and his father, a wealthy businessman, only part German. The younger Möllhausen had spent but brief periods in the Reich and, having been raised in Trieste, had spoken Italian before German. He was also fluent in Greek and French, and it was his knowledge of languages that had landed him a post in the foreign service as a translator. After a tour of duty in the Middle East and North Africa, he had been taken under the wing of Ambassador Rahn, rising with him in Hitler's Foreign Office. Relatively free of the Nazi ethic—that lethal hodgepodge of anti-Semitism and Aryan supremacy—Möllhausen was a perfect specimen to be infected by Rome fever.

The third chief with temporary offices in the Villa Wolkonsky was the head of police and Gestapo operations, SS Major Kappler.[10] The man who had so painstakingly ferreted out Mussolini was no friend of neo-Fascism. He had opposed the plan to rescue him as a waste of time, and did not shrink from telling Himmler that if the Duce was freed "he would not be able to return to power unless he ruled by the strength of German bayonets."[11] Kappler, a native of Stuttgart, had had his own variety of Rome fever for years, having come to the capital in 1939 as a consultant at the German embassy. He was trained in espionage and security, and his true mission at that time was to spy on the Italian police. While he did so, he would say later, he came "to love this country." A second fatherland, he called it after much study of "the historical basis of Italianity."[12] He collected Etruscan vases, loved roses and dogs, despised his wife, whom he was trying to divorce,[13] but cherished their adopted son, Wolfgang, an "experimental" child of the Lebensborn—Himmler's depraved scheme to genetically engineer perfect Germans by mating men and women believed to possess the purest Aryan blood.

Kappler's devotion to his second fatherland notwithstanding, there was never any question about his loyalty to the first. As with his advice on the wisdom of freeing Mussolini, he often sought to influence decisions-in-the-making, but a superior order never had a more faithful executor. "He had a certain broadmindedness," Möllhausen would say later, "but when he sensed that he was up against a traitor or an enemy of the Reich (it did not matter whether a German or a foreigner), he was pitiless and became the blind instrument of the implacable Gestapo."[14] He would soon enough show both sides of that Janus coin.

PROBABLY the most anti-Nazi Germans in Rome at this stage in the war were the men in charge of the Villa Napoleon mission to the Vatican: Ambassador to the Holy See Baron Ernst von Weizsäcker and his Embassy Sec-

retary Albrecht von Kessel. Until he presented his credentials to Pope Pius
XII, only two months earlier, the ambassador had held the second highest
position in the Wilhelmstrasse, the familiar term for the Reich Foreign
Ministry. Weizsäcker had been one rung below Foreign Minister von
Ribbentrop, but he had grown intolerant of the worst evils of the Reich, of
which he had intimate knowledge, and had asked to be transferred to Rome.
He had a self-appointed secret mission to somehow help pave the way for
the Vatican to mediate a separate peace between Germany and the Western
Allies.

If Weizsäcker kept his opposition to Nazism closely guarded, his second-
in-command Kessel, as a genteel resister, had a touch of the firebrand.
Another rare nonmember of the party, Kessel, when he judged himself securely among men of his own stripe, could barely be contained. On the Saturday night before the news of the Italian surrender, Ambassador Rahn had
given a private dinner at the Villa Wolkonsky, attended by Möllhausen,
Weizsäcker, Kessel, and a few other German diplomats. "Teddy"—as Kessel
was called by his colleagues—had unleashed one of his habitual tirades
against hated Nazism and its leaders. "Teddy, Teddy," Rahn had said with an
indulgent smile when Kessel had finished, "I see that the day is not far off
when we shall have to intervene to get you out of a concentration camp.
When will you ever learn to hold your tongue?"[15]

Now that their countrymen had occupied Rome, the time of indulgence
had passed.

EARLY in that first week, a German military vehicle drove to a halt at the
edge of Saint Peter's Square. A small number of armed paratroopers in full
battle dress got out and took up positions that were to be held around the
clock. They stood with submachine guns on the Rome side of the curved
white line that delineated the perimeter of Vatican City, in the open space
between the embrace of the Bernini colonnades. Vatican officials looked
on—some reports say in apprehension. But Hitler, for all his furor, had
weighed the possible consequences of assailing the Catholic Church and
had decided not to breach Vatican City.

Ambassador Weizsäcker had been authorized to inform the Pope that the
sovereignty and the territorial integrity of the Vatican would be respected
and the Germans would "protect Vatican City from the fighting."[16] When
the Nazi diplomat came face-to-face with Pius with these assurances, the
Pope apparently took that to mean that all of the earlier talk of his being car-

ried off to Munich or some other place of Teutonic captivity was false, and in any case he made it clear that unlike the King of Italy, "I am staying here." [17] Allied propaganda would try to portray the presence of the Wehrmacht at Saint Peter's as evidence that Pius was being held prisoner, but the troops were under strict orders never to step across the boundary line. Very shortly Vatican anxiety dissolved. The Vatican officially denied the Allied allegations, characterizing them as "unfounded rumors." [18]

"The atmosphere inside the Vatican City is one of great peace and calm," Mother Mary wrote on the 16th. "I was struck this morning by its apparent remoteness from the struggle." [19] Saint Peter's Basilica had been opened once again to the faithful. Motor vehicles with Vatican license plates circulated freely throughout Rome and all of the Vatican's extraterritorial buildings scattered throughout the city were untouched. Vatican Radio, one of the most powerful broadcasting stations in Europe, remained operational, along with the city-state's own railway line, with its direct access into the Vatican itself. Before long, American diplomat Harold Tittmann, living with his family inside the enclave, was able to report to Washington that the Germans had succeeded in giving the Vatican cause for optimism and a "sensation of relative security." [20]

Whatever comfort this sense of security may have been to Pope Pius, falling under German protection would greatly complicate his overall peace strategy. His efforts to convince the Western Allies that civilization's worst enemy was their Soviet partner had not been going well. In the period between the overthrow of Mussolini and the Italian surrender, the Vatican had sought to depict the fall of Fascism as a victory for Communism. Vatican diplomats repeatedly warned Washington during August that the demonstrations celebrating Fascism's fall were "sufficient evidence that the Communists are well organized in Italy" and that Allied policy in Italy favored "the interests of Communism." [21] With the war having turned in their favor, however, the Allies were by now all but ignoring Vatican diplomacy, toughening, not softening, their stand on Nazi Germany. There could be no separate peace in the West, they were insisting, and the capitulation of Italy had been a sturdy proof of the wisdom of the unconditional-surrender policy. In one of history's great misreadings of real-world public sentiment, Pius would continue nevertheless to try to turn the Western powers away from the unconditional-surrender formulation to reach a separate accord with Nazi Germany.[22]

Although Pius XII may have belonged, in the words of one of his closest admirers, "to that company of mortals to whom Providence has entrusted five talents," it is fair to say that communion with the real, everyday world was not one of them. He was aloof, according to the same devotee, his secretary, Jesuit Father Robert Leiber. "This aloofness remained with him throughout his life. . . . It was difficult to look into the depths of his soul."[23] At sixty-six, the Roman pontiff had long grown into an ascetic, a solitary man and a mystic. Father Leiber described him in his simple, gray-white work tunic in his unheated, drab workroom of the papal *appartamento privato*, "private apartment," driven by self-denial and a steel-like will to constant work. A large part of that work, to be sure, was dedicated to the temporal world, a search for peace marked by profound sympathies for the plight of the suffering, but always once removed.

A quality of disconnect accompanied even his piety and spirituality. With Montini, we can hear him "praying in the dead of night" at the tombs of the popes buried in the Vatican, and we know that among his prayers even in the grimmest times of the war was to find and excavate the very bones of Saint Peter. We can follow him in the 1942 film *Pastor Angelicus* (Angelic Shepherd), which he commissioned about himself—to much regret in the Vatican—a lone, ethereal figure gliding through an olive grove reading, getting into a limousine with a throne for a back seat, not seeing anything but his reading. In life, not the movie, his daily, early afternoon walks in the Vatican gardens were never to be crossed by a Vatican gardener or anyone else, all of whom were expected to discreetly disappear behind bushes. He was humble as a servant of God, pompous as a leader of men. *Sehr deutschfreundlich*, "a Germanophile," was how the Wilhelmstrasse described him the day after he was elected pope.[24] He had served his predecessor for many years as papal nuncio in Berlin, and he made no secret of his affection for Germany though not for its Führer. One historian reports the testimony of one of Pius's nephews that the Pope, alone in his private chapel, would frequently practice a form of exorcism to drive out the demon inhabiting Hitler's soul.[25] The new circumstances in Rome, however, left him totally reliant on Hitler.

With Germans occupying Rome, the Pope had been thrust into a terrible bind. His peace strategy had been predicated on neutrality toward the belligerents, and neutrality, for Pius, dictated the policy of silence in the face of Nazism's most wicked design, the systematic extermination of Europe's Jews. Until the onset of the present state of affairs in Rome, the unspeakable Holocaust, and its unquestionable burden on the Pope's soul, had nonetheless been a tragedy occurring beyond the farthest horizon. Thus, the policy of silence had been addressed to a terror that could only be poorly imagined.

This first week of the occupation, however, had seen the forces of the perpetrators of the Holocaust roll up to the very edges of Vatican City and set down their alien tentacles within the bishopric of Rome. Could the policy of silence and the prestige of the holy man behind it survive the clamorous spectacle of Rome's Jews being torn from the streets of his own diocese?

On Wednesday, September 15, far from Rome but nearer than ever and for the first time in Italy, fifty-four men, women, and children were seized by the occupiers at the lake resort towns of Meina, Baveno, and Arona along Lago Maggiore and shot or drowned, some that day and others in the days to come. They were Jews. On Thursday, twenty-two Jews, arrested by the SS, boarded the first deporation train to depart from Italy to an "unknown destination"—ultimately Auschwitz. On Saturday, other SS men of the occupation began to arrest Jews from around the northern city of Cuneo; 328 were deported.[26]

During that same week, Weizsäcker and Kessel met in the Villa Napoleon to discuss a potentially imminent crisis in Vatican-German relations. They were concerned about what the Pope might do should the SS strike within the confines of the Holy See; indeed, the two concurred that such a strike was inevitable. Although no one in the occupied city had yet received any instructions on the fate of the Roman Jews, "it was our conviction," Kessel would say later, "that the worst was to be expected."[27] Kessel proposed and Weizsäcker agreed that the leaders of the Roman Jewish community be alerted to the need for all Jews "to go into hiding or flee." It would be folly, of course, to spread such a warning themselves. A third party was sought as a messenger.

Impelled by a sense of urgency, Kessel found and met with such an angel of mercy that same evening. He was a Swiss friend of Kessel's residing in Rome, a League of Nations official named Alfred Fahrener. As Kessel had surmised, Fahrener was acquainted with some influential Jews in Rome, and the German asked him to convey a message meant for the entire community. The Jewish "colony," as Kessel called it, should disperse, he said, "leave their homes as quickly as possible."[28] Fahrener agreed to pass the word along without delay.

Kessel was greatly relieved, certain, he said later, that he had prevented a disaster, but the feeling was short-lived. Before the occupation's first week had ended, Fahrener reported having accomplished his mission as courier, but the warning was being received by his Jewish friends with some skepticism. There was "nothing to worry about," he had been told, at least for the time being. Calm had returned to the city and the Germans were behaving properly. Frankly, Fahrener added, he was inclined to agree that there seemed to be little reason to be overly concerned. Kessel flew into a rage. Establishing calm and complacency, both he and Weizsäcker knew, was part of the design, creating the preconditions for unleashing the terror. "If the Jews don't disappear at once," he shouted at his Swiss friend, "every last one of them will be deported . . . and their blood will be on my hands." He begged Fahrener to return and warn them again, but, he later said, he already sensed the presence of an attitude of fatalism, a "characteristic" of Jews and other "southern" people. The deportation of the Jews of Rome, he and Weizsäcker would agree, had become inescapable.[29]

THE PASSWORD to be admitted to Carla's apartment was *Arcangelo* and it was getting around. The tank corpsman she had rescued near the pyramid was still convalescing in her care this last week of summer, and Carla and her mother had made space in their pantry to put up two other needy soldiers. Disarmed and disbanded, the Italian army had been turned into a horde of fugitives, many begging in the streets for food and shelter at first, then seeking places to hide when ordered by the occupiers to volunteer for labor service, join them in the fight against the Allies, or be arrested and deported to Germany. Carla had emptied her late father's closets to provide civilian dress for as many soldiers as she could, and helped them find refuge among her friends, but she could take in no more than she had; she was also hiding three anti-Fascist women. Two of them were older women from the Italian North, who had been long-term political prisoners under Mussolini and now, as escapees, were again in danger. From these older women, Adele Bei and Egle Gualdi, Carla for the first time heard talk of planning for an insurrection in support of the Allied advance on Rome.

Gesmundo, the high-school teacher, returned to the apartment, too, along with a seasoned, militant Communist, Luciano Lusana, a former captain in the cavalry working now with the Military Council of the CLN. They began to speak in greater detail about insurrection and above all resistance. One day that week, Carla accompanied Adele to a pharmacy near the Piazza Navona to meet someone believed to have access to a cache of weapons. Carla lingered in the background, but the contact grew suspicious of her presence and Adele called her over, introducing her as "Elena."

When they were alone again, Adele, experienced in clandestine living, said that she had not wanted to reveal Carla's real name and somehow Helen

(Elena in Italian) of Troy had come to mind. "Do you like that name?" Carla was unsure. "What?" said Adele. "The most beautiful woman of Greece? Men fought a war over her!"[30]

Elena would be Carla's name in the underground.

SASÀ had already taken the name "Paolo." He had gone underground the day the Germans entered Rome, convinced that the record of his 1941 arrest as a student activist, though the case had been quashed, could place him in immediate jeopardy. He found a hiding place at the university hospital in the surgical pathology section, along with other young men on the run, stricken by what was being called at the hospital "Kesselring's disease"—a condition that would shortly reach epidemic proportions. The Military Council was rapidly organizing the armed resistance, and Sasà's first assignment was to help run guns to various storage places in the center of Rome, in preparation for the insurrection. One such depository was concealed in a small café and *latteria*, "milk shop," in the Piazza Navona that would one day become the world-famous bar and restaurant Tre Scalini.

During that first week, Sasà was outside the *latteria* when a municipal poster-hanger pulled up on his bicycle and began to plaster the walls with the latest ordinances issued by Commandant Stahel. People gathered to read them: a list of prohibitions—only the beginning of a series that would continue throughout the occupation—for which the standard punishment would be death. In addition to the capital offenses already designated by Kesselring, the death penalty would or could be handed down summarily for those who were caught trading on the black market, listening to enemy radio, harboring a fugitive, disseminating enemy propaganda, possessing weapons, and even violating the curfew. Sasà describes how the onlookers took the news:

> After the first couple of posters went up, a glacial silence overtook the small crowd. Grim and tense, the Romans read the threats that the occupiers were pasting on the walls of their city's most beautiful piazza. People looked at one another in irritated silence. Then as the third and then the fourth poster went up, little by little a wry smile broke here and there and by the fifth and sixth, everyone had something sarcastic to say. The truth was that to stay alive everybody used the black market, everybody knew where people were hiding, whether a homeless soldier, an escaped Allied prisoner of war, or a Jew. Everybody listened to Radio London, and at

night everybody broke the curfew laws now and then to visit a relative or friend.

"What do they take us for," a young man blurted out, "a bunch of sheep?" And the people around him burst into laughter. Surely, in that very moment, in all the piazzas of Rome, these posters were getting the same reception. . . .

Romans would still buy bread and flour on the black market, tune into Radio London, shelter those hounded by the Nazis, and commit sabotage . . . though many, for having chosen this freedom, would pay with their lives.[31]

If you were planning an insurrection, you would want Romans like these on your side.

Autumn

Rules of Partisan Warfare

The essential principles of partisan warfare: MOBILITY, SURPRISE, AUDACITY!
Soviet and Yugoslav partisans, with small forces and suffering minimal casualties, have
immobilized entire divisions and corps inflicting enormous enemy losses of men and
material.

DISCIPLINE. We must succeed in inculcating an iron discipline . . . a breach of
discipline must be punished. . . .

Do not undertake large, complicated and complex plans. ISOLATED GROUP
ACTIONS ARE TO BE STUDIED AND EXECUTED IMMEDIATELY. . . .

BEGIN WITH THE SIMPLEST ACTS, those that require only a few men, for
example: spreading four-pointed nails along the roads most frequented by enemy traffic
(you should have a model nail, if not we will send one); identify the local Fascist chiefs,
put them under surveillance to learn their movements and then attack them pitilessly.
Sometimes it is wiser to assassinate Fascist chiefs from a town other than your own so as
to confuse police searches. Cut telephone lines. Where possible, provoke landslides to

interrupt the flow of traffic. String metal wires across roads to "saw" the heads off the drivers and passengers of enemy motorcycles. These are all actions that you can do with scarce means at your disposal.

. . . The commander of the partisan band or squad must carefully evaluate simple plans [for] the three phases of an action: the approach to the objective, the attack, and the protected getaway. An ambush using automatic weapons and grenades is particularly effective when combined with acts of sabotage: blocking roads with nails, landslides, wires, tree trunks, etc.

When up against superior forces, the partisan formation must retreat to avoid engagement. But it would be an act of cowardice if a partisan formation were to withdraw in fear of weaker German or Fascist police forces sent to commit acts of violence against the civilian population. . . . In such cases the [partisan chief] has the specific duty to resist, ordering a timely response with all the arms and men in his command. *Central Military Committee Directive, PCI [Dorer: 909]*

FOUR

KAPPLER'S GAME

IN the second week of the occupation, SS Major Kappler, for his brilliant detective work in tracking down Mussolini, received the highest rewards of his career. He was promoted to the rank of Obersturmbannführer, "Lieutenant Colonel," and awarded the Iron Cross. Kappler's second in command, young Erich Priebke, was made a Captain and given the Iron Cross as well.[1] This information had been conveyed to Kappler in a telephone call, along with Reichsführer Himmler's best wishes. A final item of interest to the new Obersturmbannführer was that Himmler wished to proceed with the arrest and deportation of the Jews of Rome.

Confirmation, as promised in the phone conversation, was radioed shortly afterward. "A final solution to the Jewish question in the recently occupied Italian territories," the message said, was to be undertaken at once. The newly decorated Obersturmbannführer was to take whatever steps necessary to assure the secrecy and rapid expedition of the anti-Jewish operations in Rome. Further orders were on their way.[2]

As in the case of his objections to the plan to free Mussolini, Kappler did not approve. This new development, he believed, was yet another "gross political stupidity" of people who did not understand local conditions. Italy was not Germany, where the Jews had grown rich "off the backs of the people," he would say later. Most of the Jews, at least in Rome, were poor, orderly, and docile. True, their leaders had contacts with the "international Jewish conspiracy," but that was a matter that could be exploited for intelligence purposes and an opportunity not be lost. Moreover, persecuting Rome's Jews was likely to provoke hostile reactions among the rest of the people of the city, who were, in Kappler's view, already less than well-disposed toward the Germans. Finally, there were more pressing matters demanding his time in this period of rapidly expanding Gestapo operations in the occupied city. Rome as a strategic staging ground for the southern front had vast security implications that required his expertise and immediate attention. He was certain that Kesselring would agree. This business of a "final solution"—a phrase he had never heard before[3]—had to be taken up with Berlin.

———————

To THE overwhelming majority of the 12,000 Jews in Rome any threat of harm because of their religion seemed to have passed by that second week of the occupation. Although Hitler had spoken harshly to Italians, and Kesselring had laid down martial laws, there was nothing in these measures discriminatory against Jews and a certain reassuring calm had settled on the city. This experience of a return to normalcy was intimately shared by the 60 percent of the city's Jews, some 7,000, who lived and worked in and around the ghetto, a dense, impoverished area that followed the bend in the river at the Tiber Island. The German troops who had gone on a rampage with the capture of Rome had provoked some acts of panic among Jews[4] as well as the general population, but that activity had been brought under control by the authorities. There had been German soldiers in Rome since the beginning of the war. They were normally well-behaved, and as customers in the shops and at the stalls of the ghetto they rarely quibbled over price.[5] True, no Jew in Europe could feel completely safe, not even in Rome, but there appeared little cause for immediate alarm.

The community seeking its way through the latest storm was the most durable Jewish settlement in the Western world. The Roman Jews were the only known descendants of the people who populated ancient Rome, having lived by the banks of the Tiber for over two thousand years. Free citizens under Julius Caesar, they were enslaved by Emporer Titus only to be freed, then enslaved and freed again. In Renaissance times, Pope Paul IV built a prison-like wall around them, calling the area a ghetto, and three centuries later the emancipating Risorgimento tore their wall down. The Jews were disenfranchised once more in the age of Mussolini but surviving, entrusting their survival to God and the Book, of course, but in day-to-day practice, to their elders.

Under Fascism and the conformist imperative of the day the structure of the Jewish community had been rigidly codified, mostly by Jews themselves.

Community membership was compulsory, its benefits and obligations, such as they were, well-defined and assigned. The two most powerful positions were those of the president of the community's fifteen-member board of councillors and the president of the Rome-based organization of all the Jewish communities in Italy. They were, respectively, Ugo Foà, a former Fascist judge, and Dante Almansi, a former Fascist police official. Both men had fallen, with their many titles and honorifics, from the regime's lofty circles under the professional ostracism provisions of the 1938 racial laws and had turned to the Jewish community as a place where they could still be of service.[6] Their contribution to alleviating some of the effects of the laws had been invaluable, mainly due to their career relationships with sympathetic Fascist officials, whom they had continued to cultivate. What hardly anyone else in the community knew now, however, was that while these two authoritative figures argued that the Jews had little to fear from the occupiers—an assumed consensus founded on empty reassurances from Italian officials collaborating with the Germans—there was in fact a sharp division of opinion on this matter between them and other prominent members of the leadership.

The most intractable opponent of complacency was the Chief Rabbi of Rome, Israel Zolli.[7] A naturalized Italian, he was born in the pale of eastern European Jewry in 1881, the year of the great progroms, and the terror ran through his blood. He had in fact been thrown into a panic when the Germans entered Rome, prophesying slaughter. He began almost immediately to look for a hiding place for himself and his family. But in these early days of the occupation, he went to see both Foà and Almansi to argue for the dispersal of the Jews of Rome. The autumn High Holy Days were approaching, he reminded them, when every space in the synagogue was normally filled; the Germans could easily spring a trap and cart everyone away. He had a plan, he said: close the synagogue and the offices, withdraw all funds from the banks and use those resources to dismantle the community, to fan out the heavy concentration of Jews into the homes of sympathetic non-Jewish families, in convents and monasteries and throughout the countryside. Foà and Almansi treated his idea with scorn, urging him to spread hope, not gloom, among the faithful. After all, both men maintained, they had received assurances.

The Rabbi, who had never been a popular spiritual leader, soon enough fell silent and went into hiding, but two other prominent Jews, who were quite capable of inspiring confidence and knew infinitely more about the true dangers to Rome's Jews than anyone else in the community, were also pressing Foà and Almansi to adopt less sanguine positions. They were

native-born Romans Renzo Levi and Settimio Sorani. Levi, a wealthy in-
dustrialist, was the president of the Jewish refugee organization in Rome,
Delegazione Assistenza Emigranti Ebrei, Committee for Aid to Jewish Em-
igrants (DELASEM), and Sorani, as secretary, was its chief executive officer.
DELASEM was what Kappler meant when he spoke of exploiting links to
the international Jewish "conspiracy." It was funded by major Jewish agen-
cies in the United States and elsewhere. The Vatican was also active in
DELASEM's work of assisting Jewish émigrés in Italy who had managed to
escape countries under Nazi rule, where the deportations to the death
camps were under way.

It was through his daily contact with the Vatican, as well as the International Red Cross, that Sorani, prior to the occupation, had learned the most
horrifying details of the Holocaust. "I knew then," he would say decades
after the war, "as much as is known today. Everything."[8] Levi, as president,
an honorary post, knew as much from Sorani, and both men were prepared
for the worst when the Germans took Rome. On the evening of September
8, they and their families, furnished with non-Jewish identities, had quietly
removed themselves from their known residences and gone into hiding.
Both men continued to circulate in the community, though, discreetly
spreading warnings. Sorani also worked to conceal and destroy compromis-
ing DELASEM files, advising as many as he could of the hundreds of foreign Jews in his organization's care to attempt to cross into the territories of
southern Italy already in Allied hands—at the time not a difficult journey.
Sorani and Levi made no headway at all, however, in their appeals to Foà
that the time had come to scatter. Not even the information gathered by Sorani from his impeccable sources could persuade the fearless president to
alter his convictions. True or not, he told Sorani and Levi, "these things
can't happen in Italy."[9]

In a report that Foà wrote only two months later, he gave three reasons
why he believed that the "excesses to which the brethren in faith had fallen
victim in other lands invaded by German armies would not be repeated in
Rome." The Roman Jews were protected, he wrote, because they were "relatively few in number," the Eternal City would be respected by the occupiers, and finally, the community over which he presided was making "every
effort in order not to give any pretext for persecutions." But this document
was written after Foà went into hiding, when these considerations had already proved to be wholly in error. The report added, "Not even Italy was
immune."[10]

MOTHER MARY'S diary entry for Tuesday, September 21 included the following paragraph:

> More and more people are hiding, moving their lodgings or taking to the hills. It is still warm and mild, and the Allies are expected here shortly— but suppose they delay? The people in the hills will die of hunger and exposure. You are considered a pessimist if you think that the Allies will not be here until the middle of October. If only they could make it.[11]

The near-disaster for Mark Clark's Fifth Army on the sands of Salerno had ended well, at least for the living, with Kesselring's forces retreating on the road to Naples, yet the Allies had to abandon their target date of capturing Rome by mid-October.

That forecast had been based on information that the Germans had no long-term intentions of engaging the Allies south of Rome and would pull back to a line of defense drawn across the peninsula from Pisa to Rimini, more than a hundred miles to the north of the capital. The information had come from Ultra, the system set up by British intelligence to intercept and decode the high-level German war communications sent by the Enigma encryption machine. British cryptographers had begun to crack the ciphers even before the outbreak of war, and this secret had remained intact. Now, however, Ultra was reporting that Hitler had changed his mind. Kesselring had been arguing the case for holding Rome and stemming the Allied advance as long as possible. The battle at Salerno, where with half as much force as that of the Allies he had almost administered the death blow to the invasion, had convinced the Führer that Kesselring's strategy was correct. The Field Marshal believed that his enemy was bent on seizing Rome and planting itself in central Italy for future operations in southern France or the Balkans. Ultra was providing evidence that Kesselring would draw his main defense line north of Naples, through the rugged mountainous area around Cassino, some eighty miles south of Rome.[12]

This change of plans was both good news and bad for the Allies. The good part was that the Allied effort to tie down a substantial segment of enemy forces far away from the Allies' principal war objective in Europe— the cross-channel invasion of France in Normandy, code-named Overlord and scheduled for the spring of 1944—was succeeding. The bad part was that the mountainous terrain greatly favored the defenders. Not since the sixth-century Byzantine general Belisarius (who succeeded where Hannibal had failed) had a warrior conquered Rome from the south. And Churchill was now demanding that Rome be taken by the end of the year; if not, he said, "no one can measure the consequences."[13]

THE ALLIES immediately got a taste of what was coming on the road to Naples. As part of Kesselring's delaying tactics to gain the time needed to build his defense positions, he ordered a scorched-earth withdrawal to slow the Allied advance. On one seventeen-mile stretch of road, for example, German engineers demolished twenty-five major bridges, forcing the Allies to ford rivers and streams under enemy fire and then build new bridges to permit the movement of men and supplies. As the Allies clawed their way forward, the Germans provided a glimpse of how the battle for Rome might unfold. Under explicit orders from Kesselring, they began destroying Naples.

WHEN Peter Tompkins had landed at the Salerno beachhead he had been in the company of other OSS men who had an immediate task. They were to infiltrate small teams of expatriate Italian anti-Fascists, who had landed with them, short distances behind enemy lines to gather combat intelligence. The mission, which had proved its worth in the fighting, had been led by a French-American OSS Captain named André Pacatte, a bear of man who liked to boast of how he cut the throats of German soldiers to strip them of their uniforms to give to his agents. Tompkins in the meantime had had to postpone his plans to get to Rome, and had now joined Pacatte and another OSS officer, Henry Ringling North—the renowned circus impresario—in an attempt to investigate what was going on in Naples. A local anti-Fascist agent, a Neapolitan, had returned from the city with a report of the destruction and also of a popular uprising of the Neapolitans that was causing a German withdrawal.

The Americans and their informant set out in a PT boat, crossing the Gulf of Naples on a rainy day that early fall. It was dusk when they reached the port in a howling wind and choppy waters, stunned by what they saw:

> It was a scene right out of the *Götterdämmerung*, beyond description [Tompkins said later]. Sunken ships blocked access to the harbor. Up-ended cranes and all manner of loading and unloading equipment lay on the docks in contorted heaps. . . . Everything portside, to a depth of about 300 yards, had been blown to smithereens. All the grand hotels had been

destroyed. Every public utility was gone, no electricity, no gas, no water, and the stench rising from the broken sewers permeated everything. . . . Morning gave us a clearer picture of the devastated city, which was still being shelled from the heights of the Capodimonte district as the last of the German troops departed and units of the British King's Dragoons were entering a city that had risen up against the occupier and freed iself.[14]

Over the previous four days, about two thousand men, women, and children, aided by members of the disbanded Italian army, had indeed risen spontaneously to drive out the Wehrmacht. The insurrection had been touched off by an incident in which the Germans ordered a roundup of thousands of men to execute anyone who had been called up and had not appeared for forced labor. As the news of the roundup spread, groups of people throughout the city, with no knowledge that others were doing the same, armed themselves with weapons retained by the Italian soldiers or stolen from the Germans. The conflict escalated when one group took six Germans and six Fascists prisoner. On the third day, resistance committees sprang up everywhere, still uncoordinated and disorganized. They engaged the Germans in street fighting, hemming them into blind alleys, addling them with the hit-and-run tactics of the barefoot street urchins of Naples, the *scugnizzi*, wielding Molotov cocktails. One group seized an antiaircraft artillery emplacement and turned it on German armored vehicles, destroying eight tanks. In the Vomero district, the insurgents backed the Germans into a sports arena and surrounded them holding them at bay. Another group attacked the Cuoco barracks and forced a German surrender. On the final day, a unified command emerged, and the Germans withdrew to the Capodimonte hills, in a humiliating departure, to shell the city.

In the meantime, German demolition teams destroyed all communications, transportation, water, and power grids. Kesselring, his reputation as a city killer growing, had ordered the churches and monasteries spared, but nothing else. His forces burned and mined buildings, blew up bridges, ripped out railroad tracks, and, sinking everything in the port, rendered it unnavigable. While they retreated to their next line of defense—the Volturno River, thirty-five miles north of the city—Naples continued to burn under incendiary-bomb attacks by the Luftwaffe. For the Allies, the task at hand was clearing the port—a facility essential to the entire military campaign—so that the war could go on.

The Naples insurrection left Peter Tompkins deeply impressed. It seemed a noble ending for his mission to Rome.

• • •

Now THAT Hitler had decided to prosecute the war in central Italy, the military value of Rome became inestimable. Strategically the city was seen by the occupiers as offering four main advantages: a well-developed hub of road, rail, and air transportation to the front, a convenient base for military commands, a haven for rest and recreation, and an abundant source of civilian manpower. Badoglio's unrecognized but nonetheless useful Open City declaration and above all Rome's importance to Western civilization provided the occupiers with the next best thing to an inviolable shield from all-out attack.

On September 11, Kesselring had invited Italian workers to volunteer for German labor service. He followed with a specific appeal offering incentives "in the spirit of national and socialist justice that distinguishes the new Germany." There was no response, and so, as in Naples, he had issued a general call-up for obligatory labor service. Kesselring had decided that to build the defense fortifications in the south, he needed 60,000 able-bodied men from about a dozen provinces in central Italy. Rome was assigned a contribution of 16,440. When only 315 Roman men showed up, and much the same proportion elsewhere, Kesselring grew furious, demanding 90,000 men, nearly 25,000 from Rome. Again he achieved the same outcome, a less than 2 percent response.[15]

"The Romans in particular are making a mockery of us!" he raged at Stadtkommandant Stahel. "Start rounding them up right now!"[16]

Surprise roundups took the form of cordoning off of blocks of apartment buildings or stopping buses or trams and seizing likely candidates for labor gangs. These would continue periodically throughout the occupation, yielding diminishing returns. Roundups exacerbated the enmity between the occupiers and the people, and sent more and more men into hiding and into the ranks of armed resistance. Before long, Stahel would make his most memorable remark: "Half the population of Rome lives in the homes of the other half."[17] Kesselring, for his part, would add this "mockery" to growing contempt. He would say, "I loved the Italians too much. Now I hate them."[18]

AT 6 P.M. on Sunday, September 26, the two Jewish Presidents, Foà of the community and Almansi of the national union, presented themselves at the gates of the Villa Wolkonsky. They were immediately escorted to the office of Obersturmbannführer Kappler. The Presidents had been contacted earlier in the day by the Italian Office of Demography and Race, a bureau of the freshly resurrected Fascist Ministry of Interior, and told that their presence at the German embassy had been requested by the SS Chief of Security. Neither man knew Kappler, but on meeting him, whatever apprehension they might have felt was quickly relieved.

"Kappler assumed a rather courteous demeanor," Foà later said. "He regretted any inconvenience he might have caused. He asked about the number of Jews in Rome and went on for some minutes in general conversation, on the surface quite affably." Then his tone changed, becoming, it seemed to Foà, cutting and hard, and he said:

> You and your coreligionists are Italian nationals, but that is of little importance to me. We Germans regard you only as Jews, and thus our enemy. . . . And we will treat you as such. . . . [But] it is not your lives or the lives of your children that we will take—if you fulfill our demands. . . . Within thirty-six hours you will have to pay fifty kilograms of gold. If you pay, no harm will come to you. In any other event, 200 of your Jews will be taken and deported to Germany, where they will be sent to the Russian frontier, or otherwise rendered innocuous.[19]

Kappler later confirmed both Foà's and Almansi's nearly identical accounts, with the exception of the threat to deport 200 Jews. His version was more severe; if the ransom was not paid, he said, there would be a general roundup and deportation of Rome's Jews.[20] He may have made both statements. OSS files offer evidence that the SS Chief was actively seeking to thwart Himmler's plan to seize the Jews of Rome. Kappler's somewhat theatrical demand for Jewish gold was his own naive concoction to prevent the deportation and was substantially reinforced with the CIA release of the OSS files. Although his opposition to deportations had long been known—but only on his say-so and with evidence from some supporting material—the OSS documents reveal the extent to which Kappler and others among the occupiers sought in strange concert, when not conspiring, to avert the roundup of the Jews of Rome.[21]

Kappler's motives for pitting himself against the long arm of the Holocaust were different from the motives of those who were trying to avert a crisis in German-Vatican relations and save the Pope's prestige. Kappler's primary concern was security. There were, first of all, not enough SS police in Rome to conduct such an operation, and those available were, like him, totally inexperienced in persecuting Jews. Further, as he reported to Berlin, the non-Jewish population could be expected to be hostile in the event of a raid on the Jews, and the possibility of passive, even armed, resistance on the part of the Romans was very high. In one cable, he used the example of the much smaller number of Jews in Naples, of whom there were only 670. "Because of the attitude in the town and uncertain conditions," he wrote, "[the] action could not be carried through."[22]

His differences with the other occupiers notwithstanding, that afternoon, prior to meeting with the Jewish Presidents, Kappler had gone with Consul Möllhausen, and Stadtkommandant Stahel's approval, to see Kesselring about circumventing Himmler's order. Kesselring had had a similar experience with the Jews of Tunisia during the North African campaign, and Möllhausen had been there at the time. On that occasion, the Field Marshal had responded favorably to the suggestion of Möllhausen's superior, Ambassador Rahn, that instead of deporting the Tunisian Jews, the Germans use them in a locally organized labor service. When the SS acted in the meantime and arrested the Jewish leaders, Kesselring ordered the mobilization of Jewish workers for the construction of fortifications. The arrested leaders were released on payment of a "fine," equivalent to $400,000, so that they could organize the able-bodied Tunisian Jews into work gangs assigned to the Wehrmacht, with the result that the entire community survived.[23]

At Kesselring's Frascati headquarters that Sunday, when reminded of the Tunisian affair, the Commander in Chief was again amenable. He asked Kappler how many men he would need to round up Rome's Jews. To Kappler's estimate that it would take at least one motorized battalion, Kesselring replied, "That settles it. . . . I need all available forces for the defense of the city." He would be in favor, he said, of using the Jews of Rome for the fortification works now in progress.[24]

Whether in demanding Jewish gold Kappler was trying to apply the Tunisian solution of extortion instead of deportation, he would never say. For now, however, he sent Foà and Almansi away with a frightful lie ringing in their ears. "Mind you," he said, "I have already carried out several operations of this type and they have always ended well. Only once did I fail, but that time a few hundred of your brothers paid with their lives."[25]

Outside the Villa Wolkonsky, both men were indignant. Their old convictions dying hard, they immediately reported the German ultimatum to their sources in the Fascist police, characterizing it as a clear violation of the sovereignty of Mussolini's new government. The Fascists "were truly courteous," Foà said, "showing an understanding that merits special mention," but they could do nothing better than convince the Jewish leaders of their impotence.[26] From another aspect, however, the presidents were relieved. If the fifty kilograms of gold—about $56,000 on the 1943 precious-metals market—were paid, the Jews of Rome would be spared the horrors—true or not—said to be plaguing those brethren abroad. Saving the 12,000 Jews of Rome for $56,000—less than $5.00 per Jew—was a miniscule price to pay and in some perverse way, a vindication of their policy of watchful inertia. The difficulty however, was, in raising the ransom within the thirty-six-hour time limit. Most of Rome's prosperous Jews had by now taken the precaution of going into hiding and were as a consequence unreachable. The gold would have to come from the non-mobile ghetto Jews, and the only gold they had was in the wedding bands on their fingers, the lockets around their necks, and the fillings in their teeth.

THE SIX-PARTITE resistance committee, the CLN, would not hold its first meeting until the middle of October and throughout the occupation would never be more than a bickering coalition of politicos jockeying for power in postwar Italy. They were united only by their anti-Fascism and their contempt for Badoglio and the King. On the other hand, the CLN's Military Council, with representatives of all six parties but in practice led by the CLN's left wing—the Action Party, the Socialists, and the Communists—was organizing the armed resistance rapidly, with the Communists preparing to field the tightest fighting outfit.

Rome had been divided by the CLN into eight zones. Sasà Bentivegna, now Paolo, had been named vice commander of the IV Zone, a large part of the *centro storico*. His chief was Luciano Lusana, who also directed an information-gathering service, with Carla Capponi, now Elena, as one of his operatives. Toward the end of September, a young Communist Party organizer named Antonello Trombadori began to set up a system of armed resistance units called Gruppi di Azione Patriottica, "Patriotic Action Groups" (GAP). It was patterned after the French maquis' Unite de Choc, small and highly dedicated urban guerrilla strike forces employed successfully against the German occupiers of France. In Rome's *centro storico* the system would be called GAP Central, composed of four fighting squads, each with only three to six combatants.

GAP Central was directly responsible to the Military Council, effectively under the leadership of Riccardo Bauer for the Action Party, Sandro Pertini (a future president of Italy) for the Socialists, and for the Communists, Giorgio Amendola (the son of the popular Liberal leader Giovanni Amendola, Mussolini's nemesis, who was assassinated by the Fascists). The Partisans of the Action Party were organized in a *comitato militare*, "military committee," and the Socialists in brigades called Brigate Matteotti, but the Socialist Partisans would gain renown for the effectiveness of their extensive intelligence network.

There were also splinter underground movements independent of the CLN. The one that would prove to be the most politically influential was the monarchist Fronte Militare Clandestino della Resistenza, Clandestine Military Front of the Resistance (FMCR). It was being formed by the charismatic Colonel Giuseppe Cordero Lanza di Montezemolo, an aristocrat who had gone underground in dramatic circumstances.[27] On the extreme left of the Resistance were the Cattolici Comunisti, Catholic Communists, and in the outlying neighborhoods of Rome, the *borgate*, the powerful Trotskyite-anarchist movement, Movimento Comunista d'Italia, popularly known as Bandiera Rossa, Red Flag.

But the Partisans were undergoing a hesitant beginning. It was one thing to run guns, another to use them to shoot and kill. One member of GAP, writer Fabrizio Onofri, described what lay behind the difficulty in taking the first step in striking back:

> You have to think about what Rome had been for more than twenty years, the span of a generation. There was nothing resembling a workers' movement, and Rome's few factories, located on the outskirts of the city, were filled with spies. There were no free trade unions, no right of assembly, no free press, no free speech—just police, secret police, spies and Fascists everywhere . . . every man alone, every man for himself. There were prisons, Regina Coeli, and *confino*, and every time you tried to organize you'd fill them up. . . . Now think about Rome of that September, first with the enemy in the streets, hurling grenades to provoke terror, and then no one in the streets at all. Then there was the Rome that was waiting for the Allies: in two weeks they'll be here, they said, and they said it every day. These are the things to consider. And then perhaps you can understand what it meant for a man, whether a worker or an intellectual, when it was decided that after twenty years someone had to throw the first bomb in Rome.[28]

POPE PIUS XII viewed the autumn calm as a gathering storm. The destruction of Naples in an apocalyptic insurrection was on his mind. A new phrase had taken hold in the Vatican, *il tempo di nessuno*, literally "the time of no one," the fearsome period between the inevitable withdrawal of the Germans and the arrival of the Allies, when "no one" would be in charge.[29] The question that gnawed and required Curial attention was whether the city might fall into the hands of the Resistance—though the "resistance" was always articulated as "irresponsible [or "turbulent"] elements," or more simply, "Communists." In Naples the Nazis had left and the Allies had come the same day, but an organized resistance in Rome, with a strategy of hostile activity aimed at undoing the city's military value to the German occupiers, might easily convince the Germans to pull out long before the Allies arrived. "The time of no one" seemed nightmarish to some.

Early in October, Cardinal Maglione met with Ambassador Weizsäcker to express these apprehensions. The Germans, as the protectors of Rome and the Vatican, had the responsibility, Maglione said, to provide ample police forces for the maintenance of order. At that moment, according to Maglione's aide, Monsignor Alberto Giovannetti, the police presence in the Open City seemed "insufficient, and if they were to be further reduced, as it is being said, one would certainly find oneself incapable of preventing or repressing an insurrection." Weizsäcker agreed with Maglione and promised to speak to the military authorities.[30] He also cabled Berlin, reporting that Maglione had spoken to him of the "Communist danger that threatens the clergy of Rome . . . if the police forces and public authorities were to demonstrate themselves ineffective"[31] in the *tempo di nessuno*.

The Germans were to prove quite willing to expand the anti-Partisan police forces in Rome, and the Fascist police, eager for retribution, were agreeable as well.

A second line of the Vatican's defense against the Resistance was a direct appeal to the people of Rome. From her vantage point in the Vatican Information Bureau, Mother Mary recorded that every parish priest in Rome had been instructed to speak to his congregation in the name of the Pope. They were, she said, "to urge their parishioners to be calm and self-possessed in whatever circumstances they might find themselves, to point out that self-control and moderation were needed above all in times like these, and to say that he [the Pope] relied on them to take this advice to heart and to act upon it." She went on to say why:

This was necessary because word has come through regarding the way the Italians behaved when the Germans left Naples, firing on them from the windows. There is even a story that the owner of a flat, finding nothing else heavy enough to hand, dropped a piano from the second floor. This was the sort of thing that caused such terrible reprisals in Naples.[32]

———————

WHEN the Germans occupied Rome they emptied the gold reserves of the Bank of Italy in the amount of 110 metric tons. Kappler, who took part in that operation, knew that another 50 kilograms extorted from the Roman Jews would add little to the wealth of his nation.[33] Nevertheless, he also knew, or had heard, that the SS intelligence services were seriously short on funds, and here was an opportunity for them to draw directly from what he believed to be a link to the bottomless well of the phantasmagoric Jewish financial world.

The two Jewish Presidents, though they had no inkling of what Kappler intended to do with the extorted gold, did perceive that greed might set in and acted accordingly. By the afternoon of September 27, the day after Kappler's demand, they knew that the ransom would be met—though the individual contributions were pathetically small. The community had thrown open the doors of the ghetto synagogue that Monday morning to begin the collection in its offices on the second floor. It got off to a slow start, but only because some leaders, fearing a Nazi trick to gather everyone at the temple, were loath to spread the word among the faithful.

In the meantime, in search of insurance, Renzo Levi made contact with the Vatican to ask if the community might borrow gold from the Church. While an answer was being solicited at higher levels, ghetto Jews and many non-Jews filled the community offices to overflow. Though the majority of receipts were being written for gold contributions less than one-eighth of an ounce, it was clear that the community would soon be over the top.

In the afternoon, the Vatican sent word that the Pope himself had authorized a loan in coins or ingots of "any quantity of gold you may need."[34] It could be repaid in installments, with neither time limit nor interest. The community leadership expressed its gratitude, but informed the Vatican that the loan would not be necessary. News of the Vatican's response was kept secret for fear that it might slow contributions, but it leaked almost immediately. The loan was quickly inflated into a spontaneous, outright gift from the Pope himself that in most versions saved innumerable Jewish lives.[35]

This rumor unfortunately reinforced the Roman Jews' sense of security in living in the city of the Pope. Still worse, the rumor dampened once more all exhortations to flee; it validated Foà and Almansi's insistence that "it can't happen here."

Kappler, acceding without objection to an early request by the Jewish Presidents, had extended his thirty-six-hour deadline four hours to expire at noon on Tuesday the 28th. Sometime before eleven o'clock that morning, the scale in the community offices tipped the fifty-kilogram mark. That too was kept secret and contributions continued to be accepted. Foà in fact telephoned Kappler to appeal for another four-hour extension, which again was granted. The purpose of this deception was to minimize the success of the collection campaign and discourage any notions of ghetto wealth. As the new deadline approached, Foà finally announced to the faithful that the goal had been met. The remaining queue of contributors was sent away to pass the joyous news along. If the Germans, as people were saying, were honorable men, the news was joyous indeed. The offices were closed and the contributions counted. Nearly eighty kilograms had been donated, and more than 2 million lire in cash.[36]

Accompanied by a Fascist police escort that Foà had arranged, the two Presidents led a small delegation of Jews transporting ten boxes of gold objects, with a net weight of 50.3 kilograms. The additional 300 grams had been added in case the Nazi scale registered a total less than theirs. At the Villa Wolkonsky, Kappler refused to receive them. They were told to make the delivery at Via Tasso, 155, the building a short distance away. The former German Cultural Center, it was now the brand-new headquarters of the Gestapo in Rome. Foà and Almansi took Kappler's remoteness as an insult, and further injury was added in the Via Tasso by an impudent SS Captain, who misweighed the gold and accused the Jews of attempting to cheat the Third Reich. The Presidents maintained their dignity throughout, Foà saying at one point, "I hope to come to Germany to get this back."[37] By the time the matter was settled—a second weighing corrected the officer's error but not his insolence—an encounter that should have taken an hour was in its fifth hour, causing no small anxiety among the delegation's families and friends back in their community. Someone who saw the members of the delegation when they finally returned to the ghetto said they looked crushed but somehow unburdened, like a man "who comes back from having brought a loved one to the cemetery."[38]

•   •   •

KAPPLER continued to work with perplexing diligence on what he would later call "my last attempt at trying to avoid the roundup."[39] His own colleague in the Villa Wolkonsky, Consul Möllhausen, could not fathom why Kappler had, it seemed, upset the understanding they had reached with Kesselring about using the Roman Jews for labor. Now it was Kappler who had threatened deportation. Möllhausen had learned of the extortion from Albrecht von Kessel, who in turn had heard it from his Vatican contacts. While Möllhausen preferred not to ask questions, Kessel termed whatever it was Kappler had in mind "complete nonsense."[40] But the new CIA-released Ultra decodes of Kappler's cable traffic reveal that he had originated and had assigned a higher priority to another kind of roundup and deportation that was about to take place.

On the night of October 6, the Fascist-led colonial police (Polizia Africana Italiana), carrying out a plan initiated by Kappler and authorized by Kesselring, surrounded the barracks and armories of the Carabinieri in Rome and began arresting as many as they could. Traditionally loyal to the King, the Carabinieri had been targeted by Kappler early in the occupation as a security risk. By some unspecified "experiment," he had convinced himself of their continued unreliability and had proposed that they "be disarmed at one fell swoop because of their participation in plots, etc. and that they be removed to Germany as workers . . ."[41] More than 1,500 of the local force of 6,500 men and officers were captured in their quarters or in flight. They were carried off in trucks, herded onto box cars and deported to the Reich.[42] Kappler had tried to at least postpone the Jewish roundup because he feared that it would hinder the more important Carabinieri operation.

Thus he lost little time sending off the Jewish gold to Berlin, shipping it in a single crate directly to the new chief of the Reich security apparatus, Obergruppenführer, "General," Ernst Kaltenbrunner, second only to Himmler himself in the scheme of the Nazi police empire. He had chosen Kaltenbrunner, Kappler said later, for his reputed interest in the intelligence services and because he had had nothing to do with "all the discussions that had been going on about the advisability of executing a roundup in Rome."[43] In a covering letter, he explained why the deportation of the Jews of Rome would be a mistake. The SS, he said, would lose the chance to exploit for intelligence purposes known Jewish contacts with the Allies and with Jewish financial groups abroad.[44] Kappler also sent a cable reminding him of Kesselring's approval of using Roman Jewish labor.[45]

Kaltenbrunner, whom Kappler had never met, was as unimpressed with his arguments as he was with his gold. He cabled back a scolding that was intercepted by Ultra but not released until 2000:

To KAPPLER. It is precisely the immediate and thorough eradication of the Jews in Italy which is in the special interest of the present internal political situation and the general security in Italy. To postpone the expulsion of the Jews until the Carabinieri and the Italian army officers have been removed can no more be considered than the idea mentioned of calling up the Jews in Italy for what would probably be very improductive [*sic*] labor under responsible direction by Italian authorities. The longer the delay, the more the Jews who are doubtless reckoning on evacuation measures have an opportunity by moving to the houses of pro-Jewish Italians of disappearing completely. [Undecoded] has been instructed in executing the RFSS [Himmler's] orders to proceed with the evacuation of the Jews without further delay. KALTENBRUNNER.[46]

The gold would be found after the war in a corner of Kaltenbrunner's office, the crate never opened.[47]

```
GROUP XIII/52
BERLIN to ROME
RSS 256/11/10/43                        ✓
WGL on 6556 kcs        1902/15 GMT    11/10/43           ✓
1955/156

To KAPPLER.  It is precisely the immediate and thorough
eradication of the Jews in ITALY which is/the special
interest of the present internal political situation and
the general security in ITALY.  To postpone the expulsion
of the Jews until the CARABINIERI and the Italian army
officers have been removed can no more be considered
than the idea mentioned of calling up the Jews in ITALY
for what would probably be very improductive labour under
responsible direction by Italian authorities.  The longer
the delay, the more the Jews who are doubtless reckoning
on evacuation measures have an opportunity by moving to
the houses of pro-Jewish Italians of disappearing
completely [18 corrupt] ITALY [has been] instructed in
executing the RFSS orders to proceed with the evacuation
of the Jews without further delay.
                           KALTENBRUNNER. Ogr.
```

Copy of the intercept decoded and translated by Ultra. Kaltenbrunner's stark reprimand was unknown until the CIA release of the document in 2000.

FIVE

THE
MÖLLHAUSEN
TELEGRAM

SINCE learning of the gold episode, Möllhausen and "Teddy" von Kessel
had been in "constant communication" with each other.[1] Kessel was acting
in concert with Ambassador to the Holy See Weizsäcker, but Möllhausen, in
the absence of Ambassador Rahn, had taken it on his own to work with
Kessel in trying to fend off those who sought to liquidate the Jews of Rome.
In the confines of the Villa Wolkonsky, the Consul, along with General Stahel, had actually seen an SS dispatch to Kappler ordering the arrest and deportation of all Jews "for liquidation,"[2] and it was that phrase that had
motivated all of them—Möllhausen, Weizsäcker, and Kessel—to gain
Kesselring's support for the Tunisian solution.[3] Now that Kappler seemed
to Möllhausen to have changed his position, the diplomat had returned to
his more natural allies, Weizsäcker and Kessel. Their common objectives,
Kessel had said, were to spare the German nation "a loss of dignity," to protect the Pope from a situation in which he might have to break his neutrality
policy of silence and protest, and finally, to save the Jews.[4] Möllhausen was
in full agreement,[5] and moreover his wish to help Jews regardless of political
advantage had concrete credibility. He had recently learned that an Italian
woman friend of his in Rome, with whom he had begun an intimate relationship, was hiding a family of Jews in her home.[6] Running a suicidal risk,
he not only kept her secret, but throughout the occupation helped provide
for the fugitive family by furnishing his friend with extra ration books.[7]

The fourth member of this revamped conspiracy was General Stahel. In
Möllhausen's presence, he had characterized the liquidation message to
Kappler as *Schweinerei*, "something swinish," saying he wanted no part of it.[8]

Overcome with zeal by the job of Commandant of Rome, he had by now re-
cast himself as a political figure in the style of a flamboyant big-city mayor,
riding around town in an open Mercedes, going to what today are called
photo ops in a misbegotten effort to improve the German image in the occupied city. Failing miserably among the Romans, he had quickly grown in-
sufferable to his own kind as well and in fact would soon be relieved of his
post, shipped off to the eastern front, and not long after that, shipped home
in a coffin. His only success in Rome was in having cultivated good relations
with the Vatican, notably with the German nationals Father Pankratius
Pfeiffer, Pius's personal liaison to the occupation authorities, and Bishop
Alois Hudal, rector of the German church of Rome.[9] When approached by
Möllhausen about the need to prevent a breach in Vatican-German relations, Stahel quickly agreed that he would not permit the *Schweinerei* in
question without the express approval of the Wilhelmstrasse.

This was precisely what Möllhausen wanted, and with the encouragement of Kessel and Weizsäcker, but without consulting Rahn, on October 6
he sent an extraordinary telegram to the Foreign Office. (This would be one
of the most frequently cited documents of the Holocaust.) It was unusual
even at first glance. Marked *supercitissime!*—"very, very urgent!"—a priority
that did not exist, the highest being *citissime*, "very urgent," and addressed to
the personal attention of Foreign Minister von Ribbentrop, it read:

> Obersturmbannführer Kappler has received orders from Berlin to seize
> the 8,000 Jews resident in Rome and transport them to northern Italy,
> where they are to be liquidated. Commandant of Rome General Stahel in-
> forms me he will permit this action only on approval of the Herrn Reich-
> minister for Foreign Affairs. In my personal opinion it would be better
> business to employ the Jews for fortification work, as was done in Tunis,
> and, together with Kappler, I will propose this to Field Marshal Kessel-
> ring. Please advise. Möllhausen.[10]

Why Möllhausen advanced his September 26 meeting with Kesselring
and Kappler by ten days, not even he could explain when queried many years
later.[11] Moreover, the 8,000 residents figure and the destination of the de-
portees were both mistaken, but he certainly was correct about their one-
word destiny, which was all that mattered, of course. Even before receiving
a reply, he dispatched another *supercitissime* to Ribbentrop the next morning,
reporting to Kesselring his visit with Kappler but making it sound fresher.
Kesselring had asked Kappler, he wrote, "to postpone the planned action

against the Jews for the present time. If, however, it is necessary that something be done, he would prefer to utilize the able-bodied Roman Jews in fortification work near here." [12]

With these two cables, Möllhausen said later, he believed that he was "giving good news." Weizsäcker and Kessel had been kept abreast of the telegrams by the Consul, and they in turn informed the Vatican. [13] This was good news for the Vatican, to be sure, but from that day on the highest authorities in the Church, including the Holy Father, could have no doubt what the SS was planning for the Jews of Rome.

In Berlin, Ribbentrop was furious. What irked him most was not the substance of the message but that someone in the Reich Foreign Ministry—a high official, referring to Europe's Jews—had used the word *liquidate* in an official document. Worse, the first use of this word came in a telegram addressed to him *personally*. Ambassador Rahn, who was in Salò, was called at once. Forced to admit his ignorance of the entire affair, he promised a prompt explanation. Hoping perhaps that the decoded operative clause (*wo sie liquidiert werden sollen*) was some sort of garble, Rahn called Möllhausen, who could do no more than confirm the worst. "I expressly included in the telegram," he said later, "the word contained in the orders imparted to Kappler, precisely because it was this word that had upset me and compelled me to intervene decisively." [14]

In the meantime, Himmler was told of the meddling in Rome, took offense, and accused Ribbentrop of overstepping his authority. Ribbentrop was embarrassed. Kesselring was embarrassed. Rahn was embarrassed. Möllhausen was recalled and ordered to provide a full accounting of his behavior. Before departing, however, three days after sending his first telegram, he finally received the advice he had requested. In two "very urgent" dispatches from the Foreign Office to the Villa Wolkonsky dated October 9, addressed to Möllhausen *personally*, the Consul was told that on the basis of the Führer's instructions, the Roman Jews were indeed going to be deported and that Ribbentrop "requests you not to interfere in any way." The second telegram was clearer: the Reichsminister "insists that you keep out of all questions concerning Jews." [15]

It would take a greater effort still to save the Jews of Rome.

THE TROUBLES caused by Möllhausen's rash communications to Berlin did not end here, however. Every one of those cables had crossed the desk of a minor official in the Foreign Office named Fritz Kolbe. His job was to sort and prioritize cables of the highest order of secrecy to and from German missions abroad. With twenty years of service behind him, he was considered among the most loyal of Nazis, but for the past few months he had been secretly bringing home duplicates of many of these documents. On a trip to Switzerland in August, Kolbe had been recruited by the chief of the Bern office of the OSS, Allen Dulles, future director of the CIA.[16]

Kolbe, code-named George Wood, had been instructed in a method of transmitting his purloined secrets of the Reich to the OSS. These messages were code-named Kappa cables. Kolbe attributed great significance to at least two aspects of the Möllhausen telegram affair: the imminent roundup and liquidation of the Roman Jews and that it was to occur "on the basis of the Führer's instructions." The Kappa cables began to flow. In one of them, Kappa Cable 19, Kolbe signaled its importance. Noting that the October 6 telegram signed by Möllhausen was marked "For the Führer and Reichs Minister personally," Kolbe wrote:

> It is our wish, for reasons which will be perfectly clear, that you receive this message in its original form. For this reason, we are resorting to a described way of transmitting it.[17]

His request was respected. Only recently discovered among the CIA's OSS files, these Kappa cables, with information added, indicate the special treatment they were accorded by Allied intelligence. Only eight copies of the Möllhausen telegram were made, two of them, hand-delivered to the White House, for President Roosevelt himself.[18]

THE MAN charged with satisfying Himmler's personal interest in the Jews of Rome, an emphasis not often seen in the everyday killing routine, was Adolf Eichmann. His immediate task was to deal with the opposition coming from the Germans in Rome. There was nothing odd about an occasional diplomat, military officer, or—albeit far more exceptionally—even an SS colleague in this or that occupied territory lacking enthusiasm about deporting local Jews; it was demanding work and always an added burden on men at war. But the situation in Rome, particularly as depicted in Kappler's reports about inadequate police forces and a hostile population, seemed truly problematical. Eichmann was convinced that what was needed was a special expertise. Rome was to get Eichmann's best, Theodor Dannecker,

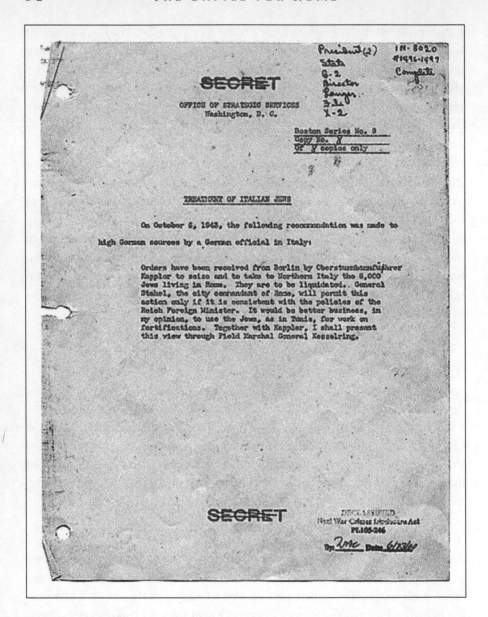

his ace troubleshooter, the thirty-year-old "Jewish expert" who one year earlier had organized and executed the *grande rafle*, the "great roundup" of the Jews of Paris.[19]

Traveling with a crack detachment of the Waffen SS Death's Head Corps, which had been placed in his command, SS Captain Dannecker arrived in Rome on October 6. His men, fourteen officers and NCO's and thirty soldiers, had been serving on the eastern front in the Einsatzgruppen,

Himmler's mobile killing squads. One of their victims would describe them as being "as tall as the gates of the Temple,"[20] those of the ghetto synagogue in Rome, which were easily twice as tall as anyone could be.

Kappler, receiving Dannecker in his Villa Wolkonsky office, would always be proud of the shortness with which he treated him. Dannecker was unflappable, however. They must have cut a frightening twosome: Kappler with his piercing steel-gray eyes, a dueling scar down his cheek, reddening, pulsating when, as now, he was bothered; Dannecker, as tall as his killing-squad men but clumsy, a tic constantly snapping his head violently to one side. Dannecker told Kappler that he had but two problems to solve: guaranteeing the secrecy of his mission and procuring the best possible list of the names and addresses of the Jews of Rome. Kappler had neither time nor men to spare, he replied, and Dannecker would have to do as all the other Germans did in Rome, deal with the Italian authorities. Later, he claimed that he steered Dannecker to the Italians "in the certainty that through the Italian police the news would be leaked,"[21] but Dannecker would show his resourcefulness by simply taking the Italians who would work with him into custody until after the roundup. Kappler, who already had the names and addresses of many of the Jews of Rome, turned over his list.

Some days later, Dannecker was back in Kappler's office, asking for his assistance on one final matter. The Waffen SS in his command was never meant to be more than a cadre. He needed more manpower, at least one motorized battalion—Kappler's original estimate. At this stage, mindful of Kaltenbrunner's admonitions, Kappler's opposition crumbled. "If Berlin did not want to listen to my reports," he said later, "I told them they would do better by removing me from Rome and sending me into combat."[22] Acting as Dannecker's nominal superior, he put through a request to General Stahel for a battalion-sized police contingent. Eating *Schweinerei*, the Stadtkommandant of Rome provided.

Dannecker was ready. The Jews would be rounded up on Saturday, October 16, beginning at one hour before sunrise in the Eternal City.

THAT DATE and time, October 16 at 5 A.M., was all that remained of the great state secret. In Rome and the Vatican and—we know now from the OSS files—in London and Washington, countless people in a position to warn the intended victims, were witnessing a countdown to tragedy. Somehow, others who were not nearly as well informed heard the countdown, too. On October 11, Cardinal Maglione's office recorded that it had received information from an Italian military intelligence agent that the Germans were planning a large roundup in Rome on the 18th, but without further detail.[23] On the 14th, Swiss diarist de Wyss spoke of "hundreds of rumours about the coming persecutions. . . . The population is half-crazy. . . . Everybody is in a cold sweat."[24] As often, Mother Mary was in the forefront of the more astute observers:

> They're at the Jews. . . . Now that they have paid their ransom, the Rabbi [i.e., President Foà] ought to destroy his register of Jewish residents in Rome. Although the Germans said that on condition of this payment they would leave them alone, how can they be trusted? The Romans are shocked and depressed; now that this sort of Jew-baiting has begun it has come home to them that they are really under the heel of the enemy.[25]

Come home to them, but not to the two most influential leaders of the ghetto Jews.

Since the gold ransom was paid, hardly a day had passed in which the Jews of Rome had not been seriously harassed by the Germans. On the morning following Foà and Almansi's delivery of the gold to the Via Tasso Gestapo headquarters, the community offices were searched by Kappler's men. They sought signs of collusion with anti-Fascists and *badogliani*, a newly coined term for supporters of the government of the King and Badoglio in the so-called Kingdom of the South. Kappler's operatives found no trace of anti-Fascism, Badoglian or otherwise, but they carted off a great deal of paper, including the complete card file of the names and addresses—the registry— of the Roman Jews.[26]

Twenty-four hours later, the Nazi scholars of the Einsatzstab Rosenberg, the erudite organization plundering occupied Europe for its art and antiquities, examined—with "suspicious attention," thought Foà[27]—the priceless holdings of the community's libraries—among the richest in the world for the study of Judaica. A few days later, Foà's suspicions, were borne out and the library was hauled away and shipped to Germany.[28] All of these things, including the seizure of the lists, were witnessed by ordinary ghetto Jews, who could only guess what they might mean. For all but the rich and the rash, however, there was, it seemed, someone with a claim to superior knowledge to advise inaction. Finally, on the Jewish Day of Atonement, Yom Kippur, one week shy of the secret date for the general roundup, several Jews were arrested. Writer Giacomo Debenedetti, himself a member of the community, recounted this initial assault in his classic 1944 article about the roundup, "16 Ottobre 1943." In the reaction to these arrests, he saw a subtle illustration of why most Jews remained inert in their homes, casting their lot with their elders:

> The wandering Jew was tired by now. He'd walked too much and could go no further. The fatigue of many exiles, of flights and deportations, acquired along the roads traveled by their ancestors for centuries and centuries had wasted the musculature of their children; their legs could drag those flattened feet no more. And then, there was, there certainly was at that time, a fifth column working away to spread "trust."
>
> For example, on October 9th several Jews were arrested. Many people were overcome with anguish; this could be the beginning of persecutions against one's person. Immediately, as if by rebound, reassuring words began to circulate (and responsible elements of the Community, without a doubt meaning well, contributed to its dissemination): those who were arrested, they said, were exceptional and special cases, a matter of individuals already well identified by their anti-Fascist activity. It was their activities that the Germans went after, not their race. The Germans, after all, were continuing to act reasonably, almost human. With their overwhelming power, with their absolute authority, *they could have done much worse.* . . . No, there was no particular reason to distrust them, to look at things so darkly.[29]

As they moved about the ghetto spreading their well-meant trust, the Jewish leadership ostensibly was acting in much the same way as those parish priests instructed by the Pope to instill calm and self-control among the Catholic faithful in whatever situation they might be. The difference, however, was one of night and day. A passive Catholic population in Rome, the Church believed, would allow the occupiers to go about their business ungrudgingly and sooner or later pack up and leave. For the Jews the occupiers' business was to round them up and kill them. Blind to this difference, Foà, Almansi, and their cohorts led the Jews of Rome into that darkness.

SIX
PAOLO MEETS
ELENA

HERE and there, the armed resistance began. A homemade grenade hurled at a German munitions convoy heading for the front down the Ostian Way and a bomb assault on Fascist militia barracks in the Fascist-chic Parioli district appear to have been the icebreakers, undertaken by Partisans of Bandiera Rossa and the Action Party, respectively. But more important, by mid-October a clear and simple strategy of resistance within Rome itself had emerged.

The underground newspaper of the Action Party, *Italia Libera*, put it this way: "We have decided to methodically inflict upon the Germans whatever blows possible, excluding no one. . . . Not only the Germans but also the Fascists . . . Spies, *agents provocateurs*, and traitors will be taken out of circulation. . . ."[1] It struck a nerve. "Idiotic writings by irresponsible elements," said the Roman Fascist daily *Il Giornale d'Italia*, calling for police action. "They think they can do with a pen what they would never have the guts to do with a more manly weapon."[2]

Mario Fiorentini, a member of GAP Central (and later the OSS) recorded how resistance strategy arose among the Gappisti. Fiorentini (code-named Giovanni), twenty-five at the time, was a mathematics major at the university. Along with his wife, Lucia Ottobrini (Maria), he was in the group commanded by Carlo Salinari (Spartaco). In early October three or four of them would hold planning meetings on one of the Tiber bridges in the *centro storico*, the Ponte Sisto and later the Ponte Sant'Angelo. He said:

The Wehrmacht had to be made to understand that they were not the masters of Rome, that they had a hostile population on their hands. We had to attack their supply lines, their vehicles whether parked or in transit to the front and their command posts. They could not be allowed to move through the city with impunity. It boiled down to this: we wanted to impose the conditions that would make Rome truly an open city. . . . [3]

This was the strategy to be pursued by GAP and the other Partisans under the CLN's Military Council, and there was a second part to its logic. The more the Partisans would succeed in rendering Rome insecure for the occupiers—striking them "in their men and in their things," they said[4]—the more they could divert the German supply-line traffic to the outlying areas of the city. These were zones under heavy Allied bombardment and formed an arena for Partisan warfare on a broader scale than in central Rome.

This was also the natural terrain of one of the most ingenious and effective "weapons" of the Resistance, the lowly four-pointed nail. A Roman Partisan named Lindoro Boccanera, who after the battle at the pyramid had found a hiding place in a military museum, at the Porta Pia, had noted among the displays of artifacts of World War I a puzzlingly shaped object of no apparent purpose. A pair of iron rods, as wide as a heavy-duty nail but twice as long, with a point at each end, had been bent in half at right angles and soldered together as interlocking vees. The result was a simple, four-pointed device that when dropped, thrown, or randomly scattered from any height or angle would always come to rest with three points making firm contact on the ground like a tripod and one point sticking straight up. Preserved from their use in the Great War and since forgotten, they were in fact a reinvention of the caltrop, a spiked weapon of the Roman army in the time of Caesar, and transformed into an infallible flatmaker.

Far worse than producing a punctured tire, slowing German traffic to the front, were the inevitable chain reactions that followed a four-pointed nail attack. An entire convoy could be immobilized when, for example, it was proceeding downhill, usually at a higher speed than normal, and rounding a curve it would roll onto a bed of, say, fifty or a hundred four-pointed nails, any one of which in such circumstances could rip a tire to shreds before a single vehicle could come to a halt. And halt they would, to recover from back-ended pileups, clear the roads, and get started again, but at the same time exposing themselves to Partisan gunfire and grenade attack. Worse still would be those gridlocks that would last until dreaded daybreak, when Allied fighter planes, strafing in the first light, would tear them apart before the sun cleared the horizon.

Boccanera contacted his Partisan comrades, and the rediscovered nail went into clandestine production in blacksmith shops, backrooms and basements all over Rome. The nails would be forged by the scores of thousands, with one blacksmith, Enrico Ferola, working nights in his Trastevere foundry, making ten thousand alone until caught with fifty kilograms of such contraband. After torture, he paid for his offense in the Ardeatine Caves. The Germans made manufacture or possession of these four-pointed nails a capital crime.

By then, the idea whose time had come was legendary. Street kids of the *borgate* would run up to German soldiers, cross their fingers like the killer nails and taunt them in song:

> *How many points, how many points,*
> *How many points has this nail?*
> *A point for me, a point for you,*
> *Four points for him!*

The "him," of course, was the Germans, and sometimes the Germans would laugh, as the kids would scamper off to safety.[5]

The first use of the four-pointed nails took place on the nights of October 10 through 13. Five squads of Partisans from Frascati and the other hill towns of the Castelli Romani spread the nails over the southbound lanes of the Via Casilina, the Via Ardeatina, and the Appian Way, snaring some twenty German trucks. Once stung, the occupiers grasped the full range of the nail's possibilities. They knew that they were up against an infernal contrivance for which there could be few unmessy remedies. While they pondered the dilemma, a fresh poster went up on the walls of Rome, particularly in the outlying districts. Reciting the usual threats, an ominous new one was added:

> We are informed that if these acts of sabotage are repeated very grave measures will be taken against those who live along the roads and in the area where such acts are repeated. It is therefore absolutely necessary that the populace, in their own interests, cooperate with the Authorities to facilitate the search and capture of those responsible.[6]

Although the barely noticed poster was not issued directly by the Germans—it was signed by the Police Forces of the Open City of Rome—it is the first written record of a retaliation threat against innocent bystanders, an act recognized under international law since 1907 as a war crime.

PAOLO had heard a lot about Elena, and what he had heard he had not liked at all. She was young, good-looking, and smart, he had been told by his friends in the underground, and she worked for Lusana's developing intelligence service, gathering information about the Germans and Fascists in Rome. She was, he kept hearing, highly cultured, from a good *borghese* family, and lived in a beautiful apartment at Trajan's Forum, in the well-known Palazzo Roccagiovine. "Everything I heard," he said later, "made me not want to trust her. Her background, her attitude, though never described to me as anything but friendly and cordial to everybody, made me judge Carla in a way that was unfair, so typical of young people and the presumptuousness of inexperience. I imagined her as some kind of coddled rich kid who was working in the Resistance only to avoid the boredom of an already jaded life. Then I saw her. . . . "

It was a morning in early October and he was on his way to a political meeting, in a great rush, he says. He had gotten on a bus at the last stop and was waiting impatiently for it to leave on its return route when he happened to see a friend of his on the street talking to a striking blond. She was slender and beautiful, he thought, dressed in a very elegant gray-green suit. His friend, Guido Rattoppatore—soon, like so many of these incipient *partigiani*, to be captured, tortured, and shot—saw him sitting on the bus and waved. The girl waved, too, then smiled.

Carla remembers the first contact rather differently:

> I was on my way to Lusana and I saw this boy out of breath running toward us; it was Bentivegna. He'd been passing by in a tram and when he'd seen his friend talking to a girl dressed in a *suit*—I was also wearing a hat—he'd gotten off to find out who she was. You know, the Latin in Italians never rests! And then he introduced himself, "Paolo." . . . Soon afterward he came to my apartment. . . . [7]

Sasà continues:

> A few days later—I'd forgotten that brief encounter and I hadn't heard a word about her since—I was asked to bring a package of underground publications to the base in Trajan's Forum. I climbed the 128 steps to Apartment 12, rang the bell in the coded way, and a young boy answered the door, looking a little worried at seeing a new face. It was Piero, Carla's

little brother, and since he knew what went on in the apartment, he was rightly suspicious.

"*Arcangelo,*" I said, giving the password. He led me into a darkened waiting room, then went inside. Later, I learned that he'd told his sister that he'd let in a "heavy-set gentleman" who had used the right password but looked like a cop. I might have looked like that to him, but it was certainly no description of me; in those days, I had a bit of a baby face, was hardly the figure of a "gentleman" and, lucky to get in one meal a day, anything but heavy-set. My friends inside were expecting me, but took no chances and prepared for the worst until one of them stole a glimpse of me and shouted a relieved "Sasà!" That was my entrance into the Capponi home.

It was a magnificent apartment. The windows faced Trajan's Column, overlooked the Forum, the Campidoglio, and you could see as far as the Janiculum. My friends, who had been playing cards with Carla while waiting for me, were seated in Louis XVI chairs. Two great mirrors from the Settecento hung on the walls, reflecting the light of the Venetian floor lamps, and a free-standing harp gave a sense of the refinement with which the home had been decorated. In front of a window was Carla's grand piano.

Carla herself was smoking a pipe. That bothered me a lot. What a show of snobbery! I thought. I did my best to mock her, to somehow offend her, not thinking that it had to do with the tobacco rationing and that a pipe was a way not to waste what was left in your cigarette butts. I behaved my worst, doing everything I could to annoy her. But Carla in the meantime got up and came toward me, with that simpatico smile of hers, so open and affectionate.

Finally, I mumbled, "I brought the printed stuff. Should we work?" Instead we started to play cards. Started arguing right away. It was love at first sight.[8]

———————

CARLA had one final score to settle with the "Latin" in her male comrades. "I wanted my own gun," she said later. "It had been steadily denied to us women by the GAP Central command." According to the leaders, all male, the urban guerrilla woman could serve best as a cover at the scene of an attack. In the moments before the attack and in the getaway, the woman would play the role of a girlfriend on the theory that two obvious lovers had only themselves on their minds. They were convinced, Carla said, that that was the extent of a woman's worth in combat. She would prove otherwise.

"I had to steal my gun. I got it from a young Fascist soldier of the GNR [Guardia Nazionale Repubblicana, Republican National Guard]. It was brand-new, a Beretta with an extra ammunition clip, all of which had been attached to his belt." She goes on:

> I'd gotten on a crowded bus with Bentivegna. We were going to [see] Luciano Lusana in the Via Salaria. The young soldier was in front of me, near the exit door, with his back toward me. His Beretta was looking right at me and I was immediately tempted. I used the crush of passengers to get as close as I could, got one hand on it, slipped it into my jacket pocket and he was none the wiser. Then, the next time the bus lurched, I slid the spare ammunition clip off his belt realizing too late that a man with a hat pulled down over his eyes was staring at me a little startled. To me he looked like a plainclothes cop and I was sure he'd seen me. Sticking my hand in my pocket, I turned to him and pressed the gun to his side. I pushed him to the exit. When the door opened, I got off with him in front of me. Bentivegna followed me. He had no idea of what was happening, but he kept a certain distance, ready to jump in if I signaled. The man broke into run and hopped onto a passing tram. In the meantime, the bus had begun to move on, but it suddenly halted and the soldier came out at the back door. He approached us, but only to search for his gun, which he must have thought had fallen out when the door was open. Bentivegna by now had understood everything. He took me by the arm, leading me forward. The driver, wanting to get going again, was rushing the soldier and we, certain we'd have no trouble now, started walking to Luciano's house. When we got there, I felt a rush of triumph as I placed the gun on a table, to show them both my very first prize of war.[9]

ON OCTOBER 15, after two days of bloodletting and 600 Allied dead, Mark Clark's Fifth Army crossed the rain-gorged Volturno River onto muddy lowland.

"Rain, rain, rain. Military operations are always conducted in the rain," read the diary entry of General John Lucas, who had just joined Clark to command the Fifth Army's VI Corps. "The roads are so deep in mud that moving troops and supplies forward is a terrific job. . . . This is a heart-breaking business. An advance of a few miles a day, fighting a terrible terrain and a determined enemy, building bridges, removing mines, climbing mountains. The men get punch drunk."[10]

At the Adriatic end of the Volturno Line, rain and superior enemy forces had stopped Montgomery's Eighth Army as well. The foul weather had foiled a surprise landing on October 3 north of the German defense position. Montgomery had succeeded in capturing the Foggia airfields, like Naples a primary objective of Avalanche, but the Eighth Army, in a state of utter exhaustion, was mud-bound by the endless flood disgorging from the overflowing Sangro River. The ferocious counterattacks unleashed by the Germans were the mark of Kesselring's determination not to yield an inch of Italian soil and certainly not a single foothold north of the Sangro.

The Allies, Montgomery concluded in reassessing the Avalanche strategy, "have made a sad mess of it," and he saw nothing but a standstill until the season changed. "Given some clear and firm directive . . . " he wrote at the time, "we would have been in Rome by now."[11] Leaving cogent prophecy in the mud, Montgomery would shortly return to England, appointed commander of the land forces for Overlord. He would bequeath the Eighth Army to his protégé, Lieutenant General Sir Oliver Leese, an uninspiring and unpopular figure destined to obscurity in the drive on Rome.

TRUE, in crossing the Volturno the Allies were thirty-five miles closer to Rome than they had been in Naples, but any satisfaction rightfully belonged not to them but to Kesselring. He had ordered the commander of the Tenth Army, Heinrich von Vietinghoff, to hold back the Allies until the same date that they actually crossed; he needed to gain the time to secure his defense fortifications. This formidable barrier, which the Allied combatants would call the Winter Line—and where scores of thousands of them would spend the worst winter of their lives—consisted of the so-named Barbara Line, the Bernhard Line, twenty-five miles farther north, and, twelve miles beyond that, the third defensive belt, the Gustav Line. Anchored on Monte Cassino and at the Garigliano and Rapido Rivers—all places that in the months ahead would become unforgettable household names back home—the Gustav Line was by far the most impregnable. It was in effect a monolith of interlocking bunkers, natural rock, and fill stretching across the Italian peninsula from one coast to the other. At Cassino, it sealed off the entrance to the Liri Valley and the ancient Casilina road to Rome, seventy-eight miles away.

FROM NORTH of the Volturno, however, Rome was beginning to look a lot farther than from the shores of North Africa, whence the bedeviled journey had begun. Early that month, Eisenhower joined Montgomery in shedding optimism about an easy march on Rome. He had undergone a "startling change," according to the official U.S. history of the campaign and warned Washington of "very hard and bitter fighting before we can expect to reach Rome." [12] Moreover, among his superiors, notably Army Chief of Staff George C. Marshall, there was a majority who were quite willing to give up the fight for Rome, much preferring to shift the fire- and manpower to Overlord, the cross-channel invasion of France.

The original goals of the Salerno campaign had been reached. Control over the port of Naples had secured Allied supremacy in the Mediterranean and the capture of the Foggia airfields provided the base for launching air strikes over almost any part of Nazi-dominated Europe. At this moment, there was almost no one in charge who could answer the question of why the Allies should not leapfrog the forces arrayed against them in Italy,[13] a war theater that could never have more than secondary status, and take on Germany in its heartland, by way of the cross-channel invasion. Roosevelt, who relied heavily on Marshall's judgment, was ready to advocate this view, and Stalin, who had been repeatedly calling on his Western allies to relieve the pressure on the Red Army in the East by opening the second front in the West, was in full agreement. It was Winston Churchill who would not relinquish Rome. "It would be impossible for us to forgo the capture of Rome," he said. "To do so would be regarded on all sides as a crushing defeat." [14]

The issue would not be decided until late November at the first Big Three conference, in Teheran, but the positions by now were known. Churchill a year earlier had conceived and advocated the "soft underbelly" theory, a farseeing approach to defeating Hitler that looked well beyond World War II. Italy would become the base from which to cross the Adriatic and thrust into the Balkan states, with the intent of bringing them to the Allied side to fight against Hitler. Less articulated at the time, but no secret, was Churchill's postwar vision of an inevitable cold war in which these newly acquired Balkan allies might be turned into a Balkan bulwark against the westward advance of Soviet Communism.[15] Stalin, who had his own dark vision of the postwar world and especially of the Balkans, found it more judicious to support Overlord than to oppose Churchill. The United States, a newcomer not only to the war but to big-power politics too, had simply not yet developed a taste for Machiavellian recipes. The Americans just wanted to win the war and bring the soldiers home.

At Teheran, the British Prime Minister would argue with Roosevelt for three days straight, attempting to convince him of Stalin's intentions to expend as many American and British lives as he could on the western front. Whether the American President pointed out the similarities between Stalin's willingness to expend Allied lives in France and Churchill's willingness to do so in Italy is not known, but in the end a compromise would be reached among the Big Three. The Allies would continue their quest for Rome, but only as a collateral effort to Overlord, for which D-Day was now early June 1944. In other words, Rome, no less coveted a trophy, was to be made that much harder to snare, because of less manpower and materiel, upping the price in British and American lives. Mark Clark, no theoretician himself and emblematic of wartime America's naiveté, would offer his hard-earned judgment of Churchill's plan: "We took a chance on Churchill's persuasive eloquence, his conviction that we could 'slit the soft underbelly of the Mediterranean.' It turned out not to be so soft."[16]

ONE of the clearest and most significant distinctions between American and British views on the war in Italy was the difference in attitude toward King Victor Emmanuel and Badoglio. The King, who had left Rome stranded in its direst hour, was now a pariah to all his people. From the shores of the Italian heel and toe to the Alpine snowline, they cried for his demise, when not crying for his head. Only a few courtiers stood by him in the impoverished phantom Kingdom of the South. Roosevelt, whose sympathies and fine-tuned sense of the American Way lay with the anti-Fascist democratic parties in Rome, kept his counsel for now, deferring to Churchill, the man on whom the Italian monarchy depended.

"I cannot for the life of me understand," Roosevelt would write to Churchill, "why we should hesitate [to support the six anti-Fascist parties]. American public opinion would never understand our continued tolerance and apparent support of Victor Emmanuel."[17]

Churchill, however, later explained that from the time of the signing of the Armistice, "I felt myself bound to work with the King of Italy. . . . On the other hand, there were the usual arguments against having anything to do with those who had worked with or helped Mussolini, and immediately there grew an endless series of intrigues among the six or seven Leftish parties in Rome to get rid of the King and Badoglio and take the power themselves. . . . I resisted these movements whenever they came to my notice."[18]

Roosevelt was willing at first to accede to Churchill's wish to postpone any action on the King's fate at least until the Allies captured Rome. But this deep divide between the Allies was having a powerful effect at Allied headquarters in Naples, notably on the OSS, with lasting implications for the Resistance movement in Rome.

LIKE the prospect of taking Rome in 1943, Peter Tompkins's original mission had faded away. With incessantly inclement skies over the Winter Line sharply restricting aerial reconnaissance, the Fifth Army needed OSS short-distance combat intelligence more than ever, and Tompkins, who had been introduced to the technique by Captain Pacatte, was now running his own operation.

He had teamed up with an Italian named Raimondo Craveri, the thirty-year-old son-in-law of Italy's world-renowned philosopher Benedetto Croce. The aging Croce, who had been rescued from the Germans at Sorrento during the Salerno campaign, had in recent months emerged as the most eloquent spokesman for the six anti-Fascist parties of the CLN. In Capri that September, Tompkins, at OSS Chief Donovan's request, had introduced the General to Croce. Asked by Donovan how the Italians and the Allies could best work together, Croce replied that it was his hope that Italy be given the chance to redeem its honor, so recently sullied anew by the flight of the King and Badoglio, by fighting side by side with the Allies. Donovan, true to his wont to act at once and then move on, took a small step in that direction by putting Tompkins together with Craveri in an effort to develop Croce's idea.

The American and the Italian devised short- and long-term operations. The first was to fill the Fifth Army's immediate frontline needs for what was called battle-order intelligence. OSS procedure at the outset, described in a recently declassified report, was to recruit local anti-Fascists from the villages along the front. Often, they were taken on in the afternoon, given need-to-know-only training, and dispatched the same night with a return rendezvous for debriefing at dawn.[19] According to Tompkins, these incursions into German-occupied territory bordered on suicide missions. Getting caught in the act meant "shot on the spot—such being the case all too frequently"—or harsh interrogation. "We also had to be careful not to re-cruit those already working for a similar, perhaps more efficient German operation aimed at fingering our men to the SS."[20]

Tompkins and Craveri soon parted company with the OSS's André Pacatte, who, in the name of trying to improve the quality of his intelli-gence, dropped the requirement that recruits be anti-Fascists in favor of employing "professionals"—usually Italian military officers with dubious motivations.

The long-range part of the Tompkins-Craveri scheme consisted of set-ting up a clandestine radio communications network linking the Partisans throughout occupied Italy to the Allies, with the CLN at the hub. In one of his earliest reports to the OSS, Tompkins explained:

> Far more and far better military (not to mention political) information could be gotten out of German-occupied Italy by making use of the un-derground movements of the various parties of the CNL [sic], rather than relying on a few professional spies (with obvious Fascist backgrounds) or adventurers out to take care of their own interests.[21]

Not only could such a system provide an instant source of deep-behind-the-lines intelligence for the Allies, but it would work in reverse as well, the Partisans benefiting from intelligence transmitted to them from the Allies. The American and the Italian saw this as a contribution to the development of a truly democratic and anti-Fascist resistance, which they, like Croce, ex-pected would restore Italian honor and determine the future of postwar Italy. "It was exactly what the King and Badoglio feared most," Tompkins said later. "And it was exactly what the British, or rather Churchill, did not want: an anti-Fascist and antimonarchic movement throughout the Italian territory occupied by the Germans and supported by the American OSS."[22]

Nevertheless, Tompkins managed to get approval from his commanding officer, Colonel Ellery Huntington, long close to Donovan, to recruit and train Italians for deployment in occupied Italy as operatives of the plan. Op-position arose at once. Tompkins and Craveri had placed their projected movement precisely in the forefront of those "Leftish" resisters whom Churchill himself opposed, and the Badoglio forces found support among the British to advance the Badoglian version of Churchill's initiative.

Already in radio contact with Montezemolo's monarchist resistance in Rome, the FMCR, the Badoglio group succeeded in imposing its own can-didates for any missions behind the lines. These men were to be drawn from the upper ranks of the Italian army, but mostly from the former military intelligence organization, Servizio Informazione Militare (SIM), a secret service of the old Fascist regime. They were in fact an unreliable band of soldiers of fortune seeking the best place they could find in the future Italy, whatever its shape or form. Compromised to one degree or another by their Fascist past, they needed to recover their political innocence. The underground, where one might succeed in pretending to have risked one's life for the nation's freedom and honor was therefore their purgatory of choice. When Tompkins would finally reach occupied Rome, he would find several of them already there, a kind of "Resistance, Inc." of political opportunists, imposters, freelance spies, double agents, and other scoundrels—all on the OSS payroll.

NOT LONG before the 9:30 P.M. curfew, Paolo and Elena stood outside Rome's Teatro Costanzi, the opera house now called Teatro dell'Opera, in the Via Viminale. There were no performances in the evenings and the street, like all streets at this hour, was nearly deserted. The pair played the part of lovers engrossed in each other. It was the first time that they were in that role, and in spite of Elena's low opinion of that ploy, her performance, as well as Paolo's, was apparently convincing.

There was a line of Wehrmacht trucks parked in front of the opera house. The occupiers used the *centro storico*, especially the most prized piazzas, as a military parking lot for everything from Tiger tanks to Volkswagen jeeps, certain that, no matter what else Allied air strikes might target over Rome, these central "parking lots" would never be bombed. But the briefcase that Paolo held was meant to end free parking in Rome.

A DAY or so before, he had seen the bomb made. He had gone to a marble-worker's shop near the Piazza del Popolo to deliver a packet of publications fresh off the underground press. The marble man was an old anarchist named Celestino Avico, a captain in the commandos of World War I. At a certain moment, Avico invited Paolo into the back room, and with due pride of craftsmanship showed him what he was working on: a length of black cast-iron pipe.

"Ever seen one of these, son?" he asked. It was a foot long, four inches in diameter, and sealed at one end with a wad of plaster, but otherwise empty. The open end looked freshly sawn from one of several much longer pipes standing in a corner.

"Can't say I ever have," said Paolo, without much interest. "What's it for?"

Avico reached into one of many similar cartons. It contained candlelike cylinders wrapped in blue paper, which he undid. "TNT," he said. Paolo was in a bomb factory. The old man filled the pipe with the easily molded waxy explosive, leaving a narrow channel running from top to bottom. "Detonator," he said, inserting a capsule and a length of fuse cut from a spool.

Paolo watched in fascination now. The last bit of TNT in the pipe did not quite fit, partly protruding. Avico picked up a massive knife and simply hacked it off in a single blow. Paolo jumped backward. The old-timer laughed. "Jesus, you don't know TNT won't blow without a detonator?" He sealed the pipe with fast-drying plaster, leaving a few inches of the fuse at the top. "This fuse burns about a centimeter a second," he said. "I gave it a ten-second burn. Sometimes there's a dead space and it burns faster. So you have to toss it, son. No hurry, but you have to give yourself that margin of safety."

Paolo had a question. "Those plaster seals on both ends, won't they blow off first, losing the force of the explosion?"

Avico looked at him as if he were a hopeless case. Wasn't he ever a soldier? he asked. Three months in the medical corps, Paolo admitted. Never left Rome. Never fired a rifle or a gun. Never touched an explosive.

"So what are you doing here, sonny? War is serious business. You have to know what you're doing, know it inside out before you put yourself and others on the line."

Paolo grew testy. "Don't worry about me," he said. "You learned it. I'll learn it." He started to storm off, turned back, and said, "I brought you some printed stuff. The idea is to distribute it. Think about that. Good-bye."

The old man stopped him and smiled. Paolo softened, smiled then laughed, mostly at himself. Avico sat him down at the workbench. "Look," he said, "TNT follows the path of *most* resistance." He picked up the bomb. "When this blows," he said, "the iron blows first, into a million splinters—takes only one to kill you." He called the bomb a *spezzone*, an outdated word from World War I that Paolo had never heard before, but which was about to enter the everyday jargon of the Roman Resistance.[23]

PAOLO and Elena stood at the side of the theater waiting and watching for the most propitious moment. Elena remembers what they talked about:

> We spoke softly, like two lovers, but we barely knew one another. He
> had shown up at our apartment and my brother had pegged him for a cop

because of the way he wore his hat; that was about all I knew. To pass the time, he told me of his love of poetry, so the first good thing was that beyond our passion for politics and anti-Fascism, we also had poetry in common, and this made being in his company more pleasurable. We began to talk about the books we'd read recently and our favorite writers. He recited a few lines from Montale, "Esterina, i vent'anni ti minacciano"; I had a preference for "Dora Marcus," and he recalled a couple of verses of that one, too, though I wouldn't have chosen those because the female character is already a woman and Esterina is a girl whose womanhood is just beginning, which was how I saw myself . . . [24]

They walked across the small piazza to the curb and the parked trucks. There were no streetlamps lit, no light visible from the surrounding buildings, and they had moved to the darkest spot. Paolo opened the briefcase, withdrew the *spezzone*, lit the fuse with a cigarette. Blue sparks jumped at them, silhouetting their bodies. They heard a hiss, smelled the biting sulfurous smoke. A few seconds had already elapsed when he rushed up to one of the trucks, placed the sizzling bomb on the gas tank mounted under the van, then fell back, taking cover with Elena. The blast shook the piazza under their feet. Windows all around them blew out, spewing glass. The truck had burst into flames, sending up a fireball that lit the baroque facade of the opera house in brilliant hues. Not a soul looked out of the windows, shattered or not. Paolo and Elena strolled away, like lovers. They went to the apartment at Trajan's Forum. Paolo slept on the couch. "I ended up in my mother's bed, sleeping very close," says Elena. "She asked me what had happened that evening and why that boy had to spend the night here, but when I didn't answer, she understood that I couldn't break the rules of the underground."[25]

SEVEN

UNDER HIS
VERY EYES

Lᴵᴷᴇ Vespasian and Titus, who set out in helmets of laurel from the Portico of Octavia at daybreak to march in triumph over Israel, Captain Dannecker's Tall Men in helmets of steel began in the same place seventy-five generations later to surround and devour the ghetto.

> In the ghetto, the beautiful ghetto—look, it was beautiful—the thing that the ghetto had was the thing that had always been there, and that was warmth. It was the warmth of families, almost all of them poor—yes, a few doing well, but that didn't change things—it was a fine, fine community.[1]

The person who spoke those words, born in the ghetto in 1921, spoke them not long before dying in Rome at the age of seventy-nine. Of the 1,023 Jews who would be arrested in the October 16 roundup and sent by box car to Auschwitz, she would be the only woman among them who would come back. Her name was Settimia Spizzichino. She survived in part because she had been selected as a human guinea pig for the infamous Dr. Mengele. And her darkest wish came true. "I made a promise when I was in the camp . . ." she said toward the end of her life, "I didn't know whether to curse God or pray to Him, but I said, 'Lord, save me, save me so that I can return and recount.' "[2] From 1945, when she was found by the Allies in a pile of death-camp corpses, asleep for two days, until she died, she spent her life recounting.[3] The story she tells of that Saturday morning under a driving autumn rain is much like the story of all the others who would be taken that day.

The family of Mosè Spizzichino, a fifty-six-year-old shopkeeper, pur-
veyor of pens and picture postcards, had like so many ghetto Jews heard
people tell them to run for their lives and had heard each telling deflated.
"This I remember well," Settimia recounted, speaking of the gold ransom
episode, "somebody among us said, 'Let's buy guns with the gold. Let's defend ourselves!' But the community said no, convinced that it was safer to
give the Germans the gold." Her mother, Grazia, fifty-four, heard the *signori* elders say so themselves and accepted that. Nevertheless the husbands
of Settimia's married sisters had gone into hiding to avoid the labor draft,
they said, and the wife of one of them, Settimia's sister Enrica, had gone with
them. That morning, when the Germans came to the Spizzichinos' third-
floor flat in the crooked ghetto lane called Via della Reginella, still living
there were Mosè, Grazia, four of their five daughters—Settimia, Gentile,
Giuditta, and the remaining married woman, Ada, and Ada's two-year-old
daughter. Ada, however, had gone out early to get a good place in line at the
ghetto tobacco shop between the two bridges of the Tiber Island, where the
weekly ration of cigarettes was to be allotted. She was there for her husband.

A single German soldier had been given the task of ferreting the Jews out
of Settimia's three-story dwelling and the noise from below was the first
warning.[4] The Spizzichinos, still in their nightclothes, thought of barricad-
ing themselves in the back room. Giuditta, the youngest, panicked, broke
from the apartment, ran down the stairs, but saw the German. She froze,
turned back, and raced into her mother's arms. The German by then was
face-to-face with them all, a list of names in his hand, giving them the pre-
ordained twenty minutes to get their lives into their satchels and pockets
and leave. Settimia acted on impulse:

> I thought that maybe I could at least save Gentile. I said that she wasn't
> Jewish, that she was our housekeeper, and I quickly turned to her and
> spoke brusquely, saying, "Ada is on the line for cigarettes," and handing
> her Ada's child, I said, "Here, bring her the baby." The German believed
> me and let Gentile go off with the baby. . . .

The remaining Spizzichinos were herded with others down the Via della
Reginella, which crosses the Portico d'Ottavia, where they were joined by
another group of prisoners. A long, single file of captured Jews was being
marched down to the Portico to wait at the gates near the ruins of the Theater of Marcellus. They were mostly women, children, and the elderly, in
various stages of dress and burdened down with useless objects from pots

and pans to pillows and blankets, taken on the assumption, falsely encouraged by the captors, that in the place where they were headed they would need them.

In a moment of confusion, Settimia's father started to drift in another direction. "Where are you going?" his wife cried. "They'll shoot you!" He had to chance it, he said, had to alert their son, who lived south of the ghetto in Testaccio. "Don't leave us," she pleaded. He left, breaking into a run. Another Spizzichino was free, but before long they saw Ada and the baby:

> Gentile had run to Ada [Settimia recounts], gave her the child, and told her what had happened. Ada got scared, was afraid for her husband, and rushed back to the house. At the corner of Via della Reginella, she was grabbed by the Germans.

They took her and the baby too.

Such were the tales of that morning and as many as not had one particular heart-wrenching feature in common. Of the Jews arrested, the women outnumbered the men by nearly two to one, and almost three out of four of the total were women and children. The reason was the widely held belief that the Germans were only after the able-bodied men for their labor. *Far scappare gli uomini*, "help the men escape,"[5] was the earliest-sounded alarm and it saved many lives. Indeed, even as the net was closing, many of the younger men and older boys were escaping at the first knock at the door, being helped by their wives and mothers to take flight across the rooftops or hide in cellars until the raid would pass. Thus there was nothing untoward about Settimia's father running off to alert his thirty-three-year-old son to escape. Untoward was the pitiful narrowness of the warning and those who had fostered the climate of "it can't happen here."

———————

THE CAPTURED Jews made to stand in the rain at the gates of the Portico of Octavia were being observed from a parked car by a German diplomat from the mission to the Holy See and an Italian princess named Enza Pignatelli Aragona Cortes. Pignatelli had been awakened that morning by an urgent telephone call from a friend who lived near the ghetto.

"Princess," the caller is reported to have said, "the Germans are arresting the Jews and taking them away in trucks!"

Pignatelli, known in certain circles for her charitable works, was shocked but perplexed. "What can I do?" she asked.

"You know the Pope," said the caller. "Go and see him. Only he can save the Jews."

Overcoming any feelings of reluctance, the Princess, who indeed knew Pius XII, had been his student before his accession, and had been received by him several times as Pope, decided to try. Lacking transportation, she called the one friend she knew whose car had not been requisitioned by the occupiers, a diplomat in Weizsäcker's embassy. The friend, Karl Gustav Wollenweber, agreed to accompany her. On the way to the Vatican, they went first to the ghetto to check on the accuracy of the caller's claim, and though even Wollenweber was stopped at the police line, they had no difficulty seeing what was happening.

According to an American journalist who interviewed the Princess not long after her story was recorded and authenticated by Jesuit historian Robert Graham, they saw "people, many still in their pajamas, being marched down the street in the rain and thrown into black-canvased trucks. They saw frightened children clinging to their mothers' skirts and old women begging for mercy. They heard screams, pathetic wails of prayer, and the slap of leather on cobblestones as some Jews tried to flee."[6]

They raced to the Vatican, and without any level of appointment, but knowing the procedure, the Princess managed to get by some startled lower-ranking officials to the *maestro di camera*, who led her to Pius's private chapel, where she found him at prayer.

"Your Holiness," Pignatelli said when a few moments later they were alone in his study, "you must act immediately. The Germans are arresting the Jews and taking them away. Only *you* can stop them."

The Pope's expression of surprise and his reply that after the gold episode the Germans had promised not to touch the Roman Jews convinced her that he was hearing this news for the first time. He immediately picked up the telephone, spoke to someone—presumably Cardinal Maglione—and showed the Princess to the door. "I'll do all I can," he said.[7]

Although the ghetto lay about a mile and a half downriver from the Vatican, Jews arrested in other parts of the city and crammed into the German trucks were passing through—and in some cases were temporarily parked— in the field of vision from the windows of the Pope's study. The closest approach, without violating Vatican territory, was on the northwestern edge of the piazza known today as Pius XII Square, about 250 yards away. The closest arrests of Jews took place in an apartment building only 600 feet from the north wall of the Vatican.[8]

The destination of all of these vehicles was the Collegio Militare, a military school fronting the Tiber, less than a quarter of a mile from the Vatican.

Here the entire catch of Jews was to be collected and processed before de- portation. Part of this hapless traffic so close to the papal apartments was thus not surprising, particularly since some German drivers, unfamiliar with the city's streets, were using the unmistakable landmark of Saint Peter's to navigate. Others, apparently in Rome for the first time, were purposely going out of their way to sightsee, to crane their necks for what might be a once-in-a-lifetime view. "The favored destination of these tourists," Debenedetti wrote in "16 Ottobre 1943," "was of course Saint Peter's Square, where several trucks stood parked for a long time. While the Ger- mans were absorbing their *Wunderbar* eyefuls with which they would one day regale some Lili Marlene back home, inside the trucks people were cry- ing out to the Pope that he might intercede and come to their rescue. Then the trucks resumed their course and even that last hope vanished."[9]

It seems unlikely, however, that the Pope was watching, much less hear- ing. Time was of the utmost importance. As he had promised the Princess, he would do all he could. The policy of silence was at risk.

THE FIRST thing he did, we know from declassified Vatican documents, was to try to stop the arrests, with the further hope of obtaining the victims' release. Secretary of State Maglione summoned Ambassador Weizsäcker and met with him during the day, probably in the morning. Apart from try- ing to prevent the expected persecution of the Jews, Maglione and Weizsäcker had been working closely on other matters in recent days, no- tably the papal wish for reinforcements of German police forces in Rome and the text of a statement to be issued by the Vatican at Berlin's request ac- knowledging the Germans' respect for the sovereignty of Vatican City. Thus, the spirit of cooperation ran high as Maglione's notes on the meeting appear to attest. The Cardinal wrote:

> I asked him to intervene in favor of those poor people. I spoke to him as best as I could in the name of humanity and Christian charity.
>
> The Ambassador, who already knew about the arrests . . . replied to me in all sincerity, saying with some emotion: "I am always waiting for you to ask me: Why do you remain in this position of yours?"
>
> I exclaimed: No, Mr. Ambassador, I would never presume to ask you such a question. I simply wish to say to you, Excellency, you who have a good and tender heart, try to save these many innocent people. It is painful for the Holy Father, painful beyond words, that right here in

Rome, under the eyes of the Common Father, so many people are made to suffer only because of their particular descent—

The Ambassador, after some moments of reflection, asked me: "What would the Holy See do if these things were to continue?"

I replied: The Holy See would not want to be faced with the need to express its disapproval.

The Ambassador observed: For more than four years I have followed and admired the attitude of the Holy See. It has succeeded in steering the boat amid all shapes and sizes of rocks without running aground and, even though it had greater faith in the Allies, it has maintained a perfect equilibrium. Now, just as the boat is about to reach port, is it worth it, I ask myself, to put it all at risk. I am thinking of the consequences that such a step by the Holy See would provoke—

These measures come from the highest level. "Will Your Eminence leave me free not to report this official conversation?"

I observed that I had asked him to intervene appealing to his sentiments of humanity. I was leaving it to his judgment whether or not to mention our conversation, which had been so friendly.[10]

In what appears to be a corrective to Weizsäcker's mild reproach of the Vatican's "greater faith in the Allies," Maglione wrote that he reminded him "that the Holy See, as he [Weizsäcker] himself pointed out, has been very prudent, so as not to give the German people the impression of having done or wished to do the slightest thing against Germany in this terrible war."[11] Adding a touch of emphasis, at least in his notes, he repeated that the Vatican "must not be be placed in a position of having to protest [but] if the Holy See were forced to do so, it would trust in divine Providence with regard to the consequences." Finally, he thanked the ambassador for saying that he would "try to do something for these poor Jews," and again reassured him that he would say nothing of their conversation.[12]

Pius's defenders have offered this document, kept secret in the Vatican archives for more than thirty years, as proof of the Pope's deep concern for the Jews, evidence that he did in fact protest the deportation. Some critics have found it to be a consummate illustration of the opposite. A cooler reading, however, might interpret it as a desperate plea to save the Jews, with the political intent also to save the papal policy of silence. Saving the silence—the cherished strategy of neutrality, the separate peace with Germany to keep Communism at bay—was of course what both men wanted. The threat of protest raised by Maglione was the transmittable slap in the face Berlin might need to come to its senses. Weizsäcker's counterthreat of provoking consequences from the "highest level" was a temporary restraining order on any papal protest. This confrontation might be regarded as the opening exchange in a historic showdown.

GERHARD Gumpert, a thirty-three-year-old legation secretary in the Villa Wolkonsky assigned to procuring foodstuffs, normally potatoes and grain, on this day would have the most important task in the concerted effort to save the Jews of Rome.

Consul Möllhausen, who had been summoned north to account for his embarrassing telegrams to Foreign Minister Ribbentrop, had placed Gumpert in charge. At about ten o'clock that morning, Kessel showed up in Gumpert's office. Gumpert was a good friend of Kessel's—and Weizsäcker's as well—but ill-prepared for the collaborative role he was now being asked to play. As chief of the embassy's economic section, Gumpert was only dimly aware of what his colleagues had been up to, but when Kessel brought him up to date he agreed to join them. Considering Möllhausen's clash with his superiors and the warning he had received to steer clear of Himmler's designs on the Jews of Rome, Gumpert, who would settle in Italy for the rest of his life, surely had Roman fever bad.

An intricate diplomatic maneuver was strung together with exceptional speed by Weizsäcker, Kessel, and Gumpert, and the Vatican was brought into the picture.[13] The plan was meant to carry out the spirit of the Maglione-Weizsäcker meeting—save the Jews and save the silence—while keeping the matter firmly in control of the Rome-based extended German "family." Thus, the threat of a papal protest conveyed by Maglione was to be reconveyed in the form of a letter from Bishop Alois Hudal, a German national and rector of the German Catholic Church in Rome. Kessel had suggested that the Vatican "lodge an official protest,"[14] but Hudal, known to be sympathetic to the Nazis (and they to him) was conveniently distant from the inner circle of the Curia and more convenient for the plan. The threat would appear on Hudal's church letterhead and not on that of the Holy See, and so it won the Pope's and Maglione's blessing. The Bishop's letter was to be addressed to Stadtkommandant Stahel, that other "family" member, who was also a practicing Catholic and a good friend of Hudal's. That Stahel had provided three companies of troops presently deployed in the roundup was probably unknown to the schemers, but by now beside the point. The Hudal letter, to be hand-delivered by Pius's personal liaison to the occupiers, another German, Father Pankratius Pfeiffer, was not intended to provoke any action by Stahel. Instead Gumpert would bring the letter to the attention of the Foreign Office.

Thus, the relatively low-ranking Gumpert, the potato-and-grain man, became the ghostwriter of the historic Hudal letter.[15] While the details of the plan were being set into place, Gumpert, with input from Kessel, dictated the kind of letter that he believed would have the most effect in the Foreign Office. When signed by the Bishop, copied to the Vatican,[16] delivered at five in the afternoon by Father Pfeiffer to Stahel (with some minor cuts made along the way), recovered according to script by Gumpert and sent as a telegram from Gumpert to Berlin later in the evening, it read:

> I must speak to you of a matter of great urgency. An authoritative Vatican dignitary, who is close to the Holy Father, has just told me that this morning a series of arrests of Jews of Italian nationality has been initiated. In the interests of the good relations that have existed until now between the Vatican and the High Command of the German Armed Forces . . . I earnestly request that you order the immediate suspension of these arrests both in Rome and its environs. Otherwise I fear that the Pope will take a position in public as being against this action, one which would undoubtedly be used by the anti-German propagandists as a weapon against us Germans.[17]

Weizsäcker, clearly the wizard behind the curtain, now activated the second phase of the plan. Allowing several more hours to pass, time for reflection or the appearance thereof, he composed the following dispatch to the same desk in the Wilhelmstrasse that had received Gumpert's telegram:

> With regard to Bishop Hudal's letter (cf. the telegraphed report of October 16 from Rahn's office), I can confirm that this represents the Vatican's reaction to the deportation of the Jews of Rome. The Curia is especially upset considering that the action took place, in a manner of speaking, under the Pope's own windows. The reaction could be dampened somewhat if the Jews were to be employed in labor service here in Italy.
>
> Hostile circles in Rome are using this event as a means of pressuring the Vatican to drop its reserve. It is being said that when similar incidents took place in French cities, the bishops there took a clear stand.[18] Thus the Pope, as the supreme leader of the Church and as Bishop of Rome, cannot

but do the same. The Pope is also being compared with his predecessor, Pius XI, a man of more spontaneous temperament.

Enemy propaganda abroad will certainly view this event in the same way, in order to disturb the friendly relations between the Curia and ourselves.[19]

The Weizsäcker telegram was sent as a night letter and would not arrive in Berlin until the next day, Sunday. It had been one long day of diplomacy. For the first time during the war a direct challenge had been raised at the highest level of Vatican and German relations. There was still a face-saving middle ground on which to back away, namely, Weizsäcker's rehabilitation of the old idea of using the Jews for labor service in Italy. In all other reports the Pope would stand eye-to-eye with the Führer. The only question would be who would blink first.

———————

ALL the talk of stopping the arrests had been rendered purely figurative hours before the Hudal request had even been delivered to its first recipient. By 2 P.M. that Saturday the last home on the list had been emptied, the last of the captured Jews transported to the Collegio Militare. The only Jew in Rome still in his own apartment after that hour, it seems, was President Foà.[20] He had received word of the raid on the ghetto and elsewhere very early that morning, had rushed to the Italian Fascist authorities to report what he termed a "premeditated crime." Accorded scarce attention, he had returned home shortly afterward. He was shocked. He was now prepared to concede that he had pursued a vain illusion. Blaming the victims—though only for lacking a "Teutonic mentality"—he saw their failure to foresee that they like their fellow Jews in Germany and Poland would suffer "unspeakable horrors" as a result of their "Italian spirit." Hiding had therefore been "more than justified," he admitted, yet for two days more he sat at home in lugubrious contemplation, waiting perhaps to be taken, and then quietly hid.[21]

SOMETIME around midnight, Obersturmbannführer Kappler filed a vivid report on the roundup for Himmler's headquarters in Berlin. Ultra intercepts, recently released, indicate what was known at the time in London and Washington. Kappler's report reads (the items in square brackets were added by the cryptographer; the question-marked items are in fact accurate):

> Action against Jews started and finished today in accordance with a plan worked out as well as possible by the office. All available forces of the Sicherheitspol. And the Ordnungspol. employed. Participation of the Italian police was not possible in view of unreliability in this respect, as only possible by individual arrests in quick succession inside the 26 action districts. To cordon off whole blocks of streets, in view both of [Rome's] character as an open city and of the insufficient number of German police, 365 in all, not practicable. In spite of this 1259 persons were arrested in Jewish homes and taken to assembly camp[s] of the military school here in the course of the action which lasted from 0530 to 1400 hours. After the release of those of mixed blood, of foreigners including a Vatican citizen, of the families in mixed marriages including the Jewish partner, and of the Aryan servants and lodgers, there remain 1002 Jews to be detained. Transportation on Monday 18[?]/10 at 0900. Escort by 30 men[?] of the Ordnungspolizei[?].

In the original transmission, the number "1002 Jews" was "1,007 Jews."[22] Missing parts of the intercept occur only in the following, final paragraph. I have placed them in brackets:

> Attitude of the Italian population was unequivocally one of passive resistance, which in a large number of individual cases has developed into active assistance. In one case, for example, the police were met at a house-door by a Fascist with an identity document and in a black shirt, he having undoubtedly taken over the Jewish house only an hour before and alleged it to be his own.[23] [As the German police were breaking into some homes, attempts to hide Jews] in neighboring apartments were observed the whole time and [it is believed that in many cases they were successful. The anti-Semitic] part of the population did not make an appearance during the action, but only the broad masses, who in individual cases even attempted to keep single policemen back from the Jews. [In no case was it necessary to use firearms.][24]

Kappler's depiction of passive resistance and some opposition notwithstanding, the fact that the roundup was carried out without a shot reveals the collective state of mind in Rome five weeks into the occupation. Rome had experienced an initiation to a horror unlike any other even under Fascism and had been chilled to its marrow. If Jews were being deported from the city of the Pope, was there no hope anywhere, for anyone? De Wyss caught the moment: "This has made a deep impression in the city . . . now, on seeing the German procedure, they are shocked and more terrified than ever, for it is generally expected that other persecutions will follow the Jewish ones."

The CLN, meeting that same day, would call for its armed resistance organizations to do battle on the streets of the city, but this was too late for the captive Jews. The underground press rolled that night. "All day long, the Germans went around Rome seizing Italians for their furnace in the north," the Action Party's *Italia Libera* would say when it materialized in letter boxes and stuffed in the folds of Fascist newspapers the following morning. "The Germans would like us to believe that these people are in some way alien to us, that they are of another race. But we feel them as part of our flesh and blood. They have always lived, fought, and suffered with us. Not only able-bodied men, but old people, children, women, and babies were crowded into covered trucks and taken away to meet their fate. There is not a single heart that does not shudder at the thought of what the fate might be."[25] A long and equally moving exhortation to bury the enemy forever came next, but the truth was that Rome was a city not yet ready for the fight.

The *Italia Libera* article may have been what Kappler meant when later that day he sent Berlin a post-roundup "survey of morale"—partially intercepted by Ultra—in which he saw sympathy for the Jews as "artificially heightened by whisper propaganda." Nevertheless he reported: "Population excited and angry after the action against the Jews. Sympathy is the uppermost feeling among the lower classes, especially because women and children were taken." There was, he noted, "growing indignation, especially against the German police." Even the Fascists were unhappy, said Kappler, but only because "the Jewish question has not been solved by Fascism."[26]

INSIDE the Collegio Militare, the Jews, sleeping on benches and classroom chairs, awoke on Sunday with one more prisoner among them. Twenty-three-year-old Marcella Di Tivoli Perugia, lying on the courtyard pavement under a nighttime sky, had given birth to a full-term baby. Twenty-four hours earlier, she and her two children had been arrested in the ghetto as her husband escaped, and now the mother of three and the new prisoner were doing as well as they ever would.

If Romans on the outside shuddered to think of that furnace in the North, almost all of those on the inside had been persuaded by their captors that they were going to a labor camp. Everyone, they were told by Dannecker himself, would be given a job, according to his or her skills, and those who could not work, the children, and the elderly would be supported by the rich Jews paying for the poor Jews. This was a way of relieving rich and poor alike of whatever valuables they might still have with them. But the general description of the coming internment, though few imagined it as less than severe, many of the poorest Jews regarded as a net improvement in their daily struggle for subsistence. Settimia Spizzichino would always remember the touch of her mother's fingers running through her hair as she said repeatedly, "Don't cry. It won't be bad at all. We'll be okay in jail. We'll eat well."[27]

On Sunday morning a Vatican official went to the Collegio Militare. The Secretariat of State had apparently learned of the release of some 250 non-Jews and part-Jews who were the offspring of a parent who was a half-Jew. These were the so-called Mischlinge, who were freed along with those seized by mistake by Dannecker on Saturday in accordance with German law. Their release, as we have seen, was reported to Berlin by Kappler. The Vatican emissary on Sunday hoped to obtain the freedom of any baptized Jews. Although Jews who had converted to Catholicism were legally no less Jewish to the Germans, such interventions had occasionally been successful elsewhere in Europe. The Vatican official learned that there were indeed some baptized Jews among the Roman prisoners, but they were not released. This effort was probably the origin of a myth that exists to this day that Pope Pius XII was responsible for the release of all 250 or so freed. The Vatican documents support no semblance of any such claim and speak only of the failed efforts on behalf of the baptized Jews.[28]

Neither is there any evidence or even logic behind Bishop Hudal's claim that he was told by Stadtkommandant Stahel on that Sunday that Himmler, hearing of the Vatican threat to protest, had stopped the arrests—just as the Bishop had requested. Since the roundup had ended as planned hours before Stahel's receipt of the Bishop's letter and much longer still before Himmler could be informed of its content, Hudal's contention was simply one more flight of fancy. Yet, such rumors flew and a few still fly.

The suggestion of protest by the Pope, who had suffered an offense too painful for words, still awaited response. To a community of churchmen who had barely gotten over fears of a Nazi invasion and an abduction of the Holy Father, these were tense moments, taking their toll on the soundness of judgments. How else to explain that the longer the challenge remained ignored, the odder the Curia behaved? When Mother Mary, with her daily presence inside the Vatican Information Bureau, wrote that "it is understood that the Pope has asked the German Ambassador to make an effort to help the Jews," it is reasonable to assume that her source was someone at least as much an insider as she, just as it is when she adds that Weizsäcker "did have some measure of success, for we hear that the women and children will be released."[29] That was written on the 19th, when the women and children were already riding in the box cars side by side with the men, 400 miles north of Rome, the whole trainload half-maddened by thirst and hunger and foul air, so Mother Mary's source was the bearer or author of falsehood. On the 19th, the threat of papal protest, as transmitted in the Gumpert and Weizsäcker telegrams, was still unanswered, and in fact lay on the same desk in the Wilhelmstrasse where it had landed, with a note scribbled by the desk man, Group Leader Eberhard von Thadden, that Foreign Minister von Ribbentrop would deal with them when he "has time."[30]

Time was the enemy of the Jews, of course, but also of the Pope. It was certainly not Mother Mary's source who told British Ambassador Osborne that his counterpart Weizsäcker had taken immediate action when threatened with the protest. His source, according to Osborne, was Cardinal Maglione himself, who then made the disastrous leap of adding that Weizsäcker's action had borne "the result that large numbers were released." Osborne was then cautioned by Maglione to keep the news of this major papal "achievement" under wraps, though he was permitted to pass it on to the Foreign Office. Osborne was told by Maglione, he reported to London, that it was "strictly for your information, and on no account for publicity since any publication of information would probably lead to renewed persecution."[31] The more the Pope's threat remained pending, the more "effective" it became.

The waiting game would continue all that week. On Monday, October 18, the captured Jews set out on the one-way trip to Auschwitz, picking up a final passenger at the point of departure. Her name was Costanza Calò Sermoneta. She had been out of Rome for some days, returning that morning to the echoes in her empty ghetto apartment. Only then had she learned of the roundup and the arrest of her husband and their five children. In her distress, she, like a small number of others, had found her way to Tiburtina Station, in the San Lorenzo district, where the twenty-car freight train containing the prisoners sat in the middle of the rail yards, bolted shut and ready to leave. Pounding her fists on the box cars and shouting her husband's name, she found her family, and in spite of her husband and others warning her to flee, she pleaded with the Germans to let her go with them, and they did. At 2:05 in the afternoon, as passengers threw letters to loved ones from cracks and airholes with pleas to the finders to post them, the train slid down an arrow-straight track pointed north and soon disappeared.

THE DEPARTURE of the death train from Tiburtina Station greatly diminished any possibility of directly aiding those captured and to that extent increased the pressure on the Pope to carry out his protest threat. The tension inside the Vatican was heightened, too. An OSS Kappa cable, a hitherto unknown message from Weizsäcker to the Wilhelmstrasse, telegraphed that day, casts a ray of light on those privileged corridors. The subject matter was the declaration Ribbentrop was seeking about how well the occupiers were treating the Holy Father. Weizsäcker had gone to Cardinal Maglione with a Ribbentrop-approved draft of the proposed declaration, but with some trepidation, it seems. He found the Vatican Secretary of State "under the influence of the Jewish arrests," he wrote, "and I had some fears about the moment being a favorable one." Weizsäcker's fears, however, were unfounded. It was the first day of a new workweek and Maglione promised to take up the Ribbentrop draft with the Pope.[32]

Pius received Osborne on that same day. Like his German counterpart, the British diplomat wondered about the strain on the Pope's policy of silence. He was at a loss to explain to himself what it would take for the Pope to make his moral authority heard. How vile would the Germans have to get, he wondered, directly asking the Pope under what conditions it would be impossible for him to stand by in Rome and do nothing; when would it be better to leave? The Pope was resolute. He would never leave Rome, he said, unless forcibly removed. Moreover, he told Osborne, he had no complaints against General Stahel or the German police; they were indeed respecting Vatican neutrality and had even helped some Jews.[33] Reporting to London, Osborne wrote that he shared the opinion of many that this German respect was based on Pius's moral influence on the large Catholic population of Germany. He had urged the Pope, he said, not to underestimate that moral authority in case "in the course of coming events an occasion might arise for taking a strong line."[34]

The Pope turned again to the issue of "insufficient" police forces in Rome. Stunningly severe measures such as the roundup were bound to exasperate the population, driving some into the arms of the "Communists."

Having received assurances from Weizsäcker that he would pursue the matter of putting more police on the streets of Rome, Pius now discussed the situation with the American envoy in the Vatican, Harold Tittmann, in an audience on the 19th. The Pope, Tittmann cabled Washington the same day, "seemed preoccupied that in the absence of sufficient police protection, irresponsible elements (he said it is known that little Communist bands are stationed in the environs of Rome at the present time) might commit violence in the city." Pius XII, according to Tittmann, hoped that this issue would be "given consideration by the Allies and necessary measures taken by them in time."

Once again, the Pope wanted the Allies to know that the Germans were respecting Vatican City and its property in Rome, but, Tittmann concluded, "he was feeling restrictions due to the 'abnormal situation.' "[35]

On Saturday the 23rd, the Wilhelmstrasse finally acted on the telegrams. In a move authorized by Ribbentrop that can be described as not entirely unfavorable to the Pope's initiative, Group Leader Thadden sent a memorandum to Adolf Eichmann about Bishop Hudal's letter and Weizsäcker's confirmation of a possible papal protest. Adopting Weizsäcker's own words, Thadden related the ambassador's opinion that the Curia's displeasure could be mollified if the Jews were to be used for labor service in Italy.[36] Eichmann, as soon as he received the memo, sent it to his superior, the highest official of the Gestapo and the man who had signed the order for the roundup, Heinrich Mueller, asking him, Eichmann later said, "to indicate to me what was to be done."[37] Mueller's reply, if any, is unknown.

By coincidence, it seems, the Thadden memorandum was dispatched on the day that the convoy carrying the captive Jews of Rome arrived in Auschwitz. Their numbers had been reduced by the deaths of three or four elderly passengers during the hellish journey and the one known escape of a young man who had seized an opportunity to jump from the moving train somewhere north of Padua.[38] As the arrivals debarked in the early morning, they were received on the platform with a certain cordiality by the "labor camp" medical director, Dr. Josef Mengele. He asked them to approach him one by one in what was called a "selection." This resulted in the formation of two groups, one consisting of about 820 men, women, and children, who, Mengele decided, were not physically fit for work. The second, the able-bodied group, was made up of 154 men and 47 women. The two groups were now separated. The 201-person work group went on foot to male and female barracks, and the other 820 went by truck to the "rest camp." It was a simple matter now to lead them into the "bathhouses," have them undress, and send them into a "shower room," where they were gassed. Minutes later, their bodies were hosed down, their hair and any gold teeth removed for shipment that same day to the Reich, and the corpses sent by elevator to be incinerated. By the late afternoon the smoke of their remains was in the Polish sky, their ashes and milled bones at the bottom of a tributary of the Vistula River. As for the work group, one member died in the first week. The others went to work, some in Auschwitz, some in Warsaw, and some in nearby coal mines. No one survived Auschwitz (after the Mengele experiments, Settimia Spizzichino was transferred to the Bergen-Belsen death camp). Fifteen men survived the external slave labor.

THE VATICAN State Secretariat had been kept abreast of the deportation train's progress.[39] Nevertheless, the papal policy of silence was reaffirmed on Monday the 25th. The threat of protest was never raised again. Instead, the Vatican, as it had done repeatedly, expressed its disapproval of the war that the Pope had tried in vain to prevent. That afternoon the Vatican newspaper *L'Osservatore Romano*, the only legal non-Fascist daily in Rome and thus widely read, carried a front-page editorial deploring the "sufferings of innocents." A second editorial appearing alongside it scolded the Germans—in rarefied language accessible only to Vatican watchers of the highest order—for that act, painful beyond words, that had taken place under the eyes of the Common Father, as Maglione had put it. "Persistent and pitiful echoes of calamities," said the Vatican editorial, ". . . continue more than ever to reach the Holy Father." It went on:

> The August Pontiff . . . has not desisted for one moment in employing all the means in his power to alleviate the suffering that, whatever form it may take, is the consequence of this cruel conflagration.
>
> With the increase of so much evil, the universal and paternal charity of the Pontiff has become, it could be said, ever more active; it knows no boundaries, neither of nationality, religion, nor descent.
>
> The manifold and ceaseless activity of Pius XII has intensified even more in recent times in regard for the increased suffering of so many unfortunate people.[40]

Clipped and translated, the editorial was sent to Berlin by Weizsäcker's embassy with a letter from the Ambassador that preserves the sense of satisfaction redolent of a master of damage control. Recalling his protest-threat telegram of the 17th, he wrote:

> The Pope, although under pressure from all sides, has not permitted himself to be pushed into a demonstrative censure of the deportation of the Jews of Rome. Although he must know that such an attitude will be used against him by our adversaries and will be exploited by Protestant circles in the Anglo-Saxon countries for the purpose of anti-Catholic propaganda, he has nonetheless done everything possible even in this delicate matter in order not to strain relations with the German government and the German authorities in Rome. As there apparently will be no further German action taken on the Jewish question here, it may be said that this matter, so unpleasant as it regards German-Vatican relations, has been liquidated.[41]

As evidence, he cited the *Osservatore* article, which he referred to wryly as a "semi-official communiqué on the loving-kindness of the Pope," and he concluded that few could understand its "roundabout and muddled style," much less as alluding to the Jews. Someone in the Wilhelmstrasse underlined the key words in Weizsäcker's letter: "POPE NOT PUSHED . . . DONE EVERYTHING POSSIBLE . . . MATTER, SO UNPLEASANT AS IT REGARDS GERMAN-VATICAN RELATIONS, HAS BEEN LIQUIDATED."[42]

The end of the unpleasant interlude in these relations came less declaratively inside the Vatican. On November 1, All Saints' Day, Monsignor Montini quoting information originating from Stadtkommandant Stahel, noted, "These Jews will never again return to their homes."[43]

For Pius XII, however, the problem of the Jews of Rome had only just begun. To be sure, the dead would never return to their homes, but the same was suddenly and dramatically true for the living. For every person of the thousand captured and deported, there were eleven Roman Jews who had escaped the net. Only the most credulous would ever again set foot where the Nazis had already come calling. There was a new breed of Jew loose on the streets of Rome, hunted in the only way possible now, one by one. Unlike the dead who had gone from one darkness to another, these were Jews forewarned, as shorn of illusions as they were of the roofs over their heads. In a city of hundreds of parish churches; well over a thousand convents, monasteries and other religious institutions; and tens of extraterritorial and quasi-extraterritorial enclaves and of course the Vatican itself, the Jews would soon come knocking at their doors.

EIGHT

FIRST BLOOD

EXCEPT for the black skies and chilling rains of the day of the roundup, it had been unusually hot in Rome all fall, heading into an *estate di San Martino*, the Italian phrase for "Indian summer." On one of those evenings, at the end of October, Paolo, Giovanni (Mario Fiorentini), and Pietro (Franco Di Lernia) were walking their bicycles just outside the Piazza Navona in preparation for a double assassination. This was to be the first operation of its kind in the center of the occupied city and it had been aimed very high. They planned to kill two ministers of the new Fascist regime, Guido Buffarini-Guidi, head of the Ministry of Interior, and Francesco Barracu, a minister in Mussolini's cabinet.

The lately constituted Partito Fascista Repubblicano (PFR), or Fascist Republican Party, had installed itself in the Palazzo Braschi, an old papal palace of some magnificence located on the Corso Vittorio Emanuele II. Palazzo Braschi is a point of an imaginary topographical triangle formed with the Pantheon and the Piazza Navona, and that area of the *centro storico* had become the hub of newly coalesced Fascist gangs. Bearing names such as "Rome or Death" and "Honor and Combat," they prowled the downtown streets, their members literally dressed to kill. Guns, grenades, and brass knuckles dangled from the leather straps and thongs of paramilitary getups topped with a black beret featuring the word *death* or a silver skull.

They were permanent hunting parties, after such prey as anti-Fascists, Carabinieri, escaped Allied prisoners of war, and, now more than ever, Jews. Those who were caught were rarely seen again, tortured and swallowed in newly outfitted dungeons of the Palazzo Braschi. The palace harbored a self-appointed police force, which committed or profited from nearly all of the city's crimes—from black-marketeering, lootings, and shakedowns to violence—in the service of political repression and violence for the fun of it. The occupiers themselves, horrified when learning of such unmitigated, and worse, unauthorized, criminality, would soon put a stop to its worst features, arresting and imprisoning the ruling Palazzo Braschi triumvirate— swaggering party bosses Gino Bardi, Guglielmo Pollastrini, and Carlo Franquinet—and forty of their accomplices, but for now the Fascists of Rome's center had become the target of the Gappisti.

This was the fourth evening in a row that Paolo, Giovanni, and Pietro had been ready to strike. The two ministers habitually dined together at a well-known restaurant, Il Passetto, in a small piazza between the Navona and the cobbled medieval lanes leading to the Tiber embankment. They had not been seen in the past three days, but surveillance had revealed that they would be there that evening with a sizable escort of bodyguards at about eight o'clock. They arrived as a burly bunch pouring out of their dark blue cars, the *signori ministri* entering Il Passetto, bodyguards posted outside. The attack was to take place when the two ministers emerged, the idea being that security would relax as time went by and passing civilians would have long gone home to beat the curfew. The Partisans were going to launch three powerful *spezzoni* and disappear by bicycle into those narrow streets behind them. In the meantime, to avoid arousing suspicion, they rode off in different directions, scheduled to return to their positions some forty minutes later.

Of the two targets, seated no doubt at their favorite table, Interior Minister Buffarini-Guidi was by far the bigger game, Barracu being an old Fascist workhorse. Buffarini, a Mussolini loyalist arrested by Badoglio in the coup and released by Kesselring, was rewarded by the Duce with this key ministry of the new regime, though only reluctantly. "He is hated even more than me," Mussolini said of Buffarini.[1] Buffarini's long-term friendship with Colonel Dollmann, however, and through Dollmann, a well-cultivated closeness to Reichsfürher Himmler, along with his role as confidant of Mussolini's wife, Rachele, made him valuable to the puppet government. His principal task was to strengthen the Fascist police nationwide in the suppression of the Partisan movement. In the thrall of some form of blackmail by Palazzo Braschi chieftain Gino Bardi,[2] Buffarini was first, at least in rank, among those who protected the party's wanton thuggery. It would have been hard to find a better Fascist target for assassination.

Yet, as Paolo, waiting for the appointed hour, pedaled his bicycle along the Tiber embankment, second thoughts were setting in:

It was my first time going under fire and I was mulling over what I was about to do. Was it worth risking my skin so out in the open? I could be killed by the bodyguards even before I got the fuse lit, or maybe I'd get the fuse lit and somehow fall off the bike still holding it, or maybe in any case I'd get killed by the blast. Who was making me do this? Why me?[3]

Nevertheless he was back in position on time and so were his GAP comrades. The ministers' escorts were in place, too, gathered around their cars and hardly on the alert. As Paolo and the others poised for the ministers to exit, they were approached by the commander of the operation, who signaled them with urgency to withdraw. Their mission had been called off, he told them when they later regrouped. Some of their fellow Partisans had just been arrested, and the fear was that the assassination of Buffarini and Barracu would become the justification for retaliation against the men who had fallen into Fascist hands. The risk of provoking the enemy into a reprisal against innocents was the most important concern in any resistance movement, and had to be addressed swiftly and decisively.

The relevant international law at the time—the Rules of Land Warfare of the 1907 Hague Convention, ascribed to by all the parties to World War II —provided for the punishment solely of the perpetrators of acts against an occupying force. Yet the Nazis, and not only they, had carried out reprisals against innocent civilians, particularly in the east and most infamously in Lidice, a Czechoslovakian village of 450 people just outside of Prague. There, in a June 1942 reprisal, all the men of Lidice were shot and the women and children deported, following the assassination of Reinhard Heydrich, second only to Himmler in the SS, and chief organizer of the plan for the extermination of Europe's Jews.

"We had already absorbed the idea that we could die," Paolo would say later, "but it seemed to us unacceptable that others, friends, comrades or men, women and children whom we did not know but were still our people, the very people we were fighting for, might suffer the brutal vengeance of the enemy stricken by us. On the other hand, were we supposed to surrender to the threat, renounce every act of war, and accept whatever military and political violence the enemy imposed?"[4]

That night Buffarini-Guidi and Barracu quietly went home none the wiser, but the Partisans' dilemma was not put aside. In the days ahead, it was the object of intense discussion and was promptly settled by the Military Council. "The problem of reprisals," Giorgio Amendola wrote in a memoir of the underground, "was raised and resolved once and for all at the beginning of the Partisan war in Italy as it had been in France and in the other countries occupied by the Nazis. To accept the blackmail of reprisals meant renouncing the struggle from the outset. One had to react to Nazi reprisals on a one-by-one basis without submitting to the enemy's threat. . . . We represented a component of a fighting army. We were in fact participants at the highest level of command of that army. . . . We had but one duty: to keep on fighting."[5]

———————

SINCE crossing the Volturno in mid-October, Mark Clark's Fifth Army had advanced no more than ten or fifteen miles by the end of November, a per-day gain best measured in feet and inches. Worse, the Allies had yet to breach the second of the three defensive belts that formed the Winter Line. The latest attacks, twelve days of pounding and running at the ring of fire from the sheer cliffs of Kesselring's mountain fortresses, had failed, sending the mule trains of the dead and wounded and the walking weary back to the mud below.

"Our troops were living in almost inconceivable misery," wrote Ernie Pyle, the war correspondent, who lived and later died with them. His eloquent dispatches from the foxholes of the Italian campaign transformed the temporal sufferings endured by the ordinary soldier into a timeless statement on the wretchedness of war.

> The fertile black valleys were knee-deep in mud [he wrote from the Winter Line]. Thousands of the men had not been dry for weeks. Other thousands lay at night in the high mountains with the temperature below freezing and the thin snow sifting over them. They dug into the stones and slept in little chasms and behind rocks and in half caves. They lived like men of prehistoric times, and a club would have become them more than a machine gun. . . . The frontline soldier I knew lived for months like an animal, and was a veteran in the cruel, fierce world of death. Everything was abnormal and unstable in his life. He was filthy, dirty, ate if and when, slept on hard ground without cover.
>
> Our men were going to get to Rome all right. There was no question about that. But the way was cruel. No one who had not seen that mud, those dark skies, those forbidding ridges and ghostlike clouds that unveiled and then quickly hid the enemy, had the right to be impatient with the progress along the road to Rome.[6]

The Fifth Army attacks to break through this middle line had been aimed at the twin peaks of La Difensa and La Remetanea. Their capture would open the way for American and British forces to pour through to the final barrier, the Gustav Line, centered at Cassino and the gateway to the Liri Valley road to Rome. Clark, continually losing manpower to Overlord, had managed to secure the newly formed First Special Service Force. Conceived as a commando-like unit, the fighting echelon of the Force consisted of some 1,500 American and Canadian volunteers. Against a defense so well dug into the cliffs and linked by invisible trails, it seemed that the only way to get by the enemy was to go in and fight man to man. Under the command of Colonel Robert Tryon Frederick, the Force had been given that mission. Frederick and his men sailed into the port of Naples in mid-November and were dispatched to the front, where they were assigned by Clark to the Fifth Army's II Corps. After a couple of days of reconnaissance to choose the assault route, they set out under cover of darkness on the night of December 1 for their first blood.

The battle for the twin peaks has been pieced together and described in a remarkable study of the Force by military historians Robert Adleman and Colonel George Walton, published in 1966 and never surpassed.[7] It was a battle soon overshadowed by the larger events to come, but Adleman and Walton permit us to see what formidable obstacles lay on the long road to Rome.

By midnight of that first day in December most of the 600-man spearhead, climbing the forbidding northeast face of 3,000-foot Monte La Difensa in a freezing rain, had reached a cleft close to the summit. They were well within range of the enemy's position, and could smell the cooking odors of the Germans' evening meal. Carrying rifles and packs whose weight would have pasted most men to the ground, they groped for cracks in the rock wall as one by one they came over the top. They had already been joined by Colonel Frederick and his staff, who were crouched on top of one another on a narrow ledge. Frederick gave the signal to move in. According to Adleman and Walton's description, based entirely on survivor interviews:

> The forward elements crept to the crest, which was a saucer-shaped area the size of a football field. There were hundreds of the best German troops here, some grouped in underground emplacements and supported by others in foxholes. The men of the Force slipped forward in the darkness, their blackened faces and dirt-stained uniforms making them almost completely invisible. Although in the distance, the rumble and cough of

artillery could be heard, the only sound being made on the crest was the soft gurgle vented by German sentries who had their throats cut by the Forcemen gliding past them in the darkness.

It was about 4:30 A.M. now, and the men were ordered to hold their fire until six. But a rockfall broke the silence. The two writers continue:

> The Germans had surrounded their emplacements with loose stone for this very purpose, and, as some of the riflemen began sliding into the ravines, the blackness of the sky was split and shattered by the flashes and noise of gunfire.
>
> A green flare went up, followed by a red one of equal brilliance. Then came a blinding flash as two magnesium flares sharply illuminated the entire scene. The men of the Force, caught in the glare, stood silhouetted like so many menacing statues. The battle was on.[8]

Fierce combat in a darkness of frozen mist went on for two hours, as the Germans unleashed their pillboxed guns and mortar. A second wave of Forcemen came over the top, bringing some relief. In one defining experience, a nest of Germans came forward waving a white flag in surrender, only to open fire and kill the officer who went to receive them. His men killed every last one of the "surrendering" Germans. Take no prisoners became the rule.

When day broke, the Germans could be seen fleeing down a slope and across a ridge to the second peak, La Remetanea, but as the victors cheered the rout from the summit basin, the daylight gave German artillery an easy target. Frederick sent his men into the vacated pillboxes for shelter, and the Force dug in.

Over the next several days, they removed their dead and went up and down the mountain to resupply, preempting a slow-to-come counterattack by attacking La Remetanea. The saddle between the two peaks proved to be the hardest to gain. One of Adleman and Walton's interviewees, Forceman Don McKinnon, recalled the onslaught this way:

> Our battle cries never ceased from the time of take-off until final attack uphill to enemy positions. I'm sure the howling and baying we did on that attack scared hell out of the Kraut; the howling was as much a release of pent-up emotions held for several days as it was a battle cry. It seemed to me that we had no thought of anything but to take that hill, and at no time

let anything stop us. . . . There was nothing skillful or intelligent, it was straight frontal and brutal, asking no quarter, giving none. The enemy was completely demoralized and withdrew under the overpowering wave coming at them. Enemy grenades were picked up and thrown right back at them, without, I believe, anyone even thinking about what could happen if it went off before being thrown back. Riflemen had fixed bayonets, and many used them. No prisoners were taken, as actually there was no chance for an enemy to give up and possibly if he had he would have been cut down by someone. His only chance was to run and that is finally what they did.[9]

After six days of fighting, the twin peaks had been taken and the tireless Frederick and his men had linked up with the British forces that had cleared the rest of way through the pass. A full one-third of the Force, 532 men, were among the dead and wounded. War correspondent Clark Lee reported that the battle had "captured the imagination of the entire Fifth Army,"[10] and the feat was hailed as assuring a major advance toward Rome. Twice-wounded Frederick was promoted to General and for his swashbuckling and courageous leadership sent on the path to legendary status when Churchill, hearing of the Force's conquest, called him "the greatest fighting general of all time."[11]

The taking of La Difensa and La Remetanca was the kind of news that, when sanitized, translated, read on the air by Colonel Stevens, and heard in Rome, made the risk of listening to Allied radio worthwhile.

"*PORCI, carogne fasciste!*" "Pigs, fascist scum!" That was the battle cry, shouted to shake off fear and hesitation, that drew first blood for Paolo. The order from the Military Council to rid the streets of Rome of Fascists was unequivocal. Nearly a month after the aborted assassination attempt on the ministers, the three Gappisti, Paolo, Giovanni, and Pietro, joined by Giovanni's wife, Maria, left Elena's apartment at Trajan's Forum on a Sunday evening, each of them concealing a short-barrel Beretta. They walked in pairs among the Sunday strollers to the Palazzo Braschi. Giovanni and Maria, in the rear, were already in the cover position. Night had fallen. Dim blue light from the streetlamps and an occasional low beam from a passing car created a glow on the beads of moisture in the late-autumn air. Some individual Fascists in uniform were among the pedestrians, but the Gappisti let them pass. Finally, a batch of Fascists came pouring out of the Palazzo Braschi, in full gangland dress, boisterous, strutting, brandishing their submachine guns, demanding a right of way through the crowd.

"If you never saw the Fascists of those days," Paolo says, "you'd have a hard time imagining them. You could see the violence they were capable of in the way they dressed, in the symbols they chose, and in their truculent ways. They were frightening, yes, but at the same time they looked ridiculous and while they made you feel utter contempt you couldn't help pitying them, too."

The group was headed toward the Piazza Venezia. Paolo recounts:

We followed them for a while, looking for a good cross-street for a getaway and a spot with no civilians around, at least not in the line of fire. When we saw what we were looking for, Pietro and I moved up fast and fell in behind them, and at a certain moment we both cried out, "Pigs, Fascist scum!" They spun around, startled but ferocious, reaching for their guns, before they even saw us. We opened fire. They did, too, almost simultaneously. One, two, three rounds fired. One of the Fascists dropped to the ground, another to his knees and keeled over. A third came up to the one lying flat on the ground, and called his name but got no answer. The others fired at us.

We kept shooting, but started running down Via del Gesù, into the little streets between the Corso Vittorio and the Collegio Romano. Somehow we had lost Giovanni and Maria, who were supposed to have created a diversionary tactic in case the Fascists went after us—which they did. We ducked into a building, behind the main door, to catch our breath and try to figure a way out of this bind. My heart was pounding like something about to explode. The Fascists came running into the same street but had lost sight of us. They stopped at the entrance to a shop adjacent to the doorway where we were hidden. A man who had seen what had happened and was himself fleeing the shooting had taken refuge in that same entrance. As the Fascists were looking around, he stepped up to them, pointing at a side street, "They went down there!" he cried. The Fascists took off in that direction. The man looked at us, said nothing, but signaled the way was clear.

They returned to Elena's apartment. Giovanni and Maria were already back. All four were shaken and sat in silence. Others of their comrades were there, but unaware of what had occurred. Paolo relived it again and again. "I had shot a man," he kept thinking. "I wasn't able to speak, not even to my friends. Now there was some kind of divide between us. I had begun my war." [12]

ELENA had been frequenting René, Rome's most famous hairdresser, whose Via Veneto salon had become the daytime gathering place for the wives and mistresses of the occupation elite. The Germans, from their crowded beginnings in the Villa Wolkonsky only three months earlier, had expanded greatly in numbers and legroom. They had moved out and requisitioned in all the high-rent districts but settled mainly in the area around the Via Veneto, with the headquarters of Stadtkommandant Stahel established in the Hotel Flora at the very top of the graceful bend in that urban slope. The ballrooms and banquet halls of the Hotel Bernini, the Ambasciatori, the Excelsior, the Savoy, and the Flora—losing war or no losing war—kept going night and day in endless, mindless celebration, and the women of the Fascist elite, the aristocracy, and the entourage of the honored Nazi of the week needed René's magic. Naturally blond Elena visited René only to slip him his copy of the clandestine *l'Unità* and debrief him of what the ladies were saying beneath his famous touch. René in fact was a precious source in Luciano Lusana's intelligence network, funneling information about the comings, goings, and doings of Nazi and Fascist high officials, and where at any given moment they might be. One such tip led to a man identified only as an officer billeted at the Hotel Ambasciatori, who would gain instant distinction in the escalation of the underground war. [13]

In the waning days of autumn the internal debate in the armed Resistance—at least among the Gappisti—had found a consensus in favor of shifting the primary target from the Fascists to the Nazis. The move was bound to incite the occupiers to harsher measures but one rationale was that it would also lift the profile of the movement in the outside world. If armed resistance could seriously challenge an occupation force of infinitely superior firepower, particularly within the perimeter of its highest command posts, it had to have a wide base of popular support to sustain such a level of operations; this would be a power to reckon with. [14] Nazi target number one was selected on the rainy evening of December 17.

The target had been observed taking daily fast-paced walks from the Hotel Ambasciatori on the Via Veneto to the nearby Ministry of War, apparently never altering his departure time and route. He wore a Wehrmacht uniform and invariably carried a bulging black briefcase. The uniform and the briefcase identified him to Elena, Paolo, Giovanni, and Maria—who had never seen him before. As he proceeded from the hotel, they fell in behind him, playing the two-couples-in-love role, though neither couple had need of pretending. They were on the southwest side of the Via XXIII Marzo—named for the founding date of Fascism (March 23, 1919) and later to be re-named Via Bissolati. They had decided to attack at the first intersection. Elena would lead the assault.

She later remembered:

My gun was in the pocket on the right side of my jacket, clasped in my hand, the muzzle pointed down and a bullet in the chamber. It was my first armed action against a man, and that to me was the sum of everything the person walking in front of us was. He was wearing the uniform of a Nazi officer and he was armed, but he was a man whose life I would have to take to get his briefcase full of documents.

At the first crossing, I hesitated. We kept on walking and when we got to the sidewalk on the other side, Paolo said to me, "At the next cross-street, you shoot, you'll do it as soon as you're off the curb." As we neared the end of the sidewalk and the officer had not yet crossed onto the next one, Paolo said, "Now." I pulled out my gun, fired straight ahead at the target, who collapsed to the ground, crying out. Paolo had fired with me. He bent down and grabbed the briefcase, which had fallen beside the man, who kept crying out something I didn't understand, which Maria later re-peated to me and translated: *Mein Gott! Ich sterbe! Helft mir!*—My God! I'm dying! Help me!

We hurried down the cross street, toward Piazza Barberini, and only then did I realize that it was drizzling and my face was wet. Paolo had an umbrella with him and opened it. All of a sudden, some Fascists in GNR uniforms sprung out of nowhere. They looked frightened, asked what happened, and when we said that somebody was shooting in Via XXIII Marzo, they ran off in that direction. That was when Paolo told me to look down and I saw that I still had my gun in my hand. He understood how upset and full of anguish I was, just as he had been when he'd gone through the same thing. I don't know how we ended up in the Galleria Colonna [arcade], which had been refitted as a bomb shelter. A lot of homeless refugees were camped there permanently with their belongings. Paolo had taken me there to be among people, in a dry place where I could let out my feelings, at least to him, which is what I did, my face still wet with rain and mixed with tears.[15]

The German died on the way to the hospital.[16] His briefcase yielded detailed maps and blueprints of power and communications grids used in German antiaircraft emplacements in and around Rome. They were turned over to the Military Council. The CLN would order the grids destroyed; the first of them, a telephone exchange located in Trastevere, was blown up two weeks later by Paolo and Elena.[17]

In the meantime, the assassination in Via XXIII Marzo marked the start of three consecutive days of bold offensives in the most heavily fortified parts of the *centro storico*—the final weekend of autumn turning the terror back on the Germans.

On the evening of Saturday the 18th, the GAP Central network led by Cola (Franco Calamandrei) bombed a favorite haunt of the German and Fascists, a trattoria near a German command post and barracks in the Prati district, killing eight German soldiers. At about the same time, Paolo and Elena and Giovanni and Maria were back in the Via Veneto area, Paolo leading an attack on the German soldiers exiting the Cinema Barberini, where twice weekly there were showings exclusively for the occupying troops.

Covered by the others, Paolo, carrying in his raincoat pocket a bulky, one-kilogram-TNT *spezzone* with an eight-second fuse, took off on his bicycle, and pulled up near a van boarding soldiers to take them back to their barracks. He lit the fuse while the bomb was still half-concealed in his pocket, but it got tangled in the lining when he tried to free it. As the fuse burned, he squandered one split second in an apocalyptic vision of hurtling into the Germans, bomb, bike, and all, before managing to rip the *spezzone* free, toss it, and pedal away. Eight Germans were dead or soon would be as Paolo felt the heat of the blast at his back and then the crackle of a submachine gun when someone who had spotted him opened fire. He zigzagged into darkness and escaped. Elena and Maria, however, were stopped near the movie theater and questioned by a suspicious German officer. German-speaking Maria quickly concocted a story that they had gone to see the film with two German soldiers. It worked.[18]

On Sunday, the Cola group made the boldest strike yet, an assault on the Hotel Flora. The Flora was headquarters not only of the occupation High Command but also the German War Tribunal and was ringed with a security contingent that included checkpoints, mounted police, and machine-gun nests. Infiltrating this barrier, GAP Central Partisans Giacomo (Antonello Trombadori), Cola (Franco Calamandrei), Piera (Maria Teresa Regard), and Ernesto (Ernesto Borghesi), were able to set off three *spezzoni*, two of which exploded, devastating the ground floor of the hotel. The Germans kept the death toll secret, admitting only to slight damage and non-German wounded. They immediately issued a punitive ordinance, however, bringing the curfew down to 7 P.M. and prohibiting the use of bicycles after 5 P.M.

A few days later, the two couples struck again—this time Giovanni leading the raid, a daylight attack on the German guard post at Regina Coeli, the Queen of Heaven prison on the Trastevere side of the Tiber. At the regular noontime changing of the guard, Giovanni made a high-speed run on a bicycle at the twenty or so Germans getting in and out of a trailer truck, tossing them a sizzling double-sized *spezzone*. While captured Partisans inside the prison—many of them newly arrested by the SS in response to the wave of the GAP Central attacks—cheered the telltale sound of the explosion, about a dozen guards fell dead and wounded.[19] In the gateway, however, Giovanni was caught in a cross fire. Fleeing the gunfire of the survivors; he made an unplanned dash across a Tiber bridge and, by pure chance, found himself biking straight into a Fascist gang gathered on the other side. Paolo and the others were too far away to be of any help, but Giovanni's luck returned when the Germans on their side of the bridge failed to hold their fire, sending the Fascists diving for cover. In a spectacular bullet-pinging run, Giovanni, head down and all his adrenaline pumping into his pedaling, rocketed through the hole the Fascists made at the end of the bridge by taking cover, losing himself and his bike in a nearby crowded street market.

The short poster that went up on the walls of Rome the next morning conveyed the German rage:

> The German Command declares: Pursuant to a new criminal attack by a cyclist committed yesterday in broad daylight against German soldiers the following is hereby ordered: from this moment on, without exception, the use of any bicycle anywhere in the territory of the Open City of Rome is prohibited. Transgressors will be shot without regard to who they are and without prior notice. The bicycle will be requisitioned with no right of compensation.[20]

The furibund authority that pronounced this latest sentence of death on anyone biking anywhere in the city was brand-new in Rome. Issuing his very first ordinance, he was occupied Rome's new Stadtkommandant, General

Kurt Mälzer, recently come to town as the replacement for General Stahel. A brutish alcoholic with a penchant for ordering people shot, Mälzer would be shunned as a boor by his own kind, utterly despised by the Romans, and ultimately sentenced by the Allies to be shot. He fancied being called the "King of Rome." The winter of the occupation had arrived.

WINTER

REPORT OF THE QUESTORE OF ROME TO THE [NATIONAL] CHIEF OF
POLICE, DECEMBER 18, 1943

A number of factors, growing more acute with each passing day, is undermining the prerequisites for the maintenance of public order in the Capital. [One of them is] the worsening food situation. Essential medicines are running out day by day, condensed milk and other foods for infants are not to be found. The black market, in spite of our efforts to contain it, continues its widespread growth along with the practice of barter, while prices have reached unbelievable levels; a liter-and-a-half bottle of [olive] oil, for example, has gone up as high as 500 lire. . . .

All this has brought on the deepest kind of malaise. . . . We are nearing the danger point beyond which lies a breakdown in discipline, disrespect of the law and the rights of others, and outright rebellion. [*Dorer: 778*]

MINISTRY OF THE INTERIOR. MORNING [POLICE] REPORTS.
JANUARY 26, 1944-XXII

Rome—During the night of 24–25 a certain Agostino Taninger and Mario Proietti broke into the nunnery of the Sisters of Alcantara in the Quarto Miglio district threatening the sisters at gunpoint. Claiming to be German officers looking for paratroopers, they searched the living quarters. After consuming much food and wine, they demanded carnal relations with the sisters. Such relations took place with the Mother Superior, 70 years old. They left several hours later, taking a radio set and more than a hundred kilograms of victuals. . . . [Dorer: Sez. IV, Approvvigionamenti]

MORNING REPORT OF THE QUESTURA [POLICE DEPARTMENT] OF ROME,
FEBRUARY 4, 1944

Yesterday morning, 600 Anglo-American prisoners were marched through the principal streets of the city. During the procession, many of them raised their right hand, lifting their index finger and middle finger to form the letter "V." Some members of the PFR [Fascist Republican Party] arrested a woman . . . showing sympathy for one of the prisoners. Also detained, at the request of the German police, was an individual of Austrian origin who . . . responded to the passing of the prisoners by making a "V" with the fingers of his right hand.—[Dorer: 1323]

NINE

CHRISTMAS IN CAPTIVITY

I N a nighttime downpour on the first day of winter, a mixed formation of Fascist and Gestapo agents made the first preventive strike against the Resistance. It came in the form of an audacious raid on three Vatican institutions known to be harboring influential anti-Fascists and military officers, labor and military service evaders, and Jews who had escaped the roundup.

The assault was led by a new man in Rome, half-German–half-Italian Pietro Koch, a twenty-five-year-old ex-officer of the Grenadiers of Sardinia. He had arrived some days earlier with a mandate from the highest police official in the new Mussolini regime, and would now begin to mold what would become the most effective and most ruthless anti-Partisan Fascist force in occupied Rome. It was called the Special Police Unit (Reparto Speciale di Polizia), better known as the Banda Koch, or the Koch Gang.[1]

One of the purposes of the December raid was to test the Vatican's reaction to a clear but only tangential violation of the vaunted German respect for the sovereignty of the Holy See. Koch, operating with approval from Gestapo Chief Kappler, was after much bigger game. The test targets—the Seminario Lombardo, the Pontifical Institute of Oriental Studies, and the Russicum Institute, a cluster of religious institutions in the immediate vicinity of the Basilica of Santa Maria Maggiore—did not have extraterritorial status, but were among the Vatican properties recognized by treaty. A property that did have such status, for example, was another seminary, the Seminario Romano, adjacent to the Basilica of San Giovanni in Laterano. It had become the hiding place of Italy's anti-Fascist elite, including CLN president Ivanoe Bonomi and the heads of four of the six parties in the coalition.

In all, hiding at the Seminario Romano were about 200 powerful enemies of the regime or Nazism, including fifty-five prominent or well-connected Jews. Thus Koch's probe was preparation for a major purge of the Roman Resistance.[2]

Shortly after ten o'clock on December 21, the self-titled "Doctor" Koch, dressed in customary foppish civilian attire, his hair matted less from the rain than from a jar-a-day habit of brilliantine, went into action. The buildings, like many ecclesiastical institutions throughout Rome, bore a warning placard issued two months earlier by the occupiers themselves and printed in Italian and German that read: "This building serves religious objectives, and is a dependency of the Vatican City. All searches and requisitions are prohibited." The buildings were surrounded by about fifty regular police as Koch and a dozen or so of his men entered the Lombard Seminary. With them were three or four of Kappler's men, including SS Captain Priebke.

There were about 110 illegals in the invaded buildings and most of them immediately tried to follow one or another preplanned escape route. Several fled over a fourth-floor bridge to another building while others hid in a "secret room" in the cellar. One man, caught off guard, played dead in an open coffin located in a chapel and another was hidden behind the ample skirts of some quick-thinking nuns attending a mass. He went undetected but the man in the coffin, according to a Vatican report, "was brought back to life" by Koch's men.[3] Those pretending to be seminarians—mostly young men evading the forced-labor and military draft—were smoked out by another of Koch's agents, a renegade Tuscan monk named Alfredo Troia, who posed as a priest and called himself Don Ildefonso. He made them all recite the Ave Maria to decide who were the imposters.

At the knock on the door to the Institute for Oriental Studies the twenty resident anti-Fascists and Jews rushed to a prearranged hiding place in the Russicum. That institution, a Jesuit school for priests training for the restoration of Catholicism in the Soviet Union, was hiding twelve others who also scrambled for safety. The search—accompanied by some thievery and much damage—went on until about seven the next morning, and when it was finally over, Koch and his men left with eighteen prisoners. The prize catch was trade-union leader Giovanni Roveda, a high official of the Communist Party. Other anti-Fascists, military officers, men with false documents, and at least four or five Jews were taken, too. An elderly Jewish man who lay dying of a heart attack suffered while fleeing to the Russicum was left behind, but not the undocumented young medical student attending him.[4]

The ninety remaining fugitives all gathered their belongings and over the next couple of days departed, taking to the streets in search of "a more secure exile," according to the account of one of the seminarians, who wondered where that place might be: "Where to go? To whom? There were terrible moments. But everyone left." [5] Some of the Jews who found no answer to those questions tried to return to the seminary but were told that it was too dangerous. [6]

AS SOON as word of the raid reached the Vatican Secretariat of State, Cardinal Maglione and others expressed deep concern. One day prior to Koch's raid the Secretariat had received information from an apparently trustworthy source that the SS police forces in Rome were about to be strengthened from the current total of 400 men to 2,000. Moreover, according to the source, a plan was afoot to use the augmented police contingent to make a thorough, house-to-house search of the city in which few ever tired of saying that half the people were hiding in the homes of the other half. [7] All able-bodied males rooted out in this way would be "loaded into freight cars." Those who resisted would be shot. Most disturbing to the Vatican was the information that convents, monasteries, and even treaty-protected Church properties would not be exempt from the search, though the last would be subject only to "pro-forma visits." Finally, the informant said, Kappler in his role as the top SS police chief in Rome had not ruled out the possibility of a raid on Vatican City itself. [8]

And now, barely more than twenty-four hours after this report was recorded, not only had three Vatican properties been "visited," but, far from undergoing a mere formality, they had been sacked. Where might the police strike next? All the recent fears of an Avignon-like exile were stirred. Was it time again to keep a suitcase packed, to rebury the Holy Father's secret papers? Could the guarantees of sovereignty extended personally by Hitler and codified directly by Ribbentrop be withdrawn by a local Gestapo police chief? Or was the reappearance of this threat the latest mischief of the "German" clandestine radio station Deutscher Kurzwellensender Atlantik, known to the Vatican as a rumor mill of recent contrivance by British psychological warfare—the source that only a few weeks earlier had "revealed" the imminent kidnapping of the Pope and his transfer to the Reich? Maglione queried Weizsäcker. Weizsäcker queried Kappler. Kappler categorically denied even thinking or hearing of any such operation against Vatican City.[9] There could be no denial, however, of the violation of the Vatican properties, and Maglione made no secret of his displeasure. The presence of Kappler's men in the raid was unknown, so the Germans blamed it on the Fascists, and since the Vatican had no diplomatic relations with the Salò regime, the matter rested—but not for Pope Pius XII.

The sudden displacement of the thousands of Roman Jews who had survived the October 16 roundup had added a significant risk to the security of Vatican City. Indeed, on the very day of the raid, convents, monasteries, and other Catholic religious institutions, particularly those near the ghetto, threw open their doors with selfless spontaneity. Others, however, turned Jews away, but in the days and weeks that followed their reluctance waned.

Pius's defenders say that he personally ordered Rome's religious institutions to provide hospitality for Jews in need of refuge. An exhaustive new study by Holocaust historian Susan Zuccotti seriously undermines that long-standing assertion.[10] She found no evidence to support it and much to refute it, discovering instead a complex and fractious attitude inside the Curia. But she also concluded that the Pope was certainly kept informed and allowed most rescue efforts to continue.[11] Not even a heartless pope—a failing that few have ascribed to Pius XII—would not have wanted to help ease the tremendous pressure on the Romans mounting day by day, particularly at a time when the civilian population might soon be called on by the Resistance to rise up against the occupiers. But some high Vatican officials sought to discourage hiders in general. Immediately after the Koch raid, for example, an anonymous member of the Secretariat, noting, wisely enough, that the Vatican should warn those in the extraterritorial enclaves that they were not at all secure, went on to suggest that hosting draft evaders was not "convenient" and that hiders of any kind in "other ecclesiastical buildings should be urged to change lodgings."[12] Cardinal Maglione took such action the very next day,[13] though it appears that no one so urged or regarded as inconvenient was actually expelled.

But Pius's acquiescence to the raid on the Vatican properties could only encourage the perpetrators of repression. With the emergence of the armed resistance, as witnessed in the December attacks against the Germans, the Pope was now forced to interpret every Partisan strike against the occupiers as the spark that might touch off the dreaded popular uprising. He was thus obliged to identify the security of the occupiers with that of the Holy See, and by tolerating the initial act of Koch's anti-Partisan police, the yoke between the Vatican and the occupiers was drawn tighter.

In spite of Pius's demonstrable compassion for the Romans—he himself, many would always maintain, the noblest Roman of his day—the closing of ranks with the occupiers compelled a more rigorous silence. The Pope had to close his eyes to Fascist and Nazi brutality, not as much to the relatively few remaining Roman Jews as to Roman Catholics and Romans of any stripe everywhere in the Eternal City.

EARLIER in December, Weizsäcker reported to Berlin that the Pope, after much hesitation, had decided that he would deliver his annual Christmas message. Pius had been extremely disappointed, said Weizsäcker, with the outcome of the late-November Teheran conference. The first summit meeting of Roosevelt, Churchill, and Stalin had reaffirmed the indivisibility of the Western and Soviet alliance and its unforgiving unconditional-surrender doctrine. The Vatican's insistence that this doctrine would lead inevitably to Germany's devastation and the advance of Communism was a position shared to some extent by many in the West, but Teheran had apparently dashed all but a glimmer of papal hopes. Weizsäcker portrayed a dispirited pontiff:

> The Pope is still trying to figure out whether he can go on with his work to influence the Western powers and how he ought to proceed. He is tenacious, but extremely sensitive where his prestige is concerned. The political motive of his Christmas message will be to turn the Western powers away from the formula of Unconditional Surrender. He plans a direct appeal to the consciences of the people in his message, disregarding their obstinate governments, in the hope that the people of America and Britain will grasp his meaning.[14]

IN THE early afternoon of December 24, Pope Pius XII sat before a Vatican Radio microphone in his private study and delivered his Christmas message to occupied Rome and the rest of the world. According to Mother Mary, "he spoke clearly and distinctly," but it is doubtful that many who heard his rather high-pitched voice directly or read his words in print grasped his meaning.[15] He appealed to the Allies for a peace based on Christian principles. Such a peace, he said, would rise above "unilateral declarations of law and justice"; it would seek not retribution but rehabilitation, and would mark "the dawning of a new spirit of world brotherhood." The Pope's discontent with the Allied peace formula was clear enough to insiders, including, it seems, Mother Mary. She saw his message as having had a positive effect "in unexpected quarters" but wondered whether it would be acted upon.[16]

Interpreters of papal nuance had an easier time with the traditional Christmas list of issues deemed important by the Pope. Broadcast along with his speech, the problems nettling the Holy Father this year included the peril of the war drawing closer and closer to the Eternal City, the losses suffered mostly by the poor caused by the Allied air attacks, and the threat to all Romans of an approaching indigence unprecedented perhaps anywhere on earth, he said. Finally, in two unmistakable allusions to the violent events of recent days—the Partisan attacks and the Fascist raid on the Vatican properties—he urged the people of his diocese to remain calm, exercise moderation, and "abstain from any inadvisable acts that might provoke even worse misfortunes." More than ever, said the Pope, it was essential to avoid the danger that the good works of the Holy See "run the risk of being caught and destroyed in a cross fire of political conflicts."[17]

IN SPITE of it all, Christmas in occupied Rome was not without some small joys. Two such pleasures came as a gift from Stadtkommandant Mälzer. The general, carousing and boozing by night, but being fat, fifty-five, and, according to Dollmann, "just laughable," might have, in some other era, made a good Santa by day. First, by edict, he tacked two hours onto the curfew for the Christmas holiday, traditionally three days long in Italy, and on Christmas Day itself he gave an elaborate dinner for—of all the people in his realm—150 guests bused in from a nearby German prisoner-of-war camp, British soldiers all. After an English-language prayer service at the American church on the Via Nazionale, which had been closed for two years, the enemy, whisked to a multi-starred Via Veneto hotel, dined on Irish stew and potatoes, drank from an individual serving of a pint of wine, and, given a glimpse of the jolly Nazi general himself, returned to their curtainless stalag with one pack of cigarettes per man. Romans, exposed to the fulsome homage accorded to the new commandant in the next day's sycophantic press, brushed it all off as misplaced vanity, but not before one wag seized the moment to offer a cruel reminder, saying, "The British boasted that they would be in Rome for Christmas: well, they have been here."[18]

Roman diarist Carlo Trabucco recorded experiencing Natale 1943 as a profoundly sad day under a leaden winter sky, a "Christmas in captivity," he called it, eased only by the company of friends, each of whom, from time to time during the day, asked the others the very same question: "When will they get here?"[19]

"THE STAGNATION of the whole campaign on the Italian front is scandalous. . . . " Churchill said to his chiefs of staff. Over the Christmas holiday,
he wrote to Roosevelt, expressing his fear of the "ruin of the Mediterranean
campaign in 1944."[20] On his return from the Teheran conference, Churchill
had fallen ill with pneumonia. Now he lay bedridden in Eisenhower's white
villa in Carthage, but still, in the first month of his seventieth year, the indomitable statesman-warlord. Brooding over the discouraging news from
the Italian front—the failure of the Fifth Army's December offensive to
plant itself on the Liri Valley side of the Garigliano and Rapido Rivers—was
no way to spend Christmas. He summoned Eisenhower and members of the
Combined Chiefs of Staff to discuss his plan to break the deadlock. True, the
avowed purpose of the Italian campaign—diverting Wehrmacht forces from
the coming Overlord invasion of France—was working, but the prime minister wanted to cash in his winnings from Stalin and Roosevelt: he wanted
Rome and he wanted it now.

His plan was called Shingle, an amphibious end-run around the Gustav
line. It would land Allied forces on the beaches of the twin resort towns of
Anzio and Nettuno, a mere thirty miles from the long-elusive prize. As
Churchill imagined it, the landing forces would be the cat claw that would
pounce on and sever Kesselring's supply line to the front, force him into
rapid retreat, and after a "battle to the climax in a week or ten days," Rome
would fall.[21]

Shingle, often regarded as Churchill's ill-starred brain child, was in fact
something worse. It had been conjured up by Eisenhower and Alexander,
elaborated by the Fifth Army staff, and, finally, killed by Mark Clark, with
the concurrence of his officers and his superiors, as militarily impractica-
ble.[22] That was on December 18, a few days before Churchill in his sick bed
heard of it and embraced it. On December 29, having removed a final obstacle to American approval, he wrote to Roosevelt, "I thank God for this fine
decision which engages us once again in whole-hearted unity upon a great
enterprise . . . here the word is 'Full steam ahead.' "[23]

D-DAY at Anzio, Churchill declared, had to be "as close to January 20 as
possible," and, as warlords usually do, he then left the details to others,
under the wing of his American eagle, Mark Clark. If it were possible to
know the precise moment that Clark's desire to conquer Rome became an
obsession, it would probably fall somewhere between Christmas and New

Year's Day, even prior to Shingle. Clark had come to believe that the British—beginning with his own superior, General Alexander—were conspiring to outfox the Fifth Army, be first in Rome, and claim a victory all their own. Churchill's newest involvement surely reinforced Clark's conviction.

A January 4 entry in Clark's war diary discloses part of his suspicion. The decision for the landing, he wrote, had been taken "lightheartedly" and without any knowledge of the pitfalls solely because the Prime Minister "had been inspired with a desire to capture Rome and had determined that Shingle would take place."[24] Clark might have complained even harder, had he known that a day after Christmas, Churchill confided in Alexander that he did "not like the idea that [Shingle] . . . should fall exclusively upon American forces."[25] A few weeks later, Churchill went even higher than Alexander. Eisenhower had been given command of Overlord and the new supreme commander in the Mediterranean was British, Field Marshal Sir Henry Maitland Wilson—to whom Churchill cabled a word of welcome and a reminder. Without a British presence in Rome's capture, said the Prime Minister, there would be "a feeling of bitterness in Great Britain when the claim is stridently put forward, as it surely will be, that 'the Americans have taken Rome.' "[26]

Clark, himself was sometimes torn. "There was a thought in the back of my mind," he said, "that 'Hell, we shouldn't even be *thinking* about Rome—all we should be thinking about is killing Germans!' " But think he did. "I must admit," Clark would say years later, "that I and all my commanders were always thinking that 'if we could just capture Rome because it's such a big milestone.' *Everything* had been so unglamorous, and here was the first Axis-dominated capital to get it before Ike went across. I didn't know of *anybody* who didn't feel that way. Whether or not now they say 'the hell with Rome' I don't know, but then there was always the feeling that Rome was certainly a great prize and the sooner we stepped out and got it, then we were in a new and final phase of the war."[27]

———————

E V E N Peter Tompkins thought of capturing Rome. That was one thought of many first entertained on the evening of January 15, 1944, when OSS chief Wild Bill Donovan, came to call. The General was passing through Naples, having just returned from Mark Clark's headquarters in nearby Caserta, and decided to invite himself to dinner and stay the night with his protégé.

Tompkins, making his stand against the British-backed faction of the OSS opposed to his organization of anti-Fascist agents, had requisitioned a dilapidated old palazzo on a back street of Naples as his base of operations. With many rooms and a friendly kitchen, the American soon found himself feeding, sheltering, and sometimes hiding a variety of aspiring political reformers and secret agents, from illiterate saboteurs to would-be philosopher-kings. The General and Tompkins shared some grievances with Mark Clark, notably opposition to British machinations in thwarting their own designs. Now, however, one week before D-Day for the Anzio and Nettuno landings, all that had changed. Donovan held back the news of those plans until dinner.

Sometime between the fettuccine and a postprandial *digestivo*, Donovan told Tompkins of the coming invasion and also disclosed that the British had agreed that all intelligence operations in Rome be conducted under the exclusive supervision of the OSS. This represented a major retreat of the more experienced and often patronizing British intelligence, SOE, or Special Operation Executive. Finally, Donovan, with Clark's blessing, had decided to infiltrate an OSS officer into Rome sometime before the January 22 landings. According to Donovan's authorized biographer, Anthony Cave Brown, the general went on to say that:

> He was looking for someone to go there and, he said in so many words, to bring the Roman resistance under OSS control and then, at a moment suitable to Allied operations, to capture the Italian capital in the name of the OSS and the Grand Alliance. Tompkins then remarked that should be an interesting assignment for someone, praying Donovan was not about to put his mark on him. But that is what happened. As if it were the most normal prospect in the world, Donovan asked Tompkins if he would go capture Rome.[28]

Tompkins doesn't remember the proposal as being quite that far-reaching, and he certainly disagrees with the suggestion that he didn't want the job, though he was, as Cave Brown writes, noncommittal that evening. Tompkins has consistently recalled being asked by the general to keep the Allies informed of just what the Germans were up to on the other side of the lines and to coordinate Partisan activities with the expected German withdrawal from Rome.[29]

It was while Tompkins and Donovan were sipping their coffee and Strega that the younger man contemplated the offer. He wondered what would become of the teams of agents he had so painstakingly put together with Raimondo Craveri but had yet to field. Would their organization fall apart, overwhelmed by the "professionals"? The former agents of the old Fascist SIM secret service who were finding a home in the OSS already had a presence in Rome. A team of three agents and a radio operator had been sent across the lines in mid-October. Their goal was to establish a clandestine radio station for transmitting intelligence but they had thus far produced sketchy results. The team leader, ex–SIM operative Clemente Menicanti had been recruited by Captain André Bourgoin, whom Tompkins considered as compromised as any of the SIM "professionals." Bourgoin, a seasoned intriguer and a French national, had been an agent of the Deuxième Bureau, but for the past twenty-five years had represented petroleum interests in North Africa. He and his cohort Captain Pacatte were now operating out of an OSS base in Corsica, running agents in and out of occupied Italy, eclipsing Tompkins and Craveri. Now, though, perhaps Tompkins's time had come. A mission as Donovan's man in enemy territory under the fire of the invasion—regarded by all as an extremely dangerous, highly prestigious, yet brief assignment—could only strengthen his hand.

At dawn the next day, Tompkins drove Donovan in his banged-up jeep to the Naples airfield at Capodichino. He had yet to give his reply and the general did not press him, but as they barreled on in a biting mist, Tompkins said yes. "From the corner of my eye," he later remembered, "I could see the General, bundled tight in his overcoat, nodding a brisk assent."

They were standing on the grassy runway waiting for the plane to warm up, when Donovan spoke again of the mission, touching on the issue of capturing Rome—and it went without saying that if not in the name of the OSS, certainly that of Mark Clark's Fifth Army. At the moment of the landings there would be a call to insurrection not only by the Partisans but by the Allies as well. A popular uprising—as had happened in Naples—could propel the Germans to a speedy withdrawal and smooth the Allied takeover of the city, but not, Donovan feared, in an all-out clash between the political parties of the right and the left. On this note, he shook Tompkins's hand, climbed into the hatch, and breaking a smile, added one last thought: "Just make sure," he said, "that when they rise up, they don't rise up against each other." [30]

Alone on the airstrip, Tompkins watched the General take off into a chill north wind, leaving him, as he noted in his diary, "with that feeling of dedication which comes when one has been entrusted with a mission by a superior being." [31]

ALREADY entrenched in Rome and preparing the very kind of politicized insurrection Donovan hoped to prevent was the right-wing armed Resistance whose leader, Colonel Montezemolo, was more informed about Allied intentions than anyone else behind the lines. Since escaping arrest in late September and going underground, the tall, steadfast chief of the FMCR, the Clandestine Military Front of the Resistance, had built a well-armed and well-trained organization to rival the CLN and lay claim to supremacy as the Rome representatives of the monarchy and the Badoglio government. The FMCR operated under the directive of "war against the German and the maintenance of public order"—the latter defined as a commitment to "secretly organize [FMCR] forces to assume control of public order at an opportune moment in the name of the government of His Majesty the King."[32]

Through its underground radio Centro X, the FMCR was in continuous contact with the seat of that government in Brindisi and by now had become the principal beneficiary in Rome of Churchill's effort to frustrate the political ambitions of the "leftish" CLN. Toward that end, the Military Front also functioned as an umbrella organization for those same ex–SIM operatives who, to the great dismay of Peter Tompkins, had been reborn in the OSS. Montezemolo had himself been a SIM agent, though Tompkins, for all his fury toward the "professionals," would always regard the forty-four-year-old aristocrat as a "gent."[33]

The FMCR had expanded considerably right after Kappler's early-October roundup and deportation of the Carabinieri. A large majority of the survivors of that raid went on to join the Resistance, most comfortably in Montezemolo's monarchist organization. With Carabinieri Major Ugo De Carolis as FMCR chief of staff, Montezemolo attracted Royalists such as Lieutenant Colonel Giovanni Frignani, the young captain who had arrested Mussolini on the steps of the Villa Savoia, and several others from the task force aiding the King's coup.

On the very day that Donovan was revealing details of the top-secret invasion to Tompkins, the FMCR began preparing its own brand of insurrection. At the first sign of any German withdrawal, Montezemolo's men would be poised to seize strategic sites such as the city's bridges, ministries, and media establishments. This monarchist initiative reached the ears of the CLN and drew the leaders of all six parties out of their hiding places to a meeting in the *centro storico* on January 18. They claimed as exclusively theirs the task of "promoting and directing the participation of all the people in the city in the battle for the liberation of Rome."[34] An uprising of one kind or another was in the air.

Although the imminent invasion and particularly its time and place apparently remained the Allies' secret, the sudden infighting in Rome was a response to persistent rumors of landings one place or another. There seemed to be an additional clue in the renewed bombing of the battered outskirts of Rome four times that week. "Something of importance must be approaching," de Wyss said.[35]

Oddly, however, when it happened, all of Rome, down to the last insider, was taken by surprise.

———

"MAJOR" Peter Tompkins, in an Italian blue sharkskin suit, loose strands of Italian tobacco carefully planted in his pockets, his well-worn shoes handmade in Capri, stood on a nighttime beach in enemy territory sixty miles north of Rome, stewing in anger. The rank of major had been temporarily bestowed for his mission; the Italian outfit, tobacco included, was part of his disguise as a titled scion of a politically irreproachable old family. The anger, authentic and all his own, was directed at Captain Bourgoin.

He had met up again with the wily Frenchman in Corsica, flying in that morning, some thirty-six hours before D-Day at Anzio. Bourgoin had accompanied Tompkins and his Italian assistant-bodyguard in a British-commandeered Italian torpedo boat, personally putting them ashore—along with six other agents headed north—in a yellow rubber dinghy. Despite orders from OSS Naples to Bourgoin, there was no one on the beach from the Rome Resistance to receive Tompkins, and Bourgoin's denial that any such orders had been received, delivered with little more than a shrug, seemed to Tompkins suspect.

With the entire party never more than a few hundred yards from patrolling German coast guards, Bourgoin, for his part, was eager to re-embark. CIA-OSS files released fifty-six years later reveal Tompkins's anger to have been more than justified. A contemporary report written by Bourgoin himself and containing false information strongly suggests that Tompkins had been left stranded in an attempt by the captain to sabotage the mission.[36]

With a small fortune of 300 gold coins (worth about $10,000) stashed in his belongings and a Beretta in his pocket, Tompkins made his way south, German checkpoint by checkpoint. He arrived in Rome at daybreak on the

21st, too conspicuously early and too tired to accomplish anything, other than seek a few hours' respite in a high-risk return to the old palazzo where he had lived before the war. The building's *portiere* and his wife had worked as household help for his parents, and counting on undying affection, he slipped into their ground floor lodgings.

> The tiny downstairs living room was dark [he later wrote], but exactly as it had always been, even to two discarded flower paintings by my mother, rescued and sentimentally hanging on the wall. . . . I crept up the narrow wooden staircase to the low-ceilinged bedroom. Dear, good old Virginia was lying on her bed, so I sat down on the quilt by her side, putting a finger to my lips.
> "How are you?" she whispered, taking my hand, as nonchalant as if I'd been out to get some groceries. "I have a little fever," [she said]. "God, but these are terrible times!"[37]

After a nap on a sofa, he made contact with two of the first-team agents recruited by Bourgoin: team leader Menicanti (code-named Coniglio), and Maurizio Giglio (Cervo), a Fascist police lieutenant in full uniform, working for the OSS as double agent. They were joined by two others, Elio Gambareri, associated with Badoglio and SIM, and Franco Malfatti, a member of the Socialist Party, who had fought against Franco in the Spanish civil war and had worked in the French underground in Nazi-occupied Paris.

Although drawn to the younger men, Giglio and Malfatti—like him, both in their early twenties—Tompkins had to overcome strong misgivings to reveal to any of them that within hours there was to be an Allied landing. First, he declared that he was under the personal orders of General Donovan and, as such, was chief of the OSS in Rome. His authority unchallenged—though he would soon learn that Menicanti had been claiming himself to be the top OSS operative behind the enemy lines—Tompkins spoke in general terms of the impending invasion and the need to act quickly to coordinate their efforts with the Partisans. Menicanti proposed to arrange a meeting the following morning with all the leaders of the Roman Resistance.

With the 6 P.M. curfew approaching, that seemed like progress enough for day one, and on the theory that the safest place in Rome for an American spy was the home of a Fascist police lieutenant, he agreed to spend the night at Giglio's apartment near the Vatican.

The next morning, the 22nd, he awoke wondering if the Allies had actually landed during the night as scheduled. No hint of any such news had yet reached Rome, and at the early meeting set up by Menicanti, it was clear that none of these purported leaders of the Resistance knew anything more than he. Moreover, it began to appear alarmingly evident from their hermetic behavior that they cared even less. Tompkins grew suspicious and found a pretext to ask for a second meeting so that he could do some checking on their credentials. "It soon turned out," he later reported to Donovan, "that they were not the leaders of the various Resistance groups, but agents associated with a particular group known as the 'Unione Democratica,' of which Coniglio and Gambareri were very active members."[38] This was a tiny "party" with little interest in either union or democracy and even less in resistance—"a *camarilla* of agents," as Tompkins described it later, "working for a group of industrialists whose prime preoccupation was the saving of certain industrial complexes from both the Germans and the Allies . . ."[39]

Tompkins, trusting his initial instincts, turned to Giglio and Malfatti for help. They disclosed their own disgust with the Menicanti group, and cast their lot with the American. Giglio, who had brought the OSS radio—code-named Vittoria—across enemy lines and controlled it in Rome, immediately gave Tompkins exclusive access, while Malfatti, for his part, had no difficulty in arranging a meeting with the Military Council of the CLN, particularly since the council had already heard of the American's presence. More important, word of the Allied landings had begun to spread and the streets of Rome were crowding up with convoys of German paratroopers speeding south. The BBC was broadcasting reports of an Allied invasion somewhere "north of the Garigliano front [at the Gustav Line] and south of Rome," and rumor had it, and had it right, at Nettuno.[40] The Roman Resistance, in fact, knew even more. Hours before the BBC transmission—while the Allies were hitting the beaches of Anzio and Nettuno—it had received the following coded radio message:

> From Allied Command. The hour has arrived for Rome and all Italians to fight in every possible way and with all forces. . . . Sabotage the enemy. Block his roads of retreat. Destroy his communications to the last wire. Strike against him everywhere continuing the fight indefatigably, without thought of political questions, until our troops have arrived. Notify all bands and parties.[41]

This was nothing less than the Allied call to organize an immediate insurrection, and as Tompkins watched the security preparations for his meeting with the Military Council on the street below him from behind a curtain in

Giglio's apartment, he knew he was dealing with the authentic Resistance. Partisans were posted in all the streets around him, he reported. They carried "parcels" wrapped in newsprint—submachine guns, hand grenades, and automatics. "Those who were to attend the meeting," he said, "appeared at intervals, unarmed, and with no incriminating documents, but followed at safe distance by heavily armed bodyguards."[42]

Present at the meeting, which took place over two hours on the 23rd, were Riccardo Bauer, for the Action Party, Giorgio Amendola, for the Communists, and Giuliano Vassalli, sitting in for Socialist Sandro Pertini, who had been arrested by the Gestapo some weeks earlier and was being held in Regina Coeli prison. The principal matter discussed was the transition period between the German withdrawal from Rome and the arrival of the Allies. This was of course viewed from one's political perspective, but a common goal was to save Rome from destruction. Apart from the inevitable devastation of street-by-street combat, no one could know the extent to which the Germans planned to mine, or already had mined, Rome. Tompkins, alone among this group, had been an eyewitness to what had happened in Naples, where the Germans had destroyed not only the port and utility facilities but also hundreds of buildings. Many continued to explode well after the Allied arrival in the city. The Military Council reported that it had come to some agreement on safeguarding bridges, utilities, and other essentials, but there were serious tensions between the Partisans of the CLN and Montezemolo's Military Front. Tompkins, though he did not conceal his anti-Fascist sympathies, believing that the Council represented the "only really effective underground," told them that his job would be purely military: "to effect sabotage against the Germans . . . what they did politically was their own damn business."[43]

The meeting had reached no firm conclusions when Giglio entered the room with a message for Tompkins received by Radio Vittoria from OSS Naples. It was an order to hold all sabotage, countersabotage, and other paramilitary actions in abeyance and concentrate solely on gathering intelligence about German movements toward the beachhead. Flabbergasted and not a little embarrassed at having to announce a "slight delay" on the military side in favor of intelligence operations, he glossed over the content of the telegram, but his reaction was hard to conceal. The Military Council seemed leery, reading his sudden change in direction, he thought, as a desire to keep the Resistance from participating in Rome's liberation. Tompkins certainly had no such personal desire, nor was it a specific aim of the Allies. Nevertheless the notion of an Allied-imposed "slight delay" at the moment when the Partisan movement was at the height of its readiness to organize an insurrection would in the postwar culture of the Resistance emerge as the enduring myth of the *insurrezione mancata*, a lost opportunity, but lost on purpose. In any case, the meeting ended "on the best of terms," Tompkins said, and as he finessed it to Donovan, "they all agreed to cooperate to the best of their ability."[44]

TEN

CHURCHILL'S
CAT

THE ghosts of Shingle lie neatly in their graves at Anzio and Nettuno—
2,300 British, 7,862 Americans, a cross or star bearing their names. A list in
marble contains the names of 3,094 Americans missing in action there.
Churchill had yearned for the capture of Rome, but his plan to end the
"scandalous" stagnation of the Italian campaign would add only more scan-
dal and stagnation. "I thought we had flung a wildcat into the [Alban] Hills,"
Churchill would cry in disappointment, "but, instead, got a whale flounder-
ing on the beach."[1] Someone would have to pay.

THEY CAME over a moonless, starlit horizon, 50,000 men, 5,000 vehicles,
the cruisers, the destroyers, the minesweepers, the submarines, the massive
air cover, and of course the landing craft—eighty landing craft packed with
men crazy with fear. Some had been at Salerno and knew what it was like to
run into the swath of slaughter; others knew it in their bones. A soldier's remembrance of the event:

> The immensity of what was about to happen struck them speechless.
> The jokes and the conversations of a few minutes ago . . . were now for-
> gotten. . . . Suddenly the shoreline rose to convulsion. Men, trees, houses,
> earth, stones were flung skywards. An intense rocket barrage had begun.
> . . . The sky was rent by an insane howling shrieking madness. A giant
> thunder filled all men with fear. The land erupted into great orange
> flames. . . . As the preliminary bombardment ended there was an ominous
> silence from the land.[2]

The water-slapping silence continued. The 800 rockets fired from out at sea in two minutes of hell had been aimed at clearing the beaches of land-mines, barbed-wire defenses, and anyone who could fire a gun. The silence continued; was it omen or simply nobody home? The landing craft opened, the men, the trucks, the jeeps, came down, British to the north, Americans to the south. It was a "very gentlemanly, calm and dignified" invasion, as the regimental history of the Irish Guards put it, observing how one company commander, "with a large black umbrella hung on his arm, stepped ashore with the air of a missionary visiting a South Sea island and surprised to see no cannibals."[3]

The Germans, at the moment, were in various stages of crawling out of bed and donning combat gear. Acting on fresh intelligence that declared an Allied landing before March out of the question, Kesselring had reduced his defensive force at Anzio to a mere company of a few hundred men—many of whom were now being taken prisoner, sleepy-eyed in their under-wear.

"We achieved what is certainly one of the most complete surprises in history," General John Lucas, the brooding commander of the invasion, wrote in his diary that day.[4] Now, from the bridge of the invasion task-force flagship, the USS *Biscayne*, anchored in mine-swept waters off the Anzio lighthouse, he was receiving nothing but comforting news. He had anticipated a bloody mess, believing his attack force far too small and ill-supplied. And that, he felt, was just one of the two strikes against him going in. Only hours earlier, the Fifth Army's three-day offensive aimed at cracking the Gustav Line had ended in colossal failure. The plan had been to draw off Kesselring's reserve divisions from the Anzio area, then break through to link up with Lucas on the road to Rome. But Mark Clark's at-tempt to cross the Rapido River had been roundly trounced, leaving him stalled with more than 1,600 casualties and a disastrous collapse of troop morale. Lucas, Clark's choice for Shingle, had been warned: "John," Gen-eral Patton had told him, "there is no one in the army I'd hate to see killed as much as you, but you can't get out of this alive."[5] He had taken that in jest but had worried like an old hen for his men, foreseeing "a fight" just to get them ashore, he wrote, "but [I] was not disappointed when I did not get it."[6]

"Old Luke" to his colleagues, "Foxy Grandpa" to the troops of his VI Corps command, the fifty-four-year-old general would not go ashore him-self until the following day. Instead, directing from the sea, he would go about his business in his famous methodical way, puffing his corncob pipe,

carrying out step one of the mission assigned by Mark Clark, seizing, securing, deepening, and widening the beachhead all day long, yard by yard, inland, north flank and south, knowing that the enemy would soon be mauling
it from every direction.

Thus did he miss the celebratory beachhead breakfast of bacon and real
eggs, served at ten that morning on the hood of a general's jeep—for generals only, to be sure—and wolfed down by 3rd Division commander General
Lucian K. Truscott, who had already taken the south flank, General Donovan, who had landed with the OSS contingent that would talk across the
lines to Peter Tompkins, and—just in by speedboat from Naples—Generals
Clark and Alexander, though Sir Harold preferred a stroll to an American
breakfast. Such was the range of pleasant choices on day one.

Missed by all the generals, however—at least in significance, it seems—
was something extraordinary that occurred during that festive breakfast. A
young American lieutenant named John T. Cummings, of the 36th Engineer Regiment attached to Truscott's 3rd Division, had landed that morning
with his unit, under orders to begin reconnaissance. Sometime after 9 A.M.,
Cummings and his driver set out in their jeep, heading north. In the absence
of any Germans, they proceeded along Highway 7, in sight of the Alban
Hills. Highway 7 was how the Allies invariably referred to the Appian Way,
the most famous of all the roads to Rome. They had still not sighted the
enemy when they could see the Tiber River. But as the first bridge came into
view, they stopped as they saw German vehicles crossing the bridge. With
the Alban Hills now behind them, the American lieutenant and his driver
were somewhere inside or very near the city limits of Nazi-occupied Rome.

"There was no sense of panic," Cummings wrote to military historian
Carlo D'Este decades later. "Apparently the people had not heard of the invasion. We stayed about an hour, met no enemy or civilian and returned to
our unit [at Anzio], made out our report and went about our regular engineer duties."[7]

The road to Rome was open. Moreover, the city was indefensible. Unfortunately, the generals at the beachhead had no knowledge of the assessment
made by Kesselring's Chief of Staff, General Siegfried Westphal, that this
was a "breathtaking situation" in which "no one could have stopped a bold
advance guard entering the Holy City." Commandant of Rome Kurt Mälzer
believed that the two SS-Police battalions guarding Rome were "of little
battle value and would never have constituted a serious danger for fighting
troops." Mälzer thought that the Romans needed "only a touch to make the
populace intervene in favor of the Allies." Colonel Dollmann expressed as-

tonishment at not seeing the Allies "push on to Rome . . . [to enter] St. Peter's Square by noon that day," as Consul Möllhausen gave orders to his Villa Wolkonsky staff long before noon to pack their bags and gas up the embassy cars.

If only by virtue of Lieutenant Cummings's report, the Allied generals knew or should have known that the road to Rome was open. That the city could not be defended was the subject of Tompkins's first Radio Vittoria intelligence dispatch that day. It provided a precise estimate of the number of German military personnel in Rome, location by location—from the command posts down to the psychiatric wards of the hospitals. The total, counting the infirm, was no more than 1,500 men.[8]

BY MIDNIGHT of D-Day, more than 36,000 men and 3,200 vehicles, 90 percent of the invasion force, were ashore. But Lucas, having seized brilliantly, kept on securing—not a wildcat but "a dear old pussy cat who purrs away," as one journalist said.[9] Kesselring would later remark that "the Allies had missed a uniquely favorable chance of capturing Rome,"[10] but at Anzio Kesselring had yet to be heard from. "The Hun was pulled back a bit," Lucas said, "but I haven't seen the desperate fighting I have during the last four months without learning something. We are not (repeat not) in Rome yet."[11]

"Don't stick your neck out, Johnny," Clark had told him before going in. "I did it at Salerno and got into trouble."[12] He had also said, "You can forget this goddamned Rome business."[13] Of all people, Mark Clark.

———————

PAOLO and Elena sat with Spartaco in a parlor of the Caffè Greco, the new developments in the highly competitive "business" of capturing Rome uppermost in their minds. Elena thought the Greco a dangerous place to meet. The Via Condotti landmark at the bottom of the Spanish Steps had been a favorite haunt of foreigners for well over a hundred years. Its polished brown opulence was remarkably unchanged since the days of Goethe, Stendhal, Berlioz, and Mark Twain, to name a few, but in these days, the Greco could do no better than draw smartly uniformed Nazis in search of the auras of old. Colonel Dollmann, with his Alsatian dog, Cuno, and his Italian chauffeur, Mario, lived down the street.

The last time Elena had been there, as Carla two years younger, she had said good-bye to a friend going off to Mussolini's war in Greece, and in the parting they had summoned up the courage to confess their love for each other. Then, after two brief letters and a photo, came the news that he was dead. That memory and the present feeling of danger in the Caffè Greco were on her mind, too, as Spartaco was giving her and Paolo their orders, announcing a dramatic shift in operations.

Spartaco had been in touch with the Military Council since the Anzio landing and the meeting with Tompkins. The American's fear that CLN cooperation had somehow been dampened had proved unfounded. The Allied call to rise up in action had in fact been embraced by the Military Council as well as the right-wing Military Front—with Montezemolo at work in reducing the conflicts between the two resistance organizations. The Council had decided, Spartaco told Paolo and Elena, to dismantle GAP Central and redeploy most of its forces in zones along the periphery of Rome. Spartaco had been assigned to command operations in the so-designated VI and VIII zones, which included the primary access roads to Rome from the south.

Spartaco appointed Paolo Commander and Elena Vice Commander of Zone VIII and ordered them to relocate in an outlying *borgata*, a working-class district of Fascist-era origin called Centocelle. What made Centocelle strategically important, Spartaco told them, was its position in the most southern part of Rome, lying between the Via Prenestina and the Via Casilina. These two roads—which led to Highways 6 and 7, respectively—were expected to be the routes of the German withdrawal. In addition there were some 150 Partisans in Centocelle, poorly armed and almost idle, in urgent need of organization.

Paolo, who had rarely been outside of Rome's *centro storico* other than to spend his summers at the family's Santa Severa beach house, had been taken by surprise and wanted to know how long he would be there.

"Until the insurrection," said Spartaco, piling on another surprise.

"Insurrection? When?"

"Immediately."

"Meaning?"

"Meaning tomorrow." Spartaco gave him the name of a contact, an address, and a password.[14]

It was only ten in the morning when Paolo and Elena took leave of Spartaco outside the Caffè Greco. The couple asked Spartaco's permission to carry out one last attack in Rome's center. Though it had been planned days earlier, it was folly to expose themselves to risk before setting out on a mission linked to the insurrection, solely for the sake of a routine *coup de main*—but folly had ridden into Rome with the news that the Allies were now close. When the wind was right, you could hear artillery at Anzio. "The Germans whom I met," an Irish priest noted, "seemed to be on the verge of panic. Within 24 hours the Allies would be in Rome."[15] Spartaco, as taken by events as were Paolo and Elena, warned them to keep the plan simple, and consented.

That afternoon, Paolo and Elena stood on the parapet at the top of a sloping street, a *salita* named after the princely Borgias. They were joined by Giovanni (Mario Fiorentini) and Pietro (Franco Di Lernia). Overlooking the wide Via Cavour, their position faced the church of San Pietro in Vincoli, built near the prison where Saint Peter was held in chains by the Romans. They waited for the German truck that always came, and when it did, it was, as always, loaded with barrels of gasoline. Paolo launched a German-made grenade that had a wooden handle. The others flung Italian- and British-made grenades. The truck blew up, killing Germans. Balls of fire illuminated the church, lit the eyes of Michelangelo's *Moses* and the tablets of law under his arms. The Partisans escaped unharmed. It was that simple.

Moments later, on a hill across from the Colosseum, Paolo and Elena said farewell to Giovanni and Pietro, who, like them, were being redeployed for the insurrection. They had been assigned, along with Giovanni's wife, Maria (Lucia Ottobrini), to remain in Zone IV, which included the *centro storico*. Paolo remembers the sadness. "We had become like brothers and sisters, bound by the same ideals, the same way of thinking, sharing the same risks and hardships. We felt safest when we were together. 'Anyway,' I said, 'the Germans have to pass through Centocelle before they get to the center. We won't leave you too many.' "[16] In the Resistance, it had become harder to say good-bye than to kill Germans.

Killing Germans had made Paolo and Elena sweat and even cry. But now there were new emotions, too, as Paolo later remembered:

> Many times when we were waiting, crouched somewhere and poised to attack, our bodies would touch, and the joy of that slight contact with the warmth of the other person would be at least as intense as the fear of the danger that lay before us. Sometimes it was she who would have to open fire, sometimes I would, sometimes both of us at once, and those moments before came to be treasured as we learned to savor something of the

beauty we asked of life. Everything we felt could be the last thing we'd ever feel, even the sun above. And when we walked down a street, passing, say, a Renaissance portico or frieze, we tried to fix its image in our mind, thinking we may never see that again. Little by little, even the simplest thing acquired new value. In the anguish just before going into action, we would take a deep breath to fill our lungs, for the last time, perhaps, with the air of Rome. Somehow we grew used to risking our lives every day and somehow our lives began to feel fuller and we had a deeper understanding of the reasons why we were fighting.[17]

THE STORY of Lieutenant Cummings's jeep ride on the open road to Rome took on a mythic quality and was embellished as often as it was repeated. The Vatican, noting that the Allies would be moving in now on two fronts, was not alone in fearing that "the Eternal City will become a new Stalingrad,"[18] but the spellbinding vision of that open read caused many in the Resistance to ignore elementary security. Euphoria was now the dominant sentiment in Rome.

Clandestine meetings that had always been held in groups of two or three suddenly grew large and unwieldy, even conspicuous. When Giuliano Vassalli, the acting head of the Socialists on the Military Council, found himself at a huge gathering of all the underground leaders openly discussing the insurrection, he wondered, "Have we all gone mad?" The most reckless, Vassalli said, were the Action Party and the FMCR, beginning with Montezemolo himself.[19] Marisa Musu, daughter of a founder of the Action Party and at seventeen the youngest of the five women combat Partisans in GAP Central was as fiery and dedicated as anyone. She later spoke of this collapse of discipline in the wake of the landing at Anzio as a "black period":

Our leaders were convinced that the Allies would arrive in a matter of days. This brought on a total neglect of the rules of vigilance. We were so eager to come out in the open that even we Gappisti no longer obeyed the rules. . . . In those few days, we were suddenly making our appointments by telephone—calls of course being consistently monitored—then meeting without taking the least precaution. To the Nazis and Fascists this looked as though there were many more Partisans in Rome and an armed resistance much stronger than they had previously imagined, and that perception produced a reaction that was much more ferocious than it had been before the landings.[20]

WHILE it lasted, about ten days, the folly provided a bonanza for the Gestapo. Kappler's two-man espionage unit had waxed into the seventy-four-man Gestapo presence in the occupied city, and Kappler, as Commander, had become the most feared man in Rome.

His once-indisputable number two, Erich Priebke, though now only one of the twelve officers in Kappler's command and lower in rank than two of them, had, like Kappler, undergone a transformation into an unplacable enemy of the Resistance. The thirty-year-old captain whose most precious years had been spent in Italy learning, as he later claimed, tolerance for one's neighbor, was gaining notoriety as a quick study in the interrogation arts these days. In the year or so since the Priebkes' second child was born in Rome and the couple, practicing Catholics, were given an audience by Pius XII, Priebke had acquired a certain reputation in the bedrooms of Fascist society's women of leisure, dubbed the white-telephone set. Erect, steely-eyed, always impeccably attired in his jet-black SS uniform, the Lothario of Parioli claimed an expertise in counterespionage and had become an aspiring Torquemada of the Via Tasso.

Every Partisan taken prisoner was regarded as the potential *passe-partout* to others still in hiding if only he or she could be made to talk. An interrogation center had recently been installed to complement the Gestapo's own twenty-cell prison in Via Tasso, 145, the north wing of Kappler's new headquarters. Priebke, in the early days of the occupation, had had some practical experience interrogating suspects in a basement of the Villa Wolkonsky, becoming familiar if not yet adept in the tools of the trade and taking a liking to the feel and heft of brass knuckles.

Now that the Partisans had stumbled, the cells of the Via Tasso would soon fill to overflow, but Priebke had already taken at least one turn in the new center, questioning the prisoner in Cell 14. Arrested on January 9, he was a Partisan of the Socialist Matteotti Brigades named Riccardo Mancini. Mancini would survive to testify against Priebke more than half a century later. He would say:

> They wanted to know the names of my comrades, and the places where we had hidden our weapons. I didn't respond. At a certain point, he—[indicating Priebke] this *being*, this individual—he got up, came toward me

and slapped me twice. This beast. I was twenty-one years old at the time and I tried to react. But they'd tied me with my hands behind my back to the door handle and I couldn't shake loose. Priebke went on hitting me, punching and kicking. Then he let loose one powerful blow, I don't know with what, and he broke my nose. I came to back in my cell, swimming in blood.[21]

The post-Anzio wave of arrests began on January 22. Kappler, leading the manhunt, returned first to where he had started months earlier, the Carabinieri and the Italian officers, now gathered around the galvanizing figure of Colonel Montezemolo and his Military Front. In the three days between the 22nd, when the Gestapo seized the sixty-four-year-old war hero General Simone Simoni, and the 25th, which saw the arrest of Montezemolo himself, about a dozen of the FMCR's most distinguished leaders, the untouchables, were arrested, incarcerated in the *Hausgefängnis* of the Via Tasso, and tortured. Their capture meant the end of the Military Front as a cohesive Resistance organization, though it would linger on ineffectively to the end. Among the others taken prisoner were the Carabinieri who had arrested Mussolini, including Colonel Frignani, whose wife, Lina, was forced to witness his "interrogation." It had already begun, when she was led into the room:

> I found him leaning against a wall with his face bloodied by the beating he had already undergone, punches and whipping; eight or ten men were still standing around him and every one of them was letting out his most bestial instincts against him. One of them had a huge ball and was pounding it against his stomach and his belly; another was sticking long needles into the flesh under his fingernails.[22]

Old General Simoni was personally received by Kappler. "At last we have the honor to welcome you here," Kappler said. He had not yet gotten to Montezemolo, and Simoni was invited to betray his hideout. Whipped, beaten with spiked clubs, the soles of his feet blowtorched, he endured, never wavering. His reply to his captors lives on in the annals of the Resistance: "My only regret is that I was not younger because there was so much more I could have done [for my country]."[23]

The worst and most protracted torture was reserved for Montezemolo, whose fortitude in withstanding the savagery of the Via Tasso torturers would induce Kappler to one day admit, "Frankly, we were moved."[24] Repeatedly bashed with jaw-busting, brass-knuckled fists, beaten with whips and chains, his bones broken in two, then ravaged by infection and high fever, the Colonel held on, dragged back and forth from the torture chamber to isolation Cell 1, an unlit, windowless room that had once been a kitchen. Rumors of his merciless treatment spread throughout the city, Vatican City included. His case, like General Simoni's and several others', would be brought to the personal attention of Pius XII.

After crippling the FMCR, Kappler over the next few days went on with equal facility to maim, if not destroy, the left, snaring the Action Party's Armando Bussi, Gappisti Guido Rattoppatore, Umberto Scattoni, Maria Teresa Regard,[25] and the mentor of them all, Gioacchino Gesmundo. In a category all his own, but arrested by Kappler for "Communist activities" that included providing false identity documents to Partisans and others, was a fifty-five-year-old priest, Don Pietro Pappagallo. Finally, on the last day of January, a mixed group of ten Partisans, from the FMCR, the Action Party, the Bandiera Rossa, the Catholic Communists, and lesser-known groups, all of whom had been arrested, tortured, and found guilty in a summary trial, were taken before a firing squad at Rome's Fort Bravetta, granted a last cigarette, and shot.

Mother Mary, writing shortly after learning of the landings at Anzio, articulated what all of Rome was thinking, that "surely the Allies will take Rome soon," adding, "I wonder if they know how, for us, every minute makes a difference."[26]

———————

PAOLO, setting out for Centocelle on January 23, went alone, with only the password and the name of a street in a neighboring *borgata* called Quadraro. Somewhere on that street, he had been told, he would find a shoemaker, who on hearing the password would escort him to his destination. Elena was to join him a day or so later. The password and, as it happened, the code name of the shoemaker were both Lupo. The trip with Lupo to Centocelle passed through two other *borgate*, Gordiani and Quarticciolo, providing Paolo with a tour of a part of Rome he had never seen before and could hardly have imagined existing. Teeming mudflats of abject poverty; dilapidated, shack-like houses deprived of plumbing, heaped with garbage and vermin—these were the dumping grounds of the people displaced by Mussolini for his architectural re-creation of imperial Rome.

There were, however, differences in character among the *borgate* that could only be discerned over time. Quadraro, for example—regarded by the

Germans as a "wasp's nest," the last resort of fugitives who could find no other place to hide—was a stronghold of the Partisans of the well-armed Bandiera Rossa. Quarticciolo had put its name on the map with the exploits of a legendary seventeen-year-old Robin Hood called the Hunchback of Quarticciolo. Handsome but deformed Giuseppe Albani led a band of anti-Fascists who, like many self-proclaimed Partisans, operated in a gray zone where armed resistance sometimes merged with armed robbery. Their bold attacks on the Germans and the Fascists were meant as much to weaken them as to relieve them of their goods. Food being shipped to the front to nourish the Wehrmacht was a favorite target and while German bread, pirated by Albani and his clan on a rampage, was sometimes resold on the black market, Albani's men more often distributed truckloads of stolen sacks of German grain to the poor, in quantities, it is said, enough to feed all of Quarticciolo and beyond.

IT WAS mid-afternoon when Paolo and Lupo reached Centocelle's main square, Piazza dei Mirti. Lupo introduced Paolo to the Partisans who had been waiting for him just outside the piazza. Their leader, a worker at the nearby Breda factory, was a man twice Paolo's age called Tonino. He had all the sandpapery ways of speech and manner of the Roman *popolani*, characterized by a voice, whether male or female, one octave lower than that of most humans and a magnificent irreverence for all things revered. Friendly enough, but surprised at being sent someone so young to command the insurrection, Tonino got right down to details. Including their comrades in Quarticciolo, he said, they could count on 150 men, who were already organized in armed squads. They had an arsenal of two machine guns, five submachine guns, about one hundred rifles, thirty handguns, a few cases of hand grenades, and a fair amount of ammunition. All of the Partisans, he said, were gathered in the piazza, waiting for Paolo to speak—fire them up with a pep talk—and they had better act fast, he said. The Germans and the Fascist police came through every now and then, and the curfew, recently lowered to 5 P.M., was coming on.

Paolo buckled, struck with an attack of stage fright. He had never spoken in public before and he was being asked to rally the men he would command. His discomfort did not escape Tonino.

"They told me you're not afraid of anything," he said with a street-smart smile.

"They told you something dumb. But it has nothing to do with being afraid. It's just that . . . I . . . I didn't prepare. . . . " That sounded as lame to him as it did to Tonino, so he added, "Okay, let's go."

They walked into the piazza. People were standing around in groups, but they came forward, slowly at first, circumspectly—public assembly of even a threesome had been banned since the first days of the occupation—then all eyes fixed on Paolo:

> There were many more than the 150 they spoke of [he says]. Men of all ages, a lot of young people, women and even small children. It was a most unusual assembly. There were even a few German soldiers on the edges of the crowd, but the men directly around me, twenty or so armed comrades who Tonino said would be at my side, told me not to worry. I put my foot up on a low wall and began to address the crowd, talking, timidly at first, about the need to correct the evil done by Fascism. Frankly, I was hoping the Germans would intervene. I was more afraid of speaking in public than taking them on. Instead, as soon as they caught on to what was happening, they were the ones to take fright. They backed away, going into a bar and lowering the shutters.
>
> I spoke about the war that was about to end, at least for us Romans, about freedom, about democracy and socialism, about the growing Partisan movement and the more humane and just society we were going to build. By the time I was finishing, the sun was setting and the cool wind that had been blowing in from the southwest began to carry the rumble of the cannon fire at Anzio. I raised my voice and it grew loud and strong as I ended with a call for their support for the insurrection. The people cheered. They rushed up around me, embraced me, shook my hand, the young people asking where to "sign up" for what they called the underground army. I had the feeling that readying the insurrection in Centocelle was practically done, that in any case my job would be much easier than I'd dared to hope.

At this point a police patrol drove up and ordered the crowd to disperse. Paolo stepped forward and said no. He told the officer in charge that the Partisans were in command here now, and if the police cared to, they could join them or otherwise simply leave them alone. The officer seemed shocked, but the patrol drove off. The next day, the same patrol returned and the Partisans and the police struck a deal. When Paolo's group wished to meet, the police agreed to disappear. When Paolo's group was not gathering publicly, the police would conduct their regular patrol.

As a sweetener, the officer and his men brought some of the Partisans with them to a police shooting range where they could train, firing sidearms and rifles.

In the meantime, Elena joined them along with a mutual friend named Vittorio Ortali, who was not part of GAP, but wanted to help organize. They would meet nightly with the Centocelle contingent at a trattoria in the piazza, not a German or Fascist in sight. A part of Rome, an ugly-duckling part, to be sure, had been freed and was looking beautiful.

"In Centocelle," Paolo later recalled, "the curfew was no longer respected. One spoke freely. Even the Allies were there, some escaped prisoners who now called Centocelle their home. There were some New Zealanders, some Australians, and even a young Senegalese from Dakar, who had been a philosophy student in Paris. But after the Anzio landing failed, when the Germans came back to the *borgata*, he was the first to be shot."

THE FIRST thing Kesselring did when taken by surprise by the landing was invoke "Case Richard," his elaborate contingency plan to deal with the unforeseen. Elements of a parachute division north of Rome reached Anzio by late afternoon and began blocking all roads to the Alban Hills and the capital. By midnight, about 20,000 German troops were in the vicinity of the beachhead. Two days later, on the 24th, the number had doubled, and by the 29th, the Allied forces were outnumbered nearly two to one, 71,500 to 41,000. Kesselring's forces stood poised to drive the invaders back into the sea.

This swift-moving, immense buildup would have far-reaching implications for occupied Rome. The entire Fourteenth Army, under General Eberhard von Mackensen, had been transferred from northern Italy to be reheadquartered in Rome, with Mackensen named Commander not only of the Anzio front but the war territory that included Rome itself. Second only to Kesselring, the aging Prussian warlord would now become the superior to the occupied city's "King" Mälzer, thus binding his fate to the fate of Rome. He was the high-born son of one of Germany's most illustrious World War I military figures, and his brother had been ambassador to Rome until replaced by Rahn. Tall, white-haired, and affecting a monocle, Mackensen was a member of the prideful caste of generals who disdained the rough-hewn Nazis, the Führer included, but there could be no doubt of his loyalty. According to his own war journal of the 29th, his mission at Anzio was to "annihilate the beachhead."

Annihilate was the word that Hitler had used in his order one day earlier. He had concluded that a German victory at Anzio would vaccinate Europe against any other amphibious invasion "by an enemy who wages a ruthless war of annihilation against the German people." At Anzio, he expected nothing short of a reversal of fortune. His forces, he ordered, were to fight "with bitter hatred . . . to drive home to the enemy that the fighting power of Germany is unbroken and the invasion of the year 1944 . . . will be crushed in the blood of British soldiers."

The German counterattack would not begin until some days later. In the meantime, while Lucas continued to dig in and consolidate his beachhead, his superiors had begun to question his pace. If seizing the Colli Laziali was the second part of his mission, when was he going to move? The question was also being asked by the officers and men on the beaches, who discussed it endlessly. "It was the only thing to do in the sodden, freezing woods," the official account of the Irish Guards records. "There was a sickening feeling of anticlimax. Every man had been keyed up for a bold, impressive stroke. . . . There were no Germans, what was stopping the Division? The men could not understand it, and the officers found it difficult to explain."

Lucas "explained" it to his diary: "The strain of a thing like this is a terrible burden. Who the hell wants to be a general?"

On the 25th, Clark and Alexander visited Lucas on the beachhead. They voiced no complaints, and Alexander complimented him "on a splendid piece of work." But privately they were less gracious. Alexander was "very much disappointed," he said later, "that Lucas had not pushed out to the Alban Hills . . ." and Clark, in his diary entry for the 26th, noted Alexander's concern. He was also aware, he wrote, that Alexander had heard grumbling from Churchill. "The Prime," Clark said, "wants an attack, Rome and a victory. . . ." So did Clark, and he knew how he would do it. Lucas had to go on the defensive, he had noted in his diary after the visit, adding, "I will then strike out and cut the German lines of communication, forcing his withdrawal out of the Cassino area. Then, I will turn my attention to Rome."

Lucas, undoubtedly sensing the underlying malaise, wrote on the same day: "This is the most important thing I have ever tried to do and I will not be stampeded."

Instead, he was soon fired by Clark and would be blamed for decades for his D-Day failure to march on Rome and far worse, for all those soldiers' graves the Allies left behind at Anzio and Nettuno. Long after Lucas's death in 1949, the limit of two divisions imposed on Lucas was, as one study stated, judged "simply too small to establish and maintain a defensible beachhead and seize the Colli Laziali [hills of Lazio] at the same time."[27]

ELEVEN

MY CURIOUS HIDEOUT

As a little boy living in an apartment of a Renaissance palace, one of the princely Palazzi Mattei that border on the ghetto, Peter Tompkins never got over his fear of the larger-than-life statues in the courtyard. He recalled that fear now as he rode past his boyhood home. He was seated in an unmarked Fascist police car driven by Lieutenant Giglio (Cervo), being spirited to a new place to hide. A few moments later, getting out of the car, he was led by Cervo to another patrician building, the Palazzo Lovatelli, and given new lodgings in a "secret room." His host was a young woman named Maria Salata, the daughter of a well-known Fascist true believer. She was also sheltering a man she introduced as Baldo Secco-Suardo, the son of a palatine count, and Baldo's friend, Lele Crespi, a ruddy Italian Air Force officer—both of whom were hiding to avoid forced labor. They all seemed pleasant enough to Tompkins, and had been vouched for as trustworthy company, but since he had been passed off on them as an escaped Allied prisoner of war, who knew who was lying to whom?

Ever since the arrest of Colonel Montezemolo, a week earlier, Tompkins had been on the run and fear ran with him, old fears and new. His mission, though he himself had never met Montezemolo, was known in detail to the FMCR leader by his association with OSS operative Menicanti and his breakaway agents Cervo and Malfatti. The situation posed a terminal threat not only to Tompkins but to the intelligence network that since the Anzio landing had begun to take shape with speed and vigor.

Ironically, Montezemolo's arrest had put the FMCR's clandestine radio Centro X off the air, leaving Tompkins's Radio Vittoria as the only Allied intelligence source transmitting from inside Rome. This had happened at the very moment of the massive redeployment of German forces at the Anzio beachhead, and the startling accuracy of the intelligence provided by Franco Malfatti's Socialist Party information service had convinced Tompkins to re-cast his mission. As the imminence of insurrection receded, the need for espionage burgeoned.

Malfatti's first report to Tompkins on the German response to the land-ing and the movement of troops to the beachhead contained vital informa-tion that, if true, could only have come from a mole well-burrowed in Kesselring's headquarters. Moreover, it identified the precise units and their deployment in or on the way to the Anzio area, information, as it turned out, that anticipated what the Allies would discover on their own only days later.

Tompkins's immediate reaction was that Malfatti might be a double agent. "How the devil, I wondered, did Franco obtain information from German headquarters in Rome!" Was the American being lured into the role of an unwitting channel for disinformation?

Malfatti apparently read his mind, offering an inscrutable smile. "You'll just have to trust me," he said. He could not reveal his sources but, he said, even in the German High Command there were men of non-German ori-gins. Some of them were children of anti-Nazis, even Socialists, who had fought the rise of Hitler and his subsequent Anschluss with Austria, the conquest and absorption into the Third Reich of their once-independent country.

Over the next forty-eight hours, relying on Malfatti, Tompkins set into motion a remarkable assembly-line operation. It was to turn out high-quality intelligence that from the outset, by its real-time nature alone, would consistently outperform Ultra in service to the front.

Although the OSS had a standing policy that agents were to support re-sistance anywhere, whether politically correct or tainted, Tompkins un-abashedly reported to Donovan that he had rejected the widespread OSS practice of employing "apolitical" professionals in favor of the idealist ama-teurs, in this case Socialist Partisans. "Personally," he wrote, "I did not have much faith in the professional spies, and eventually proved pretty conclu-sively that for reasons of their own, they often invented large portions of their intelligence, or gathered it from the recesses of their boudoirs, their convents or the back corridors of the Vatican."[1] Recruiting members of a clandestine party for intelligence purposes, he believed, had a margin of se-curity built in, since any Partisan had already won the trust of his or her comrades and was by definition acting in the interests of the group rather than the self.

Malfatti, in full agreement, was able to convince the Socialist Party leaders to authorize a detachment of up to a hundred Partisans under his command to work as the "eyes and ears," as Tompkins called it, of Allied intelligence in Rome. That number would multiply tenfold over the next two months, though the operatives, for security reasons—not least of all their own—were to know only that they were supplying the party's information service. The organizational details, which would grow to great complexity, were yet to be elaborated, but before long, as Tompkins told Donovan:

> There were Socialist eyes and ears in practically every office, on every street corner, in the farms and villages between Rome and the beachhead, on the carts and trucks that jogged along the country roads; among the laborers who built the military installations for the Germans; among the fisherfolk and sailors—everywhere in fact that human beings lived and worked, and where the Germans had to pass.[2]

Tompkins and Malfatti had just raised a pony-like glass of Aurum to toast their new network when Cervo burst into the apartment with the news of Montezemolo's arrest.

The following morning, departing the comforts of the Giglio household with an affectionate warning from Cervo's mother to "be careful," Tompkins was brought to a new hideout a few doors down from the Caffè Greco. This turned out to be a back room of a designer-dressmaker's establishment of doubtful security and in any case no place to launch a major spy ring. While waiting to be moved once again, he spent the next four days in the company of headless, stuffed mannequins, startled by every sound that could be worried into a signal of the Gestapo at the door.

Nevertheless, visits from Cervo and Malfatti kept the product moving. Malfatti delivered the intelligence in the raw, Tompkins translated, edited, and rendered his output in the lost language of newspaperman telegraphese, and Cervo, departing to wherever his peripatetic radio was that day encoded and transmitted.

On January 29, Radio Vittoria dispatched its first message of high import. It was a warning of an imminent attack on the beachhead. The details were uncommonly precise. The German plan called for a feint coming from the direction of the Alban Hills to strike at the beachhead's midsection, but the main event was to be an assault by the I Parachute Corps on the Allied left flank, an area called Pratica di Mare. The location of the I Parachute Corps base, from where the attack would be launched, was identified as being on the German side of Pratica di Mare.

The level of infiltration required to generate intelligence of this quality made the message suspect on the receiving end. "It took some time for my OSS colleagues on the beachhead," Tompkins said later, "to convince [Lucas's] VI Corps that the information was from an American officer behind the lines, but they managed to get the warning phoned to the various threatened units within a matter of minutes."[3] The momentum overcame the doubt and led to an Allied air attack. Finding the I Parachute Corps headquarters exactly where it was said to be, the bombers scored a direct hit, knocking out the corps's communications, including its ability to direct artillery fire. The attack was postponed. It was only years later that access to the German corps's war journal revealed the full extent of the damage and, moreover, confirmed the attack plan itself, but Radio Vittoria had established its credibility and found an eager audience.[4]

Dampening the good news was Cervo's report to Tompkins that his OSS rival in Rome, Clemente Menicanti, was spreading the word in the underground that he, not Tompkins, was the Chief of the OSS for all of Italy and that the American was his subordinate. Menicanti's contention was that he had been appointed in Naples by Tompkins's direct superior, Colonel Huntington. Tompkins had no knowledge of any such appointment, and worse, it would turn out to be true. His own title, conferred by Donovan, was Chief of OSS Rome, and Menicanti, refusing to recognize this, was saying that even if true, Tompkins's chiefdom was local and thus under his domain, which was national. Still worse, a third agent, one Enrico Sorrentino, yet another Italian "professional" recruited by Captain Bourgoin, was claiming an appointment, also secured in Naples, as "Chief Political Agent in Rome of General Mark Clark." To Tompkins, who back in Naples had fired Sorrentino as untrustworthy, this had all the makings of a comic opera. Three OSS chiefs suddenly staking out claims on the Eternal City, as well as on OSS financing, could only sap the authority of the OSS.

Tompkins said he wanted "no part of such shenanigans," though he asked Cervo and Malfatti to find out whatever they could about his rivals. In the meantime, they agreed to go about their business. With Radio Vittoria securely in Cervo's control, its whereabouts known solely to him, the threesome had only to stand together to rise above the others.

WHEN Tompkins was whisked away from his mannequin roommates to his new hideout, the unscheduled transfer was more of an escape than a precautionary move. One of the largest mass roundups of able-bodied Romans for forced labor—the sixth, not counting the sweep of the Jews—had been sprung that morning, and unbeknownst to the American, he was in its range.

The inevitably shrinking slave labor gangs for the needy Fatherland required frequent replenishment, but most of this day's captives would be sent first to Anzio to build fortifications. As a mark of its importance, the roundup was led personally by Kappler, his Gestapo reinforced by German infantrymen, the Fascist national guard, and a police contingent that—luckily for Tompkins—included Lieutenant Giglio. They had sealed off a vast area of the *centro storico*, and at the stroke of 10 A.M. began snatching men off the street, buses, and trams. That was the standard procedure. You were on your way to work in the morning and by evening you were in the Reich or on the western front, a rock-splitting chattel about to be worked to death. People indoors were in little danger from this routine, but there had been talk of searching buildings, and Giglio delivered Tompkins to new quarters without incident.

Ironically, Giglio's other superior, Rome's newly appointed Chief of Police spent his first day in the occupied city under arrest—one among the 2,000 conscripts nabbed in the roundup and trucked off to the Macao barracks for processing. Forty-four-year-old Pietro Caruso, *fascistissimo* veteran of Mussolini's 1922 March on Rome, had been sworn in that morning in the city's new *questura*, "police headquarters," in the Via San Vitale, which happened to be in the heart of the roundup zone. It was only natural therefore that he step outside for a look, but, taking one step too many, he was stopped on the adjacent main thoroughfare, the Via Nazionale, by an SS patrol and ordered onto a truck. Released hours later with apologies, he went into a rage back at the *questura*, calmed only by an arrangement made with Kappler. The next day he took command of an SS patrol and fifty of his own men in a two-part roundup of his design, netting another 200 unfortunate men for the Nazi labor gangs,[5] but changing little of his reputation as an inveterate bungler and a lout.

———

WITH the arrival of Caruso, chastised, vindicated, and fired up for a bigger kill, the full complement of police power was now in place for the major crackdown on the Resistance, particularly its armed left wing, that began the evening of February 1. Now that the Anzio invasion had failed to move the three principal anti-Partisan police forces, Kappler's Gestapo, Pietro Koch's

Special Police Unit, and the new Questore Caruso's traditional Fascist police apparatus unleashed three shattering strikes that first week.

Coup number one was Kappler's raid on GAP Central's "Santa Barbara,"
the organization's main bomb-manufacturing plant, installed in a *centro
storico* apartment on the Via Giulia, which confiscated "enough explosives to
blow up half of Rome," according to one German report.[6] Named for the
patron saint of artillerymen—the early virgin martyr who was tortured and
beheaded—the Santa Barbara had been conceived and operated by three
young explosives experts, a physicist, a chemist, and an architect. The last
two, captured on the premises and taken to the Via Tasso, were Gianfranco
Mattei, 27, and Giorgio Labò, 24. Core figures of the Gappisti, they were
immediately put to the extremes of torture.

Labò's thirty-five-day ordeal, during which the physical abuse he endured led to a case of gangrene, his transfer to Fort Bravetta, and execution,
was known in all its hideous details by his contemporaries. Part of it was told
firsthand by GAP Central Commander Antonello Trombadori (Giacomo),
who was arrested when he went to the Santa Barbara facility, unaware of the
raid. Nevertheless, he managed to convince Kappler's men that he had no
connection to the Gappisti, and ultimately survived. In the meantime, he
spent several days in a cell next to Labò's, glimpsing him only twice—a man
beaten to a pulp—but able to speak with him through an airhole. "I'm still
resisting," Labò said the last time Trombadori heard him. "I lay all the
blame on Gianfranco, who's dead."

Gianfranco Mattei had hanged himself in his cell, leaving a farewell note
to his parents on the back of an uncashed banker's check. He had taken his
life, he wrote, because of "very unfortunate circumstances."[7] All that, too,
was known then, along with the torture and a threat of being forced to witness his wife being raped. But it was only at the 1996 Priebke war-crimes
trial, that a significant element of the story—a high-level intervention by the
Vatican—came to light, in testimony by Mattei's sister, Teresa Mattei.

Gianfranco and Teresa Mattei were from a well-known northern family
of intellectuals, Catholics of Jewish origins. Their grandmother was a friend
of Monsignor Montini. Sometime during the three-day period between
Gianfranco's arrest and his death, she succeeded in obtaining a letter from
the Vatican soliciting her grandson's release. The letter was hand-delivered
to Kappler by Padre Pancrazio (Pankratius Pfeiffer), Pope Pius XII's liaison
to the Germans. Kappler, Teresa Mattei went on, quoting information received by her grandmother, "tore up the letter without reading it and said to
the Vatican envoy, 'This communist Mattei is extremely dangerous. Now

I'm going to turn him over to Lieutenant [*sic*] Priebke, who will get him to talk by physical and chemical methods.' "[8] The chemical methods, she explained, consisted of injecting a substance that elevated the body temperature to a level inducing a state of delirium, and her brother, an accomplished research chemist, was certain he would lose his control.[9]

The extent of such rescue efforts by the Pope and those closest to him, solicited by friends and relatives with family and other personal connections to the Vatican, is yet another measure—though largely unexamined—of Pius's dilemma: the Vatican's desire for the occupiers' protection being irreconcilable with the occupiers' oppression. There was nothing unseemly in giving greater weight to appeals coming from individuals inside the Vatican circle of intimates than to those made by strangers. The Pope could not be expected to be judge and jury in every case of a person in distress, particularly in the present situation, yet a plea from someone known by character and repute certainly merited consideration. Appeals of this nature had begun soon after the occupation, even before Princess Pignatelli's October 16 plea for the Jews, but the dramatic escalation of brutality in January sharply increased the requests for papal intervention.

The second anti-Partisan coup was scored the very next day by the Koch gang. In a manner Koch himself described as "speedy and intelligent,"[10] he began a round of arrests that closed down the Action Party's underground newspaper *Italia Libera* and would end about six weeks later with the Party bled out of the Resistance and most of its leading Partisans dead. Koch owed this success to having hired a certain Francesco Argentino, also known as Walter Di Franco, one of those ex–SIM professionals so deplored by Tompkins. Argentino, who had been taken on that very day, had infiltrated the higher ranks of the Action Party as a Partisan, and for weeks he had been informing on his comrades, choosing to speak to Koch exclusively. He then accepted Koch's offer to join the gang, because, he said later, "it corresponded to my way of thinking."[11]

It was an amalgam of like-minded thinkers that merged the forces of all three Partisan-hunters twenty-four hours later to assault the sanctuary of the Vatican properties. Again with Kappler's consent, Koch was joined by Caruso and yet another gang lord, Fascist chieftain Giuseppe Bernasconi, a certified psychopathic criminal whom even Koch later characterized as a "sinister brute."[12] Caruso's new *questura* was the base of this major operation, the target being the revered site of the martyrdom and burial of the Apostle Paul, the Basilica of San Paolo Fuori le Mura, Saint Paul Outside the Walls.

Caruso provided most of the police manpower, about a hundred men, including a squadron of mounted police—a quirk of chance that would place Lieutenant Giglio among them. The plan called for the mounted police to surround the basilica, leaving Giglio well-separated from the small group that would gain entry by a ruse dreamed up by Koch. But Giglio, without informing Tompkins or anyone else, it seems, contrived his own plan to attach himself to the entry group and assume his real function as an OSS spy.

Koch's ruse, designed for maximum surprise, was carried out by the gang's "priest," ex-monk Don Ildefonso. Around midnight, he came up to the entrance of the monastery adjacent to Saint Paul's and began to ring the bell insistently. When finally answered by a papal guard, he cried out breathlessly, "Help, help, I'm a priest being chased by the Germans!" The moment the door opened, Koch and his men rushed in and disarmed all the guards. Three other squads in groups of three or four followed, along with Questore Caruso, Vice Secretary of the Neo-Fascist Party, Giuseppe Pizzirani, and the unbalanced Bernasconi.

Blocking all exits, the invaders began a room-by-room search of the premises, arresting everyone in their path, sparing neither insult nor violence. Giglio was with them. Not only had he become an eyewitness, he had brought along a Minox, a state-of-the-art miniature camera, and was filling its fifty-framed roll of film with sensational pictures. Since Koch had brought a stenographer, in case of a need to record spontaneous statements made by those captured, Giglio's photography was thought to be authorized, particularly when they caught Italian Air Force general Adriano Monti dressed as a monk. But Koch of course knew better. The Minox was seized by Caruso, who had an eye for shiny little things of value. Giglio, slapped around by Bernasconi, was turned over to his squadron commander, who placed him under technical arrest and sent him home in utter panic to await disciplinary action.

In the meantime, Koch, as reported in a lengthy account to his superior in Milan, national Police Chief Tamburini, arrested sixty-six hiders, many disguised as priests, including, apart from the General, nine other army officers, NCOs, and soldiers, fugitive policemen, Carabinieri, and nine Jews. All but the Jews would be charged with Resistance activities.[13] According to his report, Koch also sequestered four heavy-duty trucks, a car, a Wehrmacht motorcycle, 6,000 liters of gasoline, and a vast array of military hardware, from hand grenades, rifles, and sidearms to gas masks and army cots. Finally, sometime after ten in the morning, the invaders walked out of Saint Paul's with hundreds of whole prosciuttos, salamis, and cheeses, thousands of meters of fabrics, and an unspecified number of fur coats.[14]

THE VATICAN'S indignation over the incursion into its sovereign territory surpassed its embarrassment over press reports that made it appear as if Saint Paul's was a black marketeer's warehouse. The Germans, in the person of Weizsäcker, again claiming the Reich's innocence, took the brunt of the Vatican's wrath. This anger included an alert sent to other neutral states, such as Spain, Portugal, and Switzerland, who were either courted by or otherwise important to Germany. As for the Fascists, the co-signatories of the Lateran accords, the Vatican made public its own list of violence and blasphemies committed inside Saint Paul's by the "vulgar malefactors" in violation of "a solemn Treaty by which [the Fascist state] recognized before the entire world the privilege of extraterritoriality."[15]

The Vatican's strong and unambiguous public protest, though not in the name of the Pope, was in many ways courageous, unique in the occupation thus far. It had a powerful effect in Rome. The Vatican's defense of its extraterritorial rights yielded, as anticipated but hardly guaranteed, yet another round of assurances from Berlin. Although the Germans, through Kappler, had approved Koch's probes of the Vatican's resolve, the official claim of having had no part in or prior knowledge of these raids, left Koch, and now Caruso, in isolation. Indeed, after a week or so, when the storm passed and Koch proposed going after the true objective—the CLN leadership known to be sheltered in San Giovanni in Laterano's Seminario Romano—he could muster no support, neither from the Germans nor the Fascist authorities. Such were the immediate positive aspects of the Vatican's protest. It also showed the value of unequivocal protest, particularly insofar as how it was received and accommodated by the Germans; this was all reminiscent of D'Arcy Osborne urging Pius, at the time of raid on the Jews of Rome, not to underestimate his moral authority.

Protested or not, however, the raid on Saint Paul's, by itself, sounded an alarm among those still in hiding not only in extraterritorial San Giovanni in Laterano but in Vatican City as well. A day after the raid on Saint Paul's, CLN President Ivanoe Bonomi concluded that extraterritorial status no longer afforded any security. "The advice of all the prelates who surround us," he wrote in his diary on February 5, "is to abandon this place."[16] Along with three other anti-Fascist leaders, Bonomi left on his own, following further advice from the churchmen that it would be "better to hide in private homes."[17]

But the Vatican faction that opposed giving asylum to enemies of the occupation forces was also strengthened. No longer content with having gotten Cardinal Maglione to order that hiders be urged to "change lodgings," they now sought something closer to a notice of eviction. Toward the end of the month, according to newly uncovered documents from the Seminario Lombardo, the Holy See, yielding to the hard-liners, issued a demand for expulsion. A priest at the seminary, who recorded the events of the occupation shortly afterward, spoke of religious institutions receiving "orders from the Vatican to dismiss all non-clerics." He continued:

> Why such a brutal blow? Many were in disastrous conditions: with a death sentence on their heads because they were military officers or deserters from the *repubblichina* [a disparaging term for Mussolini's puppet regime]. . . . Where could they go? . . . We didn't know what to say to them. Nor did we understand the reason for such a brutal order.
> . . . The rector tried at first to approach the authorities at the Vicariate to put the questions [of] the gravest cases to them. The Vicariate repeated its categorical order. And then the rector who had risked his life to shelter Jews, Communists, military officers, and had done the impossible, obeyed the order. . . .[18]

The Vicariate is the administrative facility of the diocesan bishop, in this case the Bishop of Rome, Pope Pius XII. On February 13 a letter was sent to Pius by Monsignor Guido Anichini, head of the Canonica di San Pietro, the Vatican living quarters adjacent to the Basilica of Saint Peter. Attached to the letter was a note made at the time by Secretariat of State official Monsignor Domenico Tardini. It is a brief but incisive account of a high-level clash over the expulsion decree.

The affair concerned the presence of some fifty fugitives then living in the several apartments of the Canonica, which was inside the boundaries of Vatican City. The residents had been ordered expelled. About half of them were ranking military officers, former government officials, and members of the nobility; the rest were Jews, all but a few, converts to Catholicism. Monsignor Anichini's letter to the Pope was an appeal of last resort to rescue them from what he called the "grave danger of being arrested and shot or deported." Indeed, expulsion meant an almost certain death sentence for the Jews and possibly the military officers, too. Noting that these fifty were part of a larger group that had been reduced when those less endangered left voluntarily, Anichini cast himself as a messenger of their "anguished invocation" to the Holy Father: "Lord, save us, we perish!"[19]

Monsignor Tardini's attachment to the letter put the case into perspective. Anichini along with another monsignor, Tardini wrote, had been summoned by the Pontifical Commission for the Vatican City State and told by commission member Cardinal Raffaello Carlo Rossi that they had to expel all their guests. "The matter caused an uproar," said Tardini, when on February 10, at a ceremonial gathering of cardinals, several cardinals "begged Cardinal Rossi and his colleagues on the commission . . . not to insist. Cardinal Rossi answered that he had spoken on the basis of a superior order. The cardinals then had Cardinal Maglione speak to the H[oly] F[ather]. In the end, those who left . . . were those who wanted to leave." [20]

The Pontifical Commission for the Vatican City State was the entity responsible for the security of the Vatican, and thus the institution most concerned with the viability of the protection agreements with the Germans. It was under the direction of three cardinals, Rossi, Giuseppe Pizzardo, and Nicola Canali. [21] Their direct and only superior was the Pope. Thus, Cardinal Rossi's reliance on a superior order in answer to those cardinals who begged him and his colleagues on the commission not to insist on expulsion would appear to be a reference to an order directly from Pius—particularly since the cardinals who were trying to overturn the order asked Maglione to speak to the Pope. But it is unclear what, if anything, the Pope said, to judge from Tardini's report that those who left "wanted to leave." [22]

These documents reveal that power in the Vatican, sometimes power over life or death, was divided, in this case into two warring camps, and that the Pope sometimes chose to support one camp and sometimes the other—an unfortunate expenditure of papal authority in those ever leaner days in Rome.

THE SECRET room that Tompkins called "my curious hideout," which could only be reached by passing on all fours through a concealed opening about a foot and a half square, grew less and less curious as it became an active base of operations. Soon renamed simply "the hole," it was there that Cervo repaired in a cold sweat immediately after his arrest as Giglio was caught using his spy camera. Contemplating going into hiding himself, he warned Tompkins of his predicament. The threat not only to Cervo but to the whole organization was indeed serious, infuriating Tompkins, but luck intervened when the film in the Minox was processed and turned up an unflattering photograph of General Monti. It showed the famous airman, though wearing a monk's habit, looking less monastic than cross-dressed, and was immediately made public, to the great delight of the Fascist press and further embarrassment of the Vatican. Moreover, Questore Caruso, already delighted, had set a proprietary eye on the pocket-sized camera, and Giglio's troubles were put to rest.

In the meantime, Tompkins, accepted as a guest in the hideout apartment under false pretenses, had felt constrained to alert the others to the mortal danger of his presence among them. His disclosure was met with equanimity by Maria, and the two men, Lele and Baldo, enthusiastically volunteered their assistance. They were eager to escape the boredom of months of idleness imposed by "Kesselring's disease," and before long became valued assets of the operation.

The remarkable work of the full-fledged spy network, overcoming deadly intramural intrigue, has received only spotty recognition and remains largely a tale of unsung heroes. They played a pivotal intelligence role in the battle to save the beachhead from extinction. Tompkins's long-classified mission report to Donovan explains that the network drew enormous energy mainly from the spirit of resistance rather than from conventional sources. It was a model of an inspired undercover apparatus probably unique in the annals of espionage, all the more so as an operation of the agency that would become the CIA. Tompkins's report stands as a rare tribute from the Allied side to the Partisan operatives, above all, but also to the people of Rome.

According to the report, the Socialist Party's Information Service had been expanded by Malfatti beyond the Partisans to include civilians, recruiting like-minded men, women, and sometimes children wherever the enemy was or might be between Rome and the beachhead. The information gathered, normally in scattered bits and tidbits, was processed in a tightly organized manner, moving swiftly from local collection points, climbing a pyramid-like structure, continually refined along the way, and finally encoded and transmitted to Allied headquarters across the lines.

One of the main tasks was a daily count of German traffic on all the principal roads to Rome. This was grueling, high-risk work, carried out twenty-four hours a day, the danger soaring during the curfew, which was often half the day long. It was a nuts-and-bolts operation, assigned mainly to the Partisans, some fifty or sixty men, sometimes more, Tompkins said, "jotting down every detail of every vehicle that passed, including type, contents, insignia, kind of troops, caliber of guns, etc. . . ."

There were part-time Partisans as well:

Farmers who brought their wares to the black market in the city [Tompkins wrote Donovan] would describe in detail German concentrations in their neighborhood, minefields, gun emplacements, gasoline dumps, the progress on the local fortifications. . . .

At the main hospitals where the wounded [Germans] from Allied bombing raids in the Alban Hills were brought, the doctors would nonchalantly gather details from their patients about who was hit and where, and what the targets were around them. And when the interns went to help the civilian wounded in the little towns around the Alban Hills they brought back detailed accounts of German installations within spitting distance of the beachhead.

Children, far back from the front, playing in the fields within eyeshot of the long-range German guns would tell their parents, and their parents in turn would tell their neighbors, and the information would be carried to Rome in the minds of peasants as they brought their baskets of goat cheese to the market. . . .

Thus dozens of carefully camouflaged ammunition dumps, gas dumps, gun emplacements, tank concentrations, and other military installations would be radioed to OSS and VI Corps headquarters and disposed of by the incessant bombing and strafing of the air corps.

Malfatti succeeded in a high-level infiltration of not only Kesselring's headquarters but also Kappler's Gestapo in the Via Tasso, the Fascist command of the Open City of Rome, the Fascist Republican secret services, the Office of Censorship, and the staffs of Rome's luxury hotels. Thus he maintained constant surveillance and eavesdropping at the haunts of the German High Command.

The pyramidal system provided for the rapid movement of the information gathered from local depositories to a central headquarters whose location was frequently changed. The raw intelligence, after screening and sorting, would be brought to Malfatti's headquarters. Adding a touch of mockery of the enemy, Malfatti worked out of the offices of a German publisher and bookstore directly across from the Hotel Excelsior on the Via Veneto, the Kurfürstendamm of an exclusive Little Berlin in occupied Rome.

Every morning, as the high-ranking residents of the Excelsior, including General Mälzer, the commandant-king himself, went off with their escorts to do the business of the occupation. In the store across the street called Domus, Malfatti and two or three others in the back room began their day, too. The information that had reached them was further sifted, checked, and condensed while the Domus employees out front sold books, unaware of the spy ring in their midst. The comings and goings of workmen and customers served as cover for armed couriers who kept the intelligence flowing. By late morning, Malfatti had produced and dispatched the first of his daily bulletins for noon delivery to Tompkins's secret room. Tompkins, assisted by Baldo and Lele, spent the next two hours evaluating the new information and preparing the most urgent messages for transmission by Cervo's Radio Vittoria to the base. His report to Donovan details the final cloak-and-daggerish step:

> The completed cables, written on thin tissue paper, were then tightly folded and carried by special messengers, inside their socks, or slipped through a ring on their finger where it could be easily swallowed. They took the messages to a man waiting at a prearranged rendezvous a few blocks away. This man, who didn't know who I was or where I lived, carried the message across town to meet another man at another prearranged rendezvous who in turn took it to wherever the radio station happened to be hidden. Thus the central messenger knew neither where the message came from, nor where it went to. If they caught the radio there would be absolutely no way they could trace the message back to me—and vice versa.

The entire process was repeated in the afternoon for the latest information. Tompkins's report concludes with an age-old spymaster's lament, a kind of Walsingham blue mood, in which he describes his "main job" as a booster of morale up against a host of reasons to sag. The work of Malfatti and his men, he said, "every day became tougher, with guys being tortured, or shot, or blown to pieces for collecting information for people [the Allies] who never seemed to keep their promises." He went on to explain:

> It was never a matter of money. All but the few top men received one dollar a day for their trouble. The top men, about five or six of them, received two dollars a day. And on this they all had to live and support their families, for it was a full day's job.
> It was not an easy job to explain away the difficulties OSS had to overcome and why they could not drop the equipment necessary for them to carry out the espionage and sabotage activities they were so ready to give their lives to carry out. . . .

It was hard to cope with their growing realizations that the Allies didn't give a damn about the Partisans, would use them so long as they served their purposes, but would otherwise treat them no better, and sometimes a good deal worse than their Fascist brethren.

But, luckily, they were mostly men who did what they did out of some deep-felt conviction. . . . whose faith in us as Americans was still child-like and untrampled-on.

Why they continued to work for us God only knows; but in spite of everything they continued to bring in more and more valuable information and stretch their organization further and deeper afield.[23]

As THE backbone of this network, these dollar-a-day Partisans could find solace, if not much appreciation, in their vital contribution to thwarting the massive German counteroffensive at the beachhead. The decisive battle took place from February 16 to 20. Hitler came within a hairbreadth of making good on his threat to drive the Allies back into the sea. Tompkins had been able to warn the Allies just as the attack began. Met with stiff resistance, the Germans drew back. Over the next three days, Radio Vittoria transmitted the positions of German units and troop assembly areas, and Allied bombers struck with an accuracy that caused another postponement of the German offensive. On February 9, Malfatti's highly placed men obtained a report signed by Colonel Dollmann, and Tompkins radioed: "SS Colonel says owing [to] retreat [from] Russia maximum effort will be made [in] Italy."

On that same day, Hitler approved Kesselring's plan to destroy the beachhead entirely—as the first stage of a more ambitious operation that would use an Anzio victory as a springboard to push the Allies back to Naples. According to captured German documents, secrecy regarding the attack was heightened, even among Fourteenth Army officers. This precaution protected the exact date and time, but a report from Tompkins sounded the alert twenty-four hours before it began. It noted that the Spezia-Rimini line of defense north of Rome had been emptied to provide additional German troops for the "attempt [to] smash [the] beachhead . . . Nazis figure maximum effort in next few days."

Unleashed the following morning, that offensive was overseen by the Führer himself, directing from his headquarters in East Prussia. His order to the troops had been read to them aloud: they were to fight until the enemy had been swept off the beach or the last German soldier was dead. In

Rome, Radio Vittoria, transmitting the output of the Partisan spotters five times daily, pinpointed dozens of targets for bombardment, resulting in hundreds of sorties on the supply lines and an unprecedented intensity of air support of ground forces. The American Tactical Air Force command appointed a special liaison office to the OSS to speed access to Vittoria's targeting.

"Enemy is less optimistic," Tompkins cabled on the morning of the 17th, "but still expecting successful big attack with arriving reinforcements." The renewed attack, in fact, penetrated the Allied defensive positions and began a direct assault on what was termed the Final Beachhead Line. Four depleted American battalions found themselves facing the equivalent of six German divisions, roughly fifteen to one. A breakthrough would split the beachhead in two—the first cut of an ax that would inevitably chop the troops to pieces.

Just after a cloud-covered sundown on the 18th, "all hung in the balance," as Churchill put it. Both sides, or what was left of them, were battered and spent. Still, the Germans, spurred on by their gains or their Führer's decree, launched one more attack in the twilight, sending a convoy of twelve tanks over a sea of churned mud against the final line that no one believed could hold. But the tanks could not cross a creek where hundreds of air raids had blown the bridge. A colossal effort had been halted by something so simple. In the dark of that Anzio night everyone on both sides knew the battle was over. The Allied counterattack over the next two days drove the Germans into disarray, sapping their offensive strength. Radio Vittoria, continuing to guide the Tactical Air Force bombers to supply-line targets, was able to report on the 21st that "Germans estimate that if present all-out attacks against the beachhead fail they will no longer be able to reduce beachhead."

And fail they did, as the fighting subsided that day. The Germans lost 5,389 killed, wounded, or missing; the Allies, 3,496.

Kesselring's Chief of Staff General Westphal blamed the failed assault mainly on an intelligence failure—the strength of the enemy's intelligence and the weakness of his own. Donovan, stressing the strength, concurred. In a letter to President Roosevelt, he said that the entire intelligence operation had saved the beachhead—though he mentioned no names, giving the collective credit to the OSS.[24]

The failure of the German offensive, however scrutinized, was the turning point of the Anzio campaign. Anzio now and for all too long would be, in the words of its most recent historian, "the bloodiest stalemate on the western front of World War II."[25]

Two days later, on February 23, VI Corps Commander Lucas was finally fired, replaced by General Truscott. He was given the task of shaking loose from the beachhead. His philosophy was that *really* good commanders sometimes have to be first-class sonsofbitches. ("It's as simple as that. No sonofabitch, no commander."[26])

Already "Axis Sally"—the treasonous, Maine-born Mildred Gillars—radio propagandist for the Third Reich, was taunting the GIs bogged down in their foxholes, calling the beachhead "the largest self-supporting prisoner-of-war camp in the world."[27]

Twelve

Hupf, Mein Mädel

The Rome to which Paolo and Elena returned after a month in the "liberated zone" of Centocelle had become an urban tundra where all illusions had withered and died. The passivist slogan about the Allies being just around the corner, now meaningless, had been reduced to drivel by an activist's graffiti on a Trastevere wall: "Americans, hold on! We'll be there soon to liberate you!"

The loss of illusion was replaced by a fear of not lasting until the end. Elena, who came back some days before Paolo, later described that winter's posteuphoric Rome:

> Growing fear and despair, hunger and sickness were wasting people away. The bombings had destroyed the ability of the municipal services to function, especially for people in hiding. Getting washed regularly was a luxury for all but the privileged living in the neighborhoods taken over by the German commands. Drinking water was often unavailable, and even the houses of the rich grew infested with germs and insects. Lice were everywhere in Rome and to catch it [sic] all you had to do was grab the handrails on a bus. You could smell the nauseating medicine for lice on the passengers, in public bathrooms, and on the people standing in lines for their food rations. We were all getting thinner and thinner, paler and paler, and the clothes people were wearing were hanging. . . .
>
> There were, however, those who still had their morning cappuccino and brioche, who spread butter on their bread when they took their afternoon tea; those who drank vintage wines with their steak and roasts or

game and baby lamb. You knew immediately who the people were who trafficked with the Fascists and the Germans. They were the only ones still driving cars; they were the well-dressed women in furs whom you saw on their way to the theater for an opera performed for the Nazi troops. The city had two categories of citizens, a minority who fraternized with the enemy, and the rest of the Romans, the vast majority, who suffered and died hoping for their liberation.[1]

The radically new set of circumstances in occupied Rome left the armed Resistance without a viable liberation strategy. All the bootstrap efforts to rescue Rome from the occupiers by creating a credible threat of a popular uprising had been exhausted by the failure at the beachhead and the reckless security lapse among the Partisans in Rome. Their negligence had filled the Gestapo prisons with the lifeblood of the underground while the parsimonious thrust at Anzio had made the call for insurrection a whistle in the dark. These failures gave birth to the bitter myth of the *insurrezione mancata*, that "the insurrection was somehow sabotaged." Marisa Musu (Rosa), the seventeen-year-old Gappista, would carry their grievance furthest in time, commenting on the stalled beachhead in a recent interview:

> Even today I ask myself how the devil they could have gotten them-
> selves bogged down at [Anzio], a place where there are no mountains, no
> large rivers, where there's nothing but flatland. How they got stopped
> there for more than four months, we'll never know. Probably, somebody
> wanted it that way . . . they knew that if they were to get to Rome at that
> moment they would have found the Resistance forces practically intact,
> thus in a position to take the city in hand or in any case be an equal party.
> At some level, somebody must have said, "Let's go slow, keep our casual-
> ties down, and another few months of Nazi terror will clear out the Parti-
> sans." I can't be sure about this because I don't have anything concrete to
> go on, but it's only that the thing seems so strange to me. . . .[2]

For the Military Council, the strategic clock on the insurrection had to be set back to zero and the firepower of the fallen or captured Partisans had somehow to be recovered. The single advantage lay in those Partisans still in the fray. Hardened by intense combat that had been extended from the city's center to the countryside, to a man or a woman, they were the match of any of the Wehrmacht's fastest guns.

In "free" Centocelle, the Partisans in Paolo and Elena's command, going on nighttime attacks to augment the daylight air raids on the supply lines, fought brazenly, dressed in Garibaldian red shirts sewn by their mothers or girlfriends. In most of the *borgate*, no German had set foot for more than a month since the Allied landing, and the greeting of choice among the Partisans was the closed-fist salute. But by February's end Centocelle, for one, could not hold on much longer, though it had not yet been retaken when Paolo and Elena had been recalled. The insurrection had been postponed indefinitely. GAP Central, the two Partisans had been notified, had been reconstituted under a unified command, Spartaco as Chief and Cola his Vice Commander. Paolo stayed on to fight to the end with his men. Elena reported to Spartaco, leaving behind a legendary status as the young, blond *inglesina*, "English girl"—because of her unusually fair complexion—who came out each night to fight the Germans. The intrepid *inglesina*, however, was in tears in the new Rome, where continuing the fight now meant leaving the apartment in Trajan's Forum, and her mother and brother. In the new Rome, the new strategy was, as it had to be, more of the old, but stripped of false hopes, now tighter, sleeker, smarter, bolder, and bigger. Now she would live in hiding, in the new Santa Barbara, in a cellar alongside a coal bin, her comrades, and bombs.

THEN on March 3, ceding prudence to rage, Elena, aiming her Beretta at a German who had just shot and killed a pregnant woman on a crowded Roman street, was pounced on and arrested. The dead woman was Teresa Gullace, a working-class mother of five, who lived on the edge of Saint Peter's Square.[3] Two days earlier, on March 1, seven hundred able-bodied men were caught in the net of the seventh major SS roundup for forced labor. Swept off the streets of the *centro storico*, they had been herded together in the military barracks along the wide boulevard Viale Giulio Cesare to await being sent to Germany or the front. As usual by now, word of where they were being held had spread fast, and the mothers, wives, and children of many of them soon began to gather outside the compound. The relatives were joined by others, too, particularly women, in a spontaneous show of solidarity. GAP Central's Spartaco and Cola were quick to perceive that the spaciousness of the boulevard, for one thing, lent itself to an all-out protest and possibly a raid on the barracks to free the captured men.

The Partisans were alerted. Elena, who had contracted pleurisy that winter and was suffering the shortness of breath that would afflict her the rest of her life, nevertheless came out of her hiding place to team up with Rosa. Along with several noncombatant GAP women, they helped organize the demonstration. By the morning of the 3rd, hundreds of women had massed outside the barracks in support of the mothers, wives, and children and their loved ones inside. The Gappisti had come with packets of freshly printed anti-Fascist flyers addressed to the "Women of Rome."

Dangerously illegal, these leaflets could only be distributed by tossing them into the air in bunches while moving surreptitiously through the crowd. With every toss, the German SS police and Fascist republican guardsmen bore down in search of the source. It was soon a tense and volatile arena, the tension heightened by the sight of the anguished prisoners. They were pressed against the barred windows, trying to locate their families, raising a din of back-and-forth shouting. Meanwhile all of the Gappisti were staked out, poised to seize any opportunity for the prisoners to break out and scatter.

Elena had just flung a batch of leaflets and was losing herself in the crowd when she heard a group of men at the windows shouting in a kind of team effort to make the sound carry above the cacophony. It was being belted out like a stadium cheer, chanted in a rhythm familiar to any Roman: "Te-Re-Sa! Te-Re-Sa!" All the other noise began to fade as the people on the street drew back to make a path for a fully pregnant woman who had been elbowing her way forward. She was carrying a small package, and tagging close behind her was a young boy. Soon the silence was complete, all eyes riveted on the woman, her chanted name now known to everyone. She had broken into a run, and she dashed through an opening in the police barricade, her son still holding on, her prisoner-husband peering out of the first-floor window. Sensing that she had only a few seconds to act, she exchanged a quick greeting with her husband and at the same time heaved the package, clearly a parcel of food, attempting to lob it to his outstretched hands. Those around him tried to catch it for him as well, but it hit the ledge beneath the window and dropped to the ground below. Elena was only a few paces away:

Teresa bent down, picked up the package and stepped back a bit to throw it again. Suddenly, to my right, I saw a German soldier on a motorcycle pulling in close by. He stopped and dismounted. In that split second a thought flashed through my mind: "Now he's going to kill her." I took a few steps closer and stood behind two Fascist guards, while the women around me had started shouting again and pushing, leaning on me, and I couldn't catch my breath, but I had my gun ready in my pocket, clasped in my hand. The German, a corporal, I think, grabbed Teresa by the arm. She yanked herself free shouting something that was lost in the cries of the crowd. He grabbed her again, this time by the clothing on her chest and practically lifted her off the ground. She seemed such a tiny little thing in the fist of a towering giant. There were shouts from the windows. Her little boy stooped down to retrieve the package and I heard an explosion. The German had drawn his Luger from his holster and shot Teresa dead.

A painful wailing filled the whole street. I had my gun out by now, and took rapid aim, my arm fully extended. I was completely oblivious to the two Fascists who jumped me, grabbing my arm, but the women around me grabbed me, too, trying to free me. I was still trying to fire when I realized that my arm was pointing upward at the prisoners. The guardsmen had me tightly in their grip but the women started dragging me and I heard somebody close to me say, "Give me the gun!" I looked to where that came from and saw it was Rosa. She had squeezed herself into the pack of women trying to pull me out of the hold on me by the guards. In the confusion, Rosa got right up to me and I let go of the gun into her hand. Finally, helped by a third Fascist, the guards overpowered the women, kicking and dragging me to the clearing where Teresa had been shot.

Brought to a guardhouse in the compound, Elena was locked inside a windowless holding room, alone and convinced she was on her way to the Via Tasso. She searched her mind for anything real or imaginary that might somehow explain the unexplainable, realizing that to the contrary she still had an unused ammunition clip in her pocket. She managed to lose it, however, burying it in the cold ashes of an unlit wood-burning heater. But now her hands were covered with telltale soot, and when she put them back into her pockets to wipe them on the lining, she felt an unfamiliar object. It was a membership card for the Fascist society Honor and Combat, and the member's name inscribed on the card was Marisa Musu. Luckily, Elena knew that was Rosa's real name and that Rosa before being accepted by GAP Central, had, like her, worked in gathering information for the Military Council. Either Rosa had been directed to infiltrate the Fascist group or the card had been forged, though it seemed heaven-sent right now. Rosa, Elena understood, had not only had the foresight to get the gun but had used the body contact to slip her the card. Now it would be up to Elena to think as fast as her younger comrade. Before long a young Fascist officer entered the room, busying himself with a notepad, and proceeded to question her.

"I'm a member of an Honor and Combat group," Elena said. "We came to keep the women calm, to convince them to go back home, that the Party would do what it could to help."

"Do you have an identification document?"

"The guards took my purse, stole it, all my money and my documents. They punched and kicked me, and you can bet I'll have the black-and-blue marks to prove that." He stared at her for a while, appearing undecided. "Look, my mother is going to worry when she hears about that dead woman who—" Interrupting herself, she "discovered" something in her pocket, coming up with the membership card.

The officer read it. "Fine," he said, "but I have to check it." He took the card.

Elena was crestfallen. It was unclear whether by mentioning her mother she had now been drawn in deeper. She pouted. He offered her a cigarette. She smiled, steadied his hand as he held the lit match for her. Their eyes met in the flickering light of the flame. She read his mind; he read hers, or thought so.

"If you like," he said, "I can give you back the card in person, as soon as we run a check on it. We can meet somewhere."

"I'd like that," she said.

A commotion erupted in the hallway. The officer opened the door. A distraught prisoner, surrounded by police and plainclothesmen, was being led down the corridor. It was Teresa's husband, being taken away, to identify the body, so said the handsome young officer. He regretted the tragedy, blamed it on the Communist women, then escorted Elena past the guards at the gates, and bid her good-bye—until they would meet again, he said.

That afternoon, a fresh, though smaller GAP Central contingent returned to the barracks on the Viale Giulio Cesare. Word of the vicious point-blank double murder of the Roman mother and the nearly full-term baby she was carrying had spread throughout the city, and by now a bed of flowers covered the bloodstained patch of sidewalk where she had been felled. A second demonstration of women, angrier than the first, was back on the street outside.

The Gappisti were there to prevent any similar incident, but one of them had a bolder, self-assigned mission in mind: vendetta. Guglielmo (Guglielmo Blasi) was a Partisan very different from his comrades. In his forties, he was twice the age of most of the others. Far from the ranks of student intellectuals, he had come out of the hardscrabble *borgate*, and more like the husband of the dead woman, he had to eke out an existence for himself, his wife, and children. He had been one of the last to be accepted as a GAP Central combatant, and though he had shown himself to be daring and courageous in action—with an infallible aim, it was said—he had gone through the rigorous screening process successfully only by covering up an inadmissible past. He had been convicted and imprisoned as a common criminal, a repeat offender, a burglar and a thief. That was under Fascism, but even now, a member of the Party and GAP Central, he was still engaged in his secret life of petty crime. Later, many of the other Gappisti would try to find the crack in the system that had allowed him through, but some would agree with Giovanni (Mario Fiorentini) who would see the flaw in their political naiveté, observing, "To us students, any member of the working class was incorruptible."[4]

The German on the motorcycle was nowhere to be seen that afternoon, and neither had any German police returned. It was left to the Fascist republican guards to keep the infuriated women in check. In the absence of his prime target, Teresa's would-be avenger showed neither disappointment nor any other sign of his intent to his fellow Gappisti. It was only when a Fascist officer, as edgy as the women, tried to force them at gunpoint to move farther back from the barracks that he stirred. Guglielmo, pulling his own gun, fired off a single round and killed him, surprising his comrades as much as anyone else. The women scattered for safety. The guardsmen opened fire, aiming for Guglielmo, but drawing return fire from all the Gappisti. Guglielmo shot another Fascist, who fell dead. The Partisans, wounding still other guardsmen, finally decamped unharmed.

They regrouped as planned an hour or so before curfew in the public market of the sprawling Piazza Vittorio. The popular piazza was their habitual place of postaction rendezvous, where they discussed their day and planned the next. Spartaco had been waiting and listened now to their account of the unexpected shootout. Guglielmo, violating every discipline, had acted entirely on his own, but to a bona fide member of the proletariat— the people to whom the dogma of their faith had assigned a historic destiny—no one, not even Spartaco, said a word.

MARCH, *marzo pazzerello*, "crazy March," a folksy reference to its capricious weather, would be Rome's cruelest month now. On the same day that

Teresa Gullace's husband had been caught in the roundup, March 1, a lone aircraft, flying low but unseen in the dark of evening, was heard over the Vatican—followed by a succession of explosions. Six small bombs had in fact been dropped only meters away from the Porta Cavaleggeri border of Vatican City and, incidentally, where the Gullace family lived. Four of the bombs scored direct hits on two of three extraterritorial Vatican properties, and the others exploded near the third such enclave, the Palace of the Holy Office. Furthermore, flying debris caused damage within the city-state itself. One person was killed. Inside the Vatican, the attack was taken as an intentional insult, a display of irreverence in defiant response, it said publicly, "to the repeated and ardent appeals of the Supreme Pontiff in behalf of the Eternal City."[5]

The blame fell naturally to the Allies, who were the only ones bombing Rome from the air. An earlier, similar incident had been exposed as the handiwork of Fascist hierarch Roberto Farinacci, but that had so infuriated the Vatican's German protectors, including Kesselring and even Hitler,[6] that no one could believe that the Nazis or the Fascists were at fault this time. In fact, a British pilot had lost his way in bad weather and mistook his target, but attempts by London to cover it up only did more harm.

Rome had already been bombed more than forty times since the first stick fell from *Lucky Lady* and devastated San Lorenzo in that July of a bygone era. Allied promises of surgical strikes to avoid damaging the city's treasures had had a tolerable level of success, though thousands of civilians had been killed and maimed.

But on February 15, far from Rome, at the Gustav Line, Allied bombers destroyed one of the treasures of the world. More than five hundred tons of high explosives reduced the sixth-century abbey built by Saint Benedict—a magnificent structure two hundred yards long—to a field of rubble on top of a mountain called Monte Cassino.

To the Vatican and a wide consensus around the world, the bombing was a senseless, barbaric act, as even the Allies would eventually concede. It was indeed a singular failure in command control[7] that yielded no military gain and provided a first-magnitude propaganda victory to the enemy. Newsreels and photographs, produced in anticipation of the bombing, had already glorified the common German soldier, who risked his life not for the Führer alone but also for civilization's precious art and artifacts. Transporting irreplaceable objects from the monastery along roads themselves threatened by Allied bombardment, the troops carried them out of harm's way. In Luftwaffe two-tone full dress, General Mälzer stood before the cameras at the turrets of Castel Sant'Angelo to ceremoniously transfer the pride of the Benedictine fathers of Monte Cassino for safekeeping in the vaults of the Vatican.

American and British Catholics agreed with the prefabricated justification, which proclaimed that the abbey was being used as a Nazi stronghold. But in Rome, Mother Mary was less "Catholic" than her coreligionists back home. She was convinced of the truthfulness of the Monte Cassino abbot's declaration that the Germans had not used the abbey at all, which, after thorough investigation, would prove to be the historical truth. As Harold Tittmann, defending his government in the Vatican, though only halfheartedly, later noted, it "caused considerable anti-Allied feeling both within the Vatican and throughout Rome."[8] The bombing of Monte Cassino drove the Pope into an even tighter embrace of his protectors. But the worst of the Nazi terror was coming.

The day after the lone bomber incident, the Allies unleashed a fierce raid, once again targeting the railyards around San Lorenzo and also the city's gas utility on the Ostian Way. Apart from the civilian casualties, bomb damage scarred Porta San Paolo, the Aurelian Wall, and the pyramid, and a direct hit on the nearby Protestant cemetery opened the grave of the nineteenth-century poet Shelley. Two neighborhood churches were destroyed and the stained-glass windows of the Basilica of Saint Paul Outside the Walls were shattered.

The Pope could not have known at that time that this was the opening shot of an extensive Allied air offensive on a scale never seen before,[9] but by now he had already entered into the closest thing to an adversarial relationship with the Allies, Washington in particular. With Rome being bombed almost daily in the first three weeks of March, the Vatican wasted considerable energy trying to reinvigorate hoary open-city proposals, rehearsing all the old arguments that had been exhausted by the old replies. Rome was being bombed because the Germans were using it militarily, Roosevelt wrote the Pope once more, and if His Holiness were to persuade them to refrain, the bombing would stop. But the Vatican saw the American President as a craftier soul. To the exegetical minds in the Curia, it seemed that riding with the American bombers were FDR's hopes of winning an unprecedented fourth term in the upcoming November elections: victory in Rome equals victory at home. A report to the Pope by New York's Archbishop Francis Spellman on his March 4 meeting with Roosevelt about the bombing issue was seen as confirmation. Speaking of the President, Spellman told the Vatican, "He says *he has decided to take Rome*."[10]

The bombs kept falling, and, according to Monsignor Giovannetti, Romans were beginning to ask why "the Allies were not doing what they should do (advance) and doing what they should not do (bombard)," and did that signal that the Eternal City could expect the same fate as the Benedictine abbey on Monte Cassino?[11] Secretary of State Maglione, the only OSS-designated "pro-American" cardinal in the Vatican, turned to the Germans to solicit a demilitarization of the city that would satisfy the Roosevelt standard. This effort produced an official "confirmation" by Kesselring of the Reich's respect for the open-city character of Rome, though he admitted that some military traffic—"restricted as much as possible"—had perforce to pass through the city. This was due to the difficulty of transiting the bombed-out roads that would otherwise be used.[12] The truth was that Kesselring was still months away from deciding whether to defend Rome street by street and, as in Naples, destroy it strategically. Since the Anzio landings there had actually been a threefold *increase* in German military movements through Rome. An eyewitness Swiss correspondent of the *New York Times* described it:

> On the Ponte Milvio, which is perpetually clogged throughout the hours of darkness, down the Via Flaminia and the Corso in the heart of Rome proper, the stream pours in unending waves of tanks, motorized artillery and trucks loaded with munitions which filter through the maze of streets to disappear into the Pontine Plains [to Anzio] or southward to the escarpments of Cassino. . . .

German command posts and other services of the rear, the dispatch concluded, have been "set up practically under the shadow of the Vatican."[13]

These advantages—safe passage through the heart of Rome and the rear zone of operations under its sheltering sky—were of course the paramount military reason why the Germans were in Rome. They were also precisely the advantages that the Partisans had fought all along to reduce and to deny to the Germans. The conflict had swelled the ranks of the anti-Partisan police forces and filled their prisons, but it had steeled their opponents and had amplified the hostility of the Romans. By March, this kind of "open city" could be held only by sheer Nazi terror, and the Partisans, trimmed to the bold and swift, struck as regularly and as self-assuredly as the Allied bombers.

PAOLO returned to GAP Central the day after the Teresa Gullace affair, moving into the new hideout and Santa Barbara arsenal. It was located in the *cantina*, "basement," of a middle-class residential building in the Via Marco Aurelio, a quiet street on a hill overlooking the Colosseum. The hiding place itself lay beyond the bottom of an elevator shaft in a coal storage room behind a heavy steel door. Only one person had legitimate access to that space, fifty-five-year-old Duilio Grigioni, the graying, affable *portiere*, caretaker to the building's residents and guardian of the secret beyond the steel door. A man who had learned to read and write in a Fascist prison, he was in fact a full-fledged noncombatant member of GAP Central.

The hideout was empty when Paolo arrived carrying a down-filled blanket given to him by his mother. It would now become a mattress, placed on a few planks of wood, and he would share this "bed" with Elena, in the company of two Gappisti married couples and two or three other Partisans. The husband of one of the married couples was a noncombatant, Giulio Cortini, a young physicist, who had escaped the raid on the Santa Barbara in the Via Giulia and was now GAP's chief bomb maker. Early in March, the execution at Fort Bravetta of Cortini's fellow explosives expert, Giorgio Labò (along with nine other Partisans captured by the Gestapo), added an unslakable thirst for vengeance to the demand for Cortini's services. Over the next few days, with more or less the same frequency as the Allied raids on the periphery, GAP Central hit the *centro storico* repeatedly, two of them major strikes, on the 8th and the 10th, resulting in curious outcomes.

The former, carried out by Elena single-handedly in the early morning, blew up a German fuel truck at a depot in Via Claudia. The explosion of 2,500 gallons of gasoline, turned the target itself into a bomb, rocking the entire neighborhood, which included the Colosseum, and the fires burned under pillars of billowing smoke all day, by chance the same day that bombmaker Labò went before the firing squad. The spectacle, which included a sighting of the legendary young blond *inglesina*, was far more enduring than the fire and smoke.

The attack on the 10th was more brazen than graphic. Paolo, Giovanni, Maria, and a fourth Gappista named Franco Ferri pounced on a procession of Fascists belonging to the same organization, Honor and Combat, whose membership card had saved Elena from certain long-term grief. The paraders were part of an armed militant wing of the group and having just come from a rallying assembly, they were marching by the Tomb of Emperor Augustus along the Via Tomacelli, singing the Fascist hymn to violence: *"All'armi, siam fascisti, terror dei comunisti,"* "To arms, we are the Fascists, the terror of the Communists." The Communists, answering the challenge, came out from what must have looked like nowhere, opened fire, killed three of them, wounded several others, and returned to the same void without a scratch. The derring-do, tales of which as usual echoed throughout Rome, had a strange magnifying effect on the perceived size of the Partisan threat, especially on the occupiers. While Kappler never shrank from his permanent anti-Partisan manhunt, Commandant Mälzer meted out the punishment for this incident to the Fascists. He banned public marches or street demonstrations of any kind by the Party, restricting future Fascist gatherings to sites indoors.

This arbitrary ruling set the stage for a dramatic event, two weeks hence in the Via Rasella.

AGAINST this tumultuous background, Pius XII spoke to the people of Rome in a public audience on the 12th. The German prohibition on outdoor assemblies did not apply to the Vatican, but in a meeting between Monsignor Montini and his counterpart in Weizsäcker's embassy, Sigismund von Braun, some days earlier, Montini mentioned the planned audience in Saint Peter's Square for Rome's thousands of bombed-out refugees and the bomb victims themselves, "many of whom have requested this favor." Among the items discussed regarding the audience, Montini noted later that day, were "free access, brief duration, [its] religious and popular nature, etc." That same morning Weizsäcker himself telephoned to say that the occupation authorities had no objections.[14]

The 12th, a Sunday, was the fifth anniversary of Pius's coronation, and his regular public audiences had long been suspended; thus there were reasons to expect a large turnout requiring external cooperation. Nevertheless, the absence of any hint of opposition by the occupiers was certainly an expression of confidence in improved German-Vatican relations. In the nearly two hundred days of their presence in the Eternal City, in which they had made themselves the scourge of the Romans, few Germans feared as they had earlier—say, at the time of the deportation of the Jews of Rome—what the Pope might say.

The Resistance had not yet reached this conclusion. A CLN proposal aimed at persuading the Vatican and especially the Pope to protest the Nazi abuses of the Romans had already been set in motion, and a demonstration was planned to be held in Saint Peter's Square that same Sunday. It would be the first of its kind and, to say the least, highly unauthorized. Such demonstrations were drawing more women—an increasing majority of Rome's visible population, as men continued to vanish in the roundups, in prison, and in hiding—especially among students, families of political prisoners, Partisans of the Catholic Communist Party and Gappisti, including Elena as an organizer. The refugees and the faithful assembled quietly in the piazza, facing the masterwork of Bramante and Michelangelo, waiting for the Pope's scheduled 3:30 P.M. appearance on the balcony high above the entrance to Saint Peter's Basilica.

How much the Vatican knew about the impending demonstration is unclear, but security measures included an armed presence of some 300 Swiss Guards, most of whom stood behind a barrier to the steps of the basilica. Any potential for violence was further reduced by the Germans, seeking to avert the threat of provocation by barring their troops from attending the audience. The Allies, however, had rejected a Vatican request in the name of decorum to refrain from flying over Rome that day as a courtesy to the Pope.

The waiting multitude inside the circle described by Bernini's colonnades numbered in scores or even hundreds of thousands.[15] Their mood reflected the bleak weather, said Mother Mary, noting that it had rained all morning and the sky had been leaden for hours. She went on:

> They were saddened by the inevitable consequences of the air raids, by the German oppression, by their disappointment at the Allies not having reached the city to free it, by anxiety for their dear ones in hiding or taken by the Germans, most of them hungry and some of them homeless, not to mention the refugees, all of them homeless and many of them hopeless.

Elena, like Mother Mary, standing among the crowd, noted the "German soldiers patrolling the borderline, almost as if to remind us of how near we were to where that area of peace ended and the afflicted city began."

Precisely at the appointed hour, the shining white figure of Pius XII stepped onto the balcony to a hushed silence. Except for a single guard and a priest, both men keeping a respectful distance, he was alone, with a bird's-eye view of the sea of people before him. A rumor had been circulating that the Holy Father would make an important announcement, perhaps, some dared to say, the withdrawal of the Germans—"a childish idea," said Mother Mary, "born of desperate desire to be rid of them." What he did say brought several interruptions of thunderous applause. The martyred city of Rome, he said, had been torn apart "down to the living flesh of its inhabitants, horribly killed, mutilated, or wounded," and he prayed, pleaded, and begged that their suffering, multiplied every day, be alleviated "by those who have the means to come to their aid." Then he continued:

> If each one of the world's cities struck by an air war that respects no limits or laws is in itself a tremendous accusation against the cruelty of such methods of fighting, how can We believe that anyone would dare to transform Rome—this nurturing City that belongs to all people for all of time, and on which the eyes of the Christian and civilized world are now focused, watching in trepidation—to transform her, We say, into a battlefield, a theater of war, thus perpetrating an act as militarily inglorious as it would be an abomination in the eyes of God and to a humanity conscious of its highest and most intangible spiritual and moral values? Therefore, We cannot but address Ourselves once more to the foresight and wisdom of the responsible men on both belligerent sides, certain that they will not want to bind their name to a deed that no motive can ever justify before history, but rather will want to turn their thoughts, intentions, desires and efforts toward the advent of a peace freed of every violence in order that they be remembered among the blessed rather than be cursed upon the face of the earth for centuries to come.[16]

The Pope ended with a prayer and a blessing for the people, who responded with loud cheering. He had not yet retreated, however, when the women's demonstration began. Mother Mary's account of what happened next differs only slightly from Elena's.

Mother Mary:

> As the throng was dispersing, shouts were heard of "Down with the Germans," and Communist manifestoes were thrown about. . . . The noise quieted down for a time, but began again among a press of people in the narrow street leading to Ponte Vittorio Emanuele [bridge]. "Down with the Germans!" "Give us bread!" they called out. Presently we heard revolver shots, and people began to run. . . . frightened men and women ran past like leaves in the wind. But nothing further happened, and we reached home safely.[17]

Elena:

> As soon as the speech ended the piazza exploded. The women cried out their protest. Small groups formed around them, the women orators im-

provising, calling for the German troops to leave the city, since they were
the cause of the American bombings. The Pope's speech, before a crowd
who had suffered not just bombardment but roundups, shootings and
mass deportations, did not even hint at the ferocious Nazi repression . . .
[or at] the hundreds of patriots who were tortured daily and then summarily executed at Fort Bravetta. The meditative silence that had preceded the
speech had transformed into a protest that continued for some time in the
piazza. People were waving [Italian] tricolor flags, red handkerchiefs, and
were crying out, "Peace, peace, out with the Germans from Italy," until
the windows closed and the pope disappeared into the impenetrable
palace of the Vatican. A patrol of Swiss Guards tried to break up the
demonstrators and the crowd dispersed beyond the colonnades.[18]

Peter Tompkins, who wasn't present but whose sources had keen ears,
noted in his diary that the people in the square were cheering the Pope with
cries for peace and that "the left-wing parties were there shouting . . .
'Throw out the Germans!' which to us was encouraging."[19]

The Allies kept out of the Roman skies all day Sunday, but the every-
other-day March bombings resumed on Tuesday, one of the heaviest days
ever.

WHEN he made the entry in his diary about the papal audience, one day
after the event, Tompkins was sitting on the sunbaked terrace of his Palazzo
Lovatelli hiding place, a hunted man recording feelings of mortality and the
awe that accompanies the approach of a Roman spring. On the same page,
he wondered how much longer his life behind enemy lines could go on. His
precarious position had seriously deteriorated in the past few days, and the
danger was even greater than he could assess.

In the first place, he had no knowledge that Gestapo technicians reporting to Kappler had begun to intercept signals from Radio Vittoria by
directional-finding instruments, and though efforts to home in on the transmitter had thus far been foiled by Cervo's practice of continually changing
the venue, several suspects had been placed under surveillance.[20] Second,
the challenges to Tompkins's authority by Menicanti on one front, by Sorrentino on another, and the enmity between the two challengers were causing a crisis for Tompkins. Sorrentino, the agent claiming to be General
Clark's man in Rome, had accused Menicanti of misappropriating OSS
funds. The amount in question was 14 million lire, half of which, said Sor-

rentino, had been meant for him. But Menicanti had raised similar charges against Sorrentino, which only added to the grand total of OSS money—in the end a staggering amount—that would disappear. Moreover, two of Bourgoin's men, saboteurs who had landed with Tompkins, had threatened betrayal to the Gestapo, seeking 500,000 lire as the price of silence.

Tompkins, reporting all of this, radioed OSS headquarters in Naples in outraged demand for clarification. "The lives of our men" are at risk, he wrote in telegraphese, "for blackmail[,] stupidity and criminal negligence."[21] The reply from the base reaffirmed his position as "chief representative of the OSS in Rome," and a second message ordered the saboteurs and Menicanti to report to separate OSS installations in northern Italy. As for Sorrentino, he dropped out of sight—to be heard of only later as a prisoner in the Via Tasso, betrayed to Kappler by parties unknown, but treachery was to become a hallmark of "the professionals" inside the OSS.

Menicanti, when confronted by Tompkins with the OSS orders for the Italian's departure, simply refused to obey, invoking his own "authority" as Chief for all Italy. Having no means of enforcing the order, the American later explained to Donovan, "I simply ignored him and went about my business." But Menicanti, who in the postliberation inquest would be described by the OSS investigator as a "very rough, ruthless 'gangster' type," was not yet finished with his own business conducted under his no-longer valid OSS title.[22] "Coniglio," Tompkins reported to Donovan, using Menicanti's code name, "then attempted to prevent the resistance groups from filing information to me, offering to subsidize them largely . . . [trying] to get the information service away from me and discredit Franco [Malfatti]."

> This was quite a serious move [he continued] because several of the social-
> ist party members resented Franco's using and endangering so many of
> the key men in the party for the very risky work we were doing. Dozens of
> them had already been arrested and over twenty had been shot.[23]

Ignoring Menicanti anyway, Tompkins, now fortified with written confirmation of his OSS position, tried to recoup his credibility in the eyes of the Military Council, meeting in mid-March with Giorgio Amendola, though the relationship would never move beyond polite discussion. With Franco, he contemplated the scarce possibilities of a raid on the Via Tasso in an attempt to free the Partisans arrested doing the legwork of their organization. Despite this setback, they still received more information than they could possibly transmit, and Tompkins had also been working with Cervo in setting up a second radio. They were well along in that project when, only twenty-four hours after Tompkins had wondered how much longer he could go on, life in Rome as he knew it received what would quickly prove to be a mortal blow.

Meeting with Cervo on March 15, Tompkins was told of a disturbing incident. Radio Vittoria's operator, Vincenzo Bonocore, had been approached by a man who had been introduced to him months earlier by an OSS agent named Paolo Poletti, who like Cervo, Bonocore, and Menicanti had been a member of the first team recruited and sent into Rome by Captain Bourgoin. On this latest occasion, the man had asked Bonocore if he was still transmitting with his secret radio. Bonocore had apparently dodged the question, but had later been passed a note left in his name at a bar he frequented in his neighborhood. The bartender had also given Bonocore a warning that the man, who called himself a Communist, was thought to be working for the Nazis. The note had requested an urgent meeting, which was where the matter now stood. Tompkins, reacting with due alarm, told Cervo to order Bonocore immediately not to leave his apartment for any reason until they could arrange for his transfer elsewhere.

The man tracking Bonocore was known in the OSS as Franco Di Walter. This was a transposition of Walter Di Franco, the alias used by the ex–SIM professional Franco Argentino, who was emerging as the Koch Gang's star Partisan-buster. Koch, in fact, had learned of Kappler's discovery of the secret radio, and Argentino, flush with his successes in infiltrating and dismantling the Action Party, had picked up the scent of fresh blood in anti-Fascist circles. The human relay system devised by Tompkins, by which no messenger could know both the origin and the destination of any message in transit, was stronger in theory than in practice. According to a report by Koch that remained buried until 2000,[24] Argentino's penetration of the Action Party had provided information about a secret radio run by a "group of spies working in collaboration with the anti-Fascists." Argentino had observed the relay activity in one particular neighborhood, concluding that it was probably in the proximity of the radio's location. "The contacts with the elements operating the radio," the report continued, "usually took place by appointments in piazzas and by persons known to each other only by their first names. . . ." Thus Argentino had been able to make the connection between Malfatti's Partisan runners and the OSS radio operator.

None of this was known to Tompkins or Cervo, but the warning delivered to Bonocore not to move was still timely. Nevertheless, within hours Bonocore was gone. He had been seen ensconced at home the night before,

Cervo told Tompkins early the following morning, but had gone to the neighborhood bar and had not returned. The Koch report makes it clear that on the morning of the 16th, Bonocore met with Argentino in the Piazza di Spagna. The urgency of Argentino's note was based on his sense that Bonocore had become suspicious and that he had to act swiftly. Bonocore himself had apparently yielded to curiosity, but when he saw Argentino this time, he immediately smelled a trap and, Koch said in his report, tried to flee, whereupon Argentino took up the chase, fired several shots, and brought in his man. "We then staked out the police officer [Giglio], who we knew had to move the radio equipment."[25]

"I'm worried about the radios," Cervo (Giglio) told Tompkins, taking leave of him that morning. "I better get them moved to a safe place right away."[26]

Radio Vittoria, along with the new radio that was being put into service to broadcast the excess of intelligence to the front, was presently located on a houseboat anchored at the Risorgimento bridge over the Tiber. The houseboat was one of several along the river, most of them private clubs operated by various civilian and military bureaus of the capital. The Risorgimento site, a recreation facility for employees of the Ministry of Finance and their families was ideal for clandestine transmissions. The ministry had its own radios sending out signals on many frequencies, which served as a cover for Vittoria, and in winter months the boat was usually empty, except for the friendly caretaker, an anti-Fascist named Luigi Mastrogiacomo.

Tompkins had counseled Cervo to use a go-between rather than attempt to retrieve the radios himself, but Mastrogiacomo, Cervo said, was under strict orders not to allow anyone into the locker where they were stored. Cervo had always jealously guarded physical possession of the radios, and he wished to keep it that way. By the evening of the next day, Tompkins had still not had any word from Cervo, and as a worried foursome—Franco, Baldo, Lele, and Tompkins—sat waiting in the hideout at a nervous game of bridge, the telephone rang. Maria, their host, picked up, listened, then passed a puzzling message to Tompkins. A woman was on the line who wanted to know "if I have bought her any honey."

"Say that you will let her know," Tompkins replied, and when Maria hung up, he turned to the others, saying, "They've got Cervo."

They also had Mastrogiacomo and Radio Vittoria. Pietro Koch was sitting on a bombshell, the greatest coup imaginable in the war against the Roman Resistance. Not only could his new prisoner deliver Tompkins and the scores of Partisans who made up the entire OSS intelligence-gathering network in Rome, Cervo was the repository of names and secrets of the many Resistance leaders who had met in his home. Cervo's radio operator had told all—and, according to Koch, offered to continue operating Vittoria as a double agent. Now, as Tompkins and the others began collecting, packing, and burning every smidgen and fiber of a life that was over, it would be Cervo's turn on the rack.

FAR AWAY from the scene, an OSS officer listening to the "professionals" would file a groundless report that the person "probably responsible" for Cervo's and Bonocore's arrests was Colonel Montezemolo, albeit under duress.[27] Even at winter's end, however, all of Rome knew that Montezemolo, two months after his own arrest and subjected to the worst agonies of the Via Tasso, had not cracked; his coveted secrets had proved unreachable. His stature as a hero of the Resistance would never flag, and he was still alive and resisting. His greatest ally was his titled cousin, the Marchesa Fulvia Ripa di Meana. This stalwart mother of six waged a daily battle for his life, and on the morning of March 19, she sat in a papal antechamber awaiting a private audience with Pius XII.

Since the day Beppo, her name for her illustrious relative, had fallen into Kappler's hands, she had not rested in her rescue efforts, moving, as only people of her station could, in the rarefied circles of a certain power in Rome. This was the power of the old, black aristocracy—black as in the color of priestly garb and old because it dated back to the time of Garibaldi and his heirs, when this faction of the Roman aristocracy was the last pillar of loyalty to a Church and a papacy stripped of their temporal rule by the wild-eyed nation-builders of the Risorgimento. Its strength greatly diminished in any tangible way, aristocratic Rome, irreducible as an essence, remained a force nonetheless. Thus, for example, by the good offices of Prince Ruspoli she had succeeded in putting her case before Colonel Dollmann, the Nazi of choice among the Roman nobility, and though little had come of it, access to the "good" occupiers was no small gain.

Time was not on her side, however, and for Montezemolo, despite her efforts, almost nothing had changed that was not for the worse. She had gone as far as plotting with others to engineer an escape, sewing conspiratorial notes into the collar of a shirt she had been allowed to send to him. Her persistence, frequent presence at the Via Tasso and above all her endless denunciation of the suffering imposed there, had irked Kappler, and she had recently received some "friendly" advice from one of his officers, Major Karl Hass, to give up the fight or face arrest. But her tenaciousness was as indomitable as her attempts to wring at least one brief visit with her cousin out of Kappler's stony rule. Early that March, Montezemolo had managed to get a message back to her. Written in an invisible ink made of lemon juice, it had been smuggled out in a thermos bottle, along with notes to his wife and children. To his devoted cousin he wrote: "Try the Pope. The Church tells us, 'knock, and it shall be opened unto you'! Go to Princess Baby Colonna and ask her to do this. I will try to hold on as long as I can." He was in fact dying.

Marchesa Ripa di Meana knew the Pope herself; like Princess Pignatelli, she had been a student of his in Rome when he was a professor of religion at the all-girls Catholic private school the Cenacolo. The Pope also knew Montezemolo, his wife, Juccia, and their children, who were living in hiding in a Roman convent, so the circle was intimate indeed. Still, it was better to go through channels, and Princess Colonna had led her to Monsignor Mario Nasalli Rocca, the papal liaison to Regina Coeli prison, who, having counseled her, had arranged the audience and was there to present her to the Holy Father. While they waited along with three other monsignori, she saw Cardinal Maglione come out of the Pope's office and go over to Monsignor Montini. Seeing Montini, whom she knew would be received by Pius immediately after her, warmed her heart, she later said, for she imagined "that the Holy Father would certainly speak to him of what I would say," and thus their good works would begin without delay.

The fact was that she had joined an invisible queue of privileged people but a waiting line no less. There were at least fifty persons of particular distinction being held prisoner by the occupiers in life-threatening situations for whom their families and friends had sought the Pope's intervention. Bringing to bear whatever influence they could muster had yielded some measure of success. Very few of those appellants, however, had reached the place in the antechamber where the Marchesa sat now. All but a handful,[28] had had their case reviewed by the Secretariat—sometimes by Montini and even by Maglione himself—and a successful outcome meant consignment with instructions to Padre Pancrazio, who as the Pope's personal liaison to the occupation authorities could plea for relief in his name. Most of these cases were currently pending before the occupation's military tribunals, and though Vatican intervention had in the meantime eased the burden on some of the victims, it had produced no dramatic results as yet. Much of this was known to Ripa di Meana, and she was well-prepared to use her advantage to the fullest. She came bearing a memorandum on why saving Montezemolo was in the Vatican's own interest and her eagerness to argue it orally was brimming.

Not long after her audience, the marchesa recalled the experience in illuminating detail.[29] She was shown into the papal study by Monsignor Nasalli Rocca, she wrote, and "behind the desk, drawn, emaciated, dressed all in white, with a shining cross of diamonds and sapphires glittering on his chest, sat Pius XII. I bowed in genuflection and approached him. He nodded for me to sit in the chair that faced him and invited me to speak." She began with one short sentence that revealed a remarkable understanding of what was perhaps closest to the Pope's own heart:

> Holy Father, I dared to come before Your Holiness to plead for a kindness that, if granted, would not only mean the salvation of one person and the joy of his family, but could have important implications for keeping public order in Rome.

Further, she pointed out that before Montezemolo's capture Rome was not, as now, bombed regularly and virtually indiscriminately, because, she said, he had been in radio contact with the Allies, directing them to targets so that the bombings would not damage the city. He had also been in control of the military resistance groups of all political parties, bar none, who were under orders from their own chiefs to heed his command. Finally, if he could somehow be freed, he would be in a position to guarantee a smooth transition of power when the Germans withdrew from Rome.

Public order. Allied bombings. Smooth transition of power. No learned Vaticanist in Rome or anywhere else, from Berlin to Washington, could articulate better than the marchesa the primary concerns of Pius XII at that moment. Montezemolo's freedom as the answer to the Holy Father's prayers, the Pope surely knew, was sincere but not excessive exaggeration. There could be no doubt that her cousin was a sterling leader and an anti-Communist force opposed to a popular uprising, though highly placed people in his own party found him less adamant than they.

The Pope, however, was inscrutable, listening carefully without questioning any part of her plea. When at last he spoke, he asked, "He's being held by Kappler, is he not?"

"Yes, Holiness," she replied, "and unfortunately we all know what that means. The tortures suffered by Montezemolo were atrocious." She saw a deeply lodged pain cross the Pope's countenance.

"I promise you," he said, "we will do everything possible for Montezemolo, really, all that is possible. I don't know what results we will obtain, but we will neglect nothing that is within our power. Leave your memorandum with me. I will read it attentively. I repeat, we will do everything possible."

She thanked him profusely and backed away full of hope, she said, all the more so when she learned shortly afterward that Monsignor Montini had in fact met with him next and had been instructed "to give his immediate attention and special regard to Beppo's case," she said. The Vatican had taken the matter to heart, she was told by someone in the Secretariat. The Pope was personally involved.[30]

The declassified Vatican documents are more precise about how the Vatican actually proceeded. After his meeting with Pius once the Marchesa had seen him, Montini made the following notes:

> See if any steps have already been taken for Colonel Montezemolo. Try to do what one can. Inform the Marchesa Fulvia Ripa di Meana nee Schanzer, Via Bruxelles 47, Rome. Cf. the attached note [the Marchesa's memorandum]: which would like us to make the Germans understand that it is in their interest as well as his to give him favored treatment; he was working for order.[31]

Some days later the case reached Secretary of State Maglione himself. A reading of the Marchesa's memorandum by a member of his staff had revealed some difficulties that needed the Cardinal's attention. "The Holy See," the unidentified reader said, "cannot approach this matter in the way she presented it . . . which would not even be in Montezemolo's interest." It could, however, write its own memorandum or alter certain parts of hers. A new memorandum was in fact drafted, but that too was held up, though some unspecified, apparently interim appeal was sent to Weizsäcker's embassy.[32] Examining the material himself, Maglione finally concluded, "The memorandum must not be sent and our recommendations must be very vague."[33] This directive was dated March 29. By then, however, Montini had already added a line to his own note: "Suspend; it seems that he was killed after the events in the Via Rasella."

MAINTAINING public order in occupied Rome, which had quickly become synonymous with anti-Partisan police work, had grown into a larger problem. The expansion of police forces of every kind to suppress an increasingly emboldened armed resistance succeeded only in striking a new balance of terror, but the maintenance of the new balance, under ever more arduous social conditions, required a new expansion of the police forces. In a city where an ordinary citizen simply trying to survive the occupation—let alone fight back—had to break the enemy's laws daily, nearly everyone was in one stage or another of becoming, in the eyes of the law, a habitual criminal in need of policing. Thus, the mere act of policing a population growing more and more adept at lawbreaking was likely to mean not more order but disorder.

Since the beginning of the year, the German police presence in Rome had been greatly augmented, dwarfing the additions made in the same period by the Fascist republican regime, namely, Pietro Koch's Special Police Unit and the aggressive new *questore*, Pietro Caruso. The Germans had brought in about 500 men, the 9th, 10th, and 11th companies of the 3rd Battalion of the SS Polizeiregiment Bozen. The regiment had been formed in October 1943 of recruits from South Tyrol. This was a German-speaking part of the Italian Alps that under the terms of a 1939 agreement between Hitler and Mussolini had been incorporated into the Greater German Reich as the Alpenvorland. The recruits were among the *optanti*, "opters," those who at that time of union with the Reich had opted for German citizenship, and when facing military service had made the further choice of serving in the SS rather than the Wehrmacht.

The Bozen regiment, divided into three battalions, was under the command of the Higher SS– and Polizeiführer for Italy, General Karl Wolff. It would later gain a reputation in northern Italy for burning villages, inhabitants included, and other atrocities against civilians committed in the name of anti-Partisan warfare.[34] The 3rd Battalion had arrived in Rome early in February, nominally attached as SS police to Kappler but in practice under Commandant Mälzer as part of Mackensen's Fourteenth Army. Polizeiführer Wolff, under later interrogation by the British, described their mission in Rome: "At the request of Field Marshal Kesselring, I had placed at his disposal . . . a police battalion of recent formation, made up of Germans from South Tyrol, to carry out the tasks of the Ordnungspolizei and to protect the Vatican."[35] These distinctions about responsibility, mission, and the character of the force, were scarcely noted at the time, but would later take on great significance.

The 9th Company was deployed south of the city. The 10th, assigned to dislodge the Partisan bands operating in the hills of the Castelli Romani, had not yet been transferred there. While waiting, this unit had been en-

gaged in Rome itself in the recent roundups for forced labor. The motorcy-
clist who slew Teresa Gullace was attached to the 10th Company. Nevertheless, the zone of operations where the 10th Company had been filling in,
urban Rome, was the territory reserved for the 11th, the newest arrival,
which was undergoing supplementary specialized training for its role.

Composed of some 160 men, the 11th Company was billeted in the Ministry of Interior's Viminale Barracks, not far from the *questura*, and every
morning the trainees would rise with the sun and march through the center
of Rome to a shooting range over the old Roman bridge Ponte Milvio. The
part of their training specific to the city concerned large-crowd manage-
ment, especially how to put down an insurrection, and that required practice
in the use of sidearms, hand grenades, and submachine guns. Another feature
of their training, which some of the recruits would grow to hate, was to learn
to sing one particular martial song in one particular way, as taught by the
Company Commander, a certain Lieutenant Wolgast, renamed and derided
behind his back as Lieutenant Vollgas, German for "full of gas." "They
wanted us to march through the streets," one of the men later recalled,
"singing at the top of our lungs, chest pushed forward like a bunch of crow-
ing roosters, in a continuous, cadenced cock-a-doodle-do."[36]

The song was called "Hupf, Mein Mädel," or "Skip, My Lassie," chanted
repeatedly. It may have sounded foolish to the marchers, but not to the Romans, who found themselves visited by a daily parade of Nazi imagery worthy of Dr. Goebbels. As intended, the figure cut by a company of SS police,
steel-helmeted men armed to the teeth, harnessed in ammunition belts and
grenades, marching through the heart of the Eternal City, bootsteps drum-
ming on the cobblestones, voices bellowing a foreign tongue in the style of
their Führer, was invasive, intimidating, and memorable—repugnant, to be
sure, but police work in itself.

Early every afternoon, following the training session, they would march
back to their living quarters, again through the *centro storico*. Except for a
short break, they had been following this routine with clockwork precision
since mid-February, more than five weeks now, and were growing very disgruntled. Songmaster Lieutenant Full-of-Gas was one thing, but the
twenty-four-hour-a-day iron discipline of Major Hellmuth Dobbrick was
quite another. Dobbrick was the Commander of the whole 3rd Battalion,
whom the men of the 11th saw as a frustrated would-be leader of an elite
corps stuck with bored military police. They had already been rigorously
trained under Dobbrick in the Alpenvorland, "*gedrillt* pitilessly," one recruit
later recalled, using a German word reserved for training circus animals.[37]

But the ordeal was almost over. The men of the 11th Company were scheduled to complete their exercises in the first week of spring.

The 11th Company's choreographed display of police power had received considerable though silent notice from the Romans whose path they crossed twice daily. Among the Romans was Gap Central's Giovanni (Mario Fiorentini). Attracted by the sound of their footfalls and their chanting, he could see them approaching from as far as the Piazza del Popolo, coming down the straightaway of the Via del Babuino, a column of heavily armed troops, stretched out a hundred yards in all, led by a squad with submachine guns leveled. Barking their guttural chant—or so it sounded to Giovanni—to the thunderous beat of their marching, they would go through the Piazza di Spagna, onto the Via Due Macelli, and pass directly beneath the window of his parents' apartment, where he was then hiding. An armored vehicle with a machine gun mounted on a platform brought up the rear, and now, looking south, Giovanni could see the column head toward the mouth of the tunnel built through one of the Seven Hills as an underpass below the Quirinal Palace. The marchers, however, never actually entered the tunnel, which had become a shelter for the bombed-out homeless. Instead, they would turn left just before the tunnel entrance and disappear into one of the narrow streets. By the third or fourth time he observed them, Giovanni noted that it was always 2 P.M. when they vanished, and the street into which they invariably turned was the Via Rasella.

SPRING

All those who are in Rome / to harm our nation's home
To plot against our Duce / who guides our Fascist future
Must first confront a band / under Pietro Koch's command
It's he who lays the brilliant plans . . . / by which we nab the Partisans
Then they face interrogation / unlucky them, a hopeless situation . . .
From the room next door you can hear the sound / of how the pleasures of the prisoner abound
If he persists and there's nothing he'll reveal / there's our man Zangheri who'll make him squeal
But just what are those cries of pain? / The work of Billi, going at it again?
Or do they come from the mighty fists / of big Pallone's massive mitts? . . .
And though the Communist's face grows sadder / in the end he tells all just to end the matter . . .
So this is Koch's squad / men strong-minded and hard
Who work for Italy's glory / and for our Fascist victory
And I, who have come to know you / shout "Onward Duce!" as heartily as you do
"Marcella" [1944] ["Hymn" of the Koch Gang; cf. Griner: 33–37]

The sun heavy with cruel light
rays embedded in the red haze of spring
Men passed like shadows on the lines of ashes and asphalt

faces that do not cling to memory . . .
Under the pounding heels
a cadence resounded on the pavement
echoing in the heart
(Only the brain left the vow intact)
At a nod from Cola it was understood
that the moment of judgment had arrived
Eyes upon us at every corner
watching, waiting
and it passed, swept away with fear
the timidity of youth
of our twenty years
Carla Capponi, "Elena" 1944 [DIR: 71]

THIRTEEN
VIA RASELLA

WHEN Giovanni returned with Maria to the cellar hideout, they told Paolo and Elena about the column of SS troops marching so brazenly through Rome. The four Partisans began to follow and clock the marchers. After the column reached the top of the Via Rasella, it turned right at the corner, onto the main thoroughfare Via Quattro Fontane and marched a final, straight line of about a third of a mile to the Interior Ministry and their barracks. The corner formed a suitable blind for an urban ambush from which the Partisans could launch several hand grenades as the column turned; then they could escape in the confusion. This "bite-and-run" tactic had become a staple by now, a reliable formula for a high rate of success, but when the four proposed it to Spartaco, he viewed it as requiring a brand-new approach. A bite-and-run strike on such a large target seemed wasted, less than a glancing blow. Here was the Via Rasella, a narrow passage between two wide streets, near the end of a long march, a tiring hill to climb and a configuration that compacted the target and reduced its room for maneuver. It was the only street on the 11th Company's route where an attack seemed feasible. The whole bellowing Bozen SS company would be funneling into a trap. Although none of the attacks in Rome thus far had employed more than three or four Partisans, Spartaco said he would make four squads of GAP Central available, some sixteen men and women, if they could be used efficiently.[1]

Thinking big was in the spring air. An even larger-scale operation was already scheduled to take place on March 23. It would combine forces of GAP Central and the Socialists' Matteotti Brigade—named for the Socialist leader who had stood between Mussolini and dictatorial power until he was murdered. The joint attack would be an unprecedented act tantamount to sacking the Fascist pantheon. On the calendar of the so-called Era Fascista, March 23 of every year was a red-letter day. It was on that day in 1919 that young Mussolini and 144 other disgruntled but kindred souls founded the Fascist movement in a meeting hall in Milan's Piazza San Sepolcro.

Thus March 23 would be the twenty-fifth anniversary of that historic day, an anniversary to be celebrated by the Fascists in occupied Rome. Such was the ardor, in fact, that party Vice Secretary Giuseppe Pizzirani was convinced that Mälzer's ban on public manifestations of Fascist pride could not possibly stand in the way of his plans for a gala commemoration. He foresaw a daylong series of events all over Rome. A morning church service to honor Fascism's fallen heroes, an afternoon parade of Fascism's many varieties of flags, pennants, and buntings, culminating in a rousing assembly at Fascism's traditional auditorium, the Teatro Adriano.[2]

The announcement of all this and more in the press, on the radio, and on the walls of Rome on the first day of spring provided the final details needed for the Partisan attack, already well along in the planning. The Military Council had been preparing at least as actively as Pizzirani to mark this special anniversary. An electrifying demonstration of the might and presence of the Resistance on Fascism's most sacred day could not but be a tonic for the sorely tried people of Rome. The Matteotti Brigade would attack the Fascist parade and the Gappisti would follow with a major assault at the Teatro Adriano.[3]

Pizzirani's plans, however, had also attracted Consul Möllhausen. In the months since his "liquidate" reprimand, he had recovered lost ground by not using the word again and keeping a low profile. But there was something about the idea of Fascists celebrating *anything* that was grating to the sensibilities of all the occupiers. "A display of Fascist pomp and ceremony on that day," the diplomat said later, "while the people of Rome were going hungry and saw Fascism as the cause of their suffering, seemed inopportune." He decided to call a meeting at the Villa Wolkonsky to discuss the matter with Dollmann, Kappler, and Mälzer. They need not have gone to the trouble of attending, since none of them, Möllhausen knew, would have a kind word to say about the Fascists, but the fireplace in the embassy's Red-and-White Room, the ritual passing around of cigars and the prewar cognac poured by men in white gloves were reasons enough to gather.

Möllhausen introduced his guests to his opinion that "to parade through the city to the sound of Fascist music and the sight of Fascist banners was nothing but a useless provocation." Dollmann agreed. He wanted the ceremonies shortened. Kappler said that politics was not his field, "but if I were asked I would say that neofascism has to disappear so that we can hold onto the last vestige of German prestige in Italy. This requires the elimination of Mussolini, and if I were charged with that task, I would know just how to carry it out." The only surprise came from Mälzer, who said he was not at liberty to ban the ceremonies. He had received word from Berlin that the Führer, aware of the rampant low regard for his ally, was insisting that the Fascists be treated as "authentic friends." The same source in Berlin, however, left the matter to Mälzer's decision. Mälzer canceled the parade, shifted the Teatro Adriano assembly to the heavily guarded Ministry of Corporations on the Via Veneto, and gave Pizzirani permission to hold the church service as planned. Pizzirani was incensed. He protested to Mälzer, then to the Duce himself, but got nowhere.[4]

When word of the cancellation of the parade and the Teatro Adriano event reached the Military Council, it had to make a swift change of plans. A new counterdemonstration was approved, scheduled to take place on March 23. While the Fascists would celebrate in the Via Veneto, the Gappisti, proceeding from a newly elaborated plan, would launch their attack in Via Rasella.

THE LEADERS of all three political parties who ran the Military Council were in agreement that the main objective of the operation in the Via Rasella, apart from injuring the occupation forces, was to provide a galvanizing show of strength against the common enemy. But the Roman resistance was never more divided than on the eve of its largest endeavor. That night of the 22nd, CLN President Bonomi, hiding in his nephew's apartment in the Trionfale district, had been brought a message from one of the six member parties, which seemed to him to signal the imminent collapse of the coalition. The issue, as had become usual, was the price that the King and Badoglio would have to pay for having abandoned Rome.

Continually inflamed by Churchill's support for the monarchy, against sharp disagreement from Roosevelt, the matter had flared up again in recent days in a surprise move by Stalin. Apparently believing he was somehow blocking a nefarious design of British and American imperialists, he granted diplomatic recognition of the Badoglio government, strengthening the King perhaps but weakening the CLN. Shortly afterward CLN leaders met to shore up their elusive unity in a resolution that would have removed the monarchy question until after Rome's liberation from Nazi rule.

While the capital shook under one of the heaviest Allied bombings, the measure was put to a vote. It drew approval from five of the six parties, with the Action Party postponing its response for four days. The 22nd was the fourth day, and the message brought to Bonomi was that the Action Party had voted no. Such was the popular resentment of the King and Badoglio that sharing the people's contempt could be turned into political gain. The Actionists, bruised and worn thin by the Koch Gang's recent arrests of its leaders, stood resolute in excluding the monarchy from any new government until the question could be decided by the people of Italy in free national elections. Moreover, invoking its unity pact with the Socialists and Communists, the Action Party showed its partners why it made sense to withdraw their yes votes, and they did. Faced with what he called in his diary entry that evening the "truly unexpected," Bonomi was ready to admit his failure to unify the CLN against the occupiers and quit.[5]

A SENSATIONAL report on the 22nd in the Fascist-run Rome daily *Il Messaggero* suggested that the Germans might soon withdraw from Rome.

Journalist de Wyss wrote in her diary, "Something is brewing." The *Messaggero* article was based on a leak from the German press attaché, who, she went on, apparently "said too much or said it too soon."[6] Other than to note the rapid spread of the withdrawal rumor and the general excitement that because of a German withdrawal the Allied bombings might end at any moment, de Wyss had nothing further to say.

But the Vatican's open-city negotiations with the occupiers had in fact entered a crucial stage. The coming warm weather was expected to bring an Allied counteroffensive, a strong inducement for Kesselring to abandon his stubborn defense in the south and shorten his supply lines by withdrawing from Rome. The efforts of the Holy See to convince the Germans to demilitarize Rome so that the Allies would halt their air raids was taking on a new logic. The Vatican was preparing for its long-sought orderly departure of the present occupants of the Eternal City. Months back, Cardinal Maglione, for one, had conceded that this transfer of power would be decided by military considerations and little else. The Pope's only concern, Maglione told both Osborne and Tittmann, was that there be no hiatus, no political vacuum that the "communists" would fill. Only a seamless transition, melding the German departure and the arrival of the Allies, could thwart such a design. The Holy Father, however, did have one specific wish. Osborne had reported it to the Foreign Office on January 26:

> The Cardinal Secretary of State sent for me today to say that the Pope hoped that no Allied colored troops would be among the small number that might be garrisoned at Rome after the occupation. He hastened to add that the Holy See did not draw the color line but it was hoped that it would be found possible to meet the request.[7]

In the light of a Roman spring, the time to decide the open-city issue seemed at hand. On March 22, what that decision might be appeared moving precisely on the course so carefully set by the Holy See.

———

IN A new but temporary hideout with a view of the Borghese Gardens, Peter Tompkins on that evening of the 22nd received his first details of the fate of Cervo. Tompkins had been on the run for nearly a week, unable to communicate with OSS headquarters, and the only further word about Cervo he had had in the meantime was that Cervo had been betrayed by Radio Vittoria operator Bonocore. What else Bonocore knew and had surely divulged was a frightful mystery no less than Cervo's capacity to remain silent. Changing addresses almost nightly, the American took the name of Roberto Berlingieri, a nonexistent distant cousin to a Fascist noble family. He had the handmade Capri shoes and could affect the necessary Tuscan accent, and in that guise he had a chance encounter with someone who had had direct dealings with that family—Gestapo Captain Erich Priebke.

Luck was on Tompkins's side, however, more than he knew. With Lele, he had gone to a crowded "curfew party"—a common all-night diversion in collaborationist circles of occupied Rome. This one was at the Parioli home of film star Laura Nucci, whom he recognized from the images of her silver-screen persona. Wrapped in furs, she lay on a sofa in a far corner of the room under the ambitious hands of a dapper SS officer. It was not until the next day that Tompkins learned that the SS man was Priebke, Kappler's chief of counterespionage, and still later of his Berlingieri connections. But the American was unnerved more than once during the evening by Priebke's intense stare. In the end, Priebke did nothing more than offer Tompkins his groping hand, click his heels while bowing slightly, and take his leave, walking a drunken zigzag to the door.[8]

News of Cervo had been brought to the Giglio family two or three days after his arrest. A boy had shown up at the Giglio home and spoken with Cervo's mother and sister. The boy claimed to have been arrested with a professor and taken blindfolded to an apartment. He had heard people screaming, and when his blindfold was removed he had seen and spoken with Cervo. He was missing several teeth, the boy said, his face badly bruised and his lieutenant's insignia ripped from his uniform. He had pleaded with the boy to go to his family, apparently expecting him to be released. The curious circumstances of the boy's story aroused suspicion, but the next morning, Malfatti reported to Tompkins that his sources had located the apartment where Cervo was being held. His men had spotted what appeared to be three dead bodies taken from the building, where neighbors had complained of agonizing cries and gunfire every night. The building was near the Termini train station, at Via Principe Amadeo, 2. The apartment was in fact the site of what had been a dismal small hotel, the Pensione Oltremare, now refitted and refurbished as headquarters for the Special Police Unit of Pietro Koch.

ANOTHER man taken to the Koch Gang's base along with Cervo and Mastrogiacomo, the houseboat custodian, was a police orderly named Giovanni Scottu, who had been assigned to Lieutenant Giglio that day. At war's end, Scottu gave a sworn deposition of the torture undergone by his superior and himself as well. Detailing in precise and horrific language six distinct sessions of torture between March 17 and 23, the deposition is undoubtedly the most quoted description of torture during the occupation, particularly by the many writers who have recounted Giglio's heroic story. Documents that have recently come to light, however, cast serious doubt on the veracity of Scottu's testimony.[9] But there is no question about Giglio having been severely tortured, and though there is ample firsthand testimony from others subjected to the Gang's repertoire of tortures, a brief reading of the accusations for which the perpetrators were later convicted leaves little to imagine. According to a postwar Court of Assize verdict, the defendants were guilty of "causing serious lesions to a large number of people they arrested committing torture in the abuse of their powers as police officers." Some of the examples cited were "kicking and beating prisoners with iron and wooden clubs and whips . . . hanging them upside down and swinging them against walls . . . clubbing them in the cardiac, stomach and genital regions . . . breaking their jaws, pulling out teeth, fingernails and body hairs . . . placing their heads in vises and tightening pointed objects on their temples; . . . they probed open wounds . . . provoked blindness and deafness . . . stuffed prisoners' mouths with ashes and pubic hairs . . . bathed them in ice or boiling water . . . abused women prisoners by inserting poles into their genitals . . ." The complete, much longer bill of particulars ends with the words "and more." [10]

As soon as Malfatti had learned of Cervo's whereabouts, he asked his sources to find out what was in the apartments directly below and above the Pensione Oltremare. Malfatti and Tompkins were of the same mind. An attempt to free Cervo by a direct assault on the *pensione*-prison had to be the next order of business.

———

IN ONE corner of the Via Marco Aurelio cellar hideout that served as the Santa Barbara munitions factory, the young physicist Cesare (Giulio Cortini) and his wife, Caterina (Laura Garroni), poured TNT. Twelve kilograms of the explosive were tamped tightly into a cast-iron casing the size of a large pail. Six more kilograms were loosely packed in a canvas sack. This was mixed with sawed-off lengths of iron pipe, about six inches long, each of them stuffed with TNT. The pail-like casing was lowered into this sack of powder and metal, and topped with a detonator and a fifty-second fuse. The whole forty-pound concoction was enough to demolish most of the building above them, but without human intervention the danger was nil. Indeed, the question of how a human could intervene in full view of the column of SS troops marching in the Via Rasella posed a problem in a multi-phased plan involving a level of complexity untried before. The solution, provided by Giovanni, stood in the graveled courtyard outside the building. It was a municipal street cleaner's rubbish cart. It had been stolen that day from a depot behind the Colosseum by Raoul (Raoul Falcioni), a Roman taxi driver older than most of his GAP Central comrades, who had distinguished himself in action. The rubbish cart, standard in Rome of those days, consisted of two silver-colored iron trash cans resting on a four-wheel chassis. The cart was empty now, but one of the cans would be filled with rubbish and the other with the bomb, then parked alongside the Palazzo Tittoni tomorrow.

Including Spartaco, seventeen members of GAP Central would have an essential part in the operation, twelve in the Via Rasella—ten in active roles and two as backup and cover. Spartaco had ruled out participation by Giovanni and Maria when he learned that they risked being recognized by an uncle of Giovanni's who lived in a street that intersects the Via Rasella, the Via del Boccaccio.

The attack was to take place in a meticulously timed sequence of three stages. Everything depended on the performance of the Partisan disguised as the street cleaner. By two o'clock that afternoon—the time determined by the Germans' unvarying routine—he would be positioned with his rubbish cart about one-third of the way down from the top of the Via Rasella, standing on the north side of the street in front of the Palazzo Tittoni. At the moment the column of troops turned into the bottom of the Via Rasella, another Partisan stationed on the south side, at the Via del Boccaccio crossing, approximately midway between the Palazzo Tittoni and the low end of the Via Rasella, would signal the street cleaner by lifting his cap. This would have two meanings: that he himself had been signaled that everything was proceeding according to plan and that now was the time for the street cleaner to light his fuse. While the column continued up the slope, and the fifty-second fuse burned away, the signalman and the street cleaner would make their getaways, the former by crossing the street to the north side and disappearing into the Via del Boccaccio, and the latter by walking away from his cart to the top of the Via Rasella, where another Partisan would be waiting with a raincoat to cover the street cleaner's uniform. They would escape together—turning the southeast corner into the Via Quattro Fontane a few seconds before the fuse would ignite the detonator. By then, the head of the column would have filed past the bomb, and the effects of the explosion would be directly felt by the first half of the line of marchers.

At this point, the second stage, three more Partisans would come out from the south side of the Via del Boccaccio intersection and attack the second half of the column, firing four 45 mm mortar shells altered to be activated by a lighted cigarette applied to a three-second fuse. They would escape by reversing their course and exiting the parallel street, the Via dei Giardini, which gave access to the tunnel.

In the third stage, another four Partisans coming from the tunnel entrance area would converge to seal off the bottom of the Via Rasella and engage the tail end of the column, doing battle and driving the Germans back until these Partisans, too, could make their escape through the tunnel. The two auxiliary Partisans would cover the getaways of those active in stages two and three.

How all this would work in practice was too unpredictable to contemplate. The matériel was shoddy, the technology ancient, guns jammed, explosives fizzled; the unexpected was the norm. The underground was a world where up was down, where only the plan could be perfected and the more you practiced, the more you were sure to die. You thought of other things.

Elena later recollected her thoughts that night. She would be one of the twelve in Via Rasella, roving for situation signals in and around the street, and finally at the top of the slope, covering the street cleaner, first with her gun and then, literally, with the raincoat. She had gone there with Spartaco a day or so earlier, just the two of them, for an on-site inspection, but in her least favorite role. He had asked her along, he said, because he needed a "girlfriend" on his arm to reduce the chances of suspicion.

Surveying the street from the top, then the bottom, Spartaco had quickly singled out the Palazzo Tittoni as the best place to situate the rubbish-cart bomb. The area around the sixteenth-century palazzo was farthest from any shops and pedestrian activity, minimizing the likelihood of civilian casualties. Then, seeking Elena's opinion, he told her that he was thinking of assigning the key role of the street cleaner to Guglielmo. Elena instinctively opposed Spartaco's idea. She related an episode in which Guglielmo and she had gone on a mission that failed because of his hesitation. Worse, with curfew coming on, he had handed her his grenades and his gun, saying that as a man he was at greater risk than she of being stopped, and when Elena, knowing that she would have to pass at least one checkpoint, had objected, he had simply shrugged and walked away. Spartaco then asked her whom she would recommend. Paolo, she replied immediately, going on to list the reasons why, and Spartaco had smiled and said, "Fine, let's do it your way. And let's hope it brings good luck to us all."[11]

Now, in pitch darkness, she lay beside Paolo in their place in the hideout. Only the rumble of the distant guns at Anzio broke the silence of the night. As she later recalled:

Stretched out on our down blanket, which by now had begun to smell of mildew, I thought about the destiny of those men who tomorrow, like they did every day, would file through that narrow, sloping street, marching in step to the song they always sang, "Hupf, Mein Mädel." Maria had translated it for me as "skip, my little girl, skip." The song also spoke of going home, of returning victoriously, but their tomorrow would have a different ending. Some of them, who knew how many, were going to die. Once again, I needed to bring to mind all the reasons why I was taking part in that attack. . . . the suffering and destruction everywhere I turned or had news of every day; of all our comrades shot or tortured in the Via

Tasso, of all those who had been deported whom no one ever heard from again . . .

In spite of these thoughts, I was unable to hate those soldiers, but I found ways to distance myself from them. At that moment my feelings were frozen, suspended, as if I were incapable of calling up all of the ways to justify what I was doing. . . . I felt we were facing an unfair fight, even with our bomb: 156 heavily armed men against a dozen kids with a pistol in their pocket and four homemade grenades. What was worse for us was that we were outlaws who had no rights and could expect no mercy. We were *Banditen* . . . and anyone could kill us or turn us over to the enemy to collect the price on our head.[12]

FOURTEEN

THE ROAR OF
THE WOLF

Romans had begun calling a beautiful day like this one *una giornata da B-17*, "a B-17 day"—windless blue skies, targets gleaming in the sun, perfect Flying Fortress weather for the U.S. Army Air Corps. But March 23 was also the second full day of spring, the warmest by far of the year—the temperature would get into the eighties—and there would be no Allied bombs today.

The bombs of March 23 were with Paolo and Elena. They had set out from the hideout near the Colosseum, separating, he with his rigged rubbish cart, she with the four mortar shells in a shopping bag sprouting parsley greens and carrot tops for cover. "I have thought of and spoken of that day so many times since," Paolo says now, "I feel I have used up all the words." As he tells it:

I had put on an old pair of socks and worn-out patent leather shoes to go with the blue street cleaner's uniform and the black-visored blue cap. The bomb was in the rubbish cart when I said good-bye to my comrades and pushed off toward the Colosseum. The cart was much heavier and harder to maneuver than I thought it would be as it rumbled over the cobblestones. I began to sweat and feel the effort, not only from the heat of the sun and weight of the cart but from the emotion of it all as well.

Nearing the Quirinale, two real street cleaners came up to me. "Hey, what are you doing around here?" one of them asked. "What's it to you?" I said. They began to laugh. "C'mon, give us a look. Let's see the prosciutto." They had me pegged as a black-marketeer, and they came up close, lifting the cover of one of the cans. I yelled at them and they laughed again. Then Raoul, who along with Guglielmo had been following and covering me at a distance, came toward us, but by then the street cleaners had lost interest in the game and started to drift away. I moved on and Raoul and Guglielmo fell back as I turned into Via Quattro Fontane, headed for the top of Via Rasella.

When I got to Palazzo Tittoni, I parked the cart, not close to the building but well into the street, so that the German column would actually have to march around it. Then I waited. It was a few minutes before two o'clock.

Elena had followed behind for a while, waiting for him to be covered by Guglielmo. She had watched him struggling with the rubbish cart, wearing himself out whether pushing the heavy load uphill or trying to brake it in descent, and she worried that trouble might arise. Then she proceeded to the tunnel entrance area, the Via del Traforo, to deliver the mortars to Francesco (Francesco Curreli), one of the three Partisans who would attack in stage two. Carrying only the raincoat now, she walked the three short blocks to the *Messaggero* building on the Via del Tritone, a thoroughfare that parallels Via Rasella.

Her last recounting was rich in detail:

As I passed Via Rasella, I glanced up the street. I didn't see anybody. It was deserted and Paolo hadn't gotten there yet. When I reached *Il Messaggero,* I saw Pasquale [Pasquale Balsamo] at the newsstand on the corner. He must have seen me looking tense and he tried to lighten my mood, flashing a friendly wink. He was the one who was supposed to signal me when to move to the top of Via Rasella, and in turn my presence there would tell Paolo that the Germans had been spotted on their way.

At the entrance to the *Messaggero* there were two plainclothesmen, easily recognized as such. I stopped to look at the copy of the day's newspaper tacked up in a display case, and with great surprise I read about an eruption of Vesuvius in Naples, thinking how caught up we were in our own lives that all else escaped our attention. I read the whole article, watching for Pasquale in the reflections on the glass and sensing that much too much time was going by. . . .

Paolo was in position but growing edgy waiting. He continues:

It was 2:20, 2:30, 2:45. The Germans were nowhere in sight. I tried to kill time, walking up and down. I was worried that my being there so long was attracting notice. I picked up the broom and began to sweep. It was one of those stiff street brooms, heavy, a bunch of twigs on a long pole. I had no idea how to handle it. I felt ridiculous, as if I were giving myself away. For weeks the Germans had been punctual. Now, no one, not even my comrades, came to tell me what was happening. It was un-nerving.

Elena:

My lingering outside the *Messaggero* had begun to arouse suspicion in those plainclothes cops, and they came up to me. "Signorina," one of them said, "are you waiting for someone?" I wasn't prepared for this, but I had already slipped my hand around the gun in my pocket, and I went on about the article I was reading on the volcano disaster. . . . It soon turned into a bit of flirting, though one of them asked me sharply why I was carrying a man's raincoat on such a beautiful day. I told him I'd removed a stain from it and was bringing it back to my boyfriend. At that point, I saw Pasquale coming toward me, and I thought he'd given the signal. I asked the plainclothesmen what time it was and when one of them told me it was 2:47, I said I was late and had to go. Pasquale went by me, whispering something that I didn't quite hear, but I couldn't look back and kept on going, my heart pounding now in every part of my body, thinking the con-clusive moment was at hand.

I turned into Quattro Fontane and looked down the Via Rasella. . . . I saw Paolo in the middle of the street, sweeping in such an awkward way that I was sure somebody would catch on. I was expecting to see the head of the column at the bottom of the street, and I couldn't understand why they weren't there.

Paolo:

I saw her cross the top of the Via Rasella and go to the corner of Quat-tro Fontane, the spot where she was supposed to wait for me. That could mean only one thing: it was time. I lit my pipe and waited anxiously for the signal to put it to the fuse. The tobacco was burning down . . .

Elena:

There were some children playing with a soccer ball in the garden of the Palazzo Barberini, and I had a horrible picture of them getting hit by what was about to happen. Pretending that I lived in the palazzo, I crossed the street to their side and shouted at them sternly, "You can't play ball in this garden! Go home and do your homework!" I guess I was more convincing than I thought I'd be. The kids dropped whatever they were doing and ran away in one bunch right down the Via Rasella.

At about 3:35, Pasquale came walking up the Via Rasella, headed toward Paolo, passing him and mumbling, "If they're not here by four o'clock, take the cart and go." It was a terrifying thought. At four, it would be an hour before curfew. He would never get the bomb back to the hideout in time, yet he could not abandon it, at least not without disarming it. He listened. No singing, no marching, no Germans.

THE MEN of the 11th Company were themselves wondering why they were behind their schedule. Today was to be their last day of training; tomorrow they were to take their assigned place in a change of guard with the men of the 10th, who had been temporarily performing their task of policing Rome. From all that the trainees had heard, Rome was to be an open city, and with the Vatican as mediator, they had been sent there as part of the demilitarization. They were to replace combat troops in the effort to prevent Rome from being transformed by the Partisans into a battlefield.[1] But there was something else in the air on this day, a premonition among them that some misfortune would strike. "That morning of the 23rd," one of the recruits, Sylvester Putzer, later said, "when they had us go out to the shooting range they stopped us from singing. Usually we had to sing. And that morning, no. If you ask me, they knew something." Konrad Sigmund, another recruit, noted that "the streets were empty, unlike other days. In my opinion, the Romans knew what was going to happen." And still another man, Franz Bertagnoll, said, "This was the first time that we were told to go out with our guns ready to fire, a bullet in every barrel."[2]

It was 3 P.M. when the 11th Company ended shooting practice. The delay had been purposeful, ordered by their battalion commander, Major Dobbrick. His direct superior, Commandant Mälzer, had of course banned the Fascists from parading through Rome on their holiday, and Dobbrick saw no reason to flaunt his own troops in what Consul Möllhausen had called a needless provocation. Moving them through the city in the quietest siesta hours of a Roman afternoon, silently, their weapons at the ready, seemed a sound precaution, all the more so since this was their final day.

ELENA, still on the Via Quattro Fontane, was standing by the gated garden of the Palazzo Barberini when she saw the two plainclothesmen again, coming toward her. "Are you still here?" one of them asked, truly suspicious now, it seemed to her. Her boyfriend was at the officers' club in the Palazzo Barberini, she said, trying to distract them from the sight of Paolo, who was plainly in view near the rubbish cart. She couldn't possibly disturb her boyfriend there, she went on; she simply had to wait. The plainclothesmen decided to wait with her. Pacing, fearing everything would go wrong, she suddenly saw a friend of her mother's walking on the other side of the Via Quattro Fontane, an elegant elderly woman with a glistening hairdo just done no doubt by René. She ran to her, glad to move away from the men, but worried for the safety of her mother's friend. After an exchange of compliments, Elena warned her to get off the street, and the woman took fright and left. Then, from the corner of her eye, she saw Guglielmo, heading for Paolo.

Paolo continues:

Guglielmo came out of a doorway just below me. "They're coming," he said, "get ready." He kept on going. I lit the pipe again. I saw Cola appear on the corner of the Via Boccaccio. He walked slowly to the spot where he was to signal me by removing his cap. Everyone else was in place. Pasquale winked at me. I knew they were coming . . .

The column was approaching the tunnel. Major Dobbrick was in his car alongside them, moving toward the front. Lieutenant Wolgast looked at the major as he went by, and received a nod. Everything was in order. They were almost home. Wolgast shouted a command. "Ein lied!" he cried. "A song!" The column turned into the Via Rasella, bursting into "Hupf, Mein Mädel."

Paolo:

I looked down the street. There at the bottom, the advance patrol rounded the corner, in their olive-green uniforms, coming toward me, submachine guns pointed. As usual they were some fifty meters ahead of the main column. They came into the street singing, not in the language of Goethe but of Hitler, an outrage to the fair skies of Rome. They passed Cola. He took off his hat. I lifted the cover of the can that was armed with the TNT and put the pipe bowl to the fuse. There was a lot of ash and it took a while to ignite. Then I heard the sizzle, the perfect-catch sound I'd gotten to know, and then came that smell of acrid smoke. I put down the cover, took off my own cap and put it on the cart—the signal to all the others that the fuse was lit and in fifty seconds the bomb would blow.

Paolo began to walk away, but at that moment, the *portiere* of Palazzo Tittoni stepped onto the street, perhaps to watch the column go by. Paolo shouted at him. "Get out of here! This place is going to be a slaughterhouse in a minute!" The man needed no further coaxing. He backed inside, but further up the street some workmen were unloading a truck. Paolo repeated the warning. They vanished.

Elena was standing alongside a handbag shop on the southwest corner of the Via Rasella and the Quattro Fontane, ready to take shelter from the blast. She goes on:

The column, marching and singing, filled the whole street until I lost sight of Paolo, who disappeared behind the first Germans to reach the top. When they drew closer to me, Paolo was able to cross the street and he came up to me. I helped him slip into the raincoat, and that was when the plainclothesmen, who had never lost sight of me, started to cross the street to go after us. I pulled out my gun but a city bus passed between us. Then came the tremendous explosion. It was followed by a violent gust of air that came at us, pushing us forward. The bus was blown off the street onto the sidewalk. The plainclothesmen turned and ran away, and we took off in the opposite direction, uphill, under a hail of gunfire ricocheting off the buildings and pelting us with chips of stone and stucco. It was from the Germans at the head of the column who had opened fire at everything in sight. Hearing the explosion of our mortar shells, we just kept running. . . .

Paolo had glanced back, and to him it seemed the entire column was lying on the ground. More than two dozen men had been killed instantly. Another thirty, dying or seriously wounded, lay among the corpses and scattered body parts. Two civilians had also been killed by the blast, a forty-eight-year-old man and a thirteen-year-old boy.[3] The Via Rasella was gutted. The rubbish cart that had stood outside the Palazzo Tittoni disappeared. A hole of about thirty cubic feet was blown out of a stone wall, and an equally large crater opened in the ground. Water surged from the wall, flowing downgrade with blood.

The second-stage mortar barrage led the surviving Germans to assume that they were being attacked from the buildings, and they turned their fire at the windows of the apartments facing the Via Rasella. Other Germans tried to escape but ran into the Spartaco-led third-stage assault on the rear, and it was not until he and his men ran out of ammunition that they withdrew. The entire attack had taken less than five minutes from the moment that the bomb exploded. It was not yet 4 P.M. when all of the Partisans had made their planned escape unharmed. Counting 60 percent casualties, the 11th Company of the Bozen SS 3rd Battalion had ceased to exist.

THE FORTY pounds of packed dynamite had created an enormous explosion heard and felt throughout the center of Rome. It rocked the Ministry of Corporations, only 600 feet away, where the Fascist commemoration was reaching its conclusion. Indeed the blast arrived like a slap across the face at the very end of the "Salute to the Duce," an oration given as the climactic event of the March 23 ceremonies by the blind war-hero-turned-poet Carlo Borsani.

The highest authorities of the Fascist hierarchy in Rome were gathered in the ministry's Great Hall of Ministers of the State. Many of the principal figures of the German occupation, under orders from the Führer to treat the fallen ally as an authentic friend, were assembled with them. Within minutes, ranking Nazis and Fascists, including Interior Minister Buffarini-Guidi, Colonel Dollmann, and Consul Möllhausen, learned what had happened, and a convoy of the highest powers in Rome was on its way to the Via Rasella.

First to arrive at the scene from the ceremonies was Questore Caruso. The pandemonium had barely abated. On the north side of Via Rasella, he saw German survivors stacking the bodies and body parts of their comrades in a row that was already about fifty feet long. He was also greeted with gunfire. The Germans, he said later, "were shooting frantically at the windows of the buildings."[4] He froze, at a loss what to do.

General Mälzer arrived next with an entourage. He had been not at the celebration but at his weekly lunch at the Excelsior with Kappler. Spotting Caruso, Mälzer demanded the presence of the Italian police and ordered his own men to begin rounding up every man, woman, and child who lived in the Via Rasella. Dollmann appeared now, as appalled as everyone else. There were puddles of blood everywhere he turned, he later said, and the street "was full of groans and cries, and shots still rang out."

Mälzer, "waving like a madman," came up to him. "Revenge!" cried the General. "Revenge for my poor *Kameraden*!" Dollmann tried to calm him, but revenge, some terrible retribution, was the only thing on Mälzer's mind.

Some Italian police had by now joined the Germans in emptying the houses on the street, not only of people but of other contents. They went from building to building kicking in doors, dragging out residents and whatever could be dragged with them. Those caught were lined up along the gates of the Palazzo Barberini, women and children herded apart from the men, all of them forced to stand with their hands above their heads. Among them was octogenarian Donna Bice Tittoni, the sole survivor still living in the palazzo that bore her husband's family name. With the ceaseless commands to keep their hands over their heads, the ordeal for most of them quickly turned into a form of torture.

These people, "trembling and forlorn," were the first thing seen by a high official of the Quirinal Palace who had come upon the scene. He left an unpublished account that preserves that moment when he turned into the Via Rasella:

> Germans, Italian soldiers, Fascists and police were running without reason from one end of the street to the other, observing the rooftops and windows. Some of them were still shooting at those heights. Everyone was shouting, everyone giving orders. On the pavement lay the many cadavers of the German soldiers, one alongside the other. Germans and Fascists kept bursting into dwellings, dragging out men to the desperate cries of women and children . . . seeking in vain to tear their loved ones away from those madmen. At a window on the third floor of the Palazzo Tittoni the head of a woman hung over the ledge and a rivulet of blood trickled down along the wall below her. She had been shot by a burst of submachine gun fire from below, having gone to look out after the explosion. The body of a horribly disfigured boy lay on the street on top of uprooted cobblestones, not far from the huge hole caused by the explosion of the bomb. A German general, overcome with convulsive weeping, was running around furiously like a mortally stricken beast.[5]

Möllhausen and Buffarini-Guidi drove up together. The Consul could scarcely believe his eyes. Civilians were being pulled from their houses and beaten in the street, and the wild gunfire was rampant and intense. Mälzer had "lost all control of himself," he said later, "and was under the influence of alcohol" from his long luncheon.

Möllhausen, who had never before been seen publicly in Rome, nor would be ever again, erupted into a violent verbal clash with the General in full view of German and Italian officials and hundreds of ordinary Romans—including the 200 Via Rasella residents lined up along the Barberini gates.

There was something about the young diplomat that discharged Mälzer's most bitter bile from the moment he laid eyes on him. "Here, here are the beautiful results of your politics!" he cried, pointing to the blood of his dead *Kameraden* on the streets. But all that was going to change now, he said, as the Consul stared at him incredulously.

"I am going to blow up the entire block of houses!" said Mälzer. "I have already given the necessary orders. I'm going to blow the whole thing up, I swear it. And I want to see who's going to stop me!"

German engineers had in fact arrived. Cases of explosives, Möllhausen saw, were being unloaded. The Consul knew that the Commandant was neither bluffing nor sane. With everyone on the street watching him, he sought to reason with the distraught general, suggesting that there were surely women and children still in the buildings.

"None of that is important to me," Mälzer retorted. "Here the houses go up in the air—even if tomorrow the diplomats get me fired!"

Dollmann stepped in again, trying to calm both men. As tears streamed from Mälzer's eyes, Dollmann tried to convince Möllhausen to leave, but the Consul continued to argue with the General.

Mälzer would have none of it. "My soldiers, my poor soldiers," he wept. "I'm going to blow up the whole neighborhood with whoever is in the houses! And you, Möllhausen . . . I'm going to throw you in jail at once!" He called to one of his officers, ordering him to get Kesselring on a radiophone to ask for full powers, and when Möllhausen protested again, Mälzer turned away from him, leaving him standing alone in the ruins of the street.

Finally, Möllhausen stormed away and got into his car. He saw Kappler arriving with some of his officers and went up to him. "That crazy Mälzer wants to blow up all the houses here," he said. "He needs to be stopped at any cost!"

Kappler said nothing in reply, his presence alone exercising a chilling effect on all. Dollmann repeated Möllhausen's warning with equal urgency, but Kappler, who regarded Dollmann as a hysteric, kept on, headed for Mälzer, observing, he later said, that the General was flushed and covered with sweat.

"You see, Kappler?" Mälzer said, indicating the row of dead. "You see what they have done to my boys? Now I'm going to blow all these houses sky high!"

Kappler signaled his own men to take charge. He told Mälzer he would proceed with the investigation, and urged him to return to his headquarters. Mälzer resisted, then buckled. As Kappler helped him into his car, Mälzer took one last look at the civilians lined up against the Barberini gates. He waved his hand across everyone he beheld, everyone listening as he bellowed to Kappler, "They are all to be shot." Then he roared away.

By 5 P.M., houses were still being searched and the mindless firing at high windows continued,[6] but Kappler and his officers had completed their investigation. The only incriminating evidence found was a small red flag and an unexploded mortar shell. From its Italian origin and primitive detonator, Kappler ruled out the instant rumor that the attack had been launched by "the English." The surviving members of the 11th Company could add nothing; they had not seen anything suspicious and first thought the bomb had come from the sky, then from one of the rooftops. Kappler himself, concluding that it had been the work of the Roman Resistance, nevertheless believed the bomb and the mortar had been launched from high windows.

With Dollmann's assistance, he now turned to the 200 civilians whom Mälzer had ordered executed. They were still at the Barberini gates, still under prodding to keep their hands up, and still expecting to die. The two Germans, however, turned them over to the Fascist police, who took them into custody for questioning. Most would soon be released.

Dollmann and Kappler departed separately, but both went to the same place: Mälzer's headquarters in the nearby Corso d'Italia. "Confusion was brimming," Dollmann later said. "Everyone had come up with his own program for expiation"—including him. The word *rappresaglia*, "reprisal," was running wild, and to Dollmann the only question, it seemed, was how much blood would flow. Mälzer, on and off the phone and cold sober, called Dollmann aside. Worried about his tantrum in the Via Rasella, he asked Dollmann to act as his peace emissary to Möllhausen to patch up any damages. Mälzer regarded Dollmann with awe; Dollmann thought Mälzer an "idiot clown," still on a rampage. Like most of the politically minded occupiers, he had already concluded that the unprecedented attack in the Via Rasella was a clever ploy to provoke an overreaction by the Germans to the benefit of the Resistance. Promising Mälzer to do his best, he left at once to join forces with Möllhausen against him.

• • •

WHEN Mälzer had telephoned from the Via Rasella requesting full powers from Kesselring, the reply was that the Field Marshal was unavailable. He was at the front at Anzio, could not be reached, and would not return until early evening. The startling news of what had happened, however, had immediately been transmitted by Kesselring's Chief of Operations, Colonel Dietrich Beelitz, to Hitler's headquarters in East Prussia, Oberkommando der Wehrmacht (OKW). By about 4:30 P.M., OKW was back on the line with Beelitz. The news of the attack in Via Rasella had been reported directly to Hitler. The Führer had been resting in his Wolfsschanze, Wolf's Lair, enjoying a rare, relatively peaceful day. On hearing what had occurred in Rome, though, he reacted with swift and stinging demands, calling for a reprisal that would "make the world tremble."[7] Relaying the Führer's rage to Rome, a staff officer at the Wolfsschanze told Colonel Beelitz, "He is roaring. He wants to blow up an entire quarter of the city, including everyone who lives there, and . . . for every German police officer killed, they should shoot thirty to fifty Italians."[8]

There had never been a reprisal in Italy. Kappler would later attest that the Germans wished to keep their losses to Partisan activity secret. But this time the magnitude of the event could not be covered up.

With Kappler present, Mälzer spoke on the telephone with General Mackensen. When Mackensen discovered that Kappler was with Mälzer, he wanted to speak with him. Mackensen had been informed by Beelitz of Hitler's reaction to the attack. The old-school Prussian militarist believed that the Führer's demands were disproportionate. He asked Kappler what he knew about reprisals. Kappler replied that he had once discussed the matter with his immediate superior in Italy, General Wilhelm Harster, who was headquartered in Verona. They had agreed that if a reprisal were ever ordered, they would execute persons in their custody who had already been sentenced to death or to life imprisonment, and if needed, those awaiting trial who were likely to receive the death penalty. Mackensen apparently took to this idea, though he later maintained that he had believed that the persons who were to be slain were all in the first category, those already sentenced to death. In any event, calling those who would be considered potential reprisal victims *Todeskandidaten*, "candidates for death," he reduced the ratio of Italians to be shot in retaliation: ten for every German killed in the Via Rasella. If there were not enough prisoners for the required number, he added, the executioners could shoot as many as there were and later falsely publicize that the full amount had been killed. The punishment was to be in the message.

They were improvising. Working from sketchy, undeveloped plans, they had begun to hammer together the prototype of a reprisal apparatus. Hanging up from Mackensen's call, Kappler and Mälzer were unsure as to what to do next. They agreed that the reprisal would require official sanction. In the meantime, Mälzer, learning that the number of Germans killed in the Via Rasella had risen to 28, told Kappler to draw up a list of 280 Italian *Todeskandidaten* to be shot.

Kappler set about his task at once. He knew from the start that he would not have sufficient candidates for death. At that moment he was holding some 290 men and women as political prisoners, incarcerated at the Via Tasso and the Third Wing of Regina Coeli prison, which had been set aside for use by the Germans. Reflecting the state of German chivalry, at least in Rome, the thought of women prisoners as "candidates" never arose. Among the males, many were not in any of the candidate categories, including fifty-seven Jews, who were awaiting deportation to Auschwitz. Moreover, Kappler was certain the German death toll would rise, which meant that to fill out his list he would need the help of the Italian police, namely Questore Caruso and the young and resourceful Dr. Koch.

———————————

KESSELRING returned from the front at 7 P.M. He had gone to Anzio to inspect the troops of Mackensen's Fourteenth Army. Plans had been drafted for a new offensive, but Mackensen had advised against it. The Field Marshal had already concluded that further action at Anzio was pointless because of overwhelming Allied artillery and air superiority and falling German morale. He had even shored up the courage to tell this to Hitler, who had evidently accepted it.

At Anzio on this day, Kesselring had evaluated the quality of his fighting men and had found them wanting, incapable of sustaining an attack. He agreed with Mackensen's assessment and decided to postpone—and days later abandon—a scheduled counteroffensive, knowing that time and the season were on the enemy's side. Stalemate would continue, for months if he chose, but the next big decision would be whether or not to defend Rome.

Such was the changed situation when Kesselring, upon returning to Monte Sorrate, his sugarloaf-mountain headquarters north of Rome, was briefed by his chief of staff, General Siegfried Westphal, on the attack in the Via Rasella and the demand for a reprisal. Over the past couple of hours, Westphal and Beelitz had compiled a full report for the Field Marshal.

There was a general consensus among Kesselring's commanders, said Westphal, that the Führer's demands were excessive but that the Romans had to be taught a lesson "in order to scare them." Mackensen, he went on, had thus lowered the ratio to ten Italians for each German killed, and Kappler had been charged with compiling a list of *Todeskandidaten*.

Kesselring called OKW. He spoke with Hitler's Chief of Operations, General Alfred Jodl. The Field Marshal agreed that he had to "achieve a deterrent effect," but the Führer's demand had been judged by those on the scene as unreasonable and impractical. He supported Mackensen's formula. Jodl asked if any of the Partisans had been caught. None had, he was told. Jodl soon ran out of questions and deferred to the men in the field. Kesselring, believing as he later claimed that he had just hung up from "an honest effort to exercise humanity," issued the following order to Mackensen: "Kill ten Italians for every German. Carry out immediately."⁹

DOLLMANN and Möllhausen agreed that the attack in the Via Rasella was a Resistance trick to provoke a reprisal against the Romans and then in turn an escalation of hatred of the Germans. They concluded that a bloodless, political solution to the affair was both imperative and attainable. They decided to adopt this approach with their superiors, Ambassador Rahn for the Consul and General Wolff for Dollmann, and continue to consult each other. Dollmann, however, when he left the embassy, realized that their greatest potential ally was the Pope. He was the one man in Rome who, if nothing else, by intervention alone could gain a critical amount of time for the hotheads to cool. He returned to his apartment to change into civilian dress, immediately set out again, crossing the Tiber in the early evening on a beeline toward the dome of Saint Peter's.

His destination was a monastery in the piazza just below the windows of the papal apartments, the seat of the Order of the Salvatorians. The man he wished to see was his old friend, white-haired Abbot General Father Pankratius Pfeiffer, Padre Pancrazio, Pius XII's personal liaison with the occupation forces. "The good padre," according to Vatican diplomat Monsignor Giovannetti, "sent by Pius XII, achieved many successes with his interventions during the occupation of Rome."¹⁰ He was on particularly good terms with Kesselring and Mälzer, and a frequent visitor to Kappler on errands of mercy.

Ushered into the Abbot General's spartan office, Dollmann needed few words to cross the divide between a man of the Reich and a man of God. Their shared Bavarian origins formed a sturdy bridge.[11] Years later, testifying in court, Dollmann described the meeting:

> Father Pfeiffer was already aware of what had happened in Via Rasella, though not of all the details. I told him that one had to expect a reprisal. It was not possible for me to say what it would be, since I myself was not informed. I expressed the hope that any reprisals would be contained within the framework of the Hague Convention.
>
> I also told the Abbot General that the Führer was beside himself with rage. Nothing had been decided, I said, but that something would happen was a certainty. I vaguely recall also mentioning that the Hague Convention provided for the execution of hostages.[12] It is also possible that in order to get the Vatican moving to take some kind of action, naturally, as fast as possible, I spoke in terms of a "bloodbath."
>
> I proposed my own pacification plan to Father Pfeiffer to present to the Pope, in order to gain time. Essentially my peace plan consisted of this: holding a funeral procession for the Germans who were killed. . . . Both the Pope and Kesselring would address the people of Rome, calling for peace. The Pope would be speaking in his capacity as Bishop of Rome. I was hoping by all this to gain time, two or three days in which to placate the agitated state of mind that reigned among the ranks of the Germans.[13]

Under cross-examination, he added:

> In the course of our encounter on March 23, 1944, Father Pfeiffer told me that he would go immediately to the Vatican. I do not know if he actually went. Only through third parties did I learn that Pfeiffer did in fact go to the Vatican.[14]

Elsewhere Dollman said that when he had made his appeal and outlined his "peace plan," Father Pfeiffer exclaimed, "Excellent! I am certain the Vatican will be very enthusiastic. And I will go at once to inform them!"[15] One could hardly imagine him doing less. A slaughter of innocents in the Eternal City would be an unspeakable affront to the Pope. This time it would be Christians, Roman Catholics, the Pope's own children, as the Romans of the diocese were called.

Dollmann took leave of Padre Pancrazio. They agreed to speak again on the following day, when they would have further news from their superiors.[16]

Pope Pius XII visits the populous San Lorenzo district immediately after the first bombing of Rome, July 19, 1943.

Italian soldiers and civilians make a last stand at the Pyramid in a futile effort to prevent the German takeover of Rome on September 10.

Publifoto

German paratroopers attached to the occupation forces stand at the edge of Saint Peter's Square, a frontier of Vatican City. The sovereignty and protection of the Holy See and the person of the pope were guaranteed, after days of uncertainty, by Hitler himself.

German anti-aircraft artillery emplaced near the dome of Saint Peter's basilica (in the background) makes clear that Rome was not the "Open City" the Germans claimed.

Dufoto

Publifoto

Gen. Kurt Mälzer, Commandant of Rome—an early master of the photo-op, when sober.

Centro Documentazione Il Messaggero

Gestapo chief Herbert Kappler, shown here at his 1948 trial in Rome.

Courtesy Massimiliano Griner, www.fabula.it/mgriner

The infamous founder of the antipartisan Special Police Unit, "Doctor" Pietro Koch.

D-Day at Anzio, January 22, 1944. GIs from the Fifth Army wade in virtually unopposed—but not for long.

OSS spy in occupied Rome Peter Tompkins (second from left) working with his Italian operatives in his Piazza Lovatelli hideout. On the far right is Franco Malfatti, whose clandestine Socialist party information service would link up with Tompkins as "the eyes and ears" of Allied intelligence in Rome.

Publifoto

Field Marshal Albert Kesselring (left) outsmiles the man he replaced as commander-in-chief of the southern front, Field Marshal Erwin Rommel.

General Mark Clark (left) and his superior, the man he would defy to be first to capture Rome, British General Harold Alexander.

Centro Documentazione Il Messaggero

Via Rasella: A German soldier watches the windows of a building shortly after the partisan attack. The assault was believed at first to have come from an apartment or a roof.

Double-agent Maurizio Giglio, a lieutenant in Rome's Fascist police and a spy for the OSS in Peter Tompkins's network. Betrayed by his clandestine radio operator, Giglio was tortured by the Koch gang.

Civilians dragged from their homes in Via Rasella are lined up as suspects alongside the gates of the Barberini Palace at the top of the sloping street.

The Ardeatine Caves, site of Italy's worst wartime atrocity, the German slaughter of 335 Roman men and boys in retaliation for the Via Rasella attack.

Among the first American troops to enter Rome proper are these men under fire, a spearhead of the 88th Division.

Infantrymen of the Fifth Army are welcomed by Romans.

Ex–SS Capt. Erich Priebke in custody fifty years after his flight from justice via the Vatican Rat Line.

"Elena and Paolo" in the resistance, wife and husband in peacetime, Carla Capponi and Rosario "Sasà" Bentivegna, in Rome's Piazza Campidoglio with their daughter, Elena, in 1951.

THE PRESSURE on Kappler to find enough prisoners "worthy of death," to use his roomier interpretation of a death candidate, increased shortly after 8 P.M., when along with telephone notification of Kesselring's order for the ten-to-one reprisal, Kappler was told that the killings must be completed within twenty-four hours. The Gestapo Chief had already been to see Caruso, demanding that the Italians provide eighty names for his list, but after a round of bargaining settled on fifty "for now." Caruso, however, in spite of his fear of Kappler, had agreed only if he could get permission from *his* superior, Interior Minister Buffarini-Guidi. More than anyone else, Caruso had taken to heart continual Allied warnings of postwar retribution for war crimes, and had begun to accumulate a stash of gold, diamonds, and hard currency to finance an inevitable flight from the losing side. Now he wished to add exculpating paper to his collection.

Before setting the first name to his list, Kappler made several phone calls to raise a shield of higher authorities. First was General Harster, his Gestapo superior in Verona. Kappler had set his sights on his fifty-seven Jews, who, he knew from recent experience, were by definition candidates for death— though guiltless and already claimed by Eichmann they did not fit the spirit of reprisal order. Harster would know what to do. As Nazi Security Chief in the Netherlands, he had overseen the roundup of Dutch Jews (and would be charged with responsibility for the death of Anne Frank[17]). According to Harster, Kappler complained that because of the urgency of the reprisal order and the shortness of time, he, Kappler, "had no other choice" but to use the Jews in his custody to complete his list. Harster was understanding. Kappler, he said later, "had done his utmost to try to carry through the principles promulgated by myself." The general could therefore "do no more than take note of this information."[18] If this sounds like only vague authorization, Kappler's version is more direct: "What do you want to do?" Harster asked. "If you can't reach the right figure, take as many Jews as you need. The important thing is to complete the list."[19]

And so the reprisal machine began to grind. The presiding justice of the German Military Tribunal in Rome, queried next, granted Kappler authorization to include anyone condemned to death or awaiting trial for a capital crime but balked on persons who, because of attenuating circumstances, had received lesser sentences in death-penalty cases. Only the Chief Justice could authorize that, he said. Kappler called him. Permission was granted. Judge General Hans Keller, under later interrogation by the British as a POW, said he had viewed the ten-to-one kill ratio as justifiable under the

German laws of self-defense. "As thanks for all that had been done for Italy," he said, "we still saw German soldiers assassinated in cold blood."[20]

In the meantime, Kappler had called in his officers and men to work with him in preparing the list. Priebke later described what happened that evening when Kappler addressed his officers:

> He told us of the incident and said that a reprisal would be made against the Italian people in the ratio of 1 (one) German to 10 (ten) Italians, and I believe that this order came from Gen. Kesselring. We were told that all records in the office were to be searched, and all those persons who had been sentenced to death by German tribunals for offenses against the German troops were to be killed.[21]

It was the start of an all-night examination of the Via Tasso prisoner files. These record cards were arranged mainly under three headings: *Spionage*, *Kommunismus*, and *Jude*, ("Spies," "Communists," and "Jews"). Reviewing them was not in itself a laborious task, but for some it also meant a search of one's soul. When Consul Möllhausen, in the nearby Villa Wolkonsky, heard that Kappler was drawing up the lethal list, he paid him a dead-of-night visit. He found him leaning over the file cards, immersed in making his momentous choices. When the two men were alone, Kappler assured him of the legality of his acts and the death-worthiness of the men who were to be executed.

"Listen, Kappler," Möllhausen said nevertheless, "if I were in your place my conscience would tremble. I do not know how I would act. But I certainly would feel myself at a decisive turn in my life." What the Gestapo man was doing went beyond war and Fatherland, said the diplomat. It was a deed for which he would one day "be called to account before the tribunal of God."

"Möllhausen, I can only promise you I will do what I am able to do. And this is what it is: For every name that I write, I will think three times."[22]

———————

NEITHER Radio Rome nor London had heard a word about the Via Rasella, but the news had reached every corner of the city. No one had heard it sooner than de Wyss. Her photographer lived in the Via Rasella, and by chance she was bringing him film to develop when the bomb went off. She had just approached the street, she wrote (while "still shivering"), "when there was a terrific explosion, then screams and yells. Then wild machine-gun fire made me spin round and run for my life, while out of a corner of my eye I saw Germans catching people who tried to escape."[23]

Peter Tompkins got the news from Lele. His first thought was that with the same audacity it would have been wiser to direct the attack at the Via Tasso, aimed at getting Kappler "and his gang of butchers." Now an inevitable tightening of security on the part of the Germans would adversely affect his own plan to rescue Cervo from the Koch Gang. "What saddened us even more was to contemplate the beauty and precision of the [Via Rasella] attack, the organization of which appeared to have been damned-near perfect!" It would not go well for the underground now, he thought.[24]

PAOLO played chess with a fourteen-year-old Jewish boy well into that night. While he and Elena had been making their getaway from the Via Rasella, he had been overcome with vertigo. Instead of regrouping with the others in the Piazza Vittorio as planned, they had gone to the apartment in Trajan's Forum, where he collapsed and passed out, restored quickly, however, by a brew concocted by Elena's mother. Elena learned now that the space she had vacated had become the hiding place of a friend of her mother, a Jewish woman, Signora Pontecorvo Pertici, widow of a well-known World War I hero. Her husband's fame had once protected her from persecution under Fascist exemption laws, but she was running from certain deportation now. Having accepted her offer to spend the night in her apartment, Paolo and Elena went there bearing a message to her teenage children. It was hardly a safe haven, but the comfort of bed and bath was something they had almost forgotten.

They had met with Spartaco on the way there, had learned that everyone was safe and that the casualties inflicted were much greater than foreseen. Spartaco's news had preyed on Elena's mind all night. "I asked myself, what would happen next? How would the Germans respond?" In retaliation for the Partisan attack on the German troops outside the Barberini movie theater, the occupiers had lengthened the curfew; for the attack on the German guards at Regina Coeli prison, they had banned bicycles; yet, for the attack on the Fascist parade in the Via Tomacelli, they had banned Fascist parades. Most often, the Germans would say nothing and simply absorb their losses in the name of the invincible Master Race. But this time, she thought, unable to shake its implications, "our attack had caused a much deeper wound to an entire German company."[25]

Had they gone too far? Cola, the Partisan who had signaled Paolo with his cap, had heard reactions from passersby in Piazza Barberini as he walked away from the postattack commotion. Many were critical, he reported, the gist being "Now they do this, now that the Germans are leaving. . . ."[26]

Gappista Marisa Musu, who had been a backup Partisan in the attack, later observed: "We knew perfectly well that we existed only because of the tacit support of the people . . . someone to close a blind eye if he sees you with a gun or someone to warn you, 'Watch it, there are Fascists around' . . . an attitude that says, 'Let's lend a helping hand to these young people trying to kill the bastards'; but when the thing exploded like it did [in Via Rasella], people got scared."[27]

"We weren't exactly jubilant," a Partisan from the Action Party said. "We understood its importance in the fight against the Germans but we worried about what the consequences might be. . . ."[28] Said another: "If you don't do things like this, you lose."[29] Many agreed but would have preferred the attack to happen elsewhere. "Right in the center of Rome; couldn't they have done it somewhere else?"[30]

"The fact remains," journalist Carlo Trabucco noted in his diary that night, "that it was a significant gesture carried out on a significant day and so all the more meaningful in itself."[31]

Mother Mary wrote, "No one knows what the consequences of this will be, nor what horrible reprisals will follow."[32]

No one, indeed, not even the Germans, not even Kappler, knew, or could know, what horror the reprisal would bring.

FIFTEEN

IL GRAN
RIFIUTO

From one or more of the 400 churches in Rome, you could hear the stroke of midnight anywhere in the Eternal City, and when it tolled for Kappler he knew he would not sleep that night. In the past hour the number of German dead had risen to thirty-two. Strict adherence to the kill-formula required a list of 320 *Todeskandidaten*, an apparent impossibility. "The moment arrived," he said later, "when it occurred to me that even if I had all the Jews in the cells of Via Tasso killed, I would not have reached the necessary number."[1]

He would handle that in its turn, however. The first surprise came when he discovered that the number of Italian prisoners sentenced to die—and still alive—came to a grand total of three. The second category, those sentenced to life in prison, contained nobody. One had to start somewhere, so he listed those category-one persons, the most compromised three: Manlio Bordoni, 23, of the beleaguered Action Party, Carlo Lucchetti, 44, of Bandiera Rossa, and Gioacchino Gesmundo, 35, the high-school literature teacher who had been both a mentor and a member of the Gappisti. Gesmundo, as mentioned, had been arrested for possession of two sacks of four-pointed nails.

In the next "legitimate" category—those with sentences for offenses that might have brought the death penalty—Kappler and his team found sixteen additional names, though they had to scrape bottom and take some who were serving a one-year term. Among them were an architect, two brothers in their twenties, a student, a carpenter, and an opera singer.

Then came the Jews. Besides his number-boosting collection of Jews who had been waiting for the next train to Auschwitz, he had an unrelated group of eight anti-Fascists who happened to be Jews as well. Since it was better, Kappler later explained, "to place Jews on the list rather than Italians, whose guilt was more difficult to demonstrate," he added them, too, bumping up his count by sixty-five names. Among the anti-Fascist group was Marco Moscati, a Roman Jew who was a member of a Partisan squad operating in the Castelli Romani.[2] The Jews who had been tagged for deportation included multiple members of thirteen families: for example, five Di Consiglios—two teenage brothers, their father, their uncle, and their grandfather—ranging in age from 15 to 74; father and son Attilio, 54, and Michele Di Veroli, 15; father and son Pacifico, 52, and Angelo Sonnino, 29; and so went the Jews.

While the feverish scramble for names went forward, Kappler made a lightning-quick visit to the Viminale barracks, where the people rounded up in the Via Rasella were being held by Caruso's men. This yielded another ten names. They were men who fit none of the candidate categories, but Kappler apparently relied on the Fascist police assessment that they were "known Communists." Among the Via Rasella ten were the artisan-owners of the handbag shop where Elena had stood waiting for Paolo, brothers Umberto and Angelo Pignotti, 29 and 34; Guido Volponi, 36, an apolitical civil servant who had been enjoying an afternoon nap in his Via Rasella apartment when the bomb exploded (he was still in his pajamas); and the family-owned-café bartender, Romolo Gigliozzi, 35. Kappler ordered the release of the remainder of those arrested. As he sped back to the Via Tasso he had at least ninety-four names.

Still far from their quota, the list-makers waded deeper into the morass of arbitrary choices. A sense of their growing desperation can be gleaned from Priebke:

The whole of that night we searched the records and could not find a sufficient number of persons to make up the number required for the execution. So, a further search was made of the records to see if there were any persons who had not been tried, but had been arrested for being . . . concerned in any outrage against German troops or had been found in possession of firearms and explosives or were leaders of "under ground" movements. These names were added to the list. Still we could not find sufficient persons. . . .[3]

What may have seemed more than half-empty to Priebke, however, was almost half-full for Kappler. Scratching away with his pen, he found and added yet another Jew to the list. He was Aldo Finzi, 52, a well-known figure in the history of early Fascism who had been the Duce's Undersecretary of Interior but had become a convenient scapegoat in the affair of the Matteotti murder. With the advent of the racial laws, rehabilitation had become impossible. A gentleman farmer, Finzi tended to his vineyards and the gardens of his villa in the Castelli Romani. The coming of the German occupiers had kindled his anti-Fascist feelings, and he had provided a base of support for the Partisans of the Alban Hills—including Marco Moscati, the Jewish Partisan whose name was already on Kappler's list.

With Finzi on his list, Kappler had run out of sanctioned categories, and if he was to keep his promise to Möllhausen, now he would have to begin to think three times. In any event, his thought process, whatever the details, led him to list the man he considered his most dangerous prisoner, the shattered but unbreakable aristocrat Colonel Giuseppe Cordero Lanza di Montezemolo. With Montezemolo named, it was a less onerous task to add thirty-seven other members of the Italian Armed Forces, most of them from the Colonel's clandestine military front: the three generals—Simoni, Martelli Castaldi, and Fenulli; the Carabinieri major De Carolis, 45; and the Carabinieri captains who had arrested Mussolini—Frignani (now Lieutenant Colonel), 46, and Raffaele Aversa, 35.

Kappler had two priests in his custody. One was Don Giuseppe Morosini, 31, chaplain to Montezemolo's military front, accused of trafficking in arms and spying for the Allies. The other was Don Pietro Pappagallo, 55, chaplain to the sisters of the Bambin Gesù convent, awaiting trial for "Communist activities." Both men had been betrayed for reward money, Don Pappagallo by a woman in distress, she claimed, in need of his help, and Don Morosini and a Partisan named Marcello Bucchi entrapped by an infiltrator promising to arrange the sale of a machine gun. Both cases had been brought to the Pope's attention. Padre Pancrazio had pleaded for clemency in the Holy Father's name. Kappler would choose only one for his list. He picked the older priest. He also picked Don Morosini's comrade Marcello Bucchi, 22. And so did Kappler's death list grow.

At about three o'clock in the morning, relying on the commitment Kappler had extracted from Caruso to provide fifty prisoners from the *questore*'s rosters, the Via Tasso contingent came within one beating heart of their goal—reaching a combined figure of 319 men "worthy of death."

There was, however, one other death-penalty-case prisoner, a perfect fit for the legitimized categories but problematical nonetheless. He was twenty-six-year-old college professor Paolo Petrucci, arrested as an anti-

Fascist on the word of an informer. He had just been tried by the German tribunal and, to great surprise, had been acquitted. He was due to be released that morning. Instead, his luck ran out. Kappler, adding the young professor to the others, completed the list: 320 men—rich and poor, doctors and lawyers, workers and shopkeepers, artists and artisans, teachers and students, men and teenaged boys from every walk of life, and a man of God to walk among them. By now, something resembling a life of its own had been breathed into the reprisal machine, and Kappler, as he later said, felt its autonomous throb: "At a certain moment during the night, I said, 'By now the wheels are turning by themselves. . . . ' "4

AT EIGHT o'clock the next morning, about halfway through the twenty-four-hour period ordained for the completion of the entire operation, Kappler's list had long been done, but Caruso had not even begun. The German had been trying to track him down for the past hour, succeeding only in leaving blistering messages for the Italian to hand over his fifty men. The slippery *questore* was in the Excelsior hotel seeking the legal coverage of Interior Minister Buffarini-Guidi's authorization. The Minister was still sleeping. Torn between incurring Kappler's wrath or Buffarini's, he woke his superior, who received him while still in bed. When the time came for Caruso to redeem the value of his "insurance policy" in an attempt to prove he was only following orders, he testified:

I told him that Kappler had asked me first for eighty and then fifty men to be shot for the attack in Via Rasella. "I defer to you, Excellency," I said. I was hoping that the minister would deal directly with Kappler. His reply to me was: "What can I do? You have to give them to him. If not, who knows what will happen? Yes, yes, give them to him." Having obtained this authorization, rather, this order, I felt relieved.5

By 9:45 A.M., however, when Caruso showed up in Kappler's office to discuss the details, much of his relief had dissipated. Koch was already there and, in contrast to Caruso, was very cooperative. In a phone conversation just prior to the meeting, Kappler had told Caruso that Koch was working on his list, which Caruso was to complete. Caruso continued to insist that he had few prisoners other than common criminals. "Then give us Jews," Kappler snapped. Now both Kappler and Koch were taken by surprise when Caruso declared that he had only one name to contribute—that of a doctor condemned to death for diverting sugar from a children's hospital to the black market. "Kappler," according to Koch, "flew into a rage, and Caruso, after writing down that name for Kappler, left. . . ."[6] Koch went with him, but not before it was understood that they would in fact deliver fifty men by two o'clock that afternoon. For Koch it seemed no problem at all. He alone would contribute thirty names, including his prize prisoner, the OSS double-agent Police Lieutenant Giglio.

———————

SOMETIME before 10:15 A.M., the Vatican Secretariat of State received a report from an authoritative source about the attack in the Via Rasella. It contained the stunning news that apart from other measures yet to be clarified, a reprisal was foreseen in which for every German killed, ten Italians were to be executed. Thus, the Vatican became the only authority outside the most privileged regions of the occupation to learn that the expected retaliation would exact such an exorbitant blood toll. The information received was drawn up in the secretariat in the customary way, though the notation of the time—normally used only on telegrams—was unique. It read:

> *Vatican, March 24, 1944, 10:15 A.M.*
>
> L'ing. Ferrero, of the Governatorato of Rome,[7] reports the following details about yesterday's incident: the German victims numbered 26 soldiers; among the Italian civilians there were, unfortunately, three or four deaths; it is not easy to reconstruct what took place because everyone escaped; some apartments were sacked and the German police took complete control of the area, prohibiting any interference by other authorities; in any case, it seems that a column of German vehicles passing through Via Rasella was responsible for provoking the Italians who then hurled grenades from the building alongside Palazzo Tittoni; the countermeasures are not yet known: it is however foreseen that for every German killed 10 Italians will be executed.
>
> L'ing. Ferrero hopes to provide further details later.[8]

The 136-word Italian-language original document lay buried in the Vatican archives until the 1980 declassification of the Holy See's wartime papers related to the 1944 period of the occupation. Previously, what the Pope knew about the reprisal and how he responded had been deduced from external evidence,[9] but with the release of this document, which was accompanied by further information from the Vatican historians who had combed the archives and selected the papers,[10] a picture richer in detail emerges.

At this moment of the morning of the 24th, the Vatican was not inactive. Ambassador Weizsäcker, at the behest of the Secretariat, was in touch with Kesselring—"repeatedly and dramatically," according to Kessel—about the reprisal, though the substance of the conversation is not known.[11] The Vatican had been gathering information since hearing of the attack the previous afternoon and by now had reached an assessment of its general significance.

If the emissary mentioned in the document was the first person to bear the news of the inordinate magnitude of the planned slaughter, it was startling news, but further confirmation of what the Secretariat already believed: that the attack in Via Rasella had been undertaken to provoke the occupiers into an excessively repressive act and increase the people's hatred of the Germans. This was what Padre Pancrazio had been told in the Vatican the night before, presumably when he went there to report his visit from Colonel Dollmann.[12] It was also, as has been seen, the opinion held by Dollmann and Möllhausen, and more or less the swift consensus of the oppositionist Germans. None of them seemed to believe that the Partisans meant to hurt the Germans as never before to extend the popularity of the Resistance.

Since the Vatican, like Dollmann and Möllhausen, believed that the chief concern now was whether the reprisal would provoke widespread outrage, it might appear that it would want to communicate this point of view immediately to the Germans of the Kesselring school. In fact, Padre Pancrazio planned to do so that morning in a personal visit with his fellow German, and incidentally his boyhood schoolmate, General Mälzer.[13] But before acting on what were little more than suppositions of the Partisans' hidden motives, a more concrete issue had to be weighed first. The priorities that guided Pius's decisions to intervene personally in extraordinary circumstances were later clarified by Cesidio Lolli, vice director and deputy editor of *L'Osservatore Romano*. Lolli, who, along with the newspaper's director, Count Giuseppe Dalla Torre, worked very closely with the Pope, stated in court testimony that:

> the Pontiff's major preoccupation was that as a consequence of [Partisan] attacks and shootings a full-scale war could explode in all the streets of Rome; this was the thing he feared and all of his interventions were aimed at avoiding that.[14]

In releasing the March 24 document cited above, the Vatican historians wrote:

> The attack in Via Rasella was a serious blow to the strategy employed by Pius XII to save Rome from ruin and chaos. Throughout the months of the occupation he had pressed the German authorities to exercise moderation while seeking to calm the impatience of the Romans.[15]

Now both "impatience" and "moderation" had been shattered. How that condition might influence this critical juncture of Pius's delicate Open City negotiations—the cornerstone of the smooth transition of power from the Germans to the Allies—no one at ten o'clock that morning could say. Yet a choice would have to be made very soon.

AT NOON, Kappler was received by General Mälzer, summoned to his headquarters to report on the status of his list. Arriving at about the same time and also called in by Mälzer was SS Major Dobbrick, the commander of the 3rd Battalion, who had escaped injury in the Via Rasella attack. Kappler, describing his all-night ordeal, said the list lacked only Caruso's fifty names but promised delivery by 1 P.M. Mälzer, making a little speech about the importance of the mission at hand, which had emanated from the Führer himself, turned to Dobbrick and said it was now up to him and the survivors of the 11th Company to avenge their fallen compatriots. He ordered the martinet major to immediately execute the 320 men on Kappler's list.

What happened over the next few minutes was undoubtedly one of the rarest episodes of Hitler's war. First, Dobbrick refused to obey Mälzer's order. Shocking Kappler as well as Mälzer, he rattled off a number of lame excuses that included an alleged ineptness of his men and their Alpine superstitions. Kappler, who was Dobbrick's nominal superior in the SS, would later file an official complaint with General Wolff,[16] but Mälzer was left at a momentary loss. Finally, he picked up the telephone, called Fourteenth Army headquarters, and spoke with General Mackensen's Chief of Staff, Colonel Wolfgang Hauser.

A detachment of troops had to be made available at once to carry out the reprisal, Mälzer said, still shaken by Dobbrick's insubordination, but receiving scant sympathy from his present interlocutor. Hauser, in fact, also refused, but unlike Dobbrick, offered no excuses. The Colonel, who would shortly be promoted to General, simply declared, "It was the police who were struck; it is the police who must make the expiation."[17] Dumbfounded, Mälzer told Kappler what Hauser had said, and when at last it sunk in, he took the Colonel's advice. Addressing himself to the policeman par excellence, he said, "It's up to you, Kappler."[18]

Kappler hesitated. His surprise could not have been greater. The thought of who would actually kill the men whose names he had placed on his list had apparently never entered his considerations. He himself had never killed anyone in his life, though he had more than proved his willingness to die fighting for the Fatherland. Five times since the war began he had volunteered for frontline service, all of his requests appreciated but denied. He was needed in Rome, said his SS superiors repeatedly. He had even gone above them directly to the Army—only to receive a record-marring reprimand. Now that the ardor had faded, he was being told to kill not armed men but the men and boys who bore the names on his list, many of whom he knew—that "dangerous" nobleman Montezemolo, old General Simoni, the "Communist" priest, Don Pappagallo, to name only 3 of 320.

Kappler tried to wriggle free. If Mälzer so ordered, he said, he would put his men at Mälzer's disposal. No, the commandant replied. As the head of the Gestapo in Rome, Kappler had the duty to set an example. This was his order, Mälzer said. Kappler agreed. He had no right to ask his men to do what he himself was loath to do.[19]

A MULTITUDE of logistical and security problems had to be resolved in the remaining eight hours, and they were immediately transparent to the man who would have to solve them. As soon as he got back to the Via Tasso Kappler called a meeting of the twelve officers in his command.

He was succinct. "Within a few hours," he told them, "three hundred and twenty persons will have to be killed." All of the officers had to take part, he said. It was a "symbolic necessity," indispensable to the maintenance of discipline. "Everyone," he later recalled, "agreed with me."[20]

Priebke was one of them:

> Kappler . . . told us that the Commander of the Police Regiment, whose men had been killed, declined to carry out the execution, and that the men from the Headquarters at Via Tasso were to be the executioners. He said that this thing was a horrible thing to do and that to show the men

that they had the backing of the officers, all the officers were to fire a shot at the beginning and a further shot at the end.[21]

Kappler spoke next of two overriding concerns, speed and security. The reprisal had to be completed by 8:30 that evening. Security was best served by secrecy. The killings had to be kept secret until the very end. "No one," Kappler said later, "could predict the reaction of the Romans if they were to discover what was taking place in their midst. The Partisans could organize an armed assault. The whole city could explode."[22]

An attack such as the one in the Via Rasella would rout Kappler's forces, which were inferior in both number and firepower to the pre-attack strength of the 11th Company. Counting only the men he intended to use for the killings, those of German nationality, he had in addition to his dozen officers and himself sixty NCOs and a single soldier, for a total force of seventy-four men. The numbers determined the method. In a chilling passage from his testimony at his 1948 trial, Kappler in one paragraph delivered a whole textbook on the methodology of multiple homicide. Since the number of his men was "much less than the number who had to be shot," he devised the following scheme:

> I calculated the number of minutes necessary for the killing of each of the 320. I had the arms and ammunition computed. I figured the total amount of time I had. I divided my men into small platoons, which would function alternately. I ordered that each man shoot only one shot. I specified that the bullet enter the victim's brain from the cerebellum, in order that there be no wasted firing and that death be effected instantaneously.[23]

The remaining major problem loomed as the largest of all, but only briefly. Executions were normally carried out at Fort Bravetta, by firing squad in the prison yard. Outdoor killings, however, left bodies to be cleared away and buried, and in this case the numbers, it seemed to Kappler, rendered that procedure out of the question. Instead, he was taken by the image of an enclosure like a grotto or a cavern, "a large, natural death chamber," he called it. One of his officers, Captain Köhler, knew of such a place only a couple of miles away. It was a network of tunnels in the Via Ardeatina, among the Christian catacombs. It had long been abandoned, but had been used recently by the Resistance as a place to hide its vehicles, until an informer reported it to the Germans. Kappler immediately dispatched Köhler to investigate its feasibility. He then gave the job of directing the execution to the fearsome Captain Carl Schütz, a man who had been overjoyed when one prisoner told him, "You have the eyes of a hyena."[24] Captain Priebke, assigned a task that would separate him from all the other executioners, was to be the keeper of the list, in charge of ascertaining that everyone named was actually executed, and vice versa.

After further delegation of details, Kappler adjourned the meeting, noting that the time was 1 P.M. By his own arithmetic, with a kill-rate already established at "not more than one minute for each man," he was safely ahead of schedule. He went to the mess hall. Not that he could eat at a moment such as this. Instead he briefed his NCOs, calmly but keenly aware of the horror and the burden he was placing on them. The solemnity was compounded when Schütz appeared with the news that another German from the 11th Company, the thirty-third, had died a few minutes before. Kappler felt duty-bound, he later maintained, to adhere to the ratio set by the order, and recalling that at least ten freshly arrested Jews had materialized shortly after the completion of his list, he decided on his own authority to mark them, too, for execution.[25]

Captain Köhler returned from his site visit to the caves in the Via Ardeatina. He had gone there with some Wehrmacht engineers, and they had concluded that it would be a simple matter to seal the entrances using explosives, and as Kappler wished, create a permanent mass tomb.

It was time to gather the doomed prisoners from the cells of the Via Tasso and the Third Wing of Regina Coeli; it was time for Caruso to name his own victims from the First and Second Wings and Koch to empty the blood-spattered rooms of the Pensione Oltremare. It was time to kill and be killed in the Ardeatine Caves.

BY EARLY afternoon, Pope Pius XII had decided not to intervene in the impending reprisal, neither publicly nor privately. The Dollmann-Möllhausen alternative of attempting to bring about a bloodless political solution by a delaying tactic had gotten no further than Padre Pancrazio's knock on the Pontiff's door. Time-tested papal silence in the name of a greater good would again prevail.

Nevertheless this was not a situation that could be left unconfronted. The extraordinary sequence of events that had begun in the Via Rasella had been judged in the Vatican as bound to bring on a time of crisis. From the Governatorato official's report alone, it was clearly beyond any doubt that a tenfold slaughter of Romans for Germans would occur, and Vatican officials feared it would strike the Eternal City harder than any airborne American bomb. The Vatican must act, and Pius had already set his response in motion.

It was still hours before the first shot would be fired in the Ardeatine Caves. It remains unclear what the Pope knew about when the killings would begin. The information released from the Vatican archives, along with the Governatorato document, however, reveal that whatever contemplation may have been given to a papal intervention, by midday of the 24th it had receded. The Vatican historians reported, first, a total absence in the Vatican archives of any other reference to the Via Rasella affair from any quarter.[26] Second, after having sifted through millions of wartime papers over fifteen years, they declared flatly that "no document permits us to establish" that the Pope or his emissaries intervened in behalf of the men expected to be victimized by the reprisal.[27] Finally, they asked what a papal emissary could possibly have done "after the bloody challenge in Via Rasella?" The Partisan attack, they noted, "deeply compromised the Pope's policies as well as his prestige among the German authorities."[28] Moreover, according to Monsignor Giovannetti, "The Germans linked this 'terrorist' action to the fate of the Open City. They threatened to reexamine their attitude."[29]

From the Vatican's viewpoint the Via Rasella incident could not have come at a worse moment. Beyond jeopardizing the open-city talks and provoking the looming massacre, it had opened the vein of every misery and evil so feared by the city-state.

Thus a work of repair—something to stop the hemorrhaging—was needed immediately and indeed was already under way. Somewhere inside the Vatican the draft of an authoritative statement, written in the lofty style of the Pope himself, was being prepared for publication that afternoon on the front page of *L'Osservatore Romano*. It would appear in a particular format, unsigned but signaling its importance by prominent placement and the use of italics. This format, called a *corsivo* and used only infrequently— especially, like this one, when bearing the title "Carità Civile" (Civil Compassion), served to convey not simply editorial opinion but that of the Secretariat of State and, ultimately, Pius XII. Such statements were normally written by *L'Osservatore*'s chief editor, Count Dalla Torre, in consultation with the Pope or the Secretariat, or both, and, according to Dalla Torre, a sharp disagreement developed between his position on this issue and the

Pope's. The final words of course would, as always, be those willed by the Holy Father. The approved version read:

> We recall that on other occasions we have addressed ourselves to the grave times through which the country is passing. Now in these anxious hours we turn specifically to Rome.
>
> Our appeal is made to the honest heart of the people, who have so admirably demonstrated their spirit of sacrifice and profound sense of dignity. Do not with violent urges shatter this attitude, which is so worthy of the virtues of our people. Every ill-considered act would have no other result than to end by injuring many innocent people, already too tried by anguish and privation.
>
> All those upon whom it is incumbent to maintain public order have the task of assuring that it is not disturbed by any attitude whatsoever that might in itself be used as the reason for reactions that would give rise to an indefinable series of painful conflicts; those who can and know how to effectively influence the minds of the citizenry—above all the clergy—have the high mission of persuasion, pacification, and giving comfort. . . . [30]

By this counsel, Pius XII hoped to send his legions of honest hearts to ward off the dark unknown that lay just beyond this day. "Carità Civile" would be on the streets of Rome by mid-afternoon.

SIXTEEN
VIA ARDEATINA

THE first of the *Todeskandidaten* were yanked from their Via Tasso cells soon after the noonday slop with what had become famous last words all over Europe, "*Los, los! Raus, raus! Schnell, schnell!*"—"Move it! Out! Quick!" Their hands were tied behind their backs and they were herded together in small groups, intentionally left to speculate on their destination. At the suggestion of Captain Schütz, Kappler had decided to keep the men's destination secret as they drove through Rome. This might make Schütz and Kappler worried that the men would cry out for help, which might bring on spontaneous attacks against the trucks by the people. "Our escort was insufficient," Kappler would say later.[1]

At least one man in the first group, however, taken from cell number 13, appeared to sense what was going on. Don Pietro Pappagallo, chaplain of the nuns of Bambin Gesù, had slept badly; he spent the morning in prayer and fasting, and when summoned by the guards, he had turned to each of his cell mates to bid them farewell in the most final form of that word in Italian, *addio.*

Crammed into trucks usually used to transport freshly butchered meat, the prisoners set out from the Via Tasso shortly before 2 P.M. About a third of a mile down the old Appian Way, the Apostle Peter once stood at a fork in the road and saw a vision of Jesus. "Lord, which way do I go?" he asked. On this day in March, at the same fork, the way on the right, the Via Ardeatina, was the way all the prisoners would go. They would head toward the old Roman port of Ardea, but would stop well before the first mile.

Situated between the catacombs of Saint Calixtus and Saint Domitilla, the Ardeatine Caves—known then as the Ardeatine sand pits—had been excavated at the beginning of the twentieth century and mined for a sandy, volcanic dust to make cement—most recently for the bunker-like buildings of what passed for Fascist grandeur. Exhausted and abandoned, the caves had three entrances, giving access to a dank and dim labyrinth of intersecting passageways ranging from one hundred to three hundred feet long, about ten feet wide, and fifteen feet high.

The executioners arrived first. Schütz instructed his men. Everyone had to take part in the killing, he said, and with scarce authority apparently threatened the lower-ranking men that anyone who refused would himself be killed alongside the Italians.[2] Like Kappler, the vast majority of the men had never killed, and many were clerical personnel with only perfunctory military training.

The trucks began to arrive, pulling into the clearing outside the caves. The back doors were rolled open, and the doomed men, momentarily blinded by the sun, were ordered to descend. They had been tied together in pairs. Among the first was Don Pietro Pappagallo, coupled with a tall, fair-haired young man. Accused of spying for the Allies, the young man had been arrested about ten days earlier carrying Italian identity papers. In fact he was a deserter from the German army named Joseph Raider, an Austrian who continued to deny the charges and maintain his posture as an Italian. At this moment he and Don Pietro were standing in a group from the Via Tasso that included General Simoni and other officers as well as Partisans. The executions had not yet begun, but by now it was clear to all what lay inside the gaping jaws of the tunnels before them. Only weeks later, Raider—the lone survivor—would write of the scene outside the caves:

There was a colonel standing in front of me, a certain Montezemolo, I believe, his face all swollen from the beatings he had undergone; he had an enormous welt under his right eye. He had a tired look about him and even his martial, heroic bearing could not hide his suffering. Everyone around him seemed to have grown old from one minute to the next, ashen and broken down by the realization that all hope was lost, stricken by an unexpected seizure of madness. In the midst of this terror, I heard someone cry out in a mournful, supplicating voice, "Father, bless us!"

Then, something happened that must have been the working of the hand of God because don Pietro, in an instant of superhuman strength, burst free from his ropes and began to pray, imparting a paternal benediction to all.[3]

The German guards rushed in to restore order, and in the confusion Raider, no longer tied to Don Pietro, made a run for his life. He scaled a slope to a field above the caves, but soon ran into the men guarding the perimeter. Recognized by one guard as a deserter from their unit at Anzio, Raider was loaded back onto a truck returning to Via Tasso. No citizen of the Reich could be allowed to die in the Ardeatine Caves.[4]

KAPPLER had been waiting for the first truckloads from the German wing of Regina Coeli, and shortly before 3:30 P.M. those prisoners began to arrive. It was time to reduce the number of Italians gathering in the clearing. He again spoke to his officers, briefly, commiserating with them as they faced their brutal task, reassuring them of its legitimacy and reminding them of the need to set an example for the men. "I was very upset," he said later. The first five-man platoon, all officers, chose five prisoners. They led them into the caves, to the rear of the central tunnel. Torches held aloft by the troops lit the way. Priebke, the list-keeper, stood at the final intersection, and when the prisoners reached him, they were made to halt and state their names. Priebke crossed them off the list.

Once stricken from the list, they were stricken from the living. They were forced to their knees and made to turn their bowed heads to one side. The executioners took their places behind the victims. A German soldier came up behind the gunmen with a torch to amplify the faint, flickering light. At Captain Schütz's command, each German fired a single round aimed at his victim's neck at an angle meant to pass through the brain and the top of the skull in instant, painless death. Or so it was imagined. Schütz cried, "Fire!"

On a hillock above the Ardeatine Caves, a farm laborer named Nicola D'Annabile, who had been working in a field and had begun to secretly observe the activity in the clearing outside the tunnels, heard the salvo of fire. He noted the time as being a few minutes past 3:30 P.M.[5]

Kappler took his obligatory turn in the second platoon. "I went to a nearby truck," he said, "and I took a victim with me. His name was crossed out by Priebke from his copy of the list. Four other officers did the same. We led the victims to the same place [where the first shooting occurred] and, in the same way, a little behind the first five, they were shot."[6]

Priebke, performing a service beyond pushing his pencil, was in the next go-around. "I went in with the . . . third party," he later confessed, "and killed a man with an Italian machine pistol."[7] Fifteen men lay dead, one and a half Germans avenged.

• • •

IF THE first three rounds of five-at-a-time killings went according to plan, the next sixty-four grew progressively less efficient. Not every victim co-operated with his executioner; some had to be subdued. One man was later found not shot but beaten to death. Before long, the system broke down completely, turning the Ardeatine Caves into a human abattoir.

When the accumulation of bodies began to block traffic in and out of the tunnels, the Germans took time out to stack them. They then hit on the macabre but labor-saving idea of forcing their live victims to stand on top of those already dead, often on the flesh of their own fathers or chil-dren or other loved ones. The freshly slaughtered men fell, layer after layer, in a pile. The murderers themselves had to climb the carnal heap to be in the correct firing position. When the pile grew too high, a second one was begun nearby.

Fortifying themselves with cognac, compliments of Kappler, the Ger-mans, drunker and drunker, became hideously sloppy. Often three or four rounds were fired into the neck area of a single victim. Heads were literally being blown away from their bodies, hitting and splattering on the tunnel ceiling. When the corpses were later exhumed, thirty-nine were found de-capitated.

Many of the Germans aimed badly. Their bullets did not pass through the brain, but only through the face, ripping away eyes and noses in a rain of blood and cartilage. Or else the bullets did only little damage, emerging from the front of the neck without having struck any vital organ. As a result, some victims were not killed instantly. They lay dying in the death heap, their lives literally being squeezed out of their bodies by the weight of the dead men above them.[8]

The already shaky discipline was further jeopardized when one junior of-ficer, Lieutenant Wetjen, refused to shoot, claiming that he felt "a revul-sion." Kappler treated him gently, reminding him of his duty to carry out orders "like a good soldier."

"It's not that easy," said Wetjen.

"Would you feel better if I were at your side when you fired?" Kappler asked. Wetjen agreed. "I put my arm around his waist," Kappler said later, "and we went together into the caves," each killing his own man.[9]

According to Priebke, that was when Kappler ordered him and the other officers to shoot a second time "to reestablish disciplinary order."[10]

Nevertheless another, still more junior officer balked. Like the men for whom all this revenge was being extracted, 2nd Lieutenant Günther Amonn was from the Alpenvorland. Called to do his duty inside the caves, he lined up with the other killers, encircled by what he estimated at that time to be 200 dead. When the command to fire was given he raised his weapon but was "too afraid" to shoot, overcome with horror, he said later. One of the Germans alongside him pushed him out of the way and did the deed for him.[11] He was the only one of Kappler's men on record who managed to avoid killing.

———————

ALL of the prisoners on the German list had been rounded up from the Via Tasso and the German wing of Regina Coeli by about 4 P.M. But the fifty men promised by Caruso and Koch were still in the Italian-run part of Regina Coeli, and Caruso's list was not yet complete. Koch had provided thirty of the fifty names—including Lieutenant Giglio and the boathouse custodian Mastrogiacomo—but Caruso had been stalling all day, hoping, it seems, for some sort of deliverance from the ghoulish demand for Italian blood.

Kappler, his patience threadbare, had sent two of his officers, Lieutenant Tunnat and 2nd Lieutenant Kofler, to the Trastevere prison with instructions to expedite the matter vigorously and in no case wait beyond 4:30. Precisely at that hour, with the Caruso list nowhere in sight, Tunnat turned savage. He backed a truck into the departure position and began taking prisoners at random. Some of them were Caruso's choices whose names had been telephoned in, but not the ten hapless men who happened to be in Tunnat's field of vision at the wrong time. They were standing in the prison registry, collecting their belongings. Charges against them had been dropped and they were about to be released. Tunnat drove off with about thirty men and said he would return for the rest. Caruso's list arrived some minutes later, and the names of the men who were taken indiscriminately were added while an equal number was crossed off.[12]

After a while, Tunnat and Kofler went back to Regina Coeli, then returned to the caves this time with Caruso's completed list and the final truckload of victims. Night had fallen. Only five prisoners remained to be executed, along with twenty new arrivals. When the last of them had been dispatched it was eight o'clock, safely within the twenty-four hour limit. Kappler sent his men back to the Via Tasso for a belated dinner and, as recalled by one of them, these words of advice: "The reprisal has been carried out; I know that it has been very hard for some of you but in cases like this the laws of war must be applied. The best thing for all of you to do is to get drunk."[13]

Carrying out the next order of business, German engineers began immediately to mine and collapse the tunnels and the entrances, less to realize Kappler's lurid fantasy of a "sepulchral chamber" than to conceal the scene of the crime for as long as possible—forever, if the perpetrators could have their way. Not more than a few hundred yards distant, a community of Silesian monks who sold religious articles and served as tourist guides at the catacombs heard two powerful explosions coming from the direction of the caves. All afternoon they had seen unusual comings and goings, German roadblocks, and trucks carrying men. Some of the monks would look into the disturbance the next morning.

For now, however, the Ardeatine Caves contained two five-foot mounds of human remains, dusted with a sandy substance shaken loose by the blasts. At least one man was not yet dead. Two months later his body would be found not to have suffered a mortal wound. A bullet had passed through his neck muscles, and if it had knocked him unconscious, or he had simply played dead, he had later gotten up from his place in the death heap, and after an unimaginable interim, made his way to a corner of the cave to die alone.

Such wrenching aspects of the atrocity would become known over time, but none would afflict so many so long as what came to be called the Error of the Five Extra Men.

In spite of all the preparatory paperwork, the meticulous adding and subtracting on the German list as well as the Italian, the checking and crossing out of names one by one, the shooters, on completion of their mission, killed not 330 men, but 335.

At his 1948 trial Kappler would blame Priebke—then safely ensconced in Argentina—saying that he, Priebke, had told him that Caruso's list was unnumbered and that there were fifty-five, not fifty, names. But the Italian list, unlike the German, survived and was placed in evidence. It clearly showed fifty names, all precisely numbered. Word of the unlisted five extra men— along with Kappler's unauthorized addition of ten names to his list after the death of the thirty-third German—would never go beyond the inner circle of the occupation during its tenure in Rome. If someone, someday, had to pay for these irregularities, everyone from Kesselring down was in tacit agreement that it should be Kappler alone.

This global cover-up began that very evening. At a late-night meeting in the Hotel Excelsior, attended by the highest officers of the occupation, including Polizeiführer Wolff, who had flown in that afternoon with further punitive demands by Himmler, Kappler reported "liquidating by shooting 335 persons."[14] But the German High Command issued a communiqué that in reprisal for the thirty-two men killed in the Via Rasella attack it had ordered and carried out the execution of 320.[15] The true number, of course, would be revealed by the Italians after the German withdrawal. But the mystery of how the "error of the five extra men" actually happened would not be solved until 1996.[16]

WHILE the German High Command crafted its communiqué, Rome and the rest of the world remained ignorant of the reprisal. Even the attack in the Via Rasella had failed to receive any notice in the press or on the radio. The only news that to some seemed to reflect the ire of the occupiers was an announcement that the daily individual bread ration had been reduced by one-third, to 100 grams. That was the weight of a single roll, an all but breadless foodstuff made from a mash of chickpeas, mulberry leaves, a substance extracted from elm trees, and a dash of flour.

In the absence of any reaction from the Germans, Paolo and Elena, after having returned to the hideout that morning, had spent much of the day discussing with their comrades plans for a series of new attacks. The Gappisti hoped to ride the momentum gained in the Via Rasella and escalate the inner-city warfare. That evening, Duilio, the Partisan *portiere*, told them that Radio Rome had not mentioned Via Rasella. By now, that seemed a sure sign, he said, that the Germans had decided "to say nothing and absorb their losses."[17]

Others, however, took a dimmer view. Mother Mary had read the Vatican's *corsivo* in the *Osservatore*, "Civil Compassion," and regarded it as portentous. She wrote of her foreboding in her diary entry that night. Summarizing the editorial's appeal to all Romans to rein in their "violent urges," which would only heap injury on the innocent, she observed that the Church was "begging the clergy and all those who can influence the people to persuade them to be strong, patient and self-controlled for their own sakes and for that of the city." With customary perspicacity, she then drew her own conclusion:

> The writer of this short appeal (published on the front page in italics) must already know something of the consequences of yesterday's occurrence in Via Rasella. Perhaps we shall know tomorrow.[18]

Learning in the late afternoon that the bloodbath, as he called it, was in progress, Dollmann had, as promised, telephoned Father Pfeiffer sometime before going into the meeting in the Excelsior. He told him that the matter they had spoken of—attempting to forestall the reprisal by papal intervention—had been overtaken by the dreaded event. In reply, the Pope's representative could only offer his regrets that he had failed to enlist the Vatican in the scheme.[19] By 11 P.M., the Vatican knew virtually everything. Minutes earlier the German High Command had released its communiqué, which was moved by teletype on the Fascist wire service, Stefani, to the newsrooms of occupied Italy and Vatican City.

It read:

> On the afternoon of March 23, 1944, criminal elements executed a bomb attack against a column of German Police in transit through Via Rasella. As a result of this ambush, 32 men of the German Police were killed and several wounded.
>
> The vile ambush was carried out by *comunisti-badogliani*. An investigation is still under way to clarify the extent to which this criminal act is attributable to Anglo-American incitement.
>
> The German Command has decided to terminate the activities of these villainous bandits. No one will be allowed to sabotage with impunity the newly affirmed Italo-German cooperation. The German Command has therefore ordered that for every murdered German ten *comunisti-badogliani* criminals be shot. This order has already been executed.[20]

ALTHOUGH this communiqué was transmitted at 10:55 P.M. on the 24th, the news of the worst atrocity ever committed in the Eternal City, or anywhere on Italian soil, traveled with a strange leadenness, slow even by the standard of its day. Radio Rome would not air the dispatch until four o'clock the next afternoon. The Fascist daily newspapers, publishing the Stefani dispatch without comment, would follow their regular publication schedule, appearing at noon, but that left a news gap of some thirteen hours. At the *Osservatore Romano*, however, the delay was welcome, as a minor but exceedingly rare crisis arose between Chief Editor Count Dalla Torre and the Holy Father.

The Fascist press could withhold comment to gauge reaction on how best to kowtow, but not the Vatican's own newspaper. Yet another test of papal silence, perhaps the most difficult of all, was in the making. As was not the case before the reprisal, the Vatican could not claim ignorance; there could be no ambiguity in the statement that the order had "already been executed." The German communiqué was sitting on the teletype in Vatican City. Someone had to tell the Pope. Hundreds of the Pope's fellow Romans—mostly Catholics, his own diocesans, many known to him personally, men for whom at one time or another he had exercised some measure of his far-reaching powers, trying to rescue them—had now been slain. Never in modern times had any supreme pontiff been so meanly disregarded by a secular power in Rome. He had to be told.

The grim messenger was Nasalli Rocca, the monsignor who had acted as Marchesa Ripa di Meana's chaperone in her audience with the Pope to save Montezemolo. As confessor to the prisoners of Regina Coeli, Nasalli Rocca had made his daily call at the prison on the evening of the 24th. Sensing a certain disquietude, he was told by a guard that the political prisoners in the Fourth Wing wished to see him, and when he got there he was greeted by a terrified group of male and female inmates. All that afternoon, they said, scores of their cell mates had been taken away, told they were going to a labor camp, but those left behind had since learned that the others had all been shot. Nasalli Rocca later said:

> I was shaken and incredulous, but some of the prison guards were able to confirm that these executions had taken place, though they knew few other details. I remained in the prison until seven the next morning, March 25, and about nine o'clock, for reasons having to do with my position as "prelate-attendant" [to the Pope], I went to the Pontiff Pius XII (we were alone) and I related to him what I had heard in the prison. The Holy Father raised both hands, burying his head in a gesture of astonishment and pain, and he cried, "What are you telling me? It cannot be!"—in a way that made it clear to me that he knew nothing about what had happened.[21]

Nasalli Rocca was assigned to try to gather further information, but Pius XII had a deadline. By that hour, Count Dalla Torre had written a front-page editorial for that day's *Osservatore Romano*. He planned to run the text of the German communiqué followed by the comment, again in italics to signal high authority. Dalla Torre's article, however, was far from what the Pope wished to say. For someone who had worked very closely with the

Holy Father, in a day-to-day relationship over years, the count was bruised by Pius's displeasure. Dalla Torre knew every nuance of the papal policies and through convoluted and often coded use of language knew how to express them in the printed word. But this time he had somehow misjudged how Pius would react.[22] The count later recalled the response to his draft of that morning with evident bitterness:

> When the Ardeatine Caves infamy occurred, I raised a vibrant protest against the bloody vendetta. But the piece was revised and reduced to a general censure of such tragic violence . . . the fear was that an already very grave situation would worsen.[23]

——————————

A FEW minutes before noon on March 25, Elena stood in the same place near the Via Rasella where two days earlier she had waited for the column of German troops to arrive. She was outside the *Messaggero* building, waiting now by the glass cases where today's edition of the newspaper would shortly be posted. Paolo was with her, and a small group of passersby was gathering for the same purpose, though one of them was a Gestapo agent sent to monitor public reaction to the news that was about to break.

All four pages of the wartime-sized single-sheet paper were displayed when the clock struck twelve. The lead stories on page one had nothing to do with Rome: the Allies being "decimated" at Cassino and Anzio and further eruptions from Mount Vesuvius. But halfway down the front page, an untitled, three-paragraph box, right-of-center, its boldface characters still wet with ink, leaped, as it still does today, at the hungry eye: "Via Rasella" in the first paragraph, "*comunisti-badogliani*" in the second, and "ten-for-one ordered shot" in the third, yet hardest-hitting of all were the final words, "This order has already been executed."

For the rest of her life, Elena would be asked to describe how she felt at that moment. Mostly, she would speak of her anguish and despair and her first thoughts that the Germans must have killed the Partisans captured in recent days, her friends, her comrades, and her teachers. When she remembered it at her life's end, she said:

> It was as if the entire city had fallen on us, crushing us in an agony so much worse than the long wait leading up to it. There was the communiqué and then nothing else, no comment, no explanation of the way or where they had been "executed." Not a word about whom they had killed.

Were they men chosen from those in prison or chosen at random from the roundups of the days just before our attack? . . . No names, not even what kind of people they were, chosen for what we knew at once not to have been an execution but truly a massacre.

Visceral pain and overwhelming outrage were what Paolo felt:

My first impulse was to take revenge, to kill, call it what you will, to show them that we had not been broken, that the Resistance was intact, more resolute than ever. Now I understood, in a way I never knew before, how beastly an enemy we faced.

But for Elena, in a certain sense, the Resistance had fallen short.

A slaughter in reprisal had never followed any of the attacks against the Germans, but we asked ourselves how they had been able to transport such a massive number of men to the place of execution without the Resistance knowing anything about it in spite of being in a state of alert. . . . The Germans had rushed to murder all those hostages, hidden the bodies somehow, and left their families without a word, so that everyone would suffer the torment of not knowing whether their own loved ones were among the victims.

Indeed, as the news spread wildly now throughout Rome and beyond, the laconic announcement of what the Germans had done, but not to whom or where, would prove to be the cruelest blow of all. By the very nature of the occupation of hostile territory, everyone from the Pope to the wretched have-nots of the *borgate*, the entire population of the city, knew someone who might have been among those slain. The Germans, particularly Kappler, used this uncertainty as a stranglehold on the city, withholding the list, allowing profiteers to circulate false or otherwise unreliable lists that were selling for as much as 1,000 lire. When some two weeks later the Gestapo began sending out notices to families to collect the belongings of prisoners who, for reasons unstated, had died on March 24, the letters—mailed not at once but piecemeal and with excruciating slowness—were in German only. Finally knowing the truth added to the grief of all, even those whose loved ones had been spared. By some remarkable shuffle of the deck of evil, the 335 people picked to die represented a nearly perfect cross section of the social makeup of the Eternal City.[24] That meant that even after the names were revealed, almost all of Rome *still* knew someone, or at least knew *of* someone, who lay dead in the Ardeatine Caves. The city that had fallen on Elena had fallen on all.

––––––––––––

THE *Osservatore Romano* came out a few hours after the *Messaggero* with the same German communiqué and the first public appraisal of what it called in its front-page headline "the Deeds in Via Rasella." Appearing only twenty-four hours after calling on the Romans to repress their "violent urges" or pay a terrible price, the Vatican newspaper looked rather prescient to close watchers, if not supremely informed. Count Dalla Torre's editorial, completely rewritten and handed down, was printed immediately below the Stefani dispatch. It now read:

> In the face of such deeds every honest heart is left profoundly grieved in the name of humanity and Christian sentiment. Thirty-two victims on the one hand; and on the other, three hundred and twenty persons sacrificed for the guilty parties who escaped arrest. Yesterday we addressed a sorrowful appeal for serenity and calm; today we repeat the same request, with more ardent affection, with more fervid insistence.
>
> Above and beyond the strife, moved only by Christian charity . . . we call upon the irresponsible elements to respect human life, which they have no right whatsoever to sacrifice, to respect the innocence of those who as a consequence are fatally victimized; from the responsible elements we ask for an awareness of their responsibility, toward themselves, toward the lives they wish to safeguard, toward history and civilization.[25]

Hardly a platitudinous condemnation, the Vatican by these unmistakable words had issued a perverse declaration of good and evil. While Count Dalla Torre, interpreting what he believed to be in the heart of the Holy Father, had wanted to protest the infamy of the Nazi atrocity in the Eternal City, the Holy Father had deemed not the Germans of the Ardeatine Caves but the Partisans of the Via Rasella the "guilty parties." The victims of the reprisal, the *Osservatore* had been made to say, had been "sacrificed for the guilty parties who escaped arrest." Not only had these "irresponsible elements" killed the thirty-two; in avoiding capture they were the cause of the slaughter of the 320 innocents.

There would seem to be only one way to read this statement. It was meant to assail the "irresponsible" armed Resistance and remind the "responsible"

occupiers not to stray. But it had unforeseen repercussions, the most surprising of which—an angry reaction from Kesselring—jeopardized the
Vatican's immediate interests.

Kesselring, the man who had ordered the reprisal, lost no time in raising
a protest of his own against the *Osservatore Romano*'s editorial. The Field
Marshal strongly objected to the implication that the victims had been innocent hostages, insisting on a fictitious status as convicted criminals sentenced to death. At a Sunday meeting of his staff called the day after the
editorial appeared, he demanded that the Vatican be reproached. He considered the editorial to be "against the Germans" and based on "an extraordinary twisting of the facts," according to his Chief of Staff, General
Westphal. On Kesselring's orders, Westphal and Colonels Beelitz and
Zolling drafted a stern letter for the Field Marshal's signature. Weizsäcker,
who had called Kesselring's attention to the editorial, used the letter to express the Field Marshal's dismay to the Vatican. With the Open City negotiations under review by Kesselring, the Vatican was made keenly aware that
it had misspoken. While rejecting Kesselring's interpretation of the article,
the Vatican sought to soothe his vexation by adding another measure of silence. "The Vatican," Westphal said later, "never said anything further."[26]

"THEY have shot Cervo," Malfatti reported to Tompkins late on the afternoon of the 25th. He had learned that Giglio had been unable to stand on
his own when carried off from Regina Coeli with other prisoners. Slain
along with him, Malfatti said, were twelve other men of their network.

Malfatti craved vengeance, but Tompkins, he frankly admitted later, felt
frightened and "horrible as it may seem . . . relieved." Cervo's death, he said,
in the belief that he had not talked, was an escape from endless torture, and
for Tompkins and his agents it was a release from "the constant fear that he
might not be able to refrain from giving us away." But he agreed with Malfatti. Their fallen comrades had to be avenged. The attack on the Pensione
Oltremare had to go forward. In his diary he wrote, "We are planning a little surprise for the brutes that torture people at Via Principe Amadeo 2, in
the form of 80 pounds of dynamite."[27]

AS THE shock wave created by the news of the massacre continued to buf-
fet all of Rome, Spartaco called the Partisans of GAP Central together. The

Germans had to be shown that the Resistance had not been broken, that reprisals would not pay. Agreeing to identify themselves as the Partisan group that had carried out the attack, they issued a statement declaring that they had engaged the German column in an "act of war," as part of the armed Resistance's campaign to drive the occupiers out of Rome. As for the 320 innocent Italians massacred by the Germans, the Gappisti intended to answer their cry for revenge, which they promised to be "pitiless and terrible! We swear it!" They concluded with a show of resolve:

> In reply to today's lying and intimidating communiqué from the German Command, the Gap Command declares that the patriotic and partisan guerilla actions in Rome will not cease until the total evacuation from the capital on the part of the Germans.
>
> The activities of Gap will be increased until the armed national insurrection routing the Germans from Italy, the destruction of fascism, and the winning of Independence and Freedom![28]

To back up these words, Spartaco ordered an attack, preferably of Via Rasella proportions, to be launched, if possible, at once. The Gappisti had already been studying such an action, an out-and-out assault on the Germans who guarded the Gestapo's prison wing in Regina Coeli. It was a complex, high-risk operation. Back in December, they had successfully attacked the changing of the guard outside the prison (the attack that brought the ban on bicycles). Security measures had been tightened thoroughly by the occupiers, but that security required deploying and thus exposing many more guards. The Gappisti had in fact concluded that any similar action would be virtually impossible, but had found the expanded contingent highly vulnerable if assaulted while on the move, rather than outside Regina Coeli. Following a fixed route through the center of Rome, the Germans were crowded into the trucks going to Regina Coeli twice daily to relieve the men on duty there. The site chosen as the battlefield was the Largo Tassoni, a large clearing giving onto two bridges over the most prominent bend in the Tiber. Spartaco gave his assent. The foursome of Paolo and Elena and Giovanni and Maria would be augmented by two other Gappisti. Although it would be less spectacular than the Via Rasella attack, the combatants had decided among themselves that this one—with its potential for an extended street gunfight—would be seen as pitiless payback. There were to be no German survivors.

The attack was set for noon on the 26th, and the Gappisti were already fielded when, only minutes from the appointed hour, a messenger arrived. The mission had been postponed. They were to disperse at once. The reason given was that the Military Council had been directed by the CLN to suspend all armed operations because of an internal dispute that had developed after the news of the reprisal. Paolo, for one, saw it as a sign of capitulation to Nazi intimidation. Elena had an urge to disobey, to proceed with the attack as planned on the pretext that the messenger had arrived too late—but it was only a passing thought.

Nevertheless, their suspicions about intimidation were true. Apart from reaching into every corner of Rome with the announcement of the catastrophic reprisal, the Germans, through the acumen of the authors of the same communiqué, had succeeded as never before in driving a wedge into the Resistance. The use of the previously unheard-of phrase *comunisti-badogliani*—attributing the Via Rasella operation to a joint venture of the Communists and the Badoglio-monarchist wing of the Resistance—although nonsensical, could not have been a more perfect instrument to set one group against the other, the political right against the left. The occupiers could only guess which side had actually struck, but in accusing both, they likely hoped that one would seek to disown the other and thus undermine whatever unity existed between them. They were right.

In an emergency meeting of the full leadership of the Military Council and the CLN, held twenty-four hours after the public disclosure of the reprisal, one of the right-wing parties argued that the CLN should issue a denial of having been responsible for the Via Rasella attack. By coincidence, CLN president Bonomi, disgusted with the endless bickering of the incompatible marriage of the anti-Fascist right and left, had resigned the morning of the Via Rasella attack. His judgment that the coalition was near collapse seemed a prophecy fulfilled as a second party, the centrist Christian Democrats, added its own demands for more control of all Partisan operations. A majority held, however, voicing support of the Via Rasella Partisans and favoring the assumption of full responsibility by the CLN. But the required unanimity appeared beyond reach, and the CLN fell silent, more silent than the Pope.[29]

DOLLMANN and Möllhausen seemed to have been proven wrong while Kesselring's strategy seemed to reap demonstrable gains. They included still another proof of the imperturbable equanimity of the Vatican, an enfeeblement of the Resistance, and the widespread numbing of the populace. True, the people's hatred had reached new heights, but the hated parties—from Kesselring and Mälzer to Kappler and his Gestapo cohorts—could content themselves with the latest telephone intercepts by the Fascist police, in which Romans calling Romans were heard to make remarks such as these:

- The Germans did right. . . .
- You can blame those scoundrels who threw the bomb. . . .
- Those idiots! . . . they'll do anything to turn Rome into a battlefield. . . .
- Ten for one? Too little! . . .
- Well, that's 320 of them who won't make trouble anymore. . . . [30]

It mattered little to those to whom such reports were circulated that more than 90 percent of Romans had no telephones and that 100 percent of the population, telephone users or not, were aware that every word was monitored and could be used against them.

On the day after the release of the reprisal communiqué, that first Sunday of spring, the carrot followed the stick. The German Command announced sweeping measures "to deprive the Anglo-American enemy of every pretext for the senseless bombardment of the city of Rome." The German threat to the Vatican's open-city negotiations evaporated in a declaration by the occupiers that there would be "no military traffic of any kind through the city and in the city." This would create difficulties in prosecuting the war, said the Germans, but the decision had been taken anyway, "in the interest of the city of Rome and for the good of the civilian population." There was an "if," however:

> If, therefore, *comunisti-badogliani* elements, as happened March 23, try to disrupt these far-reaching provisions and if other circles misinterpret these measures, the German High Command will be forced to take such military actions deemed necessary in the interest of the conduct of war operations in Italy.
>
> *With this, the fate of Rome and its civilian population, apart from the conduct of the Anglo-Americans, is placed exclusively in the hands of the people of Rome.* [Emphasis in original.][31]

In a separate press release to foreign correspondents in Rome, the Germans sought to clarify their position, saying that since their troops and war matériel were no longer permitted to enter or pass through Rome, the Allies

SEVENTEEN

THE SMILE

Less than five years after the battle for Rome, Mark Clark, reflecting on the final drive for what he called "the great prize," wrote in his memoir that when spring came to Italy that year, after six months of bitter fighting since the landing at Salerno, all he had to show for it, apart from having "eliminated a great many Germans," was a gain in combat experience and a new song. If the war had been decided on musical merits, he said, the Germans would have won with "Lili Marlene," the enchanting worldwide favorite that proved irresistible to the GIs as well. But in the meantime, Irving Berlin had brought his *This Is the Army* show to entertain the troops in Italy and had written the Fifth Army's own song. "He's somewhere on a beachhead," says GI Joe's girl waiting for the Fifth Army to come home. "I can see him in a bathing suit, basking in the sun." [1]

Clark did not fail to notice, however, that all this, at winter's end, had come at the terrible price of nearly 90,000 Allied casualties, a thoroughly exhausted army, and a two-front stalemate that had turned the containment strategy on its head. The plan to tie down German troops in Italy in support of the cross-channel Overlord invasion had resulted in the siphoning off of more and more *Allied* forces to a point where General Alexander asked, "Who is containing whom?" [2]

In late March, after another colossal Allied failure to breach the Gustav Line, the third in as many months, the Germans emerged more in control than ever. Kesselring was gaining a reputation of invincibility. Allied military operations beyond maintenance of the status quo were virtually halted at the Cassino front, as were those at Anzio, to give the weary troops a rest could have nothing to bomb and the Romans would be held responsible for any future Partisan attacks.[32] The occupiers' sole objective was "the saving of Rome from destruction."[33] Either Rome would truly be an open city now or the world would know whom to blame for its destruction.

Diarist Carlo Trabucco marveled at how the occupiers could disregard what Romans saw happening with their own eyes in the streets and piazzas all over the city, namely "that the Germans are everywhere in Rome."[34] Mother Mary assessed the wishful-thinking factor. The German withdrawal, she wrote, "is repeated by everyone, high and low, wise and foolish, diplomats, market women, journalists, bus drivers, priests, shop girls. They are going, they say. Oh, yes, there is no doubt about it. Just a few would remain to police the city. And what might that mean? Well, they didn' know."[35]

Nevertheless, in the coming weeks, the Germans removed some detachments, and the Allies stopped bombing. The Germans took credit. The Vatican took credit. The Resistance took credit. But troubles mounted for the Romans.

and their commanders time to rethink and reorganize. For Clark, though, the onset of spring hastened the day when they, that is, *he*, would be truly on the road to Rome. It was fair to say, he wrote, "that the arrival of warm sunshine on that bleak, mountainous landscape made a difference." Redeployment of the British Eighth Army from the Adriatic to Cassino and the positioning of the Fifth Army closer to Anzio—and "the great prize"—massed greater strength for a renewed offensive, and, said Clark, "We got a song."[3]

General Alexander had concluded that the only way to crack open the Gustav Line was by applying overwhelming brute force. To achieve that, he estimated, the number of troops he needed had to be three times more than those arrayed against him. Once the breakthrough had been accomplished, according to Alexander's plan, the German's Tenth Army defenders would be compelled to move north. At the same time, Clark was to move his forces along the western coast to link up with a breakout at Anzio. Finally, the advancing Fifth Army would cut off and destroy the retreating Germans before they could reach Mackensen's Fourteenth Army south of Rome.

The essential element of the Alexander plan was the care and feeding of Kesselring's ego, feeding it the poison of deception. Alexander would build up his three-to-one advantage and then some by moving in his Eighth Army under cover of darkness to join the men already there. With a total of thirteen divisions in place—more than twice the number vouched for by German intelligence—Alexander would then proceed to rout the four divisions that Kesselring had decided was all he needed, under the prevailing ratio, to sustain the impasse at Cassino.

For the Allies to alter the established balance of power without detection, the German Field Marshal had to be made to believe that the highest Allied strategists had at last conceded that they could not take Rome from the south. The Allies would have to appear to start all over, this time with the sun in their eyes. Testing whether Kesselring would succumb to the myth of his own invincibility, they devised a complex cover operation to create the illusion that they were preparing a new amphibious landing, this time at Civitavecchia, north of Rome. The extent to which the deception succeeded would be measured by the number of troops Kesselring kept at the shoreline waiting for the phantom invasion.

Fewer of these machinations were known, and fewer were understood, in Washington, when, in the first days of April, Clark was summoned home. He traveled cloak-and-dagger style to avoid adding mystery to the playlet being acted out to mislead Kesselring. Clark was spirited across the Atlantic to be received by General Marshall, but always undercover. Thus, he could meet with his wife and his mother only in the backseat of this or that unmarked car or at a military airfield. He was allowed but a few days' rest in a remote cottage in West Virginia, then flown to a secluded estate in South Carolina to brief President Roosevelt (who, Clark said, "was quick to offer ideas . . . for reaching Rome"), then flown back to Washington, hustled into a small, closed-for-the-day restaurant along with a group of Congressmen to whom, on Marshall's command, he told everything, "even explaining," he said, "exactly how we were going to capture Rome."[4] All of America wanted Rome, he concluded, wanted it before the cross-channel invasion now scheduled for six weeks hence, and wanted America's Fifth Army in Rome first, alone—even if, he would very soon feel constrained to tell Alexander, that meant ordering his troops to "fire on the Eighth Army."[5]

D - D AY for Operation Diadem, the code name given to the final push for Rome, was set for May 11. Meanwhile the Mediterranean rainy season brought raindrops the size of Ping-Pong balls—and the gullies of Anzio filled with this seasonal downpour and death eternal. The Germans shelled and strafed the beachhead day and night, and out of Hitler's famous arsenal of high-tech secret weapons came radio-guided glider bombs and killer "butterflies," bombs that wafted in, seeking human flesh.

"For those who served there," military historian Carlo D'Este writes, "Anzio was quite simply a never-to-be-forgotten horror. For sheer misery, for danger, for the uncertainty of whether one would live or die, Anzio had few peers. What made Anzio different from other campaigns was the close proximity of every single Allied soldier and sailor to the fighting. The beachhead was so small that no one in it was safe."[6] One regimental history offers this description:

> The drenching rain, which never seemed to stop, had swollen the stream in the bottom of the gully to a deep flood and filled the trenches up on either side of the stream with water, which came up to the knees and stayed. . . . at night the venturous enemy parachutists crept up to near the edge of the gully and lobbed grenades into the trenches. . . . graves were dug into the lower slopes of the gully, and every day the swelling flood washed away the rough crosses of wood made from "compo" boxes and with them the earth from the tops of the graves, gruesomely revealing a khaki-covered arm.[7]

Subtlest and yet crudest of all was the sultry, sexy-voiced expatriate American from Ohio named Mildred Gillars. She called herself Midge; the boys on the beachhead sometimes called her the "Berlin Bitch," but the GI-given name that stuck and by which she was known worldwide was "Axis Sally."

"Hello, suckers," the star of Nazi radio would often say at the start of her nightly broadcast from Berlin, *Home Sweet Home*. A pop tune usually followed—one of her favorites for Anzio listeners was "Between the Devil and the Deep Blue Sea"—and then some "friendly" banter for the troops to mull on, such as, "I'm afraid you're yearning plenty for someone else. But I just wonder if she isn't running around with the 4-Fs way back home." Or, "Heard about Private Jones? He had all his guts blown away by a Schuh mine last week, but went on living twelve hours. Nasty things, Schuh mines." When she knew her program could be heard in the States, she would identify a living, captured GI by name, serial number, and hometown, and would speak of him as having been wounded, "assuring" his mother, "Well, I suppose he'll get along all right—the doctors don't seem . . . I don't know . . . only time will tell." Turning up the sex, the forty-three-year-old counterpart of the Pacific's Tokyo Rose would sign off, "Got a heavy date waiting for me."[8]

Then there was Gusville. That was the new name of the village of Borgo Sabotino, captured from the Germans by a unit of General Robert Frederick's First Special Service Force. Gusville, christened by and for the unit's commander, Lieutenant Gus Heilman, was situated about a quarter of a mile from the front, *inside* enemy territory. The new occupiers made Gusville their home and Heilman their mayor. His job-approval ratings soared with his first official act—opening a saloon.

Gusville's main drag was Tank Street, a stone's throw from Prostitute Avenue, itself within walking distance of a condom depot for residents, who managed to liaise with Italian farmers' daughters and sometimes their wives. Gusville had a daily newspaper, weekly church services, no black market, no strikes, no unemployment, but, as in all earthly places, there were death and taxes, especially death. Living under the skin of Mackensen's Fourteenth Army, Gusville suffered an inordinately high mortality rate, though that of the surrounding enemy zone was far higher. At night the men of Gusville joined their fellow Forcemen in the specialty that had earned them the name Black Devils. According to their most thorough chroniclers:

It was here that they perfected their technique of gliding black-faced through the lines at night, slitting the throats of the Germans that they found, and leaving a sticker posted on each dead man's helmet which read "You May be Next."[9]

Killing Is Our Business was their motto, Take No Prisoners their creed. "They revel in danger," wrote one journalist, romancing the legend, ". . . they make desperate silent killings, and come back as dawn streaks the Italian sky, bloody, weary, torn but grimly satisfied."[10] Last ones back were the men of Gusville, lingering after the kill to perform a community service, stealing. Emptying the enemy stores to restock Gusville's bar and larder was an endless chore, even though the population of Gusville always declined. Eighty-nine men were killed, missing in action, or captured. Thus would Gusville one day be reclaimed by the Borgo Sabotinesi. A higher glory in a far larger arena awaited General Frederick and his First Special Service Force.

WHEN the German High Command publicly disclosed having carried out the ten-to-one retaliation for the attack in the Via Rasella, a second, more specific communiqué was issued by Kesselring to his troops. To the instruction to crush the "villainous bandits" expressed in the first communiqué, a modus operandi was added. "Partisan and sabotage activity of anti-Nazi elements," it said, "must be expected in all parts of Italy. The formation of Partisan groups is to be neutralized by continual supervision of the civilian population . . . mutinous happenings must be reported by quickest possible means." The instructions went on:

> In such cases [we] will act with remorseless severity. Commanders, all grades, must counteract the blind faith of the German soldier in the civil population of foreign countries. It must be hammered into every man that every civilian may be either an agent or a saboteur, who uses the trusting nature of the German soldier to do him harm.[11]

If the German soldier was too bighearted for his own good, Kesselring later admitted that he too had been at fault, having until then treated the Partisan movement too lightly. The same applied to civilian populations. The man who had confessed traveling from love to hatred of the Italians had learned by now that wherever there were areas "infested" with Partisans, one had to regard "every civilian of either sex a fanatical assassin." The Partisans themselves, mostly "riffraff who robbed, murdered, and pillaged," contradicted every principle of clean soldierly fighting, he said. True, he said, there were a few "irregularities" on the German side as well, "perhaps three or five cases" that did not turn out to be lies or exaggerations, but when the guerrilla warriors gave fight they forgot all human decency. "Their southern temperament could run riot, their 'patriotic' mission combined with vicious instincts . . . ran amok without restraint, doing their nefarious work everywhere."

He had therefore concluded, he said, that the Partisans represented a critical threat to his lines of withdrawal, and now he had to "repair omissions." Measures already in place were intensified, notably Gestapo activities—what he called "police observations of resistance nuclei"—and encouraging existing Italian dissent from Partisan acts by "political appeasement . . . [of] influential persons," the latter activity being something done best "with the cooperation of the Vatican and the Italian princes of the Church." [12]

What was new were Kesselring's orders to treat the Partisans and their civilian constituency with the same ferocity applied at the front. Adopting Hitler's 1942 directive to the commanders on the eastern front for combating Partisans ("use all means without restriction—even against women and children"),[13] Kesselring asked the Führer for absolute authority in dealing with the Partisans in Italy. This was a special preserve of Reichsführer Himmler, entrusted in Italy to SS Polizeiführer Wolff, but despite strong opposition from the SS, such authority was granted. Now at the pinnacle of his powers, Kesselring immediately showed his resolve not to stop in the Ardeatine Caves. In his very first order as supreme commander in Italy of *everything*, he declared:

> I will protect any commander who exceeds our usual restraint in the choice of severity of the methods he adopts against Partisans. In this connection the old principle holds good, *that a mistake in the choice of methods in executing* one's orders is better than failure or neglect to act. [Emphasis in original.][14]

Thus were "excesses," a universal euphemism for *crimes against humanity*, now to be "protected," a coded synonym for *rewarded*.

EIGHTEEN

ROME MUST STARVE . . .

THE secret that Kappler had hoped to keep eternal—where the bodies lay—was unraveling, albeit slowly at first. A single word was in the air, heard in murmurs everywhere in Rome but not quite understood, an unfamiliar place called Ardea.

Three of the Silesian monks who had heard the explosions at the caves went the next day to investigate. They found the entrances sealed, but the blasting had left a new, raw opening, a narrow passageway. They followed the trail of an electric wire lying on the ground, making their way inside by candlelight. Seeing nothing else unusual, one of them, Don Giovanni Fagioli, scaled an earthen mound covered with freshly fallen volcanic dust and was able to look into a parallel tunnel. "On the other side," he said later, "I saw a pile of cadavers. It was about two, two-and-a-half meters wide, and just as high, and you could see arms hanging here, legs hanging there, heads hanging, too, really. I crossed myself, then got down and told the others to have a look. I didn't say what was there, just to have a look." [1]

The monks reported at once to their superior, who with equal urgency ordered that the Vatican be informed. [2] Over the next few days, the Silesians revisited the site along with a few Romans who were drawn there by little more than rumors and utter desperation. The only secret still intact was who in fact had been slain.

In the meantime, someone who lived near the Via Ardeatina had called the police to report a terrible stench permeating the sparsely populated neighborhood. That news made its way to Questore Caruso, who passed it on to Kappler. He told Caruso that he would "have the inconvenience eliminated."[3] He ordered that the city's garbage collections be dumped at the entrances to the caves, hoping to mask one smell with another, and, as an added preventive, a sign was posted forbidding entry on pain of death.

Nevertheless, more and more Romans, tolerating the inextinguishable smell of death and the threat of death itself, continued to come, though the passageway itself was now covered by swarms of giant flies. The mourners arrived bearing flowers and were forced to lay them on a thickening field of garbage until the unspeakable profanity drove them to sweep the filth to one side and hallow the naked ground with prayer.

> Again the massacre of the catacombs of Domitilla [wrote diarist Tra-
> bucco]. The people speak of it every day, even aloud. . . . So near to the
> dead of the catacombs who for 2,000 years have slept in peace, there are
> now 320 patriots who lie without burial, without a sign of pity, without a
> name. . . . When we will be able to honor the 320 martyrs—still unidenti-
> fied because up until now there has not been a single official notification
> given to the families—a pilgrimage without end will go to the *Fosse
> Ardeatine*.[4]

Apparently unsure of what to call the reprisal when he began this entry, dated March 31, the journalist ended with the phrase *Fosse Ardeatine*, the first recorded use of the name by which the Ardeatine Caves massacre would from then on always be known to Italians—the word *fosse* invoking not only the caves but also the death inside them.

On that same day, the Friday before Palm Sunday, the Vatican sent two high officials to the Governatorato of Rome—the municipal administration in charge of, among other things, the disposal of garbage and unclaimed cadavers. Churchmen requested that the city authority try to arrange that the victims be properly buried. They received no other reply than a shrug of the shoulders.[5] Later that day, coincidentally or not, the Germans sent a truckload of soldiers to the Ardeatine Caves to close the passageway. A series of window-shattering explosions rocked the area, sealing the opening, chasing away the flies, containing the cadaverous smell, and collapsing some of the tunnels in a landslide of dirt, sand, and garbage. The victims, beneath it all, were indeed buried. As long as the Germans were in charge, there would be no more violation of their graves.

· · ·

NOT UNTIL the voice of Great Britain's most famous Italian-language speaker, the BBC newscaster who called himself "Colonel Stevens," was heard in Rome to speak favorably of the Via Rasella attack did the right-wing leaders in the CLN and the Monarchists begin to worry about being isolated. Other Allied broadcasts added to their concerns, referring to the Via Rasella Partisans as "Italian patriots," and, to be sure, all condemned the German atrocity. It had taken several days for the Allied news programs to sort out wild rumor from fact—leaving themselves open to enemy ridicule—but the popular Colonel Stevens, a favorite of Italians taken by his amusingly British-accented delivery, got it reasonably correct and gave the rightists, particularly those who had wanted to disown the Via Rasella operation, second thoughts.

Before long, they agreed with the other parties to issue a unanimous protest written by ex-president Bonomi and signed by the CLN. Backdated to hide their hesitation and dissension, and probably not the work of Bonomi, it was an eloquent call for unity and action, uncharacteristic of the niggling CLN. It read:

> Italian men and women! A crime without a name has been committed in your capital. Under the pretext of a reprisal for an act of war by Italian patriots, in which it lost 32 of its SS, the enemy has massacred 320 innocent persons . . . without any kind of trial, without religious assistance or comfort from their families: not executed but murdered.
>
> Rome is horrified by this unprecedented slaughter. It rises in the name of humanity and condemns to abomination the murderers, and equally their accomplices and allies. But Rome will be avenged. The atrocity that has been consummated within its walls is the extreme reaction of the beast that feels itself about to fall. . . .
>
> Italian men and women! The blood of our martyrs must not have flowed in vain. From the grave where the 320 Italians—of every social class, of every political creed—lie united for all time in their sacrifice, a solemn call is raised to each of you:
>
> All for the liberation of the Patria from the Nazi invader! All for the reconstruction of an Italy worthy of its fallen sons![6]

The dissenters might not have come on board were it not for a much more powerful unifying event that occurred contemporaneously—an epoch-making turnabout by the Communists. Party Secretary Palmiro Togliatti, who had spent the past eighteen years living in exile in the Soviet

Union, surfaced early in April in the Allied-controlled Kingdom of the South to make a breathtaking announcement. Still using his code name, Ercole Ercoli, the singular and plural Italian forms of Hercules, he proclaimed that winning the war came first. The Communists were ready to join hands with the Monarchists—including the King and Badoglio—and every other anti-Fascist party in a government of national unity. Dissolving all dissent on the right, Togliatti's *svolta*, a shift rightward deemed "wonderful" by Bonomi, did indeed work wonders. In rapid succession, Bonomi withdrew his resignation, the King announced his abdication—accepting postwar free elections to determine the fate of the monarchy—and, finally, Badoglio was named to head an Allied-approved government of all six parties, thus closing the rift between Churchill and Roosevelt. Left to nurse the wounds of disillusionment were the Communists' closest allies and the Communist Party members themselves. While most anti-Fascists of the left, especially those of the armed Resistance, believed they were fighting for an Italy rooted in a democracy of ideals, Togliatti's Herculean feat had given them a glimpse of a more likely future, a democracy of just deals.

THE WRITER Elsa Morante later remembered occupied Rome in its crepuscular days, though it seemed to endure forever then:

> In the last months of the German occupation, Rome took on the look of certain Indian metropolises where only vultures get their fill of food and there is no count of the living and dead. . . . The people had fallen silent. The daily news of roundups, torture, and butchery ran through the neighborhoods echoing like death-rattles with no way to respond. . . . And even the exalted mirage called Liberation was shrinking to a tiny dot of foolishness, a topic of sarcasm and ridicule. Indeed, it was said that the Germans, before abandoning the city, would blow it all up from its very foundations, and that miles and miles of sewers had already been mined underground. . . . But, in the end, inside the isolated city, sacked and besieged, the true master was hunger.[7]

Although the sharp reduction in the bread ration announced on the day following the Via Rasella attack was seen as punishment for all, the occupation authorities had acted out of necessity. The food supply in Rome, Ambassador Rahn had informed Berlin at the time, was sufficient for "only two or three days ahead," and the biggest problem was replenishment.[8] Allied bombardment of the rail yards had forced the Germans to transport food-stuffs by truck, but the need for these vehicles to service the front had in-creased and they, too, were prime targets for Allied air attack. To further stretch the food rations, the occupiers had agreed, said Rahn, to "remove" a portion of the consumers—an unspecified number of refugees, students, and unemployed—which would mean more roundups and deportations.[9]

The famous lazing cats of Rome, from the ancient ruins of Palatine Hill to the backyards of Trastevere, were gone. What few other edibles re-mained, not always properly labeled, could be had only on the black market. In early April, exasperation took on a new form, starting with a group of women queuing at a bakery for their measly new ration of the hated *pane nero*, an ersatz dark bread. Hours had passed and not one person had been served when a verbal protest turned violent. Overrunning a Fascist police guard, the women broke into the bakery and stripped it of sacks of the white flour reserved for a privileged few, filling their shopping bags and smocks with the flour. When several such uprisings erupted over the next few days in other neighborhoods—including the *borghi* in the shadow of Saint Peter's—women in the Resistance began to organize them, calling on their sisters everywhere to take to the streets and "demand your right to live!" The women's "assaults of the ovens," as these bread riots quickly came to be called, continued throughout that month, leading to clashes with more and more Fascist police and finally the Germans themselves. Then the shooting started. In the Ostiense neighborhood, south of the pyramid, women and children raided a bakery that serviced the German troops stationed in Rome. The SS seized ten women, dragged them onto the nearby bridge over the Tiber, the Ponte di Ferro, and made them face the river. Then they were shot to death by submachine-gun fire.

The plan to reduce the number of food consumers by other means was initiated by Kappler and managed with characteristic economy of move-ment. Many of the bakery raiders were women who lived in the densely pop-ulated working-class Quadraro district in southeast Rome. But to Kappler they were only the latest nuisance to be identified in a district known to the occupiers as a "wasp's nest" of Partisans and other dangerous anti-Germans. Consul Möllhausen called the area the last refuge of those who could find no other place to hide in Rome. Straddling the Roman consular road Via Tus-colana, Quadraro was a gateway to Anzio and Cassino. At least three armed Resistance groups operated against German military traffic to and from the fronts: the CLN's Action Party combatants, the Gappisti of the so-called

VIII Zone, and the independent Bandiera Rossa Partisans. It was also a kind of urban Sherwood Forest for the populist, apolitical but anti-Nazi Hunchback of Quarticciolo and his gang.

On Easter Monday, the boy bandit for unknown reasons had teamed up with some Partisans in an attack on the Via Tuscolana in which three Germans soldiers were killed. On the pretext that the Romans had failed to learn the lesson of the High Command's "hard reply" to the attack in the Via Rasella, the occupiers activated their removal plan as a response to the incident. One week later, in the predawn hours of April 17, Kappler, leading his men and additional forces of the Wehrmacht and the paratroopers, completely surrounded Quadraro and proceeded to conduct the largest roundup of the occupation. In a careful search of every house, the Germans nabbed some 2,000 men and boys, packed them into the neighborhood movie theater, and subjected them to a selection process to recruit the most able-bodied of the lot. About 750 of them, between the ages of fifteen and fifty-five, were promptly shipped to the north, removed from their place at the table of the Roman food supply, and, according to the pink poster that went up on the walls later that day, "assigned to a productive occupation in the German war effort directed against Bolshevism." Half of them never returned.[10]

AS LATE as April 22, the Vatican was still imploring the German embassy to help in relieving the anguish of the families who feared their loved ones had been among those killed in the Ardeatine Caves by providing a list of victims' names.[11] But several days earlier, the Gestapo had begun sending out next-of-kin notifications. Little by little, it no longer mattered that the grim message inside was in German only. The mere receipt of a letter with the Via Tasso, 145 return address and the March 24 date alongside the victim's name erased all hope at a glance. The well-placed families—the Montezemolos, the Simonis, and several others—received the news from other sources long before the notices arrived, but none more directly or earlier than the Giglios. As soon as he had learned of his son's arrest, Cervo's father, Armando, had gone to see Questore Caruso himself. As a high official in OVRA, the Fascist secret police, the senior Giglio had expected at least to ease his son's situation, and in any case, had he known that Cervo faced execution, it was more than likely that he could arrange that his son be spared the pending trial. But he had arrived too late, Caruso told him, while almost certainly holding back the news that the OVRA chief's son was not on Kappler's list but on his own. Neither Koch nor Caruso had been aware of Armando Giglio's ranking position in the Fascist regime, which meant that Cervo, put to the limits of torture, had gone to his death protecting not only Tompkins and all he knew about OSS operations on both sides of the front but his father as well. By forgoing rescue, Cervo had in fact surrendered his own life to save his father from any hint of suspicion.

Weeks before receiving the official notice from Via Tasso, the Giglio family boldly placed its own death notice in the March 31 edition of *Il Giornale d'Italia*. Lieutenant Maurizio Giglio, it said, only twenty-three years old, "died on the 24th last most suddenly." To those who had the greatest need to know, a clearer signal that Cervo had not talked could scarcely have been devised.

Despite Cervo's extraordinary self-abnegation and loyalty to the Tompkins-Malfatti network, Tompkins himself was in a more precarious position than ever. Much of his trouble came from his own side. Surrounded by betrayals and suspect agents, Tompkins began to harbor a galloping fear that the man who had become his archrival, Menicanti, was also a threat to his survival. Trying to reestablish radio contact with the base, he found himself in a fierce but unilateral spy-versus-spy struggle with Menicanti for control over a single radio transmitter, two radio operators code-named Siria and Iris, and a unique set of radio crystals, the technology that gave access to the correct frequency for transmission to headquarters. Since Tompkins had the radio but not the crystals, while Menicanti was in the opposite condition, both were vying for the services of the operators—who had been allied to the now missing Sorrentino, the self-proclaimed representative of Mark Clark.

Plans to attack the Pensione Oltremare and to avenge Cervo were abandoned now as Tompkins scrambled to keep afloat in the morass of his drastically altered circumstances. With the help of the resourceful Malfatti, he was able to establish a new cover identity as a corporal in the Italian Colonial Police (PAI)—narrowly escaping being taken for an imposter and a Jew in the required physical examination by inventing a medical history of a cured venereal disease to explain his circumcision. In the meantime, he pursued his objective of setting up the radio. One of his agents had succeeded in infiltrating Kesselring's headquarters, so there was no shortage of intelligence in need of timely transmission. The entire effort, however, collapsed in mid-April, when his protector in the PAI organization—a plan-ahead officer scrounging for anti-Fascist credentials in preparation for the inevitable ar-

rival of the Allies—was arrested by the SS, and Menicanti made an attempt
to kidnap Siria and Iris and their radio. Tompkins, seeking a peace meeting,
feared a Mafia-like trap when Menicanti sent word that he would agree to
such an encounter only if he were to name the time and place. As the American reported to Donovan, he reluctantly accepted, and was indeed shaken
on arrival, finding himself "surrounded by a bunch of thugs," he said,
though unharmed. He went on:

> [Menicanti] tried to reaffirm that he was the real boss. But when I re-
> minded him that sooner or later the Allies would arrive and that he would
> have to answer for his actions, he agreed to turn over the necessary mate-
> rial to Sorrentino's agents.[12]

Filing his own report to the OSS only two months later, Menicanti told
his side of the tale:

> At that moment, Mr. Tompkins tried in every way to hinder my efforts
> to find this radio operator and his set, for reasons absolutely unknown to
> me. He said to everyone that I was a very doubtful person, and probably a
> double agent, a traitor in the service of the SS. These rumors immediately
> created to me all sorts of difficulties and also aroused suspicion among my
> agents and friends, causing me to lose a great deal of time, thus preventing
> me from working more efficiently. I don't believe that it is interesting to
> the OSS to tell you in detail all the difficulties and the nuisance of Mr.
> Tompkins' behavior against me.[13]

Two days later, Menicanti backed out of the agreement, teaming up with
yet another Italian SIM agent recruited into the OSS by Captain Bourgoin.
The new man was a Sicilian aristocrat named Raimondo Lanza di Trabia,
also known as Dr. Antonio Lima, who had recently arrived in German-
occupied Italy with his own radio operator and was now in Rome. One
month earlier, Lanza di Trabia had been arrested in Allied-occupied
Palermo, wearing an American Army uniform—with authorization, however, by the OSS. Investigated by the U.S. Counter-Intelligence Corps, he
was described as a "notorious Fascist" who had lived with Mussolini's son-
in-law, Count Ciano, was a lover of Ciano's wife, Edda Mussolini, and was
a "secret emissary of Mussolini . . . and other leading Fascists."[14] Nevertheless, Menicanti welcomed Dr. Lima, as he called him. Tompkins, for his
part, decided that Rome was not big enough for all of them, and leaving a

skeleton organization behind, he set out with five of his men to cross the lines once more, head for OSS headquarters, and "get the whole thing straightened out."[15]

————————

PAOLO and Elena and the other Gappisti had been preparing actions on a scale no less imposing than that of the Via Rasella attack—losing sight, perhaps, of a sound principle of Partisan warfare, adopted as their own when it had all begun: not undertaking large, complicated plans. The foursome of Paolo, Elena, Giovanni, and Maria, for example, had formulated just such a plan for a raid on the Via Tasso to be carried out in conjunction with the Socialist and Actionist combatants. Gaining secret access to neighboring rooftops and terraces, they had found a way to penetrate Gestapo headquarters and launch an attack in which the prisoners would be freed and armed by the Partisans and would thus overwhelm and subdue Kappler and his men. While they waited for approval from the Military Council, another complex operation that was to begin with a common burglary as a ploy and culminate in the assassination of Questore Caruso was set into motion the first week in April but quickly crushed by police action. A shoot-out ended in the capture of three Gappisti, Rosa, Pasquale and Ferdinando, who were charged with burglary, then quietly released by a high police official, who was secretly cooperating with the CLN.

The authentic burglar among them—GAP Central's idealized working-class Partisan, Guglielmo—conceivably might have made a difference, but he had not participated in this action. Instead, the hiatus created by suspended, canceled, and aborted operations had caused him to drift back to his dark side. Idle since the Via Rasella attack, Guglielmo, well into the curfew hours of April 23, was busily rifling through the bureau drawers of an apartment he and an accomplice had broken into. They had already pocketed 7,000 lire and were still looking when they were interrupted by the occupants, the *portiere*, and before long some of the neighbors. The accomplice, whom Guglielmo never named, had the only gun between them, and he managed to escape with all the money, while Guglielmo, "armed" with only an ammunition clip and a jimmy-sized crowbar, was overpowered and conducted to the local station house in the Appio district of south Rome.

In his pocket was a document allowing him freedom of movement during curfew. It was authorized by the SS, but as an easily ascertainable forgery it now became a one-way ticket to the Via Tasso. Guglielmo asked to see

Caruso, and it took no longer than a couple of hours and a telltale word or two for a meeting to be arranged.

Face-to-face with the Questore, he was asked to provide some kind of proof that the information he had was authentic. Guglielmo disclosed the plan to assassinate Caruso, rattling off the minutest details about Caruso himself, including the restaurants he frequented and the address of a secret apartment he maintained in Rome. The Questore was convinced, but apparently still unaware of the quality and extent of the traitor's knowledge, turned him over to Koch, who would reap all the credit for the prize catch of the occupation.

GUGLIELMO, who had been struggling to keep himself and his family alive on the 750-lire monthly payment from GAP Central plus the proceeds of his occasional thievery, was now potentially worth many millions of lire. A fortune in reward money was at his fingertips but the price of cashing in was certain death administered by his ex-comrades. The solution to his dilemma was clear. Telling all that he knew about GAP would soon exhaust his value to the enemy. Even naming the names he knew, not just code names, would be of limited use, since nearly all were in hiding. He would instead go back to the Resistance as a spy.

Koch liked the idea. Guglielmo returned to the street. The one fellow Gappista he knew where to find was his oldest and most trusting friend, Raoul. Over the next several days, beginning with Raoul, who unwittingly led him to other people and places in the organization, Guglielmo and the Koch Gang virtually dismantled GAP Central along with the GAP organization of VI Zone, where Guglielmo had worked earlier in the occupation. Captured in a series of arrests were GAP commanders Spartaco and Cola, and among several others Duilio, the Partisan *portiere* of the Via Marco Aurelio hideout, though the place was empty when raided. The arrests in themselves were reason enough to abandon all hiding places, but at the same time Guglielmo's betrayal had become known. Koch had just transferred his group to new headquarters in the more commodious Pensione Jaccarino, and, it appears, a lapse in the new security arrangements had allowed Cola to escape through a bathroom window.

What had saved Paolo and Elena and Giovanni and Maria was time gained by their disciplined use of their code names and Cola's warning. Koch, however, was now aware of Paolo's central role as the street cleaner in the Via Rasella, and he more than doubled the price on his head, to a

record high of 1.8 million lire, making him the occupation's public enemy number one.

Somehow, Koch sensed correctly that Spartaco, as commander, and Duilio, as caretaker of the hideout, knew more than the others and could lead him to Paolo. Both Paolo and Elena had entrusted Duilio with letters to be delivered to their mothers in the event of their death, and Spartaco knew as much, too. Thus the worst of the inevitable tortures were directed against them. Hog-tied and immobile, Duilio was made to lie on the floor, stomped on with cleated shoes, his ribs breaking one by one, kicked and battered until he lost consciousness, only to be awakened by buckets of ice water thrown in his face, as Koch's men bombarded him with questions: "Who is Paolo?" "Where is Paolo?"

Spartaco, with a storehouse of other information and stronger physically, was treated worse, if possible, particularly after spurning Koch's personal gesture of peeling off 1 million lire as a down payment to his prisoner for Paolo's true identity. Spartaco spit in his face.

Following the first wave of arrests, most of the prisoners were sent to the Via Tasso to await trial and, since none of them ceded to torture, a mandatory death sentence. The search for Paolo and the others who had eluded the decimation of GAP Central was intensified. It almost succeeded when a suspect apartment in the Piazza Bologna was raided by Koch's men. They found only an open window, but a moment earlier Paolo and Elena had been there. Paolo later recalled:

> Our life had become a hell. We were hunted like wolves, continually changing our place of refuge, going for days on end without eating because contact with our command centers was sporadic. Our plan to attack the Via Tasso, which had been reinforced and had become an impregnable fortress, was discarded. Finally, we received word that we would be sent out of Rome, to join the partisan brigades in the mountains.

While waiting for specific reassignment, they were ordered to remain closeted in their latest hideout. It was an order they found impossible to fully adhere to. Paolo continues:

> We had been profoundly transformed by the long struggle. The hunger, the unease, and the anger toward the enemy, toward the betrayal, and the pain we felt at the thought of our comrades who were about to be killed, seemed like a host of reasons why we should disobey. It was impos-

sible to simply lower a curtain separating us from the life we'd been leading all these months. The need to go out on the streets of our city to still
feel part of that struggle was something we couldn't shake.

Above all there were two objectives we felt duty bound to pursue: punish Guglielmo and free our comrades. Hungry and poorly clothed, we
walked the streets of Rome, our guns in our pockets, our hands curled
around them and the safety undone, ready to fire.

In the meantime, Antonello Trombadori, the Partisan who had founded
GAP Central and had been arrested by Kappler, was back in his place of
command. He had escaped from a forced-labor gang at Anzio and was now
reorganizing GAP. The lust for vengeance would have to be contained and
rechanneled if the Roman Resistance was to be worthy of its name.

STARVING cows and sheep, down from the Alban Hills with the refugees,
could graze on the new spring grass in the Villa Borghese and the other
great parks of the city, but by the beginning of April, Romans began dying of
hunger.[16]

Reducing the number of mouths to feed, by both "reprisal" and "removal,"
did nothing to alleviate the approach of famine in Eternal City. Neither did a
German plan to use boats in Venice instead of Wehrmacht trucks to transport
food to Rome under the Vatican flag. Both Kesselring and the Pope approved,
but the Germans worried about the Vatican "capitalizing on this by propagandizing,"[17] and the inadequate system remained in place. The Vatican was
left "propagandizing" its own "economical soups" program—low cost for
some, free for the very poor. But the king of propagandizing food was General Mälzer. The gourmand commandant was the jovial Nazi general seen in
newsreels and news photos distributing foodstuffs free in one or another
Roman piazza. As soon as the cameras left, the same packages were often
taken back by the Germans, snatched from the hands of the recipients.

For their part, the Allies kept bombing and strafing German trucks, un-
caring about what they might contain, and even whether the trucks were
German. Many of the vehicles carrying food on the roads to Rome were, in
fact, owned and operated by the Vatican, and clearly marked as such, but it
was nearly impossible to identify them from bombing altitudes. As for the
strafing, the Germans were known to stoop to painting Red Cross and hospital markings on their trucks. The Allied position, as with regard to recog-

nition of Open City status, was that the occupiers were wholly responsible for the fate of the Romans.[18] In the case of feeding the population, any relief of that burden by the Allies would free up enemy resources to be turned against them militarily. The same held true for any scheme to bring in food by sea.

The idea that military considerations greatly overrode humanitarian ones was put to the test on April 29. A convoy of more than fifty trucks bearing legitimate Vatican insignia and transporting food to Rome was attacked by Allied aircraft and severely damaged. A Vatican protest was promptly transmitted by British Ambassador Osborne to London. Some days earlier he had warned the Foreign Office that unless the Vatican was permitted to provide at least an adequate supply of flour, or the Allies did so themselves, "we shall be inviting a catastrophe."[19] The tocsin signaling the threat of mob violence, being sounded for almost a year by Vatican diplomacy, was finally being heard. Now, citing Cardinal Maglione's words, Osborne wrote: "Famine, with all its unknown consequenses, is now hanging over the city of Rome." The use of trucks was the only way of maintaining the food supply. "It cannot be believed that the Allies wish to deprive the population of this ultimate means of subsistence."[20]

The British, who had been more adamant than the Americans on these issues, wavered. Foreign Secretary Anthony Eden placed the matter before Churchill. Rome was not just another occupied city, he said. It was also the capital of the Catholic world and one that would, he hoped, shortly be host to the Allies. "Is it really in our own interest," he asked the Prime Minister, "to risk reducing the population of Rome to starvation with all resulting political and social consequences from which we shall be the chief sufferers when we occupy the city?"[21]

Churchill replied, "Foreign Secretary. It is with pain that I write these words. Rome must starve till freed."[22]

NINETEEN

SHIMMERING CITY

Diadem, the regal-sounding code name of Alexander's breakthrough strategy, went operational on the starlit night of May 11. A thousand cannons and a thousand tanks stood ready. The encouragement by deception had continued until the last moment. Allied after-dark routine along the Gustav Line was maintained. Patrols went out as usual; artillery shells were lobbed as the night before. In the meantime, troops continued to mass behind the Fifth and Eighth Army lines in the night shadows. Then came the hour before midnight. Mark Clark, at the head of his II Corps, later recorded a vivid description of what he saw:

> At 11 o'clock about a thousand big guns from Cassino to the sea fired at approximately the same moment. . . . The ridges in front of the Fifth Army seemed to stand out momentarily in a great blaze of light, sink again into darkness, and then tremble under the next salvo. It was perhaps the most effective artillery bombardment of the campaign. It simply smashed into dust a great number of enemy batteries and vital centers. . . . [1]

CBS war correspondent Eric Sevareid, watching the same demolition of the Gustav Line, later described it this way:

> The moon was high and full and impartially illuminated both sides of the front, blessing and betraying both defenders and attackers. It lighted the way for the men who crawled on their bellies up the Italian drawbridge toward Fortress Europe; it exposed them to Europe's jailers, touching

with iridescence coat buckle, water bottle, gun shaft, and wide young eyes. From Cassino to the sea on the central front the soft spring earth shuddered and heaved in grunting convulsions; the venerable olive trees burst their trunks, bent beneath the blasts of air, and then, half erect, exhibited to the moon their leafless limbs, thin and naked as the arms of an obscene hag.

The first blow for the freeing of Europe had fallen in the night. . . . [2]

———————

AT DAWN the bombers took to the sky, pulverizing Kesselring's headquarters, for one, and burying the Gustav Line in its own rocky substance. Although the Wehrmacht troops put up strong resistance on the floor of the Liri Valley, the Allies finally crossed the Garigliano and Rapido Rivers, never again repelled. With the thousand tanks behind them at last gaining traction on dry land, all the old obstacles, along with the myth of Kesselring's invincibility, began to topple. Never had the Nazi Field Marshal been more surprised than now. He would spend his remaining years blaming others, but within the first forty-eight hours of Diadem, the impasse had been breached. On the 16th he gave the fateful order to Tenth Army commander Vietinghoff, saying, "We shall have to give up Cassino." [3]

The swift breakthrough, sealed by the startling advance of the Fifth Army's French Expeditionary Corps, was as much a triumph for Clark and Free French leader Marshal Alphonse Juin as it was for Alexander and his Chief of Staff, General John Harding. Harding had authored the plan, but Clark had proposed the one move least expected by the Germans— an attempt to dislodge them from the mountains that dominated the valley. Control of these heights meant control of the roads to Rome beneath them.

In this, Marshal Juin gave Kesselring a lesson in a higher form of invincibility. Three of Juin's four divisions were French colonial troops trained in mountain warfare, and the most skilled of all were the 8,000 Moroccan irregulars, the feared Goumiers. Men whose weapon of choice was their knife, whose uniform was their flowing striped burnoose, and who moved across treacherous terrain at a runner's pace, they produced the surprise of surprises. They were the first to penetrate the enemy defenses, traveling fastest and furthest, swarming over ranges believed by the Germans—and by the bulk of the Allies, too—to be all but impassable. But they quickly overran the enemy's positions, crushing all resistance, and, by eliminating Kesselring's vantage points, assuring that the rupture of the Gustav Line was irreversible.

With rare exceptions, even detailed accounts of the Goumiers' military prowess by historians of the Italian campaign end here.[4] But a poignant episode in the trauma of the last days in the battle for Rome is described by renowned novelist Alberto Moravia and the film made from his book *Two Women*. An early investigation by the postoccupation government in Rome reported more than 700 cases of "carnal violence" committed by Juin's Goumiers in the adjoining province of Frosinone.[5] Few of the peasant families that populate most of the region were spared.

A woman from the Frosinone town of Esperia, identified only as Giovannina M., told the investigators:

> We were expecting the liberators and what we got was something else, a people of another breed. How ugly they were! They seemed possessed by demons. They robbed what little we had left and ran havoc over the people. They had been given a free hand at the front and they did all those dirty things to the men and the women. It was a slaughter. . . . The mountain was crawling with them. They came out of every nook and cranny, taking all the women they saw and carrying us off into the brush . . . escape was out of the question. . . . There were officers with them, white men, the French, and they didn't do a thing to stop them. We were a joke to the commanders . . . they told us that the only way you could make the Moroccans move on was to let them do what they do.[6]

Concetta C. said:

> They came here by the thousands. You could see them moving down the mountainside, looking like tiny ants from far away, but really a plague going through, creating hell for three days. They were an ugly, filthy lot, rings through their noses, long robes, eyes bulging. All over the mountain you could hear the screaming and the groans. The French in command were with them when they got to where we were and went on their rampage. Two of them threw me to the ground, but when they realized I had my period they ran off. . . . Do you know how many old women died just from the pain of what they did? No other soldier behaved like them. It had nothing to do with the color of their skin. They were beasts and that's how they conducted themselves. The Germans, even though they took the animals and destroyed everything when they withdrew were better behaved. And these Moroccans were supposed to be our liberators! Some liberation! They were sent to free us, sent to help us, and did these disgusting things.

They took the children and had their way with them. The youngsters tried their best to fend them off. But what could they do? There were always three or four of them on top of one. Our husbands, brothers, fathers, anyone who tried to come between them, were beaten back and killed.[7]

WHEN Mark Clark, who could have had only the vaguest notion of the voracious nature of the Goumiers, later called their feat the "key to success" in the quest for Rome, he was of course referring exclusively to their military performance.[8] Conquering Rome had always been Clark's objective, and higher still was the goal of being first inside its gates. But now that the barriers were crumbling, his vision of the Fifth Army leading the triumphant entry into the Eternal City was all.

The breakthrough at the Gustav Line, which had so brightened the lives of all who had planned it, marked the moment that the final showdown between Clark and Alexander began. Diadem had been conceived by Alexander, and agreed to by all, as a kind of one-two punch that could knock out the enemy even before the Allies reached Rome. The breakout at Anzio—phase two of Diadem—would be timed to link the forces pouring out of the beachhead with the Fifth and Eighth Armies heading north through the Liri Valley. Alexander's strategy—expressed in General Harding's blueprint—cast the linkup as a unique opportunity to cut off Vietinghoff's retreating Tenth Army from Mackensen's Fourteenth. Such a separation opened the possibility of the unified Allied forces enveloping and destroying both enemy armies and perhaps even ending the war in Italy right there.

To achieve this goal Harding had proposed Operation Buffalo. It specified that the troops breaking out of Anzio would move eastward through the Alban Hills, with the goal of blocking the German route along Highway 6 at a town called Valmontone. By this maneuver, if successful, a classic pincer would clamp the Tenth Army between the Allied Cassino forces advancing behind them and the Anzio forces in their path.

Operation Buffalo troubled Clark. Apart from all other considerations, Clark wrote, "we wanted Rome prior to the beginning of Eisenhower's invasion of France, and that time was getting very close."[9] By "we" he referred to General Marshall and President Roosevelt as well as himself. On the other hand, Churchill, who had begun the "soft-underbelly" war in the first place, was fully behind Alexander in a decisive battle at Valmontone "fought to the finish."[10]

Thus Clark, who had long since discarded his faith in Churchill, greeted Alexander's decision to attack at Valmontone with scarce enthusiasm, arguing that it was seriously flawed since there were other roads by which the Germans could withdraw. Moreover, the Valmontone plan appeared to him a stalling tactic—confirmation of his worst fears—as clearly reflected in his diary entry for May 5, the day he learned of Alexander's intentions: "I know factually," he wrote, "that there are interests brewing for the Eighth Army to take Rome, and I might as well let Alexander know now that if he attempts anything of the kind he will have another all-out battle on his hands; namely, with me."[11]

The hidden agenda in Operation Buffalo, Clark believed, was to open the way for the Eighth Army to beat him to Rome. Eighth Army Commander General Oliver Leese, who was continually jockeying to gain space for his troops at the Fifth Army's expense, was in Clark's view almost as much an enemy as any of Kesselring's men. According to the official U.S. history of the campaign, Clark was convinced that Diadem, as plotted by Alexander and Harding, put Leese out in front in the race for Rome. The Fifth Army's only hope of getting to Rome before the Normandy invasion was to head out of Anzio straight for the capital.[12]

> We had massed all our strength to take Rome [Clark wrote]. We were keyed up. . . . We not only wanted the honor of capturing Rome, but we felt that we more than deserved it; that it would make up to a certain extent for the buffeting and the frustration we had undergone in keeping up the winter pressure against the Germans. My own feeling was that nothing was going to stop us on our push towards the Italian capital. Not only did we intend to become the first army in fifteen centuries to seize Rome from the south, but we intended to see that the people at home knew that it was the Fifth Army that did the job and knew the price that had been paid for it.[13]

It had come down to this: the choice between a plan to end the war in all of Italy and a plan for Mark Clark to win the race for Rome and claim the trophy for America. The outcome would depend on whether the Fifth Army, when it reached Highway 6, made a right turn or a left. Neither plan, to be sure, was even close to being foolproof, and the choice did not belong to Clark but to Alexander. With practically everybody else trying to get into the act, as Clark put it, there would be squabbling in the days ahead. Whatever else might be decided, no one was renouncing a place in the starting gate for the run to be first in Rome, and the field was crowded. Apart from the American contenders—the Fifth Army's VI Corps at Anzio and II Corps at Cassino—and the British, the formidable New Zealanders, Juin's fleet Free French, the Free Poles, the Brazilians, and an assortment of other

United Nations armies all had visions of being in the finish-line photos, if not the winner's circle itself. "I had my hands full," Clark said.[14]

ALTHOUGH the likelihood of a general insurgency with "irresponsible elements" taking control of the Eternal City seemed to have ebbed in the recent repression, grief, and hunger, the Vatican's anxiety about the approaching change in government had never been higher. The organized assaults on the bread ovens portended all-out food riots. A CLN-sponsored general strike on May 3, though hardly a success, did see scattered stoppages and slowdowns in several workplaces, most notably by the typographers at the Fascist-controlled daily *Il Messaggero*, along with an ominous display of red flags.[15]

Still, many Romans and even some of the leading figures of the occupation would have been shocked or at least taken aback to discover that on May 10 the Holy Father, only weeks after the Ardeatine Caves massacre, granted a secret audience to Supreme SS Polizeiführer Wolff. True, Wolff was the man most responsible for the safety of Vatican City and the Pope himself—and maintaining order in Rome—but he also served Himmler, formerly as his Chief of Staff and now as the Commander in Chief of the entire police and persecution apparatus in all of occupied Italy. For years now, the SS had been singled out by the Curia as a particularly unsavory institution of the Hitler regime. Its officials were generally unwelcome in the Vatican, though some contact was necessary to pursue humanitarian aims.

Polizeiführer Wolff's protégé, Colonel Dollmann, had been the go-between for the May 10 papal audience. Whether it was through Dollmann, a poor keeper of secrets, or someone else, the meeting became known soon afterward and famous in the annals of Rome under the occupation. But what the Polizeiführer and the Pope actually spoke of when alone behind closed doors has only recently come to light.[16]

Wolff had sought this audience, he testified in 1972, because he regarded the foreign policy of the Third Reich as having lapsed into total confusion, and he believed that the Pope was "especially suited and would want to mediate an early end to the war with the West, which by then had become senseless." As Wolff described it, the meeting with the Pope came about thanks to Princess Virginia Agnelli, of the family-owned Fiat automobile company. The curious set of circumstances had begun when the police had arrested Donna Virginia, caught committing the Fascist crime of speaking in English on her tapped telephone. Leaping to her rescue, as he would for any princess in distress, was Colonel Dollmann, who asked Wolff to order her release, to which he consented without delay. In gratitude, the Princess asked Wolff, according to his testimony, how she could repay his kindness, and aware of her standing in the black aristocracy, he told her of his desire for an audience with the Pope, whom he had never met before.

"Tomorrow at noon. The Pope wants to speak to the General," Donna Virginia told Dollmann by phone the day before Wolff's next visit to Rome, displaying either her own influence or the Pope's enthusiasm, or both. Keeping it all secret demanded that Wolff go the Vatican in mufti, but he had traveled only with his uniforms and had to borrow a suit, shirt, and tie from Dollmann, a stylish dresser but a head shorter than he. "Naturally, he looked awful," Dollmann said. "He was famously handsome, very tall, a true Siegfried."

Accompanied to the papal antechamber by Father Pankratius Pfeiffer, Wolff was given a speedy lesson in papal protocol, and at a certain moment Pfeiffer told him that although the Pope himself would never ask, His Holiness hoped Wolff might do him a favor. The son of an old friend of the Pope's late brother was a prisoner in the Via Tasso, arrested, Pfeiffer said, "because of his radical left-wing tendencies," and facing the death penalty. The prisoner was Giuliano Vassalli, who had been captured a month earlier by Kappler's men. Vassalli was known to Wolff as a high-ranking Partisan, but was unaware of the details, such as his relationship with the OSS by way of Peter Tompkins and Socialist intelligence operatives of the Tompkins-Malfatti spy network. Moreover, the General and, ironically, the Pope, knew nothing of Vassalli's high position as the Socialist member of the tripartite Military Council, nor that the Council had authorized most of the urban guerrilla operations in Rome, including the Via Rasella attack. Nevertheless, while Wolff assured Pfeiffer that he would do what was possible to honor the papal request for Vassalli's release, he went on to warn him that the Pope might regret it.

After Pfeiffer had introduced him to the Pope and withdrawn, it was Pius, Wolff later stated, who initiated the audience by asking him what he thought of the situation in Germany. "From the Pope's own words I could sense the sincerity of his sympathy and how much he loved the German people." He went on:

> I then told him that, in my opinion, the political and military might of Germany and the Western powers would eventually be wasted away in this senseless war between them, and that Germany would plunge into chaos, while the real conflict with the East went on, leaving us in a state of

total exhaustion. I expressed my conviction that he, the Pope, was the right person to engage the Western powers in a search for an early end to this war, though the terms would have to be honorable, since I would not want to appear as a traitor. I was firmly committed, I said, to carrying out the mission entrusted to me to the very end . . .

The Pope replied, saying that he was happy to hear such an honest and open-minded appraisal of the situation, which corresponded to the reality in Germany and generally speaking in the West. At this point, I stated explicitly to His Holiness that to achieve the aims I had just expressed—an early end to the war with the West—I would be ready to risk my own life, but, because of the danger I faced if my efforts were to be misunderstood, I would also be jeopardizing the lives of my family. . . .

The Pope told me that naturally it was not easy to test the waters regarding the possibilities of a compromise peace. The main difficulty lay in the fact that a part of the Allies bore an attitude that was not only anti-Nazi, but to some extent also anti-German, in the sense of a prejudice that first of all had to be overcome, and that would take time. . . . The Pope said he would do everything possible to support my efforts, as my view corresponded to his own ideas on the matter, and that he would keep me advised through Father Pfeiffer as to when it would be possible to meet again. . . .

When Pfeiffer reappeared, Wolff took leave of the Pope, who in bidding his own farewell reminded him that he had embarked on a very difficult road, fraught with peril to his life. It was then, Wolff admitted, that he lost himself in a distraction, a misstep. In his words:

> As I took my final leave, I was standing at a certain distance from the Pope, and I instinctively raised my hand in a Nazi salute. It happened really spontaneously, because over the years I had become unused to civilian dress, but it was meant as a sign of deference. At that instant, Father Pfeiffer took me by the arm and told me as we left that the Holy Father would understand and take it in the right way.

Wolff never saw Pius XII again, but the search would go on for the coveted separate peace—that Holy Grail of World War II that receded with the westward advance of the Red Army—the "compromise peace" for which the Pope had squandered so much of his moral capital to obtain so little. Indeed, now it was with the improbable threesome of Dollmann and Wolff in the forefront and Pius XII as a spiritual partner[17] that the quest would continue—taking on a vigorous pace a year later when the two Germans would make contact with Allen Dulles, head of the OSS office in Switzerland. Initiating an increasingly complicated endgame, they would conclude a "compromise peace" with the Allies that would do honor to none who had sought it and would be nothing more than the unconditional surrender of Kesselring's armies in Italy one week before the end of the war in Europe.

WHEN Giuliano Vassalli, not long after the Ardeatine Caves massacre, fell into Kappler's hands, his fellow Socialist, spymaster Franco Malfatti, took the usual precaution of dropping out of sight. He attached himself to Peter Tompkins's party heading for Allied territory, but the attempts at crossing the lines were leading nowhere. By the second in week in May, having tried all the points of the compass, by land and by sea, the fugitive travelers had had to retreat and were back in Rome. The situation Tompkins had hoped to resolve had taken a turn for the worse.

The so-called skeleton organization he had left behind had been picked still cleaner by further arrests, and the effort to set up radio contact with OSS headquarters behind the lines at base appeared to be dead. Sorrentino, the bogus representative of Clark in Rome, had in the meantime reemerged but only long enough to be captured by Kappler. He would never have been sorely missed by his own side but after one night in Via Tasso, he betrayed one of Tompkins's most trustworthy agents, the Roman Partisan Arrigo Paladini.

Menicanti and the Allied-certified "notorious Fascist" Dr. Lima had found a new way to turn OSS operations in Rome into cash. They had begun issuing "American" documents to those who felt in need of political detoxification before facing the anti-Fascist future. For 1,000 lire, a seal of the United States would attest to the good works performed by the document holder as a freedom fighter in the anti-Nazi underground. Since the CLN, by the turnabout of Togliatti's Communists, had wheeled to the right to accommodate Badoglio and the monarchists, many of these same born-again customers were being successfully pitched by Menicanti to add luster to their new credentials by opposing any form of insurrection when Rome changed hands. In this regard, the Rome to which Tompkins had returned was looking like the Rome Donovan had had in mind when many months back he had warned Tompkins to "just make sure they don't rise up against each other."

With Tompkins a de facto castaway, the OSS in Rome had become a den of cutthroats and thieves, a travesty of what Tompkins had set out to create. The intelligence coups in the weeks following the Anzio landings had died for want of a radio. His latest and perhaps most vexing frustration was being powerless to convey the steady flow of daily German intelligence bulletins being accessed by his agent in Kesselring's headquarters. One such bulletin had reported that six clandestine radio stations, sent behind the lines by the Fifth Army, had been infiltrated by German counterespionage and were transmitting false information to the Allies. A final attempt to reach OSS headquarters through the radio facilities used by a British agent Tompkins had used in the past brought news of his arrest as well.

"The water seemed to be rising all around," Tompkins later reported to Donovan. "Franco and I decided . . . [to] attempt to cross into Switzerland, as our days were definitely counted, and we had no hope of establishing contact with the base."

That decision was altered the following day, however, when on the morning of May 12 the BBC announced the massive Allied assault on the Gustav Line. Tompkins had just received word from his man at Kesselring's headquarters of the extent of the Germans' surprise. They were still expecting a second attack, an amphibious landing north of Rome, and though Tompkins could only guess what the Allies were planning, this was something they had to know. The decisive spring offensive had clearly been launched; there would be precious intelligence continuously. There had to be a way to send it. He would stay in Rome to find the way.

EVEN the telephone-owning class was going hungry now. The same telephones in Parioli and the luxury hotels around the Via Veneto that had carried the voices of people praising the Nazi way of administering law and order now carried mainly complaints. The messages can still be "heard" in the intercepts:

Here a Roman *contessa* receives a call from an unidentified *signora*:

SIGNORA: How are you doing?
CONTESSA: What do you expect . . . anything new?
SIGNORA: Nothing. We're dying of hunger! Everywhere there's this terrible hunger! Tonight, I can't even stand on my feet. The only thing I've eaten all day is a slice of bread! They're just letting us starve to death!
CONTESSA: We can't go on like this!

From a phone owned by a duke of the well-known Pignatelli family, a woman named Maria speaks to an unidentified woman:

MARIA: How are things?

SIGNORA: I'm dying of hunger! I have nothing to eat here except some artichokes!

MARIA: If you don't starve to death, you're bombed to death!

Two women in conversation, one of them the wife of an army general:

WIFE: I hear the salt ration has been cut.

SIGNORA: You can't live anymore. In their hurry to cut down, we're the ones being cut down.

WIFE: What can you do?

SIGNORA: In Rome it's become unbearable. You never could live on air and you still can't.

WIFE: All we can do, dear, is hope!

Rome had become a city where the rich began to envy the poor. Calls to the offices of the rationing authority of the Governatorato reveal a recurring theme.

A *signora* calls the complaint department:

SIGNORA: I have disability supplementary rations for sugar, pasta, [olive] oil, and I haven't received anything for April nor this month either.

EMPLOYEE: There hasn't been a distribution order yet.

SIGNORA: What your office is doing is really not fair, because the workers . . . get all these things, and the poor sick people, who are dying of hunger, don't even get medicine . . . they get nothing.

A "law-abiding citizen" apparently has the clout to reach an inspector in the same department:

SIGNORA: Nothing for people with sicknesses?

INSPECTOR: Not yet.

SIGNORA: When does that mean? When we're dead? In April you didn't give us anything. In May, likewise . . .

INSPECTOR: Madam, it's not my fault.

SIGNORA: All you do is think of the workers. That's because you're afraid of them, because they raise a stink and rebel. . . . The law-abiding citizens

have to die. That's the reality of it! The rest is all lies, all bluff, all deception.
. . . What a life! What a cross to bear! From this, you die!

Finally, an unnamed *signore*, a gentleman resident of the Grand Hotel,
one of Rome's finest, calls a certain Signorina Brandi to tell her of experiencing a form of rude awakening:

RESIDENT: A curious thing happened to me yesterday morning. At about
ten o'clock, I was going to mass at Santa Maria degli Angeli and I was eating
a half of a sandwich with some paper wrapped around it. I was down to the
last bite when a rather well-dressed young man came up to me and asked,
"Are you having your breakfast?" I kind of smiled and he said, "You wouldn't
have a little piece of bread for me?" I was simply mortified because there was
nothing left. His face got all flushed and he asked me to forgive him, and he
just went on his way.

SIGNORINA: Poor soul. He must have been really hungry. It certainly is
terrifying, all the more so since, as you say, he seemed an upstanding sort of
person.[18]

In the second half of May, the Fascists and the Germans stepped up their
food handouts in the piazzas of the neediest and most volatile districts, distributing packets of either flour or rice in neighborhoods such as Trastevere,
Garbatella, and Testaccio. With the Allies on the move, the air raids on German targets had been intensified again, and though American bombs continued to cause civilian casualties, the German presence was resented. The
elitist fear of the common Romans rising up loomed once more, and the
flow of free belly-filler staples to the masses became the latest moat around
the citadels of power. A sign of the level of anxiety was recorded by one diarist. "General Mälzer," he wrote, "could not refrain even now from having
the photographers there, but this time he did not have the soldiers retrieve
the food after the photographs had been taken. The madman, who had ruled
Rome like a Nero, was nearing the end of this reign of terror."[19]

YET the terror reigned on. On April 3, the day Socialist Partisan commander Vassalli had been arrested, Don Giuseppe Morosini, the priest who,
of the two imprisoned in the Via Tasso, was not chosen by Kappler to die in
the Ardeatine Caves, went before the firing squad at Fort Bravetta. It was
the first execution in the ten days since the massacre, but the pace quick-

ened, with eighteen men slated to die at the same killing ground over the next few weeks—among them Vassalli's cousin Fabrizio Vassalli, of the Matteotti Brigades. The Socialists were to be especially hard-hit in the post-Ardeatine period, notably at the leadership level, with the arrest of the distinguished trade unionist Bruno Buozzi and the assassination of Eugenio Colorni, the head of the Party's underground newspaper, *Avanti!*

The scourge of the Roman Resistance, Kappler, had graduated from relatively innocuous police work beginnings into a stereotypical Gestapo homicidal chieftain. But he was outdone by Pietro Koch, who would rack up 435 arrests in his four months in Rome. Together, though rarely working together, they had by now all but demolished the most vigorous part of the Roman underground, despite extraordinary feats of endurance by many of their prisoners in withstanding torture.

Kappler would always deny that he personally tortured his prisoners, and Koch would only admit to conducting interrogations patterned after what he called "the American third-degree."[20] After the war ended it would be difficult to determine who did what to whom except in the case of Captain Erich Priebke. His years of heeling to Kappler had transported him to prominence as the subtlest and most effective grand inquisitor of the Via Tasso. His own subsequent denials might have gone further had it not been for the recent arrest of Peter Tompkins's agent Arrigo Paladini.

Paladini had been an artillery officer who had fought at the pyramid, then crossed the lines to join the OSS, recruited by Captain Bourgoin. Code-named Eugenio, he had been sent back in November, under Captain Pacatte's command, to work with the Partisans north of Rome. He had been reassigned to Menicanti's and then Sorrentino's operations, growing increasingly disenchanted with the shenanigans of both men. After Cervo's capture, he sought out and teamed up with Tompkins, above all in the effort to reestablish radio communications with the base. Now, delivered up by Sorrentino, he was in Priebke's hands. Paladini would leave a rare account of Priebke as self-taught tormentor with a signature style.

"I remember Captain Priebke's interrogation method perfectly," Paladini wrote. "He hit me in the chest and in the testicles with his trademark brass knuckles that he used on the prisoners." Having undergone three Priebke interrogations and several more conducted by others, Paladini observed the differences:

> Priebke was never offensive or vulgar in the way he addressed me and
> he never lost his temper. His recurring line was, "I'm sorry, but with me

you're going to have to talk. You will be shot anyway, but you can avoid needless suffering." He said this often, but then added another threat: "If you don't talk I will be forced to shoot your father." In the third interrogation, speaking in a cutting, icy tone, he told me that my father's execution had already taken place. . . . It wasn't really true, however. My father had died in a concentration camp months earlier, but I didn't know that. . . .[21]

Only two years later would Paladini learn that. Until then he would feel himself responsible for his father's death, believing that Priebke had in fact had the elder Paladini shot because of his own refusal to talk. For the rest of his life, his widow would later recall, he would often awake in the middle of the night screaming.[22]

———————

ELENA was both sick and starving, spitting blood from the lung ailment she had contracted and doubling over with cramps brought on from attempts to drink water after five days of not eating. That was how Paolo had found her when he came down to Rome from the hills of Palestrina to bring her back to the *macchia*, the natural habitat of guerrilla warriors, where the fight was shifting now. The raging urge to kill the traitorous Guglielmo Blasi, now an operative of the Koch Gang, had developed into a less emotional plan to assassinate Koch himself. But that plan, too, had had a betrayer.

While Elena, stricken by her illness, sought a respite to recover, Paolo had departed. He had been named by the CLN as military commander of all the Partisan groups operating between the Alban Hills and Cassino, including those of the other political parties in the area, the Socialists, Christian Democrats, and the CLN's new partner, the Badoglio military front. Having established contact, he had returned for Elena, finding her in worse condition than ever. But the next morning—it was the day of the breakthrough at the Gustav Line—they set out together to do battle in the path of Kesselring's armies.

It would be a long day's journey they would always remember. Taking the Via Casalina, Highway 6, knapsacks on their backs, they traveled by bicycle on the flat and by foot on the upgrades. "I put her on the bar of the bike," Paolo later recalled. "She was so light, I could have pedaled uphill as well, if I'd been in shape, but I was tired and hungry myself." The mid-May sky was cloudless and ablaze with a summery sun, patrolled by Allied aircraft looking for anything German on the ground, swooping down and attacking the occasional military vehicle that went by. The asphalt was pocked with bomb craters new and old, and the drainage ditches running alongside the road were filled with burned-out trucks and cars, cleared from wherever they had been hit. Some of them had the rotting corpses of German soldiers inside.

At about noon, a distant rumbling behind them soon grew into the ear-splitting din of a formation of low-flying fighter planes dropping at a sharp angle of attack. To Paolo and Elena it seemed as if they themselves were the target, but just beyond them lay a stretch of railroad tracks and a small building already half-destroyed. The aircraft now barely above their heads opened fire. The couple dove into a gully just under the strafing, landing in the shade of one wispy tree and in one another's arms, clinging to life. Suddenly, a spray of machine-gun bullets hit the tree like a chain saw, slicing the trunk in two. The treetop, bearing a bloom and the new leaves of spring, fell on the gully, burying Paolo and Elena. They were completely covered but uninjured.

> We just stayed there [Elena remembered], lying still, waiting, expecting the planes to circle for another strafing. With a deafening roar, they came in low again, the leaves above us trembling in the rush of air. But they held their fire, gaining altitude and at last disappeared in a bank of clouds. We remained lying on the ground for a few minutes, close to one another, still overcome with fear; then, unexpectedly, Paolo began to kiss me. It came as such a surprise. We had both been so frightened and then we were both embracing, thinking that this journey might separate us forever.[23]

Paolo doesn't remember a fallen tree, only diving for cover from the strafing and holding on to dear life together in the shade and the fragrance of wild rosebushes. Their daughter would be born in February; they would name her Elena.

It was dusk when they reached Palestrina, exhausted and above all famished. A farmer offered them milk, which they nursed until they slept, thinking it "the best thing in the world." Over the next few days, Paolo took command of a motley brigade of farmhands, draft dodgers, and a band of Russian prisoners escaped from a German camp. By night they fought the Germans going to and from the front, the front itself drawing audibly closer each day. Their ranks began to grow. Elena began to heal. Paolo recovered lost vigor. "Within a short while," he recalls, "we were profoundly transformed. Life in the open air, the help we got from the farmers, the sense that danger was not quite as close as it had been in the guerrilla fight in Rome, and most of all the feeling that the end was near had restored the strength we needed for that last battle."

One morning, Paolo and Elena could see uneven movement on the mountain trails of Palestrina. Clusters of German soldiers hobbling, trudging along, some heading northwest, some northeast. Disheveled and dirty, they were downtrodden men, trying to make their way to Rome. The last battle had begun.

———————

AT SIX o'clock on May 23, a misty morning at Anzio, the Germans were again taken by surprise when the Allies turned on the big guns once more. In a matter of hours, General Truscott's VI Corps, four months and a day after landing, burst out of the beachhead, leaving the young blood in the sand behind them. Although two British divisions were with them, they were forces attached to the Fifth Army, making the breakout an all-American enterprise, a distinction that had grown in importance to the Americans.

Smashing through hastily scrambled-up enemy resistance, Truscott moved swiftly but bewilderedly, trapped in the cross fire of an unequivocal order from Alexander to head east for Valmontone and the defiant will of Mark Clark to lead the Fifth Army northwest, into the Alban Hills on a straight line to Rome. Truscott would remain confused, but Clark's defiance had ballast, British ballast. Back in September, when the Fifth Army alone had fought most of the ferocious battle to hold on to the bridgehead at Salerno, Clark had discovered Alexander directing his press officers to claim most of the credit for the British forces. Repressing his resentment, Clark had sought advice from Montgomery. It was their first meeting, the start of a long friendship. Montgomery advised Clark, "From time to time you will get instructions from Alex that you won't understand. When you do, just tell him to go to hell."[24]

The showdown now had erupted on the eve of the breakout, when Clark moved to the beachhead to be at Truscott's side. Clark had been shocked to learn of Alexander's peremptory directive to Truscott, and though it had come from his own superior, Clark viewed it as Alexander "trying to run my army" and, worse, as yet another proof of British machinations to rob him of Rome. Clark had confronted Alexander, again arguing that the Operation Buffalo plan to wipe out the German Tenth Army by interception on Highway 6 at Valmontone "couldn't be done."[25] But he had been unable to sway Alexander and had softened his own position. The American now counseled a "flexible," see-how-it-goes attitude, while maintaining a readiness to exploit either way, depending on events. Alexander, never less than polite, apparently took that as no threat to his ultimate authority, and the matter was put aside. But Clark read it otherwise. In the name of flexibility, he was going to Rome.

His problem, however, grew larger than life over the next two days with the spectacular success of the Fifth Army. The II Corps, which had broken out of the Gustav Line and, as envisaged in Diadem, advanced north along the west coast, linked up with Truscott's VI Corps as the German defenses on both fronts—Mackensen's Fourteenth Army at Anzio and Vietinghoff's Tenth Army to the south—began to falter earlier than expected. According to the official Fifth Army history, by the morning of the 25th, "the scene was one of hurried retreat [by the Germans]." Enemy resistance along the route to Valmontone had crumbled, and "the first objectives of Operation Buffalo were all in our hands by the evening of 25 May. Here as on the southern front our victory had been quicker, less expensive, and more devastating to the enemy that had been hoped. . . . Thus far our attack was a superb success."[26]

The inescapable consequence of such success, with Valmontone beckoning to be taken, was that cutting off Highway 6 and trapping the Tenth Army seemed all but certain. Alexander's planning appeared to be flawless, sprung from a vision in a crystal ball, and Clark's see-what-happens position seemed already obsolete. That was when the American made an audacious decision.

Historian Carlo D'Este, who had access to primary material never seen by earlier writers and who has written the most thoroughly researched military study to date of the battle for Rome, assessed the significance of that "memorable day" of May 25. "Mark Clark," he states, "the commander who had made the capture of Rome his raison d'être, had earlier that afternoon deliberately committed what must rank as one of the most misguided blunders made by any Allied commander during World War II. About to win a stunning victory that would not only have gained him the glittering prize of Rome virtually without a fight but would have earned him immortality as a great battlefield commander, Mark Clark suddenly dismembered Operation Buffalo and in the process sparked a controversy that continues to this day."[27]

D'Este goes on to characterize Clark's decision as a calculated act "as militarily stupid as it was insubordinate."[28] What Clark actually did was to go right *and* left, instead of choosing between the left turn toward Rome and the right to Valmontone. The major thrust of the VI Corps was now northwest to the Alban Hills, while a small contingent made for Highway 6 so Clark could avoid disobeying Alexander's order. D'Este, examining parts of Clark's diaries kept secret for nearly half a century, removes all doubt that Clark used deceptive tactics to forestall being overruled, but no level of analysis can predict the outcome of a battle never fought. The answer to how the German Tenth Army might have fared remains stuck in the what-if parlor game of history. Kesselring's resolve and Hitler's orders to keep the escape route for the Tenth Army open at all costs were bound to stiffen accordingly. Moreover, no amount of gainsaying can alter the plus side of Clark's decision.

Alexander would never speak of insubordination, instead uttering disingenuous expressions of disdain. "I had always assured General Clark in conversation," he later wrote, "that Rome would be entered by his army; and I can only assume that the immediate lure of Rome for its publicity value persuaded him to switch the direction of his advance." Alexander's assurances were less than credible.[29] Clark's suspicions about everyone else were not unfounded. Rome, not Valmontone, was the prize, not for the cheap-sounding "publicity," but, as recognized by Roosevelt and Stalin as well as Churchill, for the intangible propaganda effect of its capture—infinitely mightier than that of cutting Highway 6. The drive for Rome energized soldiers. But the prize would lose its value the moment Eisenhower's Overlord would hit the beaches of Normandy. "You see," one Fifth Army officer told military historians Adleman and Walton, "we had been through this bitter winter at Cassino. . . . Now, the prospect of taking Rome was like sunshine, breaking out after four months of being locked in a kind of dungeon. Even before Rome was captured, the jump-off attack was a tremendous psychological lift. Down to the lowest private there was a sort of resurgence of spirit. I remember the feelings of my fellow officers that by God we weren't going to let the British get there first!"[30]

LISTENING to Radio London in Rome, Mother Mary, with her unfailing acumen, saw through the high-handed hypocrisy. The Allies were coming nearer, she noted, but were still on the far side of the Alban Hills, the last line of German defense. She wrote:

A BBC commentator says breezily: "Rome, of course, is a prize, but how much better for General Alexander to surround Kesselring and settle his hash before entering the city." Oh yes? Is it? We are not strategists, armchair or otherwise, but we have a practical knowledge of the urgent need of liberating Rome.[31]

That was her diary entry for June 1. A day earlier, Fifth Army General Fred Walker, commander of the 36th Texas Division, had discovered a gap in the Caesar Line, that final barrier to Rome. It lay on the slopes below the town of Velletri, a stronghold in the heights of the Alban Hills defense perimeter under Mackensen's Fourteenth Army. This would not be the final battle. Men who had been through it all, up from the landings on Italian shores, were not home yet and some would still die. But correspondent Eric Sevareid, who was with the men at Velletri, the Eternal City no more than a dozen miles and a single obstacle away, makes that distant time live again. He wrote:

> Velletri . . . is an ancient town, and Nero once sent his favorite mistress into exile there, but the tired and dirty men of the American 36th Division didn't know about that and they wouldn't have cared. They had been dug in the vineyards before the town for several days, harassed by snipers and machine guns around them and eighty-eights from the German batteries above Velletri. They had to take the town somehow, they had to break the highway-railway defense belt here because these slopes formed the last German breastworks defending Rome. . . .

In a predawn incursion on May 31, two regiments of the 36th crossed the enemy line, capturing the single German guard post without firing a shot. When Mackensen heard of the breach some hours later it was too late. His counterattack was swiftly rebuffed, his forces surrendering Velletri to the Texans the next day. Sevareid recorded a moment of uncertainty when the shooting stopped:

> One Italian entered a house, immediately ran out in panic and shouted, "Tedeschi!" meaning there were Germans inside. Americans burst in and found, in the dim lit room, a large mirror and nothing more. The excited Italian had been confronting himself. The conquest was over in a few minutes. Reporters walked through the streets, prickly with shrapnel, to a house on the outer edge. Inside were four GIs, their rifles hardly cool, playing poker in their shirtsleeves while two Italian girls heated their C rations on the stove. A few hours earlier they had been cooking at the same stove for the Germans.

With Velletri gone, the Alban Hill defense line was irreparably penetrated and our Divisions smashed into the disorganized Germans around
to the left, down Highway 6 and to the right—Rome lay shimmering and
undefendable straight ahead. Many outfits deserve the credit for the
whole operation, but those of us who were present will always remember
the men of the 36th, climbing silently in the night behind the enemy,
armed with little but their American competence and a personal faith in
their quiet, retiring general who had never let them down. If Generals
Alexander and Clark received the key to the city of Rome, it was General
Walker who turned the key and handed it to them.[32]

Walker and the 36th, which had been shunned as a hard-luck to bad-luck
division in a string of setbacks going back to Salerno, had gained a new reputation. They would be celebrated now as having opened the way to the
gates of Rome. Clark's own diary records his chief of staff saying that the
news of Velletri's fall "caused us all to turn handsprings,"[33] the head of Fifth
Army presumably among them.

TWENTY

ROME ETERNAL

WOULD Rome burn? Would the Colosseum fall—as in the ancient prophecy "When falls the Colosseum, Rome shall fall / And when Rome falls—the world"?[1] Few people believed that Hitler would pardon the capital of the traitor-nation he had vowed to punish—not while his own capital was burning and falling, bombarded almost nightly by enemy air power.

The Romans, who had come to feel the Führer's wrath, believed what they saw and heard, the window-rattling thunder coming out of perfect skies, the distant fires already encircling Rome. "The Germans would resist to the extreme," went the rumor cited by Elsa Morante, "and anyway they would first blow up all those famous places they had mined, and the Pope was getting ready to flee along with the Vatican's fleet of armored planes to someplace unknown."[2]

The Pope in fact was said to have told Polizeiführer Wolff in their secret audience that he would never leave Rome voluntarily, adding, "My place is here, and here I will struggle on to the end for the Christian commandments."[3] But down to the last moment Pius XII and the vast information-gathering apparatus of the Vatican would have no inkling of whether the Germans would defend against the Allied advance on Rome. The truth was that no one would know with any certainty, not the Allies, less so the Resistance, and not even the Germans. In the end, only Mussolini would express his desire to see Rome flattened into rubble like the abbey at Monte Cassino, and only the Pope would lift his voice in a warning of damnation, deeming that "whosoever raises his hand against Rome will be guilty of matricide before the civilized world and the eternal judgment of God."[4] Others, belligerents or allies, would agree on a more practical approach: Rome must be saved, unless it must be destroyed.

The tired contrivances for an open city would die hard, but seemed already buried when on May 27 Ambassador Weizsäcker asked Monsignor Tardini if the Vatican had a concrete plan to rescue the city. The answer was a flat no, but, Tardini explained, the Holy See would proceed from a simple premise: to the Allies, it would say, "Do not attack"; to the Germans, "Do not defend." Reporting on his meeting, Tardini wrote:

> At this point, I said that *personally*, not only am I certain of the good intentions of the German government, but I am likewise persuaded by the [military] tactics of Field Marshal Kesselring that . . . at a certain moment he will abandon Rome. This observation, a casual remark on my part but spoken in a tone of, you might say, certainty, brought an instant and spontaneous reaction from my interlocutor. Shaking his head in disagreement, he said, "No, I don't have this impression," adding that in his view, Kesselring had no intention of simply walking away from Rome. At this, I immediately objected, "But if he remains in Rome, that will provoke attack—and ruin!" The ambassador, smiling wryly, replied: "The attack on Rome will depend on Roosevelt's standing in the next elections." [5]

It was a cryptic remark that, despite lengthy parsing by the papal pundits, would never be understood to anyone's satisfaction. But the Vatican worried that by defending, Kesselring could force the Americans to damage Rome and so turn American Catholic voters against Roosevelt, which would somehow help the Nazi cause. This fear that political interests on one side or the other would now be a factor in the preservation of Rome brought out the Catholic hierarchy in America, led by the archbishops of New York, Chicago, and Philadelphia, to warn against turning Rome into a battlefield. The Catholics of America, they declared, stood united behind Pius XII in his tireless effort to save his diocese, "the Mother Church of Christianity." [6] The Holy Father was no doubt grateful for these kind words, but a Gallup poll taken at the time showed that three out of four Americans, Catholics included, approved bombing *anything*, be it historic or religious, or both, for a military necessity—powerful affirmation of Roosevelt's well-known position. [7] Thus could the Colosseum fall.

• • •

MARK CLARK thought less about saving Rome than getting there. After penetrating the Caesar Line at Velletri, he turned the full brunt of the Fifth Army on Valmontone and Highway 6. It was too late to attempt the cutoff of the German Tenth Army but not to order his men "to destroy, discourage, disrupt, disorganize, and any other ds you can think of, any enemy forces" as part of the new mission to roll through Valmontone and take a left on Highway 6, while killing as many Germans as possible on the way into Rome. Finally conceding Clark his due, Alexander moved the Eighth Army out of his way. The British would pass east of the city. Rome, unshared, would be Clark's at last. "The agreement gave me a good deal of satisfaction," Clark said. "Now all we had to do was go out and get Rome." [8]

Like everyone else, Clark was unaware of whether the Germans would withdraw without a fight. "Do not know if the Krauts are going to defend," he said in a telegram to his men as they began the final approach. "It is urgently desired that private and public property in Rome not be damaged. Firing into Rome depends upon Krauts. If opposed, Battalion Commanders and higher Commanders have power to eliminate same by fire and movement." [9]

To his endless consternation, Clark would still have to dodge others trying to sneak into the line of the Americans entering Rome. Even a British contingent, in spite of the orders to steer clear, would make a breakaway try, and the French, the Poles, and a handful of Yugoslavs would, too. But the nature of the race had changed. For the Fifth Army it had become a question of which *American* unit would cross the finish line first, the VI Corps coming over the Alban Hills or the II Corps up Highway 6—a sporty-sounding endeavor but deadly serious in the event. For Clark, however, now it was above all a race against the clock. D-Day for Overlord was imminent, but he was unaware of the actual date, certain only that it could be counted in hours and that he was alone among his top men in knowing how close the outcome would be. The Germans were falling back, but a tough, rearguard resistance to delay the Allied advance was succeeding. "Pray hard tonight," Clark told his Chief of Staff on the eve of the final push. [10]

THE GERMAN rearguard action to impede the Fifth Army's passage through the Alban Hills was itself under attack by the Partisans in Paolo's command. Paolo and Elena were operating according to a plan that was to culminate in the much-discussed insurrection. It was, to be sure, now or never. At Palestrina, the Fifth Army was in their backyard, the shells shrieking over their heads. The Partisans' objective was to descend from the hills with the Fifth Army, escorting the Americans into Rome. At the same time, they were to distribute arms to civilians along the way, organizing a rolling uprising. Although such an entry was far from Mark Clark's mind, the Military Council had in fact reached this agreement with the Allied Command, the latter committed to supplying the weapons. Radio London was to signal the moment to swing into action by broadcasting the phrase, "The snow has fallen on the mountain." [11]

By the beginning of June, Paolo and Elena had returned to Rome for further instructions. Their fellow Gappisti Giovanni and Maria, they were told, had already linked up with Free French Marshal Juin in the mountains southeast of Rome, and were attached to an Eighth Army unit. Paolo and Elena were then sent to make contact with the couple to prepare a site suitable for a nighttime parachute drop of weapons and munitions. [12] As for the insurrection, final go-ahead depended on the message from Radio London. In the meantime, they were to continue to follow the current Allied directive to all Partisans to help clear every path for the Allied march on Rome. That was June 3, but by then, Paolo and Elena, along with the contact who briefed them, were working in a vacuum. The word had not yet reached them that on the 2nd the CLN and the Military Council, right, left, and center, along with Badoglio and his King, were at last in perfect accord with one another and the Allies: the snow of insurgency would not fall; the Togliatti doctrine, finding a patch of common ground where even Stalin and the Pope could stand, would prevail. There would be no insurrection in the Eternal City.

ON THE next day, June 3, Kesselring received orders from Hitler on what to do with Rome, though what the Führer ordered would never be clear. The man who had almost always insisted on a fight to the death and had already buried whole cities is often credited with saving Rome. But Kesselring, a city-slayer himself, though on a lesser scale, would need the credit of having saved Rome more than his irredeemable leader would and, when it was safe to do so, would arrogate it all to himself. "I refused to budge from my determination to keep the battle out of Rome," he would later write, letting his readers imagine who was trying to budge him. [13] A more plausible scenario than those of a sentimental Führer or a paladin Kesselring is that Hitler left his commander on the scene the freedom to decide Rome's fate in the same manner as proclaimed by the Allies—according to military necessity.

Kesselring's exit strategy supports this pragmatic approach. The moment he decided to pull out was the same moment that the guessing game of whether he would defend or not intensified. All day of the 3rd, while many Fascists were burning documents, gathering their nest eggs, and slipping out of town, Kesselring continued to move men and materiel to the front. It was to look like occupation business as usual, and pleasure too: that evening General Mälzer, at Kesselring's beckoning, led a showy entourage to the opera for a performance by the world-renowned tenor (and Nazi-fraternizing) Beniamino Gigli in *Un Ballo in Maschera.*

Meanwhile, at 10:30 P.M., Weizsäcker, playing his part, met in the Vatican with Monsignori Montini and Tardini. The two prelates, an hour or so earlier, had been informed that the German withdrawal was not imminent. Now, the ambassador told them that he had just conferred with Kesselring, whose dearest wish was to save Rome and with that in mind had formulated a proposal. All that was lacking was an assist from the Vatican to obtain the consent of the Allies. The historic center of Rome, mapped out to include its greatest treasures, would, according to the proposal, be recognized as an open city by both belligerents. The Vatican officials immediately saw the offer as a ploy. It appeared aimed at creating a corridor of safe passage for a German retreat, leaving the rest of Rome a battle zone. In a remarkable airing of a long-standing grievance, the Pope's men all but accused the Germans of deceit—occupying, not respecting, the Open City to supply the front. Nine months of violations had continued right up to that same day, they noted, having observed artillery moving through the *centro storico* in the predawn hours. They doubted that the Allies would agree not to set foot where the Germans had gone before them. Nevertheless they would notify them of Kesselring's proposal and see what, if any, counteroffer it might bring.[14]

Weizsäcker, unruffled by what amounted to a papal scolding, stuck to the script, saying that there was no urgency. Kesselring was calm, unhurried. It was nearing midnight when the German ambassador left the Vatican. At that hour, as Monsignor Giovannetti, the junior man at the meeting, noted in his account, just beyond Saint Peter's Square where it gives onto the Via della Conciliazione, German Tiger tanks rumbled on the pavement, in yet another violation of the Open City. But for the first time in all those months of traffic to the front, there was a difference: they were going the other way.

• • •

THAT NIGHT, Mother Mary posed a question to her diary: "Are you imitating the small boy who whistled when going down a dark alley when you want to repeat that it will be all right? That the Germans . . . will fade out of Rome silently, will fold their tents like the Arabs, or however else the poets would express it[?] Yes, I think it is a comfort to do so, or even to write it. Here goes, again: *I do not think that the Germans will make Rome a battlefield.* (But the fighting is very close tonight.)"[15]

———————

ELEFANTE! Italian for the code word "Elephant"—signifying the Allied entry into Rome—had been radioed from London on the 2nd, but the liberators were yet to be seen.

From the first hour of Sunday, June 4, to daybreak, Carlo Trabucco, unable to sleep because of the noise and his excitement, watched thousands of German vehicles converge under a brilliant full moon, lining up at the Ponte Milvio to cross the Tiber.[16] They rolled onto the Via Cassia and the Flaminia, the consular roads that had carried the Romans of olden times to triumphs in the land where these soldiers yearned to return even in defeat.

"The Huns are retreating!" de Wyss recorded with unjournalistic elation. "The Huns are leaving the city!" She had heard an Allied Radio report that the German lines in the Alban Hills had been breached and that the road to Rome was open. "I ran upstairs to the terrace, from which, with binoculars, I had an excellent view. There is no doubt. They are retreating! My heart beats. Finally they go away! They are retreating!"[17]

In the Vatican, the office of the Secretariat was going through the formalities of transmitting Kesselring's latest open-city proposal to the Allies. In the meantime, Monsignor Giovannetti kept an eye trained on what was unfolding outside:

The soldiers were retreating orderly, but they looked spent and humiliated. . . . They had requisitioned anything with wheels, private cars, horse-drawn taxis, even oxcarts with the oxen. It was an interminable procession. Some were marching with huge, overstuffed backpacks, carrying their weapons in their hands. The people stood by and watched them, saying nothing. A few boys offered them something to drink. Soldiers who for nine months had fought with valor against a superior enemy . . . passing by, showing all the signs of a terrible battle. How many of them still believe in the promise of Hitler's Thousand-Year Reich?[18]

Elsa Morante would write of an endless line of trucks going through the Piazza Venezia up the Corso:

They were packed, brimming with German soldiers, blackened with soot and stained with blood. The people stared at them, saying nothing. They looked at no one.[19]

De Wyss, daring for the first time to take out her camera, was taking pictures:

Finally I saw the beaten German army retreating. There were lorries and wagons so overloaded with soldiers that they all hung around in bunches; carts with soldiers, also soldiers on horseback, peasant vehicles crammed with dead-tired men. Once soldiers passed riding oxen, and finally came endless rows of those going on foot. Their faces gray with fatigue, eyes popping out, mouths wide open, they limped, barefoot, dragging their rifles after them. I remembered the same army entering France —contemptuous, almighty, trampling over the weaker. I remembered being thrown into a ditch by them. Now I was witnessing their defeat. My jaws clenched.[20]

Watching in the *centro storico*, Mother Mary, unlike Monsignor Giovanetti, saw disarray, noting that "the defeated Huns were escaping in disorder." She wrote:

The Germans went on, wild-eyed, unshaven, unkempt, on foot, in stolen cars, in horse-drawn vehicles, even in carts belonging to the street cleaning department. There was no attempt at military formation. Some of them dragged small ambulances with wounded in them. They went, some with revolvers in their hands, some with rifles cocked. . . . Whereas last September they came with machine guns trained on the Romans, it was a different matter now. They were frightened. They had a clear idea of the strength of the underground movement, the power of the armed patriots and their determination to take action when and if necessary.[21]

ON THIS day of freedom's battle won, Paolo and Elena had shed their *noms de guerre* like skins left in the sun, reemerging as Carla Capponi and

Rosario "Sasà" Bentivegna, though forever changed. A reassignment to monitor the German retreat had brought them back to San Lorenzo to stand in the rubble where the bombs had fallen from twenty angels over Rome one summer ago. Now the couple wore the distinguishing armband of the Roman *partigiani*, the green, white, and red of the Italian flag, with the full name of the CLN spelled out around it. They were among the many Partisans, all of them armed, in the front ranks of the people lining the way of the German withdrawal. There would be no insurrection, but in the past twenty-four hours, the Partisans had been given a new role and their orders were clear.

Early that morning, Allied leaflets had rained from the skies with a message from General Alexander to the people of Rome. The liberation was at hand, and the citizens of the Eternal City were asked to stand "shoulder to shoulder" in a common cause. "Do everything in your power," the liberators said, "to prevent the destruction of the city." Among the items on a long to-do list of counter-sabotage activity were blocking the detonation of mined bridges and government buildings; protecting the lines and facilities of communications, the power grids and public utilities, and rail and motorized transportation; and assuring free passage for the Allies to pursue the enemy. The Romans were to remove any barriers or other obstructions on the roads and in the streets. The message, repeated all day on Allied Radio, concluded:

> Citizens of Rome, this is not the time for demonstrations. Obey these directions and go on with your regular work. Rome is yours! Your job is to save the city, ours is to destroy the enemy.

It was a tall order for a severely tried, malnourished populace. The single admonition in the same message to "hide your food" was almost eloquent in revealing the true state of affairs and probably the advice most observed. The Resistance fighters, however, had by now received these Allied instructions as firm orders from their own commanders. In spite of internal dissent and the unhealable disillusionment of the *insurrezione mancata*, the military arm of the Resistance at that moment was the most powerful, disciplined, and battle-ready force in Rome—more so than even the spiritless Germans in retreat. In accepting the responsibility of guarantors of a peaceful withdrawal, the Partisans would in fact take de facto possession of the city, stepping into the hiatus between the German departure and the arrival of the Allies. The situation so dreaded by the political right and most of all by the Pope—Rome in the hands of the "irresponsible elements"—was about to occur, though it would begin and end that afternoon, a monumental fear reduced to a pinprick of pleasure not pain.

———————————

IN TERMS of the "responsible" parties, a power vacuum already existed and had since the start of that day. The diplomats in the two German embassies in Rome, the Villa Wolkonsky and the Villa Napoleon, had either already departed, including Consul Möllhausen, or, as in the case of Weizsäcker and Kessel, would simply move into the accommodations afforded by the Vatican, replacing the Allied representatives, Tittmann and Osborne. Commandant Mälzer was still in Rome that morning, no longer "king" but immobilized, last seen by one of Tompkins's agents "stinking drunk, cackling in lousy French and in a state of funk." Dollmann, as was his style, took a melancholy stroll around the city to bid farewell to his favorite Berninis and Bramantes, and, on Kesselring's orders, departed for Florence. Kappler was still burning documents in the Via Tasso early that morning, but Priebke, who had already sent off his wife and their two Roman-born children to his next destination, SS headquarters in Verona, now set out alone in his two-seater Fiat. His first stop was a last rendezvous with the Fascist flame of the silver screen, Laura Nucci. Much later, as an old man awaiting trial in a Roman prison, he would remember that sweet-sorrow good-bye:

> I was feeling very sad that day. We had come to Rome as allies and were leaving in defeat, the American troops at our heels. In the early hours of that morning, I was in my "Topolino," heading for Via Ruggero Fauro, a quiet little street in the Parioli district of Rome. I wanted to say farewell to Laura, to see her for the last time. While I was driving, I thought of all the times I had been in that street, always in the evening and always in civilian clothes, with my trusty Mauser hidden in one boot. Now, she would see me in uniform, armed to the teeth. . . .
>
> Our last good-byes were very brief. We had to leave Rome in a rush. I went down the stairs without looking back. But Laura ran after me all the way to the car, crying, "Wait, wait for me, I'm coming with you. . . ." She was practically begging. I got behind the wheel, turned away from her and took off, catching up with my companions. . . . [22]

At about the same time, the Koch Gang fled in a column of cars headed for Milan and further infamy, while Questore Caruso, he too in the company of a convoy of henchmen, took off in the same direction. Speeding away in a powerful Alfa Romeo and packing a small fortune that included a rather mysterious collection of women's jewelry, he saw his getaway end just outside of Rome. He was caught in an Allied strafing near Lake Bracciano, veered off the road, and crashed into a tree. The bumbling police chief, seriously injured, was rescued and rushed to a hospital still in German-held territory, but this last bit of luck would run out a few days later when local Partisans would hand him over to the Allies.

Sometime before noon that Sunday, Kappler, passing under the life-sized portrait of the Führer in the lobby for the last time, finally left the Via Tasso. Alone and abandoned, the surviving prisoners remained locked in their cells, unfed and unaware of their reprieve. Three days earlier, on June 1, the Fascist authorities informed the Vatican that they were willing to release not only the five political prisoners in Regina Coeli for whom the Pope had intervened but everyone in their custody. They expressed a fear, however, that the Germans would object, and sought the Vatican's help. Monsignor Montini recorded speaking to Weizsäcker about the matter but not the result.[23]

One possible result was that on June 2, which coincided with Pius XII's name day—Sant'Eugenio on the church calendar—Partisan commander Giuliano Vassalli was summoned from his cell in the Via Tasso by Kappler. "You can thank the Holy Father," Kappler told him, "that you're not being sent to the wall, which is what you deserve, Vassalli, right?" Vassalli, who had been expecting execution, was unaware of the Pope's intervention, but wasted no time inquiring further, when Father Pfeiffer suddenly appeared and Kappler turned him over to the papal emissary, saying, "Don't ever let me see you again."[24]

On the next day, however, six other Partisan prisoners, members of the monarchist Military Front, did go to the wall, taken from Regina Coeli to the firing squad at Fort Bravetta. That same evening of the 3rd, as the general retreat of the occupiers began, fourteen prisoners at the Via Tasso, their hands tied behind their backs, were put aboard a truck heading north. They were an odd mixture of men that included the trade-union leader Bruno Buozzi and three Italian operatives of the OSS: Tompkins's agent Edmondo Di Pillo; Vincenzo Bonocore, the radio operator who had betrayed Cervo; and the self-appointed Fifth-Army representative, Enrico Sorrentino, who had sold out another Tompkins man, Arrigo Paladini. Paladini himself, suffering two broken ribs, was among those who boarded a second, larger truck crammed with about thirty prisoners in all. The truck carrying Buozzi and the others departed first, proceeding in the outward flow along the Via Cassia, but a few miles out of Rome it halted at the suburban hamlet of La Storta. The prisoners were made to descend behind some trees, forced to their knees, and one by one slain in the bullet-to-neck manner used by Kappler in the massacre in the Ardeatine Caves.[25]

In the second truck, Paladini was in the company of the Gappisti turned in by Guglielmo Blasi, including Spartaco, Raoul, and Duilio, all of whom, like Paladini, were under a sentence of death by now and physically gutted. This truck, however, either by breakdown or sabotage, had failed to depart, and these men were again locked in their cells, this time unguarded, miraculously spared, a key-turn or a battering ram away from freedom. They did not have long to wait, for they were rescued within hours by an unruly crowd of Romans drunk on liberation air.

KESSELRING'S endgame—rearguard resistance to slow the Allied advance until his troops had been safely withdrawn—had choked the one-way traffic on the roads to Rome all day long. The run for the prize crept along Highways 6 and 7 and other roads, cheered on by the Romans along the roadsides, but at times there was only standstill. Eric Sevareid, preparing a home-bound live broadcast of the great event, later recalled the scene from his own position at noon:

> Rome was just ahead, yet all the city proper was obscured in haze and smoke. Guns and smoke sounded loudly near us and from somewhere in the city came the dull sound of explosions . . . There was a curious feeling in the air; a combined spirit of battle and holiday. Reporters sat typing with their machines balanced on their knees. . . . People hung out of every window and gathered before every gate. The girls and children tossed flowers at the two lines of slowly walking American soldiers, and bouquets were now displayed on the turrets of our tanks.
>
> Two old women approached me as I was typing. They insisted upon shaking my hand. One held out a blond baby for me to kiss. . . . There was singing on the road, and a wedding party came along, walking toward the rear in the middle of the highway between the two lines of troops. The bride was all in gray with hat to match, and she carried flowers in her arm as though she were stepping down the aisle of a church. One or two of the soldiers threw her a kiss, and a few shouted gratuitous advice. . . .
>
> Rome was falling, and all the world was waiting and watching. It was a day of climax and portent, a day for history.[26]

On Mark Clark's orders, a number of task forces had been formed to lead the way, each led by spearhead units. When they met German resistance on one road, they shifted to another, but this also heightened the overall confusion. At the head of the pack, at least most of time, was General Robert Frederick's First Special Service Force, the Black Devils of Anzio, or, as the Germans had dubbed them more famously, the Devil's Brigade. They had been given the mission of capturing the bridges to assure pursuit of the enemy even beyond Rome. One of Frederick's advance patrols, sixty men in eighteen jeeps, had actually penetrated Rome on the 3rd. Attacked by snipers and machine-gun emplacements, they had managed nevertheless to reach Cinecittà—the Hollywood-like motion picture lots on the Via Tuscolana edge of the city—where they had spent the night, only to be driven back the following morning behind the city limits in an attempt to advance.

Adding to the sporadic clashes with the enemy was the danger of friendly but-not-that-friendly fire. In one tense confrontation, a British thrust from Highway 6 to steal first place was stopped by a traffic jam artificially created by a quick-thinking American. Moreover, several exchanges of gunfire erupted between the Fifth Army and other Allied units, and there was "a little fire fight," in the phrase of one American commander, between his men and Frederick's Forcemen, "due to [a] misunderstanding between the two forces."[27]

As a consequence one or another unit of the Fifth Army would claim to be among the first in Rome. The unofficial honor, in many accounts, would go to Frederick's First Special Service Force, which would enter the heart of the city in the early evening. Frederick, himself wounded twice that day, would add two Purple Hearts to his military decorations, establishing a record-breaking total of nine for the Italian campaign—the most wounded-in-combat general in American history. One of his men, Forceman Thomas Garcia, would earn the distinction of being endlessly quoted for his remark on seeing the Colosseum for the first time. "My God," he cried, "they bombed that too!"[28]

But on the afternoon of the 4th, General Frederick, like everything else on Highway 6, was standing still when a jeep carrying Mark Clark and II Corps Commander General Geoffrey Keyes pulled up beside him. Clark, just down from the Alban Hills, the prize now so close, wanted to know what was holding things up. A welcome distraction then arose as one of the photographers traveling in Clark's entourage drew attention to the reflector-studded blue highway sign just beyond them. It read, "ROMA." It was in fact a city-limit marker on the Casilina, approximate at best, but if you were reading it you were probably not in Rome, whereas if you were looking at the blank reverse side, you might be. It was awe-inspiring, in any event, and, in a flash, so to speak, a famous photo was taken. Then Clark turned to Frederick and said, "Golly, Bob, I'd like to have that sign in my command post."

Frederick himself went to retrieve what was now a museum-class artifact, but at that moment a German sniper, with three generals in his crosshairs, cut loose. The first bullet tore through the sign, and the rest of the volley went over their heads as they dove into a ditch. The shooting went on for several minutes, and as the generals crawled on all fours to a safer position, Frederick finally had his best answer to Clark's vexing question. "That," he told Clark, "is what's holding up the First Special Service Force!"[29]

Clark left them, though not before registering a redundant reminder that "we've got to get in there." Frederick asked Keyes why Clark had been so impatient. "Well," said Keyes, "France is going to be invaded from England the day after tomorrow and we've got to get this in the paper before then."[30]

INSIDE the city, an order of unknown origin had set the curfew hour for 6 P.M. Few Romans paid it any heed, but at that hour, though the sun was still high in the western sky, the streets were eerily empty. The German pullout had thinned to a few stragglers, among them the snipers and machine gunners giving up the fight with but agonizing slowness. Carla and Sasà had been on duty at the Porta San Lorenzo gateway outside the Piazzale Tiburtino, assigned as were their comrades to prevent last-minute enemy mischief. But the Germans had left by now, without incident, and the men, women, and children of the neighborhood were gathered in doorways, the Campo along the wall of Verano cemetery and outside the San Lorenzo basilica, waiting for the Americans.

When at last a single American vehicle entered the Piazzale Tiburtino, people barely moved, looking on in suspicion, unsure whether the newcomers were friend or foe. Sasà and some other Partisans went up to them. The soldiers had camouflage on their helmets and their uniforms were covered by a layer of dust that hid the markings. They looked overcome with fatigue, Sasà recalls, and somewhat leery themselves under the stares of the crowd:

> They said something in English, but drew only blank looks, even from those of us who had studied it in school, and the way they said "yes" sounded like "yeah"—a little too close for comfort to a German "ja." But

when one of them took out his pack of cigarettes, and we saw the word *Camel* there was no longer a shred of doubt, and the people went wild with joy. They came running from all over the piazza and the adjacent side streets, shouting at the top of their lungs, "The Americans are here!"

THE AMERICANS kept coming and the shouting never stopped. An aspiring American journalist, Army Sergeant Jack Raymond, wrote and filed his report inside Rome that night. Obscure even then, it nevertheless survives, as wide-eyed and fresh as when first pecked out:

> ROME, June 4—The mighty armored columns of the last Armored Division which all day had pressed forward along Highway 7 and smashed every delaying attempt by the Jerries was finally stopped in the streets of Rome by a jubilant-crazy populace.
>
> Tanks that had weathered enemy artillery, Mark VIs and self-propelled guns were forced to halt on Via Appia for fear of endangering the lives of the civilians who swarmed about them, shouting, screaming, weeping, laughing—delirious with excitement.
>
> It was 1930 hours. A woman shouted in English, we have been waiting all day. A soldier responded: "We've waited longer."
>
> Within two blocks inside the city the first tank commanded by Lieutenant Henry Schoberth, Versailles, Kentucky, was just a mountain mass of human arms, legs and bodies. Children and old men—and even an old lady at least 65 years old—clambered aboard oblivious to the danger of grinding tank tracks. . . .
>
> The inevitable bambini showed up demanding caramelli [*sic*]. Young girls kissed every soldier they could lay their hands on and one tiny blond succeeded in mounting the turret gun of a light tank.
>
> Every thoroughfare was lined with cheering crowds. . . .[31]

Electric power had gone out late that afternoon, and when night fell, the moon was veiled in a mist. Though the celebrations continued, sometimes in pitch blackness, it was not until daybreak that the city exploded in the fullness of its joy.

———————

ON MONDAY, June 5, 1944, the army that had launched bombs by the thousands on Rome would itself be bombarded by all the flowers of spring, hailed by two million people starting life anew.

"Wherever the troops entered," Mother Mary wrote, "they were cheered, applauded and showered with blossoms. A rain of roses fell on men, guns, tanks and jeeps." Her own first sight of the liberators, after a night of listening to the clamor and the clapping in the darkness beyond the convent, came in the early morning, "dramatic in its simplicity," she said.

> Opening a window at about six o'clock, I saw one little jeep with four American soldiers in it, making its way slowly and soundlessly along the street. No one else was about. The thing looked so solitary, yet so significant in the cool stillness of dawn. I had it all to myself for a few seconds. It was so small, yet so secure; a vignette on a page of history; a full stop at the end of a chapter of oppression and fear.[32]

SASÀ awoke beside Carla at dawn in San Lorenzo, and went out while she slept. There was still a threat of sabotage and they remained under orders, but he had been given an additional assignment of leading a squad of Partisans to surprise and arrest a number of Fascists known to be in the district. Even before calling on the first name on his list, however, he sensed he had been sent on an errand conceived in an excess of zeal. These were people as victimized by poverty, the Nazi occupation, and the war as anyone else in San Lorenzo, families who cowered, trembled, and wept for mercy now at the sight of the Partisan armbands, paying for their "Fascism" in fear. After three such visits, he aborted and returned to the command post. If there was Partisan work still to be done in the liberated city, he said, it would have to be more worthy than something that smacked of the past they had fought to put behind them. But work of any kind was far from his mind that day.

"Everything had changed from one minute to the next," he said. "The Americans kept coming and the streets of San Lorenzo filled with more peo ple than anyone could have imagined, but it was clear that many of them were coming out from months of hiding. They were ashen and dazzled by the sun, but moments later, they were animated, joining in discussions; they looked happy, almost unscathed."

FROM sunrise on came the "big entry," as Sevareid called it, the main body of Mark Clark's Fifth Army taking Rome. "Many great cities were liberated after Rome," the General wrote, "and the spectacle was nearly always the same. But to me this entry was a new thing and I found myself having to hold tight to my emotions."

Everyone was out on the street, thousands upon thousands from the out-lying areas walking toward the center of the city. A vast murmurous sound of human voices flooded everywhere and rose in joyous crescendo at every large avenue we crossed. There was a gladness in all eyes, and now and then, as when a German sniper in his green-daubed cape was marched out of the Colosseum, remembrance of hate contorted the faces, even the young children uttered savage cries, and the fists that had held bundles of flowers were doubled in anger.

The Piazza di Venezia was jammed with a monstrous crowd, and our jeep proceeded at a snail's pace, while flowers rained upon our heads, men grabbed and kissed our hands, old women burst into tears, and girls and boys wanted to climb up beside us. One tried to remember that they had been our recent enemy, that they were happy because the war was over for them as much as because we had driven out the Germans, that noncom-batants such as I had no right to this adulation. But one tried in vain. I felt wonderfully good, generous, and important. I was a representative of strength, decency, and success. . . . [33]

IT WAS still early morning when Mark Clark made his triumphant entry into Rome. All of the more or less elaborate schemes to formally deliver the city to the Americans disappeared in the planning, as the head of the Fifth Army, like any unchallenged conqueror—and one who had outconquered Hannibal—needed only to take the prize in hand. In the fifth decade of the twentieth century the day had arrived when all one had to do to proclaim a reality, was, as General Keyes had said, "get this in the paper." Yet, it was one thing to march on Rome, but quite another to know where in Rome to go. Certainly Clark did not know, and he said so, but he saw the logic in the sug-gestion of one of his generals to arrange a meeting with his corps command-ers in what Clark called "town hall." He could not have made a more appropriate choice, the town hall in this town being the venerated Campi-doglio, the Capitol, site of the ancient Senate of the People of Rome, at the summit of Capitoline Hill. Here, at "the head of the world," as it once was called, Brutus had addressed the Romans after the slaying of Caesar, on this hill of the caesars and emperors.

Without a trace of fanfare, Clark and his officers entered the jubilant city in a small convoy of jeeps, transported body and soul. Unrecognized in the endless parade, they wandered through a maze of side streets, "while we craned our necks looking at the sights," said Clark, apparently delighted most of all when they lost their way. As generals are last among men to ask directions, they ended up in Saint Peter's Square, where they stopped and gawked.

Caught in the act, Clark heard someone say "Welcome to Rome" in English, and when he looked around he saw a priest. "Is there any way in which I can help you?" the clergyman asked.

"Well," Clark replied, "we'd like to get to Capitoline Hill." The priest was happy to point them the right way, thanked them all for saving Rome and introduced himself, saying he was originally from Detroit. "That's sure nice," said Clark. "My name is Clark."

The priest smiled and went on his way, taking no more than two or three steps before he wheeled and cried, "*General* Clark?"

In the meantime, a crowd of Romans had gathered, as much in awe as the priest, and a boy on bicycle offered to lead the way to the Campidoglio. "He did," Clark later said, "pedaling along in front of our jeep and shouting to everybody on the street to get out of the way because General Clark was trying to get to Capitoline Hill . . . and by the time we reached a point opposite the balcony where Mussolini used to appear for his major speeches the road was blocked by curious and cheering people."[34]

The "point opposite" is the magnificent Aracoeli steps—a stairway to heaven, in Latin—atop which sits the Campidoglio. Clark, in his memoirs, goes on to recount a kind of anticlimax to it all: how when he got to the great palazzo, it was locked. He stood there pounding on the door, "not feeling much like the conqueror of Rome," an evanescent figure left to console himself on this "curiously varied . . . historic day" with the thought that "anyway . . . we got to Rome before Ike got across the English Channel to Normandy."[35]

Others, however, witnessed something else, a final Clarkian moment in the battle of vanities for Rome.

Alerted by the Fifth Army's public relations chief that the General would hold a press conference, the war correspondents rushed to the Campidoglio. They found Clark receiving his top commanders, including Truscott, Keyes, and Marshal Juin, in a round of handshakes in the piazza overlooking Rome.

"Well, gentlemen," Clark said, turning to the reporters, photographers, and newsreel cameramen. "I didn't really expect to have a press conference here—I just called a little meeting with my corps commanders to discuss the situation. However, I'll be glad to answer your questions. This is a great day for the Fifth Army and for the French, British, and American troops of the Fifth who have made this victory possible."[36]

Clark omitted any reference to Alexander and the British Eighth Army, for which he would be widely ridiculed from that day on. An implacable Eric Sevareid, among the newsmen present, would be harshest. "That was the immortal remark of Rome's modern-day conqueror," he wrote. "It was not, apparently, a great day for the world, for the Allies, for all the suffering people who had desperately looked toward the time of peace." Clark was as unapologetic then as later. Sevareid recorded another uncharitable remark, uttered by a colleague: "On this historic occasion, I feel like vomiting."[37]

SOMEONE with a more substantive grievance on that day was Peter Tompkins. After nearly three months of being cut off behind the lines and boarded up nail by nail into isolation by the treachery of his rivals, Tompkins now found himself in a further predicament. He knew none of the OSS officers arriving with the Fifth Army. They were the newcomers of a restructured and restaffed organization. Many of his strongest supporters, who would later attest to the critical importance of his work in Rome, had been transferred to London for the Overlord invasion, and he was as much a stranger to the arriving agents as they were to him. Worse, the Menicanti group had managed to ingratiate itself at Tompkins's expense, and when in the coming days the American would accuse them of sabotaging his operation and criminal activities, they would counter with charges that he was "completely mad."[38]

Thus all his groundwork of recent weeks, identifying and setting in motion an apparatus for tracking down the Nazi spies purposely left behind in Rome, would be disregarded, and his efforts to secure living quarters, office space, and transportation for postliberation counterintelligence operations would be misinterpreted from the first day. Moreover, with the senior officers now entering Rome vying for the choicest accommodations, Tompkins was transformed into their man in Rome, not an intelligence agent but a full-service real-estate agent. "The first service they wanted was women," he recalls. "I had finally got an apartment all to myself, and that night when I got home this young American brigadier general comes out of my shower, into my living room, demanding to know what the hell I was doing there. Then his aide shows up in riding boots and breeches with these girls, one on each arm, everybody ready to party. I stormed out, went straight to Clark's new headquarters and told them that no goddamn brigadier general was going to get my place. He moved out but not the wild-west atmosphere of those first days in liberated Rome."

———————

AT 2:30 that afternoon, Carla and Sasà stepped out of the building that until that day had been the offices of the newspaper *Lavoro Fascista*. The clatter of the printing presses was still going strong, but now the pressmen were putting out the first nonclandestine edition of the Communist Party's *l'Unità*. Carla and Sasà had been there for the past few hours setting up a security system to protect the new occupants and the presses. In addition to the spies who were Tompkins's concern, the Fascist regime, it was known, had left squads of terrorists and saboteurs in the capital. A new war, longer and bloodier than the campaign that had just ended in Rome, was beginning in the path of Kesselring's retreat.

By chance, the requisitioned palazzo, located at the top of the hill that rises from the Piazza Venezia, stood directly above Trajan's Forum and the apartment building of Carla's family home. It had been months since she had seen her mother and younger brother, and a longer absence had separated Sasà from his parents. It was to their respective families that both of them were heading now, stopping for a moment in the adjacent Via delle Tre Cannelle at the *fontana* of the same name, the Fountain of the Three Spouts, before parting. Going home, though only for a while, they were both facing an emotional reunion, more so for Sasà since his mother and his stepfather were completely unaware of the life he had led underground. They believed he was hiding from the labor draft, safely ensconced in the Vatican.

Carla and Sasà had stopped in the quiet, semicircular sidestreet to drink from the fountain and for a brief respite. They were about to go off in different directions when they saw two men in military dress, but worn irregularly, angrily tearing down the posters and banners on a wall of the building where they had been printed and put up that day. They bore the slogans of the moment: "Long Live the Allied Armies!" "Long Live Free Rome!" "Long Live Free Italy!" Both men were carrying holstered sidearms and wore ammunition belts, and in the absence of any markings on their uniforms, Carla and Sasà suspected that they might be the very stay-behinds to whom they had been alerted. Moreover, while the couple had been in the building, they had heard reports of skirmishes in the northern part of Rome.

As the men continued to rip away the posters, Sasà rushed toward them, shouting at them to stop. They turned to him and stared.

"Why are you doing that?" he asked.

"I'm doing what I want to do," one of them countered in a hostile tone.

"No, you've got it wrong, my friend," said Sasà. "What you want to do is what you did up until a few hours ago. Now you're under arrest." He indicated his CLN armband, which carried police authority.

Carla, who had come up behind Sasà, cried out, "Watch it! Watch it!"

From the corner of his eye, Sasà could see that the other man, who had been standing off to one side, had drawn and pointed his gun. Carla, Sasà knew, was unarmed, having left her pistol in the building. He took a backward leap, just as the gunman got off two rounds, and the movement saved him. In the meantime, the first man pulled his gun from his holster as Sasà reached for his own weapon in the right-hand pocket of his trousers, and it was suddenly a matter of who had the faster draw. Sasà cut him down with the first bullet before the man could even fire. Still in the firing position, he swung around to the second shooter, only to see him turn and run. Sasà took after him, but the man got away.

Returning, he saw that the first man lay dead on the ground and a small crowd had gathered. Among them was a Partisan wearing the armband of the Military Front. Sasà reported what had happened. A Fifth Army Military Police patrol then stepped in. Their jeep had been parked at the top of the street, and one of the MPs, who claimed to have witnessed the entire clash, shook Sasà's hand. No one doubted that it was an open-and-shut case of self-defense, and before long, both Sasà and Carla were again on their way, adding death in freedom's first afternoon to the burdens they were bringing home.[39]

————

No one in liberated Rome had been more unburdened that day than Pope Pius XII. So certain was he that he no longer had anything to fear from either the irresponsible or the responsible parties that for the first time in the tortuous history of the Open City he raised a strenuous protest against a violation on the ground. At ten o'clock that morning he had come to his study window to bless a small group of Romans from the adjoining neighborhood, who had assembled in the piazza below to acclaim him. He had done much the same three hours earlier, but this time he saw an American tank parked near one of the Bernini colonnades. He was not going to tolerate the Allies using Rome to move troops and matériel. According to Monsignor Giovannetti, the Pope telephoned the Vatican Secretariat three times to have the

tank removed. "This was the first manifestation of several resolute and per-
severing interventions by the Holy See to preserve the open-city character
of Rome even after the arrival of Allied troops," said Giovannetti.[40] Continual denunciations of Allied "violations" would get him nowhere now. They
might have had greater moral force had he begun with the Germans back in
September.

To the exhilarating peal of church bells cleansing the Roman air of the
calamitous sounds of bombs and mortar that clung like grime to memory,
tens of thousands of Romans were gathering in Saint Peter's Square by five
o'clock that afternoon. Since midday, groups of boys and girls had been
going about the city in loudspeaker trucks repeating the message hastily
printed on the signs they posted and handed out door-to-door. "Come to
Saint Peter's at 6 P.M. to thank the Pope."

The piazza was full when Mother Mary arrived sometime before six, and
by her formula that meant a congregation of 300,000 souls. As usual, she
evoked the scene in a few telling strokes of her pen:

> The afternoon's sun slanted across the roof of the Basilica, spilling tor-
> rents of golden light on the sea of color below. With the flags and banners,
> it looked like a herbaceous border in full bloom. Soldiers in battle dress
> provided an olive-drab background for the whole.[41]

Though the GIs in the piazza were gray-faced and dusty in their combat
clothes, they looked on in boundless wonderment. "I didn't know there was
anything so beautiful," an American infantryman in Saint Peter's would tell
a *Stars and Stripes* reporter.

A similarly ebullient Carlo Trabucco, who in a perverse manner wished
that the unmentionable "man from Piazza Venezia" could have seen what
the *real* enthusiasm of the Romans was like—not the kind whipped up by the
Duce's henchmen—saw this crowd in Saint Peter's as a plebiscite of what
people of every political stripe were feeling for their Pope. "The red flags of
the Communists were numerous," he said, "and numerous were the socialists, countless the Christian Democrats, and the anonymous crowd was simply immense.[42] And when the white-robed Pope—"the White Father,"
Trabucco called him—appeared on the central balcony, the roar of the multitude rose to the heavens again and again while he spoke.

In one of his shortest and most plainspoken speeches, he declared that
yesterday's fear had been replaced by today's new hope, that instead of
unimaginable destruction Rome had been granted salvation, and that "the

Eternal City had been saved by divine mercy inspired by the intent of both belligerent parties to seek peace not affliction." The Pope thanked God, the Trinity, and Mary, Mother of God, for saving the Romans, and he bowed before Apostles Peter and Paul for protecting the city in which they, too, had impregnated its soil with the sweat and blood of their martyrdom. Finally he called on the Romans to put aside all thirst for vengeance and strive for brotherly love. "*Sursum corda!*" he cried. "Lift your hearts!" Then, after blessing a kneeling crowd, he turned and left the balcony in a wake of white silks and the roar of popular acclaim.[43]

Among the Americans in the piazza, even hard-boiled Sevareid could not escape succumbing. Although he insisted on being free of any feelings of awe toward the Vatican, which he regarded as "inclined to Fascism," the splendor and pageantry, the sense of spectacle and theater, left him profoundly stirred, he said. In the Pope's words thanking his "side" only, while commending the Germans as much as the Allies, Sevareid saw no analogy to Mark Clark's stingy praise. But, apart from the Pontiff's showmanship, he was impressed, he added, "by his political genius." Pius XII had in fact found a perfect mix for both attributes. "By inference," Sevareid perceived, "he took credit for the fact that the city had been spared."[44]

The Vatican would call this Pope *defensor civitatis*, the "defender of the city" in the terrible time of Nazi-occupied Rome—a weighty crown of glory that would prove increasingly heavy to wear.

―――――――

S A S À went home to family warmth and love that evening, but it was nothing like he had imagined. His parents' joy could not be faulted, but he was not ready even to begin to tell his story. Before long, he went out again, back to his comrades at *l'Unità*. Carla had come back, too.

When she had arrived at the lobby of her apartment building, she had caught sight of her mother and brother on their way out. She had stopped in her tracks, but they had kept walking, failing to take note of the drawn young woman ahead, almost passing her completely until her brother shouted, "Carla!" They embraced, kissed, and wept. "You're all skin and bones, my darling," her mother said. And heavy was the heart that beat inside, Carla would recall.

Carla and Sasà spent all that night working at the newspaper, helping to get out the next day's edition, nodding off in between, as in clandestine times. Here, among their scarred comrades, some just out of the Via Tasso or Regina Coeli, others not seen in months, survivors of one or another harrowing experience, there was an air of festivity, a great need to catch up, even a taste perhaps of the happiness they found missing elsewhere.

"In this climate of camaraderie, of freedom won," Sasà remembers, "we felt relaxed and serene, lifted by a great will to live. After all, we were already prepared for the hard times coming. The war would go on and we knew where our battleground would be."[45]

Carla said:

> I knew what we could expect: difficult times, maybe miserable times, but now, we would face them with a certainty. The future would not be a place where you could only beat your head against a wall, not a prison of the spirit and the flesh, but a window that had at last been opened looking out on all the world; and anything you wanted was in that open space, waiting for you to begin to fly, the way a child dreams of flying, above a garden, above a cabbage patch, over roses and wisteria.[46]

THAT NIGHT Roosevelt went on the air. Banner headlines around the world had already told the story, but the ring of triumph in his voice was hardly lessened as he declared the first Axis capital captured and final victory assured. Yet, he cautioned, a hard fight still lay ahead. "One up and two to go," he said, taking aim first on Berlin, then Tokyo. In the captured capital, it was already morning when the American president spoke, the morning that all eyes took aim with him—all headlines, too. It was D-Day on the beaches of Normandy. Eisenhower's forces had crossed the English Channel; the great invasion of Fortress Europe proper was under way. To the south, the bulk of the Allied armies were already well north of Rome, engaging the Germans.

Although under temporary Allied military administration, liberated Rome had been given back to the Romans. There were pieces missing, mostly people—the victims, dispatched or deported—but much remained intact. The Colosseum had not fallen, and a civilization had been saved, for Rome had again been tried and found eternal. But the wounds ran deep, and it would be a long time before a San Lorenzo poet, writing in the Romanesco dialect in and of the place where it had all begun, could compose this song:

> *In nineteen hundred and twenty-two*
> *We had a government—I don't remember who*

Then we had a march—I don't remember where
But it was called—I don't remember what
And for twenty years we participated
In many wars—I don't remember which
But, one fine day, we were liberated
By—I can't remember who.[47]

EPILOGUE

The Resistance is written in our DNA.

Antonino Intelisano, Chief Prosecutor, Military Tribunal of Rome

I. JUSTICE POSTPONED

Liberated Rome was Camel cigarettes, white-flour bread, and olive oil at one-thirtieth the black market price, but the Romans did not forget those missing from their table. There had been a solemn promise made by the Allies in November of 1943. Meeting in Moscow, Roosevelt, Churchill, and Stalin had declared that war criminals would not escape justice; they would be pursued to "the uttermost ends of the earth . . . brought back to the scene of their crimes and judged on the spot by the peoples whom they have outraged."[1] In Rome it would be a promise a long time coming.

Of all the crimes committed by the Nazis during the occupation (with one minor exception) only one was prosecuted. On the other hand, whatever the offense, the same perpetrators were complicit to them all, and justice for the victims heaped in the Ardeatine Caves would provide retribution. The steely prediction made by Carlo Trabucco that when the Romans would be free, a "pilgrimage without end" would go to the Fosse Ardeatine came to pass without delay. It began in the very first days of the liberation. Morning to night the two kilometers from the start of the ancient Appian Way, past the church of Quo Vadis, and forking down Via Ardeatina to the caves, the roads were lined with whole families of mourners bearing flowers, walking into the all-pervasive stench.

At the same time, U.S. Fifth Army Colonel Charles Poletti, the Allied Regional Commissioner for Rome, appointed a commission of American and Italian officials to conduct an inquest of the Ardeatine crime. One of its principal tasks was assigned to a team of experts who were to exhume the bodies and attempt to identify them. This work was led by Rome's top forensic scientist, Attilio Ascarelli, professor of legal medicine at the University of Rome and director of the police academy, the Superior School of Police. Ascarelli, a Roman Jew who had gone into hiding during the occupation, was the uncle of two of those killed in the caves, and he undertook his labors with a "religious fervor," he said, not only to rescue the victims from a limbo of uncertain identity but to crush any hopes held by the Germans that the full horror of the atrocity escape disclosure.[2] His team of highly specialized physicians, notably in exhumation hygiene and body identification, supported by paramedics, firemen, and workmen, numbered 110. Why he needed that many became clear from his account of the first visit inside the caves, late in June. Picking their way under torchlight through the landslide debris caused by the explosions, they were able to get only a glimpse of bodies in the depths of one of the tunnels by crawling through a parallel tunnel and climbing a ladder. In his final report, Ascarelli wrote that what they saw was beyond words or imagination:

> Two enormous shapeless heaps of cadavers, from which arose an unbelievable smell of rottenness, of rancid and decomposed fat. It penetrated and permeated one's clothes to the point that it became necessary to take precautions by wearing special garments, gloves and boots, and to shield the respiratory tract with gauze masks soaked in deodorant. And even that was not enough.
>
> . . . Little could be seen of the bodies, but through the mixture of volcanic dust, soil and the decomposed cadaverous fat that covered the corpses, there emerged a foot, here and there a pair of shoes, there a skull, whole or crushed, now a limb, now a piece of tattered clothing. Insects swarmed among the scattered limbs. Myriads of larvae fed on the rotting flesh. Numerous large rats darted from the unburied and unguarded remains, and even from the fragmented heads.[3]

The grisly effort of reconstructing human forms from degrading flesh and restoring each individual's identity went on for six months. Visual identification of the remains by the victims' families failed almost entirely. Nevertheless Ascarelli and his team, in an era long before DNA analysis, working from items found on the bodies, such as wrist watches, rings, and clothing, produced remarkable results. They succeeded first in determining that the number of victims was 335 not 320, and of the total they positively identified 322.[4] Two other victims were named but could not be matched to the remaining thirteen bodies. They also were able to unravel some of the deepest secrets of the killers, as described above in Chapter 16—the labor-saving slayings carried out by soldiers who stood on the bodies of those already shot, the decapitations, and the sloppiness and drunkenness of the executions squads. This cruel and unusual conduct would later become an essential part of the prosecutions' cases in the coming trials.[5]

ASCARELLI had not yet published his report, but the thirst for vengeance could not have been greater, and never would be, than on September 18, 1944, when the first defendant brought back to Rome to account for his role in the crime was due to go on trial. Ex-Questore Caruso, delivered by the Partisans of Viterbo, had been in custody all summer in Regina Coeli, the same Roman prison from which he had sent fifty inmates to die in the Ardeatine Caves. That was the main charge against him, but by now, photographed in his cell reading the Bible, he had repented. A bishop would be called to so testify. The crowd that gathered outside the Palace of Justice, which included kin of the victims, would have none of it. Calling for blood, they stormed the courthouse, and when they discovered that Caruso had not yet arrived they settled for a lesser "evil." Someone among the frenzied avengers had recognized the man who had been the warden of Regina Coeli during the occupation, Donato Carretta, and he was seized and dragged from the courtroom. Carretta, in fact, had secretly aided the anti-Fascist prisoners and the day of the massacre had resisted the removal of the men on Caruso's list. He was to have been the prosecution's main witness but was turned into yet another innocent victim—seized and murdered by an unstoppable lynch mob.

Caruso was put in the dock two days later. The trial was over by the early evening. He was convicted and sentenced to death the next morning, and driven to Fort Bravetta in the afternoon to go before a firing squad of twenty Carabinieri. "Aim well!" he cried out to his executioners. They did. According to an American eyewitness, "It sounded like one shot."[6]

ON THE first anniversary of the liberation, June 4, 1945, Pietro Koch was tried in a makeshift courtroom at the University of Rome by an Italian High Court of Justice formed to punish Fascist crimes. He too was sorry and asked for forgiveness, abandoning his hitherto unshakable atheism in a declaration of his belief in God. Like Caruso, he had a prelate ready to vouch for his faith, along with four men from the Action Party who would say that they had not been tortured, but when the first of them to take the stand, the Italian film director Luchino Visconti, admitted to having been browbeaten under a death threat, the defense called no further witnesses.[7] Koch was found guilty that same day for a host of high crimes against the Resistance, including torture, deportations, and "handing over numerous patriots to the German SS to be massacred in the *Fosse Ardeatine*."[8] The sentence was death by firing squad.

In the final two days of his life, Koch spent most of his time smoking, chatting, and even joking, but above all explaining the reasons for his "mistakes." He had never been a Fascist, he said in an interview in his Regina Coeli cell, driven instead by a "spirit of adventure." Now there was nothing left for him to do but plead "forgiveness from God, forgiveness from all those he had made to suffer, forgiveness from all Italians."[9] To Monsignor Nasalli Rocca, he confessed that success had gone to his head, "reached" by ambition and power. He asked the priest to pray for him, for "I feel the weight of the tears of many mothers!"[10]

On the morning of the execution, after bidding Koch a final farewell, Nasalli Rocca was summoned with great urgency by Pius XII. "Hurry," said the Pope, pressing a rosary into the Monsignor's hand, "go at once to Lieutenant Koch and bring him my forgiveness, my blessing, and this rosary." The Holy Father had received a handwritten apology from Koch for having violated the sanctuary of Saint Paul's Basilica; he was still holding the letter as he dispatched Nasalli Rocca. Tears welled in the condemned man's eyes when the future cardinal delivered Pius's good wishes along with the rosary. "Father," Koch said in a breaking voice, "these hands of mine are drenched in blood and unworthy of touching the Holy Father's rosary." He asked him to place it over his head, which Nasalli Rocca did, promising to ask the Pope to grant him one last request, a blessing for his mother.[11]

In the early afternoon, kneeling in the grass at Fort Bravetta, Koch received the last rites, then rose and calmly took his place before the firing squad. He refused the proffered blindfold. Seventeen rifle bullets tore through him, removing the entire cap of his skull and hurling it over the wall behind him. He was not yet twenty-seven years old.

DESPITE liberation and the immediate abrogation of the Fascist anti-Jewish laws, the Jewish community in Rome was undergoing additional pain and confusion unwittingly brought on by the Allies. As part of the de-Fascistization process, one of the first measures taken by Regional Commissioner Colonel Poletti was to dissolve the two main bodies of Jewish leadership, the councils headed by presidents Foà and Almansi. They were branded as Fascist-controlled organizations, and an "extraordinary commissioner" was named to organize the free election of a new council. In the meantime, Chief Rabbi Zolli, who had been demeaned and ostracized by Foà and Almansi, was ordered reinstated, but the old guard fought on. A bitter controversy arose over Foà's failure to destroy the community's lists of the names and addresses of Rome's Jews. No one disputed that they had fallen into German hands, but the ex-president maintained that they had not been used in the October 16, 1943, roundup, which would be proved untrue, and in any case it was a defense as unworthy as his later attempts to sanitize unfavorable documents.[12]

The community was further traumatized some months later. On February 13, 1945, Rabbi Zolli stunned all of Rome and the world by undergoing baptism in the Roman Catholic Church. As his baptismal name he chose Eugenio—the given name of Pope Pius XII. He was given a post in the Vatican Library. People of all faiths, some with delight, some with rancor, sought to explain his conversion, reaching a consensus of sorts in viewing it as an expression of gratitude for the Pope's efforts to save the Jews of Rome. Zolli himself denied this. He esteemed the Pope, he said, but he preferred to emphasize an epiphany he had experienced in liberated Rome's main synagogue while presiding over the Yom Kippur services in the fall of 1944. The temple was filled with Roman Jews as well as American and British Jewish soldiers when his mind's eye, he said, was drawn beyond the congregation to "a vision of a meadow sweeping upward . . . [where] I saw Jesus Christ clad in a white mantle," and words formed in his heart, saying, "You are here for the last time."[13]

The departure of the old rabbi cleared the way for a compromise between the ousted but still powerful old order and the Allied democratization effort. Elections were held to form a council free of "Fascist hangers-on," as Colonel Poletti's representative put it. Foà and Almansi were in fact prohibited from holding any office in the community, but the new leaders showed where their loyalties lay, slowly rehabilitating the old. As soon as the Allies began to lose interest, the ex-presidents were elevated to honorary positions.

In the summer and fall of 1945, the survivors of the Holocaust returned to Rome. Of the 1,023 who boarded the cattle-car train to Auschwitz from Tiburtina Station on October 18, 1943, only Settimia Spizzichino and fifteen men were still alive, though on average they had lost half of their body weight in the interim. Details of their collective travails in some twenty labor and concentration camps had been gathered in interviews by various officials. They had then been given a second-class train ticket and a bar of soap for the journey (and a packet of razor blades for the men), and came home one by one. Although the "martyrdom" of those who had been taken from Rome in the roundup would live on, engraved in marble and dutifully commemorated year after year, the returnees, whose eyes had seen what had been consigned to memory, who had breathed the smoke particles of those "martyrs," and who had the indelibly inked numbers on the skin of their forearms to prove it, were promptly forgotten.

———————

IN NOVEMBER of 1946, Rome was the venue of the trial of Generals Eberhard von Mackensen and Kurt Mälzer. They had been brought from England, where they had been held and interrogated as prisoners of war. Because of the International Military Tribunal and the Nuremberg Trial of Major War Criminals, Mackensen and Mälzer, instead of being tried by the Italians, were to face a British tribunal installed in the capital. Two witnesses had traveled back to Rome with them: Field Marshal Kesselring, who would testify for the defense, and Colonel Kappler, the prime witness for the prosecution. Both of them were due to be tried as well. The three Wehrmacht officers, insisting with abiding indignation on their innocence, were hoping to cast all blame on the SS, Kappler in particular.

Mackensen, in a statement to his interrogators in England, claimed to have done the Italian people a service by supporting the decision for a ten-to-one kill ratio as opposed to earlier demands for a higher figure. "I certainly saved the lives of other people," he said.[14] Mälzer stated he had almost nothing to do with the affair, although he admitted being "very excited" in the Via Rasella, personally affronted by the Romans because "I had done all I could in favour of the population." Thus, he might have made some threats about blowing up a building, but he had no such power, no control over Kappler, and no knowledge of how and where the executions were carried out. His only role was that of a messenger, who transmitted the order for the reprisal from Mackensen to Kappler.[15] Moreover, both defendants were adamant in their contention that Kappler had told them that the victims were already under a sentence of death or were prisoners who would have been "liquidated" by the SS, reprisal or no reprisal.

This latter position became the crux of their defense. Kappler had misled them. The prosecution, calling Kappler, maintained the opposite: He had told both defendants that he did not have enough death-sentence prisoners and that he would have to compile a list of persons "worthy of death." The defense lawyers countered that their clients had broken no law. The reprisal was justified as legal redress sanctioned by international law, namely the Hague Convention of 1907 on the rules of land warfare, of which both the Allies and Germany were signatories.[16]

Twelve days after the trial had begun, Mackensen and Mälzer were found guilty and sentenced "to suffer death by being shot." Mälzer's neck turned crimson. Mackensen slowly removed his monocle and dipped it in his vest pocket. Roman men and women burst into tears. The prosecutor, Colonel R. C. Halse, was swamped like a hero by women in black. They kissed his hands and thanked him profusely, expressing their eternal gratitude.[17]

The sentences, however, were not carried out. They were twice reduced and finally canceled, though Mälzer did not live long enough to enjoy his freedom. Mackensen was released in 1952; he died at age eighty in 1969.

"IF General von Mackensen is found guilty, then I am guilty, too," Kesselring had declared, and in February 1947 that proposition was put to the test.[18] Defiant, the supreme commander was also tried by a British military court, this time sitting in Venice. Aside from the charge of responsibility for the Ardeatine killings, a second count accused him of "inciting and commanding" his forces to kill Italian civilians, specifically 1,078 unarmed persons, including schoolchildren and babies.[19]

On the first count, Kesselring adopted the Mackensen defense of blaming Kappler, in this instance asserting that the Gestapo chief had personally told him that there were enough death-sentence prisoners to fill his list. He had therefore acted humanely, said his lawyers, in seeking certainty that the victims had already been convicted of capital offenses. The legality of the reprisal under international law was also alleged, and the Kesselring defense added a new element by introducing a "second order" from Hitler's headquarters that relieved Kesselring of any role in the killings other than passing on the first Führer order, messenger style. Neither of these orders existed in written form, but one of Kesselring's officers testified that the "second order" declared that the executions were to be carried out by the security forces of the SS, namely Kappler.

The judge advocate, a neutral adviser to the tribunal, told the court that if it believed that a "second order" or any other evidence shifted responsibility to Kappler, then "you are bound to acquit the accused."[20] But Kesselring was found guilty. Moreover, the court ruled that the executions in the Ardeatine Caves had no basis in any law and thus constituted a war crime. Pronounced guilty of the second count as well, Kesselring was sentenced to "death by shooting."[21]

He was astonished. It was "incomprehensible," he said, that the testimony of his officers was not believed. His efforts to assure that the reprisal be carried out under law ought to have been considered by the court "as an honest act of humanity." Kesselring's bewilderment over the verdict did little to mar the satisfaction of Italians, and the trademark grin he wore in a prison photograph while awaiting execution was only a reminder of who was due to laugh last. But the old warrior's plight and his plaintive cries of "utterly unjustifiable persecution" resonated greatly with the old warrior Churchill, and for that matter, Kesselring's onetime foe Alexander. Both men, in retirement now, expressed their dismay to the new British Prime Minister, Clement Attlee, with Alexander vouching for Kesselring as a worthy opponent who fought "hard but clean," which, incidentally, was more regard than he would give Mark Clark in his war memoir. Eight weeks after his conviction, Kesselring's sentence was commuted to life. Then, while he worked in a prison factory making paper bags and suffering further insult, he said, by his physical proximity to "professional criminals" and "the worst felons," his sentence was further reduced, and in 1952 he was released.

The protests and demonstrations in Italy went on for days, but he found honor in his own country in the time of its awakening to the paucity of "good" Germans among the Hitler generation. The man who followed the Ardeatine atrocity with unprecedented orders for public hangings and summary executions of civilians and the burning of villages—encouraging excesses that included 100-to-1 kill ratios ("*I* will protect any commander who exceeds our usual restraint in the choice of severity of the methods he adopts against Partisans"[22]), who regretted his own "usual restraint" as having taught him that "in the future such scruples will have to go by the board"[23]—all in the name of protecting his soldiers from the Partisans—underwent a remarkable cleansing of his war-criminal status after his release. "The Germans can today legitimately admire [Kesselring]," Shelford Bidwell wrote in a 1989 essay that went beyond praising the Field Marshal's performance on the battlefield to characterize his conviction as a miscarriage of justice.[24] Carlo D'Este would find his allegiance to Hitler and Nazism "misguided," but "history will certainly judge Kesselring as an honorable and able soldier." [25] Such a judgment, however, will have to reconcile his nature as the unrepentant *Soldat bis zum letzten Tag*, the "soldier to the last day," of the title of his memoir—on the final page of which he rejects any suggestions that there was something wrong with the German Army of Hitler's time, or any other time, as "more than I can take." [26] Kesselring died in 1960.

KAPPLER, after spending ten months in Regina Coeli, went on trial in May 1948. It was Rome's first and only prosecution under the Moscow Declaration, and thus, according to its terms, he faced the judgment of the people whom he had outraged. Those people were now the constituency of the fledgling Italian republic, and in judging Kappler they would be represented by a Rome-based Italian military tribunal.

Five of Kappler's men, two officers and three NCOs, were to stand trial with him. Another officer, Kappler's longtime number-two man, Captain Priebke, was to have been tried with them, but he had vanished. He had escaped from a prisoner-of-war camp in Rimini—a breakout that had apparently gone unnoticed for months.

A second count charged Kappler with extorting fifty kilograms of gold from the Jews of Rome. The accusation of the relatively petty crime— abuse of office to make an "unfair profit with considerable patrimonial damages to the Jews of Rome"—was the closest anyone would get to obtaining justice for the monstrous roundup, deportation, and extermination of the Jews caught in the October 16 *razzia*. The man most directly responsible for the roundup of Rome's Jews, Captain Dannecker, had been captured in Germany by U.S. forces and in December 1945 hanged himself in his cell. [27]

Kappler would be found guilty of the extortion charge for no other reason than having "acted without the authorization of the competent authority." [28] As for the Jews of Rome, a commemorative plaque would one day be affixed to the facade of the Collegio Militare, the military school by the Tiber where the rounded-up Jews had spent their last night in Rome.

Turning to the Ardeatine crime, Kappler took the stand in his own defense. He spoke for eight full days. Except for attempts to hide the most ghoulish and most damning features—acts for which there could be no legal defense—he would emerge as the most reliable witness to the making of the massacre, describing every cog and wheel of what was meant to run like clockwork and instead ran amok. At the same time, no one but he himself

could have done him more harm. His precision rendering of the details of
mass murder brought cries of agony from the public crowding the courtroom. Many of them were those closest to Kappler's victims, but the pain
was seen in the eyes of the judges, too.[29]

The defense sought to drain the flood of emotion by arguing matters of
law, adopting the deathless warhorse of the military man taking refuge behind the barrier of having no choice but to obey superior orders. It was the
Via Rasella attack that was illegal, and the reprisal was a legitimate act sanctioned by the Hague Convention of 1907. It mattered little that the first
Nuremberg trial of the Nazi hierarchy had rejected such a blind concept of
duty, overturning any remnants of the old laws. Indeed, in the Kappler trial,
all five of his codefendants were acquitted, specifically on the grounds of
"having acted in the execution of an order." Kappler, however, was found
guilty on all charges.[30]

Despite the conviction, the court's ruling on the legalities of the Via
Rasella attack and the reprisal would have lasting repercussions. While declaring the Partisan strike against the occupiers an action undertaken by a
military formation sanctioned by the legitimate Italian government, the
military judges held that out of necessity the Partisan movement at the time
had to act "in the orbit of illegality." Thus the attack itself, though courageous and an act of patriotism, was illegal and by definition, the court said,
provided a justification for a reprisal. Nevertheless, the court determined,
the reprisal in the Ardeatine Caves was a long way from qualifying as legitimate; it was in fact a war crime, the court said, if only because of the extreme
cruelty in the way the men were killed.[31]

Kappler was sentenced to *ergastolo*, the equivalent of life imprisonment
with almost no possibility of parole and the severest penalty under the postwar Italian constitution. He received an additional fifteen years for the gold-
extortion charge. But on August 15, 1977, Kappler escaped—with assistance
from his wife and doubtlessly others—and returned to Germany, where the
seventy-year-old ex–Gestapo chief died in his native Stuttgart the following
year.

———————

FROM the day after the Ardeatine reprisal, when the *Osservatore Romano* declared that the victims had been "sacrificed for the guilty parties who escaped arrest," one by one the facts of the Resistance movement began to be
altered in its disfavor. The triumph of the Resistance in northern Italy far

exceeded anyone's expectations. An extraordinary but difficult beginning in Rome had grown into a Partisan army, 150,000 strong and fully recognized by the Allies. In city after city civilians rose up in insurrection to expel the Germans ahead of the Allies—the Resistance forces proclaiming the liberation of Italy on April 25, 1945, a day of pride that would become a national holiday.

A year later, in the nation's first free election since pre-Fascist times and the first ever for women, the winning but small majority restructured Italy as a republic and adopted a democratic constitution strongly influenced by the anti-Fascism of the left wing of the Resistance. In a country where millions of surviving Fascists had been subdued, often harshly and sometimes unjustly, where a monarchy had been politically and physically ousted— though not the disgruntled monarchists—and where the Communist Party had emerged as the largest in the West, the politics of postwar Italy quickly became dangerously polarized, and the constitution was regarded by a large segment of the population as unrepresentative.

Thus the stage was set for an old-fashioned culture war, with its timeless strategy of restoring lost power and prestige by rewriting history. The revisionist rhetoric, contemptuous of truth, marched in lockstep with recurring episodes of violence, ranging from attempted coups d'état to terrorism, right, left, and state-sponsored, and a resurgence of neo-Fascism with an eternal flame of nostalgia as its symbol.

In the meantime, adding to the discomfiture of the revisionists were the honors bestowed by the nation's leaders on the Partisans. In the immediate postwar period, authorities of the new republic had established who had served the country as a "partisan combatant"—certifying more than 6,000 in Rome—and had recognized their military operations against the occupiers as the acts of patriots. Many were awarded military honors, and a few, such as Carla Capponi, received the nation's highest decoration, the Medaglia d'Oro for Military Valor. Sasà and Franco Calamandrei, who had commanded the Via Rasella attack, were awarded the Medaglia d'Argento, again for Military Valor.[32]

By 1994, however, when Romans were virtually alone in commemorating the fiftieth anniversary of their wartime ordeal, the revisionists, it seemed, had had their day in court. Some learned scholars among them had risen above the morass of propaganda and had posed legitimate questions. Was the Resistance simply an insurgency against an invader, they asked, or was it also an Italian civil war, on the order of the American civil war, in a nation divided over fundamental beliefs? Many Fascists, particularly those of the new generation, had fought and given their lives to regain Italy's honor after defeat and humiliation, and was that not the moral equivalent of what the Partisans claimed as theirs alone? And, finally, had the Partisans united or divided postwar Italy?

But after half a century, one of the major controversies of World War II in Italy appeared spent, the passion cooled, the players fading away. Then a seemingly unrelated telecast in the United States refocused attention on those events as never before. In the program, a trim, eighty-year-old grand-fatherly-looking man was seen getting into his car on a quiet street in Bariloche, Argentina, when a TV newsman walked up to him with his microphone extended and asked a fateful question. "Señor. . . . [I'm] Sam Donaldson of American television. May we talk to you for just a moment?" And the man, a respected citizen of a picturesque town in the foothills of the Andes, where he had lived for nearly fifty years and was known to friends and neighbors as don Erico, said yes. Don Erico was deftly unmasked by reporter Donaldson as ex–SS Captain Erich Priebke, a war criminal and fugitive from justice since 1947.[33]

Priebke was placed under house arrest, and for reasons convenient for the governments of Italy and Argentina was extradited to Italy.

It soon came out that Priebke, under his own name, had managed to live a lifetime of freedom unclouded by fear as the genial proprietor of Bariloche's Vienna Delicatessen. Prospering in Argentina, Priebke had traveled widely on a German passport, including vacation jaunts with his childhood-sweetheart wife, Alice, to New York, Paris, and twice to Italy, second-honeymooning in South Tyrol and, in 1978, spending three days in Rome "to re-visit places of the past," he would tell a reporter. His peregrinations as a Nazi on the lam would be pieced together as he grew increasingly garrulous. He had escaped a British prisoner of a war camp at Rimini, and then, hiding in a monastery, he waited his turn on a long, unholy queue behind the Mengeles and Eichmanns to be spirited out of Europe. Again like the others, he was assisted in fleeing the Continent via what U.S. intelligence called the Rat Line, a subterranean activity of the Vatican's refugee-aid operations that was run by Nazi-sympathizing prelates—a fact that Priebke publicly acknowledged at the time of his recapture. "I want to thank the Catholic Church for their help," he told the Buenos Aires daily *Clarín* in May 1994. It was an indiscretion he has been trying to rectify ever since.[34]

Former U.S. Justice Department Nazi-hunter John Loftus estimates that in those postwar years approximately 60,000 war criminals disappeared down the Rat Line to Argentina—"the single largest smuggling route for Nazi war criminals." Another resident of Bariloche, Priebke's neighbor, was a former Nazi officer named Reinhard Kopps, who had been a major player in the Rat Line. Kopps had assisted Bishop Hudal—the German prelate who was a go-between in the Vatican's protest threat during the roundup of the Roman Jews—in providing false identities to countless fugitives. Kopps admitted that he had an office in the Vatican. By the end of 1946, Loftus and coauthor Mark Aarons wrote, "the crush of escaping Nazis became so large that the Vatican's top agent in the 'refugee' network, Father [Krunoslav] Draganovic,[35] was commissioned full-time to arrange documents and transportation to Argentina and other South American countries."[36]

Priebke's case was typical. Traveling with his wife and two small children, he was given a Red Cross passport, courtesy of the Vatican, and safe passage out of Genoa. The Priebkes crossed the Atlantic on an ocean liner named *San Giorgio*, arriving in Buenos Aires with a "few dollars," he says.[37] Despite that meager beginning, safe passage stayed by his side. From waiting tables in a German-style beer hall to mongering sausages in Bariloche until retirement, it took only a one-word lapse, that abominable yes to Sam Donaldson, for safe passage to cast him aside.

In May 1996, the eighty-two-year-old Priebke was in the dock of an all-too-tiny courtroom back in Rome. Even before the proceedings got under way, the outlines of Priebke's defense were well known. "We did what they ordered us, you know. That was not a crime," he had told Donaldson in the original interview. The tired but effective obeying-orders stratagem would be hauled out once again. Three months later the Military Tribunal of Rome found Priebke "guilty but not punishable"; he had obeyed a superior order. He was to be released immediately, the court said.[38] The verdict was denounced throughout Italy and worldwide.

But a second chance to get it right arrived some months later when the Supreme Court of Cassation annulled the verdict. It had found evidence that Priebke had been freed by an unabashedly biased tribunal that had harbored an intent to absolve the defendant even before the trial began.[39]

The retrial was held the following summer. But there was an astonishing difference—another captured Nazi in the dock. He was older, higher-ranking in the SS, and had led a much more colorful postwar life than the daily white-apron grind of Bariloche's Vienna Delicatessen. SS Major Karl Hass, an exceptionally spry eighty-five-year-old, had been Kappler's intelligence chief and had killed two men in the Ardeatine Caves. Officially deceased, Hass had been tracked down by the prosecutor, acting on an inadvertent tip picked up from the garrulous Priebke gossiping with the media. After escaping Allied custody as a prisoner of war, Hass had remained in Rome, hiding in monasteries and helping his fellow Nazis down the Rat Line. One reason he had stayed behind was that while sheltered in a monastery he had been given a chance to continue his intelligence work, as a spy for the United States, and later for the Italian secret service in the Cold War.

No friend of his name-dropping codefendant, Hass was a star witness for the prosecution. In the Kappler trial, the court had concluded that the five men killed in the caves whose names were not on any list had been the result of a counting error, implicating list-keeper Priebke. Hass, however, now revealed the deep secret that had been covered up all these years: The Error of the Five Extra Men.

> At the Ardeatine [he testified], Priebke was there with the copy of the list. He got the people down [off the trucks] and canceled out their names. At a certain point, one of the prisoners was not on Priebke's list. At the end, in fact, there were five extra men. That was when Kappler said, "What do I do with these five? They've seen it all." I don't know if it was Kappler himself, or Priebke, or who—I don't believe it was Kappler— . . . I don't know who killed these five people.[40]

There it was: a simple solution, yet plausible enough to withstand any challenge. First there was one, then two, and so on. One by one, they were shunted aside, watching the others enter the tunnels, hearing the shots, again and again, five at a time, made to wait and made to wonder all those bloodletting hours what their own fate might be. After all, when there was one, then two, the killers could not know how many extras they would end up with. Only at the end would they decide what to do with these interlopers who had no authorization to be there because they were not on the list. And then, at the end, there were five, doomed for no other reason than having "seen it all."

On July 22, 1997, the Military Tribunal of Rome rejected the defense of obeying orders. The panel then defined the killings in the Ardeatine Caves as both a war crime and a crime against humanity under international law, punishable by *ergastolo*, life without parole, and not subject to any statute of limitation.[41]

The sentences, however, were reduced for both men, in consideration of their age and other extenuating circumstances. Priebke was to serve fifteen years under house arrest, and Hass was released on time served that same day. Although there were cries of too much leniency, and some of too little, the reaction to the decision among the families of the victims and the prosecution was satisfaction. "Even a sentence of a single day," said Chief Prosecutor Antonino Intelisano, "can be enough when it is a statement that we have not forgot."[42]

II. *DEFENSOR CIVITATIS*, THE UNFINISHED STORY

Twenty years would pass before anyone would dare to question publicly what Pius XII had done during the war. In the summer of 1944, Pius reached the summit of his prestige. In an age of dictators and the cult of personality, the Pope tightened his grip on Church power. "I don't want advisers," he told Cardinal Tardini. "I want people who do as I say."[1] When Maglione died that August, Pius assumed the office of Secretary of State. Never again in his lifetime would he hear an unkind word about the silence so perfectly kept in the name of neutrality even when freed from any restraint imposed by his relationship with the German occupiers. Indeed, the opposite was true. Some leaders of world Jewry could not still their urge to render homage to Pius XII, from World Jewish Congress official Aryeh Kubovy's 1945 appreciation-donation to the Pope's charities to Israel's Golda Meir's tribute to Pius following his death in 1958 for having "raised his voice in favor of the Jews."[2] As for *his* Jews, those rounded up under his very eyes, Pius's closest survivors lived to hear the Chief Rabbi of Rome, Elio Toaff, articulate what it had meant to the Jews of Rome to experience "the great compassionate goodness and magnanimity of the Pope during the unhappy years of the persecution and terror, when it seemed that for us there was no longer an escape."[3] And a decade later, in 1967, an Israeli diplomat, Pinchas Lapide, would discover by spreadsheet arithmetic and an abacus-like mind-set that Pius XII had saved the lives of "as many as 860,000 Jews."[4] By then, however, the Pope's efforts to rescue Jews during the Nazi times had undergone a dramatic reevaluation. An impassioned debate erupted in 1963 with Rolf Hochhuth's play, *Der Stellvertreter,* *"The Representative"* in London and *"The Deputy,"* in New York.[5]

By this time Pius's wartime aide, Monsignor Montini, was Pope Paul VI, who lost no time in defending his predecessor against the onslaught unleashed by the playwright. In a statement published at the time of his ascent to the papal throne, Montini maintained that public protest would have been "not only futile but harmful"; Pius XII would have been guilty of unleashing "still greater calamities involving innumerable innocent victims, let alone himself."[6] This justification would be seconded by nearly all of the Pope's defenders, and would invariably draw a unanimous reply from the critics that it was all but impossible to conceive of anything worse than the Holocaust that actually happened. The intensity of the clash of indignation prompted the normally hesitant Pope Paul to take two bold countermeasures. He waived the Vatican's seventy-five-year rule prohibiting release of its archival documents, promising publication "wholly and completely" of its World War II papers, and second, he initiated the process of sainthood for Pius XII.

Published piecemeal, the eleven-volume set of wartime documents was not complete until the early eighties, and even the Vatican admitted it was a mere sample of the whole—"edited according to exact scientific standards," one spokesman attested.[7] Historians were still far from consensus about Pius's activities when controversy flared up again in the mid-nineties. Pope John Paul II initiated a series of apologies for the fact that there were "too few" Catholics who opposed the Nazis, but he also formulated the strongest defense of Pius XII yet by advancing the case for his canonization. He had in fact planned Pius's beatification—the penultimate step to sainthood—as a central event of the Holy Year 2000, but a new outcry led to postponement of this plan.

A Hochhuth-like storm struck again in the fall of 1999 with the publication of John Cornwell's international bestseller *Hitler's Pope: The Secret History of Pius XII*. A Catholic-affairs writer and senior researcher at Cambridge's Jesus College, he had set out to rescue Pius's reputation from harm's way by telling the "full story," and, received by the Vatican as a paladin, was granted access to still-secret archival material. Waylaid along this route by what he uncovered, Cornwell was thrown into a state he described as "moral shock," which he preserved in the timbre of every page of his book. Behind the silence, he found evidence that convinced him that Pius was a "deeply flawed human being," afflicted with anti-Semitism and "a habitual fear and distrust of the Jews . . . the ideal Pope for Hitler's unspeakable plan."[8]

While controversy raged over the Cornwell book, the Vatican agreed to participate in an unprecedented international commission of Catholic and Jewish scholars, again to study the Vatican's wartime silence but as never before. Three historians were appointed by the Holy See and three others by an international committee representing Jewish organizations, including the Anti-Defamation League, B'nai B'rith, and the World Jewish Congress. The six scholars were authorized to undertake a critical examination of the

eleven volumes of Vatican wartime documents "to raise relevant questions and issues that, in our opinion, have not adequately or satisfactorily been resolved by the available documentation."[9] One year later, the commission submitted its report, positing forty-seven such questions and issues, and in July 2001, following the Vatican's denial of access to the documents that might provide the answers, disbanded.[10]

The four-decades-old great debate is not even a debate anymore but a polemic in which the Pope's defenders can do no better than cite decades-old research of deflated credibility while the critics, locked out of the Vatican's wartime archives, are driven to search for documents that might lend support to sweeping but irrelevant condemnations of the Catholic hierarchy from Saint Paul to John Paul.

The trouble lies in the central conundrum, attempting to understand Pius's silence in terms of the Holocaust. From Hochhuth on, virtually every researcher, sooner or later, feels obliged to set sight on German-occupied Rome and examine the Pope's reaction to the roundup and deportation of *his* Jews, under his own windows, as Weizsäcker famously telegraphed Berlin. The Pope's policy of silence emerges as immutable and can be either defended or attacked, but not seriously disputed.[11] This is the "given," the starting point of the "great debate." But the history of the full nine months of the German occupation of Rome, as this book attempts to show, reveals a pope of many silences with multiple variations. His silence in the autumn extended beyond Rome's Jews to his silence in the winter of Rome's Nazi repression. He was silent in the spring of the Ardeatine Caves massacre of his children, his fellow Catholics, and in the summer of liberation, the season when his silence had been emptied of any meaning. Moreover, there were silences that predated the Holocaust as Fascism bonded with the Church, and there were those of the postwar period, in the tens of thousands of Nazi fugitives saved by the sheltering silence of the Rat Line.

To be sure, nonsectarian papal silence in the service of Vatican "neutrality" has long been recognized, though invariably added to the list of justifications for the silence on the Holocaust as a tactical feature of the "larger" strategy of mediating a separate peace in the West. Failed or not, in the light of Stalinist totalitarianism, even some critics would agree, Pius's position was tenable. But far less reasonable is the Vatican's silence in occupied Rome. The *moral* failure of this strategy, which was based on Pius XII's committing one of the great misreadings of history, is evidenced by the relationship between the Vatican and the Germans occupiers—a Faustian pact by definition. The papal obsession with protecting the physical integrity of the

Vatican City-State by any means, against enemies less real than imagined, was fulfilled in exchange for papal silence, not one silence, but one following another, a whole range of silences for the whole range of Nazi and Fascist brutality in Rome.

LONG AGO, in the first storm over the silence, one of Pius's subtlest critics, historian Leon Poliakov—later to be joined by many Catholic writers— stated plainly that the Pope should have lifted his voice simply because it was the morally right thing to do, whatever the consequences. More than ever, that appears to be the judgment of history.

The search for the historical Pius XII is perhaps more relevant today than ever. When, in September 2000, John Paul II beatified "the good pope" John XXIII before a joyful 100,000 pilgrims in Saint Peter's Square, a sec- ond pontiff received the same recognition. The other pope was to have been Pius XII, but to deflect the recent outburst in the old controversy, Pius XII was replaced with Pius IX, the nineteenth-century tyrannical anti-Semite still scorned by Jews everywhere. His beatification stirred up a predictable international protest of significant proportions and, as a kind of test case that survived the furor, probably helped advance his successor's cause. In any event, the vehicle of Pius XII's elevation remains ready.

Pope Pius XII as a saint, a modern day role model worthy of emulation for the one billion Catholics worldwide, would close the case forever, with immediate far-flung repercussions for Catholics and non-Catholics, partic- ularly Jews but other faiths as well. Pius's secular works would be sanctioned as wise and fruitful by his Universal Church. His deeds would be singled out for imitation and veneration; virtue would be found in a passivity that was sometimes indistinguishable from complicity before the acts of perpetrators of crimes against humanity; foresight would be seen in his conversion of silence into the currency used to buy protection for a cherished but inani- mate place in the sun; and, finally, upheld by the Church would be the recti- tude of his silence of silences as having forestalled still greater calamities even while European Jewry was being systematically devoured. He would be credited—as his defenders say he must and his critics say he does not deserve—with saving the lives of thousands of Jews, saving the Romans, and saving Rome.

There would be a Saint of Silence, but the divine grace that is supposed to shine in such a servant of God would light nothing in its path.

Chronology

ROME, SUMMER 1943–SPRING 1944

July

19   Rome bombed for the first time during the war.

25   King Vittorio Emanuele III arrests Mussolini and names Marshal Pietro Badoglio head of a new, military government.

27   The long-suppressed anti-Fascist political parties from right to left form a Committee of Opposition demanding the dismantling of the Fascist Party, press freedom, and the release of all political prisoners.

August

4   Badoglio makes a secret bid to the Allies to extricate Italy from a war it can no longer sustain. Meanwhile, Hitler pours additional troops into Italy.

14   Following a second Allied bombing, Badoglio declares Rome an open city—a demilitarized zone—an idea originated and promoted by the Pope. The new regime takes no steps to demilitarize, and the Allies reject open-city status.

30   Three of the anti-Fascist parties on the left, anticipating a German onslaught, set up a Military Council in preparation for a civilian resistance movement.

September

3   Rome signs an unconditional-surrender "armistice," to be kept secret until the imminent invasion of the mainland.

8   Eisenhower airs the news of Italy's capitulation, as U.S. General Mark Clark's Fifth Army begins amphibious landing operations at Salerno, south of Naples. Badoglio orders Italian troops to end hostilities against the Allies, but to oppose attacks from "any other quarter."

9   As German Supreme Commander in Italy, Kesselring moves on Rome, and the King, Badoglio, and key ministers flee the capital under cover of predawn darkness, leaving no one in charge. The opposition committee reconstitutes itself as the CLN, the National Liberation Committee, calling on all Italians to resist the Germans.

10   The historic last stand of both civilians and army regulars at the Pyramid of Cestius succumbs to superior force, as German Tiger tanks sweep them aside. The armed Resistance, born like the Roman phoenix, symbol of the Eternal City, goes underground.

11   Kesselring declares Rome an open city, blatantly militarizing it more than ever, proclaiming it a war territory, and placing the citizenry under his command.

Summary executions are decreed for nearly every infraction. The Vatican queries the German ambassador regarding Berlin's position on the extraterritorial status of the city-state.

12   A task force of German paratroopers swoops down on central Italy's highest mountaintop and rescues Mussolini from captivity to Hitler's waiting embrace in Munich. Within days, the Duce forms the neo-Fascist Italian Social Republic (RSI), propped up in the northern Italian lakeside town of Salò by German fire-power.

13   Hitler offers assurances that the Germans will respect the Pope's sovereignty and "protect Vatican City from the fighting."

25   SS Lieutenant Colonel Kappler, Gestapo Chief of the occupied city, is advised by Himmler that the roundup and deportation of Italy's Jews is to be undertaken at once, beginning with Rome.

26   On his own initiative, Kappler summons Roman Jewish leaders Foà and Almansi, demanding fifty kilograms of gold against the threat of deportation. Two days later, they comply.

OCTOBER

6   Some occupiers attempt secretly to save the Jews of Rome, most notably Consul Möllhausen, who sends a telegram of objection to Berlin—not so much to spare them from the Holocaust as to deflect a potential crisis in German–Vatican rela-tions. Pope Pius XII has refrained from public condemnation of the distant slaughter of Europe's Jews, but with the Germans at his front door, a papal protest appears inevitable.

9   The Möllhausen telegram draws a sharp rebuke from Foreign Minister von Ribbentrop, mainly because Möllhausen has used the word *liquidate* when refer-ring to Himmler's order to deport the Jews. This is the first time someone in the Foreign Office has used this term in an official document, and news of the Consul's misstep is leaked to the Vatican (and intercepted by British intelligence and passed on to London and Washington). Only the target, the oldest Jewish set-tlement in the Western world, remains unaware of the Reich's intent.

16   In a house-to-house sweep of the ghetto and other neighborhoods, more than a thousand Jews are seized during the morning and early afternoon, many are dragged away in the line of sight from the Pope's own windows. Two days later the Jews are shipped by rail to Auschwitz.

28   When the Pope fails to follow through on a veiled warning of public condemna-tion of the deportation of the Roman Jews, German Ambassador von Weizsäcker declares the threat of papal protest "liquidated."

NOVEMBER

15   After gaining less than fifteen miles in one month since crossing the Volturno River, General Clark orders a two-week pause in operations to give his troops a chance to recover from general fatigue.

22   Roosevelt, Churchill, and Stalin relegate the Italian campaign to secondary im-portance. Eisenhower is shifted to England to command Overlord, the cross-

channel invasion. Churchill nevertheless convinces Roosevelt of the enormous psychological and political value of capturing Rome.

DECEMBER

17   Rome's armed Resistance begins to strike the German occupation forces directly, designating central Rome, with its heavy concentration of occupation forces, as a prime attack zone. Taking the lead are the Partisans of the recently formed GAP Central—four units of the clandestine Communist Party's highly disciplined military arm, GAP (Patriotic Action Group).

21   Responding to the rise in urban guerrilla warfare, a mixed formation of Fascist and Gestapo agents makes the first collective raid on the Resistance. Three Vatican institutions known to be harboring influential anti-Fascists and military officers are targeted.

JANUARY

1   Returning to England, Churchill has just gained Roosevelt's support to move "full steam ahead" on a battle plan code-named Operation Shingle. Aimed at breaking the deadlock on the southern front, Allied forces are to land behind enemy lines on the beaches at Anzio and Nettuno, a mere thirty miles from Rome.

22   Operation Shingle achieves a complete predawn surprise, the Allies hitting the Anzio beaches and meeting almost no resistance. The road to Rome appears wide open. A plan to link up with Fifth Army forces coming from the south and march into Rome aborts, however, as attempts by Mark Clark to cross the heavily defended Rapido River end disastrously.

23   In Rome, OSS spy Peter Tompkins meets with the CLN Military Council to plan an uprising, but is interrupted by orders radioed from the front to postpone the insurrection due to a "slight delay." The Resistance leaders grow wary of Allied intentions. Meanwhile, news of the Anzio landing creates a state of euphoria among the Romans, but has a calamitous effect on the Partisans, who fall victim to a general lapse in security measures. Over the next ten days, the Gestapo succeeds in arresting key Resistance figures on both the right and the left.

FEBRUARY

3   Rome police chief Pietro Caruso and his Fascist police force, working jointly with the Koch Gang and Kappler's Gestapo, conduct the most audacious violation of Vatican sanctuaries thus far, raiding the extraterritorial Basilica of Saint Paul's Outside the Walls. The Vatican raises its strongest protest of the occupation, but the Germans deny complicity.

15   An Allied air raid destroys the sixth-century abbey founded by Saint Benedict on top of Monte Cassino.

MARCH

12   Pius XII, marking the fifth anniversary of his coronation, holds a public audience in Saint Peter's Square for Rome's thousands of bombed-out refugees and bomb

victims themselves, drawing a crowd of some 100,000. Pius addresses his remarks solely against the Allied bombings—"an air war that respects no limits or laws"—and the looming threat of all-out destruction should the Eternal City be turned into a battlefield.

17   OSS double agent Maurizio Giglio, a lieutenant in the Fascist police but working for American spy Peter Tompkins, is arrested by the Koch Gang, betrayed by his radio operator. Now, with Giglio in enemy hands and aware of every detail of his activities, Tompkins goes into deep cover.

23   Timed to the 25th anniversary celebrations of the founding of Fascism, GAP Central carries out its boldest and largest assault. A heavily armed column of 156 SS police marching through Via Rasella in the center of Rome is attacked, leaving 32 dead and scores of wounded. Notified within minutes, Hitler demands a reprisal that will "make the world tremble." That evening, SS Col. Dollmann meets with Pius's personal liaison to the occupiers, Fr. Pfeiffer, to alert him to what he calls an imminent bloodbath. Pfeiffer agrees to immediately inform the Pope, who, Dollmann believes, could "thwart or delay" the reprisal.

24   Sometime before 10:15 A.M., the Pope's Secretariat of State receives a report on Via Rasella from an Italian official close to the German High Command; it warns the Vatican to expect that for every German killed, ten Italians will be executed. In the meantime, Kappler and his officers have prepared a list of 320 men to be slain. Later that day the executions are carried out in Rome's Ardeatine Caves.

25   The news of the massacre is announced at noon. A few hours later, the Vatican newspaper, *L'Osservatore Romano*, appears with the same text, but unlike the other, Fascist-controlled papers issues a comment. Refraining from any word of condemnation of the Nazi atrocity in the Eternal City, the *Osservatore* declares the Partisans "the guilty parties," whose "deeds in Via Rasella" had caused the sacrifice of 320 innocent victims.

April

1   Bread riots begin in Rome.

7   In the Ostiense district, a group of women and children raids a bakery that serves the German troops stationed in Rome. The SS captures and kills ten of the women.

23   GAP Central Partisan Gugliemo Blasi is arrested and found in possession of forged SS documents. He opts betrayal and for the millions of lire in reward money for the heads of the most wanted Partisans. He aids in the capture of his GAP comrades. GAP Central is disbanded.

May

3   A CLN-sponsored general strike achieves some work stoppages and slowdowns. The CLN is induced to put aside its differences with the Badoglians in the name of national unity.

10   The Chief of the SS police and persecution apparatus in all of occupied Italy meets secretly in the Vatican with Pius XII. Alone with the Pontiff, General Karl Wolff offers his services to advance the Pope's wish to mediate a compromise peace. Pius thanks him for his support.

11 Whiting out a starlit sky over Monte Cassino, Allied artillery launches Operation Diadem, General Alexander's innovative plan for smashing the Gustav Line by brute force. A swift breakthrough is led by the Fifth Army's French Expeditionary Force.

23 Phase two of Diadem—a breakout at Anzio to unite the forces of the beachhead with the American Fifth and British Eighth Armies heading north through the Liri Valley—again catches the Germans with their guard down.

25 Ordered by Alexander to cut off the German retreat route, Clark sees this as a ploy to allow the British to beat him in the race to capture Rome. In a decision bordering on insubordination, Clark turns the bulk of his forces toward Rome.

JUNE

2 Pius XII goes on the air. "Whosoever raises his hand against Rome," he proclaims on Vatican radio, "will be guilty of matricide before the civilized world and the eternal judgment of God." Will Hitler abandon Rome without a fight? The CLN and the Military Council, right, left, and center, along with Badoglio and his King, have reached an accord with one another and the Allies. There will be no insurrection in the Eternal City.

4 Shortly after midnight, German forces begin to leave Rome, heading north. Sometime in the late afternoon, one of the spearhead units formed by Clark passes through the south gate of Hadrian's wall.

5 Mark Clark makes his triumphant entry into Rome without a trace of fanfare, as American troops are showered with flowers and cheering throngs. More than 100,000 citizens and soldiers heed the call heard everywhere in the city to gather in Saint Peter's Square "to thank the Pope." The ascetic white-robed figure commends the Germans as much as the Allies for inspiring divine mercy to spare Rome from destruction. He calls on the Romans to renounce all lust for vengeance, blesses the kneeling throng, and withdraws from the roar of good feelings, leaving others to articulate the inference that he above all others merits the Vatican-bestowed title of *defensor civitatis*, defender of the city.

THE VALUE OF THE LIRA

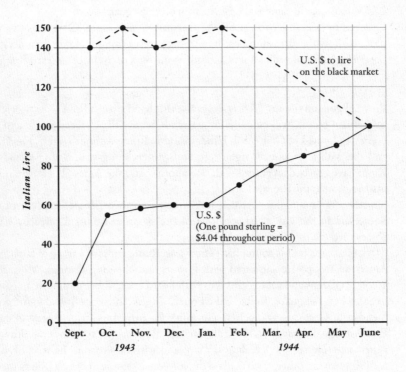

U.S. $ to lire
on the black market

Italian Lire

U.S. $
(One pound sterling =
$4.04 throughout period)

Sept.   Oct.   Nov.   Dec.   Jan.   Feb.   Mar.   Apr.   May   June

1943   *1944*

PACELLI V. KATZ ET AL.

In 1974, the first of five penal proceedings was initiated in Rome against me as the author of *Death in Rome* and the screenplay of the film based on the book. I and my two codefendants, the film's producer and director, Carlo Ponti and George P. Cosmatos, respectively, were charged with "defaming the memory" of Pope Pius XII, who died in 1958. The charges, dealing specifically with the Ardeatine Caves massacre, were pressed by the Pope's niece, Countess Elena Pacelli Rossignani. In *Death in Rome*, though none of the Vatican's wartime documents had yet been released, I had presented circumstantial evidence that Pius had known of the impending massacre and made no discernible attempt to prevent it. The basis of this conclusion came from six separate sources, though no single element was conclusive.[1] My efforts to obtain additional information at the Vatican, the primary source, were to no avail.[2] Nevertheless, I felt justified by the weight of what was known then in concluding that Pius XII behaved in this case as he had in others, maintaining a well-elaborated policy of silence as the lesser of two evils. In the end, I left the question open, awaiting the accessibility of the Vatican archives.

Whether I had written a book and a film that constituted the commission of a crime of high insult in the Eternal City or I had exercised my right of free speech guaranteed by the Italian constitution was the only substantive issue in the case, but the longevity of the proceedings, and a certain amount of ongoing attention, provided fertile ground for the revisionists. The Vatican had reacted strongly to my assertion in the book that the Pope had had advance warning of the reprisal. Even before publication of *Death in Rome*, a Vatican spokesman stated that the charge would be "simple to disprove because it is a vicious lie."[3] That was in 1967, and the Vatican's public promise, reported in the *New York Times*, to do the disproving in the *Osservatore Romano* "after the book was published,"[4] had been left unfulfilled for seven years, which made the court action appear as the response.

Indeed, to disprove that the Pope had any knowledge of German intentions is precisely what the prosecution in the first trial tried to do, and the court, the Tribunal of Rome, spared neither effort nor expense in its quest. Apart from sitting in the capital for nearly two years, it traveled and reconvened in the fortress-prison at Gaeta to take testimony from Kappler, then still serving his life sentence; it traveled beyond Italy's frontiers, reconvening in Germany to hear from Colonel Dollmann, and again beyond frontiers to Vatican City itself to gather the recollections of Cardinal Nasalli Rocca. At last, when it had heard everyone—some two dozen witnesses—the Tribunal arrived at what it called the "one and only truth" ("*un'unica verità*"). It declared that "in the hours that preceded the Calvary of the Ardeatine, the Pontiff knew nothing of the order for the reprisal and the way it would be carried out."[5] Found guilty, we defendants were sentenced to a combined total of twenty-eight months in prison.

On appeal, a panel of three judges overturned the verdict of the Tribunal. The reconstruction of the events related in *Death in Rome*, which it called "a contribution to the history of the period," demonstrated that I had fairly exercised the right of historical inquiry guaranteed by the Italian constitution, "and therefore Katz must be exonerated of [the charges]."[6] Ruling similarly regarding the film, the court on July 1, 1978, acquitted all defendants.[7] This judgment, however, as permitted under Italian law, was itself appealed by the prosecution. In the meantime, the Governatorato document—quoted above in full, in translation, on p. 241—surfaced from the Vatican's own archives, and the question of whether the Pope knew was settled. This document proved beyond any doubt that at least five hours and fifteen minutes before the first man was killed in the Ardeatine Caves, the State Secretariat of His Holiness had been authoritatively informed that it was "foreseen that for every German killed ten Italians will be executed."

Stripped of its "one and only truth," the case nevertheless limped on in the higher courts. The appeals court proceeding that had concluded in acquittal was declared a mistrial, but the case against the film was thrown out. In my retrial, the original question of whether the Pope knew of the coming reprisal was not and could no longer be at issue by virtue of the new Vatican document. Instead the prosecution attacked the "tone" of the book (read only in a third-party translation) as defamatory. That served as proof enough for the retrial court, which found guilt by reason of an "intention to denigrate" the Pope.[8]

Acting on my appeal to the highest court in Italy, the Supreme Court of Cassation brought an end to the affair exactly ten years after it began. It annulled the retrial verdict and dismissed the case entirely on the grounds of an amnesty dating back to 1970.[9] That meant that none of the preceding trials had any basis in penal law, since the alleged crime had been rendered "nonexistent" ("*estinto*") before the first indictment. The court left open the possibility of a civil damage suit, which Pius's family decided not to pursue.[10]

SOURCES AND NOTES

This book is based to a large degree on sources that became available years after the battle for Rome.

Just as the international controversy over *The Deputy* convinced the Vatican to break long-standing regulations of superannuated secrecy and declassify a sizable selection of its wartime papers, it took an act of the U.S. Congress—the 1998 Nazi War Crimes Disclosure Act—to shake loose the innumerable pages of particularly sensitive OSS secrets from the CIA. I was given access to primary material concerning the Ardeatine Caves war crime because of my trial, as described in the previous pages. The Priebke affair of the mid-90s became a significant new source of knowledge of Rome under the Nazis.

Even the studgiest Italian archival sources have by now substantially lowered the access threshold.

I was only imprecisely aware of the extent and nature of the new material on the Italian side when, in the spring of 2000, I began the Rome-based research for this book, but the time could not have been more auspicious. For the past five years, I discovered, a task force of professional and volunteer researchers had been sifting through the newly or recently opened files, not only in the Roman archives, but also in Germany, the U.K., and the U.S., twenty archives in all. Sponsored by the city of Rome, the researchers had been collecting documentary materials pertinent to the nine months of the German occupation. The project had been promoted by a historical society known as Irsifar (Istituto Romano per la Storia d'Italia dal Fascismo alla Resistenza), and the documents gathered, which numbered in the tens of thousands, touched every aspect of the period from the events leading up to the fall of Fascism to the Allied liberation of occupied Rome and its aftermath.

Of this collection, 1,370 documents were selected as representative of the whole, though they included some well-known classic material, such as Giacomo Debenedetti's narrative of the roundup of the Jews of Rome. An edited version of this sampling was subsequently put on a CD-ROM, packaged and distributed with a slender volume of essays (*Documenti della Resistenza a Roma e nel Lazio*, Rome: Biblink Editori, 2001), while the complete and unedited collection, called the Archivio Dorer, was retained by Irsifar to be catalogued and eventually made available to scholars. To my good fortune, my own arrival at Irsifar fell between the moment the selection of the 1,370 documents for the CD had been completed and the moment the entire Dorer archive was shut down indefinitely for the cataloguing. Thus, for a period of several weeks—too brief, to be sure—having stumbled in at the right time, I was alone with it all at my fingertips, enjoying the fruits of perhaps a hundred man-years of research.

In the end, however, even the complete collection was itself a selection from a larger whole. I had to track down the originals, at least those that would be cited, not only to verify them but to learn what had not been selected. The task was made easier by the diligence of the Dorer researchers, who recorded the precise provenance of every document.

I was fortunate to have had long-standing relationships with several of the principal figures of the story, some of whom I had interviewed repeatedly.

Finally, a word about the older sources. The primary and secondary works cited here need no further elaboration, with the exception of my use of my own archives. This as yet uncatalogued collection of written and audiovisual documentary research materials specific to the German occupation of Rome and to my trial, dating back to 1964, is located at the Biblioteca Comunale, Piazza del Comune, 52020 Pergine Valdarno, Italy, and is accessible to scholars by written application only to the chief librarian. The archive also contains notes of conversations with persons I had interviewed for my books *Death in Rome* and *Black Sabbath*, and, much later, *Dossier Priebke*. Further, there are interview notes for articles, book reviews, and so forth with people named in this book. When I quote interviewees directly, particularly Carla Capponi and Rosario Bentivegna, I often cite the pages in their memoirs that correspond to the citation in question; there are some differences, however, most of them minor, based on my notes. Capponi died before I completed my manuscript, but I have had the opportunity to review with Bentivegna every incident and quotation attributed to him. The same is true with Peter Tompkins.

ABBREVIATIONS USED

ARCHIVES AND DOCUMENTS

ACS	Archivio Centrale dello Stato, Rome.
ADSS	*Actes et documents du Saint Siège relatifs à la seconde guerre mondiale*, 11 vols., Vatican City: Liberia Editrice Vaticana, 1965–81.
ASC	Archivio Storico Capitolino, Rome.
ASL	Archivio del Seminario Lombardo, Rome.
Dollmann ms.	Unpublished manuscript by Dollmann written in 1948 and appended by hand when given to me in 1965.
Dorer	Documenti della Resistenza Romana.
EP Afragola	Priebke's sworn statement, taken when he was a prisoner of war, August 28, 1946, at Afragola, near Naples (Dorer: 633).
FO	Foreign Office (U.K.).
Foà-Almansi reports	Three reports by the Roman Jewish community and the Rome-based union of Jewish communities of Italy regarding the Nazi anti-Jewish persecutions of the occupied city. The first two are by Foà, dated November 15, 1943, and June 20, 1944. Almansi's is dated August 15, 1944. (Title C Documents are in the archives of the Centro di Documentazione Ebraica Contemporanea, Milan.)
FRUS	*Foreign Relations of the United States, Vol. II. Europe, 1943*, Washington, D.C.: Government Printing Office, 1964.
INQ	Inquest of the Ardeatine Caves Commission. The principal report of the exhumation and identification team led by forensic scientist Attilio As-

carelli was originally published in A. Ascarelli, *Le Fosse Ardeatine*, Rome: Palombi, 1945. A revised, expanded edition, the sixth, was published by the Associazione delle Famiglie Italiane dei Martiri (ANFIM) in 2001.

IRSIFAR   Istituto Romano per la Storia d'Italia dal Fascismo alla Resistenza, Rome.

Kappler
sentenza   Transcript of the final verdict in THK, handed down January 10, 1954, by the Military Tribunal of Rome after several appeals. The 30,000-word text is published in the full 2001 ANFIM edition of *Le Fosse Ardeatine*.

KT   Transcript of Kappler's 1961 testimony in the Eichmann trial, taken at the military prison in Gaeta, Italy, June 27, 1961. I have used the original, but an English translation is available at *www.nizkor.org*.

NARA   National Archives and Records Administration, Washington, D.C.

OSS   Office of Strategic Services (NARA collection of CIA release 2000–2002).

Priebke-Hass
sentenza   Transcript of the 120-page verdict in TEPH, handed down by the Military Tribunal of Rome and filed on September 13, 1997.

PRO   Public Records Office, London.

RG   Record Group (NARA file-location designation).

RK appeal   "Corte d'Appello di Roma: Motivi di appello": An 88-page brief motivating the appeal of the lower-court ruling in TRK.

RK ARC   Archives of Robert Katz.

RK sentenza
appello   Transcript of acquittal verdict in TRK, handed down by the Court of Appeal of Rome, July 1, 1981.

RK sentenza
tribunale   Transcript of lower-court verdict in TRK, handed down by the Tribunal of Rome, November 27, 1975.

RK sentenza
corte suprema   Transcript of final verdict in TRK handed down by the Supreme Court of Cassation, September 29, 1983.

TAK   Trial of Albert Kesselring, in UNWCC.

TEP   Trial of Erich Priebke, transcript deposited at Tribunale Militare di Roma, Viale delle Milizie, 5/C, Rome.

TEPH   Trial of Erich Priebke and Karl Hass, transcript deposited at Tribunale Militare di Roma, Viale delle Milizie, 5/C, Rome.

THK   Trial of Herbert Kappler et al., transcript deposited at Tribunale Militare di Roma, Viale delle Milizie, 5/C, Rome.

TMM   Trial of Eberhard von Mackensen and Kurt Mälzer, in UNWCC.

Tompkins
papers   Peter Tompkins's personal collection of documentary material and his unpublished manuscripts pertaining to his OSS career.

Tompkins
report   Peter Tompkins's Report to General William Donovan of March 5, 1945, in OSS.

TPC   Trial of Pietro Caruso. Transcript in Z. Algardi, ed., *Il processo Caruso*, Rome: Darsena, 1945.

TPK   Trial of Pietro Koch (see MG, below).
TRK   Trial of Robert Katz et al. (later Katz alone). Transcripts of all five Katz
             proceedings are deposited in Rome at the following courts, listed with the
             year of the verdict:
             1. Tribunale di Roma, Sezione Quarta Penale, 1975.
             2. Corte d'Appello di Roma, Sezione Prima Penale, 1978.
             3. Corte Suprema di Cassazione, Sezione Sesta Penale, 1979.
             4. Corte d'Appello di Roma, Sezione Terza Penale, 1981.
             5. Corte Suprema di Cassazione, Sezione Quinta Penale, 1983 (offi-
                cially deposited January 4, 1984).
UNWCC   United Nations War Crimes Commission, *Law Reports of Trials of War
             Criminals*, vol. 8, London: H.M. Stationery Office, 1949; see also Web
             Genocide Documentation Centre, *www.ess.ac.uk/genocide*.
WO   War Office (U.K.).

**FREQUENTLY CITED OR REFERENCED PERSONS INTERVIEWED BY ROBERT KATZ,
AND DATES OF INTERVIEWS**

AKi   Albrecht von Kessel, 1967*
CCi   Carla Capponi, 1965–2001*
CS   Carlo Salinari, 1965*
DG   Duilio Grigioni, 1965*
ED   Eugen Dollmann, 1965–1975*
EFMi   Eitel Friedrich Möllhausen, 1967–1981*
GA   Giorgio Amendola, 1965*
GG   Gerhard Gumpert, 1968–1975*
HK   Herbert Kappler, 1974*
MF   Mario Fiorentini, 1965
MNR   Cardinal Mario Nasalli Rocca, 1975*
MT   Michael Tagliacozzo, 1967–1968
MTM   Maria Teresa Regard, 1996*
PB   Pasquale Balsamo, 1965–1990
PT   Peter Tompkins, 1965–2003
RB   Rosario Bentivegna, 1965–2003
RL   Renzo Levi, 1967*
SS   Settimia Spizzichino, 1967–2000*
SSo   Settimio Sorani, 1967
*= deceased

BOOKS

A&W-1   Adleman, R., and Walton, G., *The Devil's Brigade*, New York: Bantam
             Books, 1967 (paperback ed.).
A&W-2   Adleman, R., and Walton, G., *Rome Fell Today*, New York: Bantam Books,
             1970 (paperback ed.).
ACB   Cave Brown, A., *The Last Hero: Wild Bill Donovan*, New York: Vintage
             Books, 1984 (paperback ed.).
AG   Giovannetti, A., *Roma, città aperta*, Milan: Ancora, 1962 (diary format but
             written years later).

AK   Kesselring, A., *A Soldier's Record*, New York: William Morrow, 1954.
AP   Portelli, A., *L'ordine è già stata eseguita: Roma, le Fosse Ardeatine, la memoria*, rev. ed., Rome: Donzelli Editore, 2001.
BS   Katz, R., *Black Sabbath: A Journey Through a Crime Against Humanity*, New York: Macmillan, 1969.
CC   Capponi, C. *Con cuore di donna*, Milan: Il Saggiatore, 2000.
CD'E   D'Este, C. *Fatal Decision: Anzio and the Battle for Rome*, New York: Harper, 1991.
CDS-1   De Simone, C., *Venti angeli sopra Roma*, Milan: Mursia, 1993.
CDS-2   ———, *Roma città prigioniera*, Milan: Mursia, 1994.
CT   Trabucco, C., *La prigionia di Roma*, Rome: S.E.L.L., 1945.
DIR   Katz, R., *Death in Rome*, New York: Macmillan, 1967.
DP   ———, *Dossier Priebke: L'Anatomia di un processo*, Milan: Rizzoli, 1997 (available in Italian only).
ED-1   Dollmann, E., *Roma nazista*, Milan: Longanesi, 1949.
ED-2   ———, *The Interpreter: Memoirs of Doktor Eugen Dollmann*, London: Hutchinson, 1967.
EFM   Möllhausen, E. F., *La carte perdente*, Rome: Sestante, 1948.
ES   Sevareid, E. *Not So Wild a Dream*. rev. ed., New York: Atheneum, 1978.
FHS   Katz, R., *The Fall of the House of Savoy*, New York: Macmillan, 1971.
GDB   Debenedetti, G., *16 ottobre 1943*, Milan: Il Saggiatore, 1960 (amplified ed. contains his related essay "Otto ebrei").
JC   Cornwell, J., *Hitler's Pope: The Secret History of Pius XII*, New York: Viking, 1999.
JS   Scrivener, J. (pseud.), *Inside Rome with the Germans*, New York: Macmillan, 1945 (see p. 362).
MC   Clark, M., *Calculated Risk*, New York: Harper, 1950.
MdW   Wyss, M. de, *Rome Under the Terror*, London: Robert Hale, 1945.
MG   Griner, M., *La "Banda Koch": Il Reparto Speciale di Polizia 1943–44*, Turin: Bollati Boringhieri, 2000.
MSD   Davis, M., *Who Defends Rome?* New York: Dial Press, 1972.
OC   Chadwick, O., *Britain and the Vatican During the Second World War*, Cambridge: Cambridge University Press, 1988 (paperback ed.).
PT-1   Tompkins, P., *A Spy in Rome*, New York: Simon & Schuster, 1962.
PT-2   ———, *Italy Betrayed*, New York: Simon & Schuster, 1966.
PT-3   ———, *L'altra Resistenza*, Milan: Rizzoli, 1995 (available in Italian only).
RB-1   Bentivegna, R., *Achtung Banditen!: Roma 1944*, rev. ed., Milan: Mursia, 1983, 1994.
RB-2   ———, and Mazzantini, C., *C'eravamo tanto odiati*, a cura di Dino Messina, Milan: Baldini & Castoldi, 1997.
RB-3   ———, and De Simone, C., *Operazione via Rasella*, Rome: Editori Riuniti, 1996.
RDF   De Felice, R., *Mussolini*, 8 vols. Turin: Einaudi, 1965–1998 (paperback ed.).
RPC   Capano, R. P., *La Resistenza in Roma*, 2 vols. Naples: Macchiaroli, 1963.
RT   Trevelyan, R., *Rome '44: The Battle for the Eternal City*, New York: Viking, 1981.

ing but the bombing of Rome should consider their duties in respect of the unprecedented crime against humanity of Hitler's campaign of extermination of the Jews." (Quoted in OC: 216.)

11. See communications of March 1, June 15, 28, 29, 1943, *FRUS:* 915, 918, 923, 925.
12. CDS-1: 252–253.
13. Retired San Lorenzo housepainter Anselmo Ricci, quoted ibid.: 254.
14. Exchange of letters in *FRUS:* 926, 931.
15. *FRUS:* Tittmann to Hull, July 26, 1943.
16. CDS-1: 246.
17. Puntoni, P., *Vittorio Emanuele III*, Milan, 1958: 139–140 (diary entry of July 19, 1943).
18. One of the planes that bombed Ciampino that day was a B-24 dubbed *Delta Rebel No. 2*, with its world famous gunner on board, Clark Gable.
19. Puntoni: 126 (diary entry of March 16, 1943).
20. Mussolini, B., *Il tempo del bastone e della carota*, Milan: Edizione FPE, 1966, 47.
21. For the summit and Ambrosio's meeting with the King, see Deakin, F. W., *The Brutal Friendship*. Rev. ed., New York: Harper & Row, 1966: 411–425.
22. Document in CDS-1: 279.
23. CDS-1: 182.
24. Monelli, P. *Roma 1943*, rev. ed., Milan: Longanesi, 1963: 244.
25. Deakin: 444.
26. Kirkpatrick, I., *Mussolini: A Study in Power*, New York: Avon, 1964: 534 (paperback ed).
27. For Mussolini's version, see his *Il tempo del bastone:* 64–65; the King's is in Bartoli, D., *La fine della monarchia*, Milan, 1947: 234; cf. Puntoni: 144–145.
28. RB-1: 18, RB-2: 149.
29. It was published in wartime Britain in 1945 and appears in many bibliographies but has received little attention. The diary entry cited here is dated July 26, 1943: 48.
30. OSS: RG 226, CIA, Box 6, Doc/D 987: 6.
31. ED-2: 232.
32. Bullock, A., *Hitler: A Study in Tyranny*, rev. ed., New York: Harper & Row, 1960: 637.
33. JC: 313.
34. Text in WSC-5: 99–100.
35. The second bombing, on August 13, targeted more or less the same areas as the first. On the following day, the new government, spurred by the Vatican, unilaterally declared Rome an open city to much public approval. A recently surfaced document signed by Badoglio, however, reveals that he did little more than order a study of how to demilitarize to make the self-proclaimed open-city status acceptable to the belligerents (Dorer: doc. 104).
36. Montgomery diary, quoted in CD'E: 35.
37. In contrast to the Red scare raised by Badoglio, the opposition was representative of the full political spectrum, from Monarchists and Christian Democrats to Socialists and Communists. The group would shortly evolve into the six-partite Comitato di Liberazione Nazionale (CLN), or National Liberation Committee, the basis of the Italian Resistance movement.
38. Dorer: doc. 94.

39. Garland, A., and Smyth, H. M., *Sicily and the Surrender of Italy*, Washington, D.C.: Government Printing Office, 1965: 509.
40. Quoted in CD'E: 38.
41. OSS RG 226, CIA, Box 6, Doc/D 987: 14; cf. ED-2: 258–60.
42. *FHS*: 354.
43. Ibid.
44. Ibid.: 355.
45. Ibid.: 356.

TWO: THE PYRAMID

1. La Pasionara, a Spanish communist revolutionary whose real name was Dolores Ibarruri, was world famous at the time as a heroine of Spain's civil war. Said by her enemies to have once cut a priest's throat with her teeth, she was regarded by the left as a kind of female Che Guevara. See CC: 96–97.
2. Ibid.: 33.
3. AP: 119.
4. RB-2: 158.
5. On the tortuous capitulation negotiations see Garland & Smyth: 526, MSD: 438.
6. Lochner, L., ed., *The Goebbels Diaries*, Garden City, N.Y.: Doubleday, 1948: 492.
7. ED-2: 262–263.
8. MSD: 438.
9. At this hour, the King and the rest of the absconding party, after a misadventurous Keystone Kops dash across the Apennines, pursued by visions of being hanged by the side of the road if caught by the Germans, were aboard an Italian warship, the *Baionetta*, steaming south on the Adriatic but still unsure of where they would land. Later in the day, they would debark circumspectly at the port of Brindisi, in the heel of the Italian boot. Here, where the ancient Romans had once set out to conquer the world, the King, under the aegis of the Allies, would establish the capital of his short-lived "Kingdom of the South."
10. MdW: 106.
11. Born Jessica Lynch in Brooklyn, N.Y., Mother Mary is deservedly one of the most consulted diarists of the occupation but cited almost exclusively, even today, by her pen name, Jane Scrivener. Her self-imposed anonymity, however, kept for thirty-six years, was revealed posthumously by British writer Raleigh Trevelyan (in RT), who described her as "a woman of spirit, humourous, once a champion squash-player."
12. JS: 4–6.
13. Alvarez, D., and Graham, R., *Nothing Sacred: Nazi Espionage Against the Vatican 1939–1945*, London: F. Cass, 1997: 84.
14. ADSS 7: 611.
15. Vatican historian Father Robert Graham (writing with coauthor David Alvarez), believes that the Pope sought to avoid a recurrence of the bloodshed of the 1527 sack of Rome, when 147 Swiss Guards died in Pope Clement VII's escape from the German and Spanish troops of the Duke of Bourbon (Alvarez & Graham: 84).
16. Of the abundant material on Persichetti, see especially MSD.
17. Ossicini, A., *Un'isola sul Tevere*, Rome: Editori Riuniti, 1999: 197–198.

18. CC: 100–101.
19. Garland & Smyth: 531–532.
20. JS: 6–7.
21. MdW: 106.
22. CC: 103.
23. JS: 9.
24. One of the original posters remains on public display in Rome at the Museo Storico della Liberazione.
25. Text in F. Watts and N. Ausubel, eds., *Voices of History*, New York, 1944: 343.

THREE: ROME FEVER

1. This almost certainly included at least one suicide attempt. Mussolini feared being handed over to the Allies for prosecution—which in fact was a condition of the part of the armistice, the so-called long terms, kept secret until years after the war. The same fear was shared by Hitler and was one of the motivations of his quest to rescue his Italian counterpart. See the first chapter of the final volume of Mussolini's most thorough biographer, Renzo De Felice (RDF 8).
2. Lochner: 512–515.
3. It actually had the opposite effect. The German forces at Salerno reacted to Italy's defection with a fury, while Clark's invasion force, hearing the announcement while in transit to the landing site—according to official naval historian Samuel Morison—"proceeded to relax, mentally and otherwise" (Morison, S., *Sicily-Salerno-Anzio, January 1943–June 1944*, Boston: Little, Brown: 252).
4. CD'E: 39.
5. Ibid.: 40.
6. Hugh Pond, *Salerno*, Boston: Little, Brown, 1961: 204.
7. Tompkins later edited a collection of Shaw's letters to Molly Tompkins, published as *To a Young Actress*, New York: Potter, 1960, and *Shaw and Molly Tompkins in Their Own Words*, London: Blond, 1961.
8. PT: cf. PT-3: 7–17.
9. EFM: 71.
10. Officially, Kappler was in the SD (Sicherheitsdienst, or Security Service), but in practice he did the work of its overlapping bureau, the Secret State Police, the Gestapo.
11. *DIR:* 27.
12. THK, testimony of May 31, 1948.
13. As is revealed in the newly released OSS documents, he also had a mistress, a Dutch woman named Helen Louise Brouewer, trained in espionage at the SD school in The Hague (OSS RG 226, Entry 210, Box 9).
14. EFM: 114.
15. Ibid.: 56.
16. Telegram from Ribbentrop to Weizsäcker, October 4, 1943, in Friedländer, S., *Pius XII and the Third Reich*, New York: Alfred A. Knopf, 1966: 182.
17. Graham, R., "Voleva Hitler allontanare da Roma Pio XII?" in *La civiltà cattolica*, March 1972: 454.

18. *DIR:* 14.
19. JS: 21.
20. Telegram to Secretary of State Hull, October 25, 1943, in *FRUS:* 951.
21. See memoranda of Apostolic Delegation at Washington to State Department of August 18 and 20, 1943 in *FRUS:* 944–946.
22. One of the newly released OSS intercepts of German cable traffic between Rome and Berlin (OSS RG 226, Entry 226, Box 534, #1576—Kappa) echoes Weizsäcker's well-known reports on the Pope's position at that time—often contested as self-serving by Pius's defenders—but this one has a curious twist. "The Pope's dream," he wrote, "is a union of the old civilized countries of the West with insulation of Bolshevism toward the East in the same way that Pope Innocent XI unified the continent against the Moslems . . ." Innocent XI, who promoted the seventeenth-century Christian war against the Turks to a victorious conclusion by his support of a pact between the King of Poland and the Holy Roman Emperor, was beatified in 1956 by Pope Pius XII.
23. Leiber, R., "Pius XII," in Bentley, E., ed., *The Storm over the Deputy*, New York: Grove Press, 1964: 174–175.
24. Staatssekretär: Vatikan, Reich Foreign Ministry memorandum of March 3, 1939; text in Friedländer: 21.
25. JC: 273.
26. SZ: 150–151.
27. AKi.
28. AKi; see also *BS:* 27.
29. AKi. Fahrener's prominent Jews were far removed from the indigenous Jewish leadership. The "colony" referred to by Kessel was a small group of foreign Jews who worked in Rome-based nongovernmental international organizations. In addition, among those converted to Catholicism, a few were employed at the Vatican. Warnings from Fahrener, and from Kessel himself, did in fact induce some of these Jews to go into hiding. (See *BS:* 44–45.)
30. CC: 106–109.
31. RB-1: 39–40.

FOUR: KAPPLER'S GAME

1. Fifty years later, at Priebke's war-crimes trial in Rome, evidence would emerge that he was awarded the medal under false pretenses—a claim that he had been shot and wounded in the course of the Mussolini investigation. A fellow officer, however, testified that Priebke, drunk at the time, had climbed over a fence, and his gun went off, nicking his finger. (See *DP:* 125.)
2. KT; see also *BS:* 48.
3. KT.
4. In one hitherto unknown and uncharacteristic incident, on the evening of September 9, a gun shop in the center of Rome was broken into by a group of Jews led by a woman named Elena Di Porto, and seventy hunting rifles and ammunition were stolen. Di Porto was arrested when attempting a second such break-in shortly afterward (Dorer: docs. 139, 140).

5. Seventy percent of Jewish heads of households were either itinerant peddlers or shopkeepers (*BS:* 13).
6. Fascist anti-Semitism had been codified in November 1938 in the "Measures for the Defense of the Italian Race," patterned after the Nazi Nuremberg Laws. Italian Jews were banned from public service, schools, and universities, from marrying "Aryans" and engaging in most economic activities, and were otherwise excluded from non-Jewish Italian society.
7. See Zolli's memoir (*EZ*). For the long-running Zolli affair see *BS*.
8. His informants were the high Vatican officials Monsignori Angelo Dell'Acqua, Cipico, and Umberto Dionisi, and the International Red Cross representative in Rome, Count De Salis. Sorani had also received reports of Nazi atrocities from U.S. representative to the Vatican Tittmann (SSo).
9. SSo, RL.
10. Foà-Almansi reports.
11. JS: 26.
12. CD'E: 43–45.
13. Quoted in CD'E: 45.
14. PT-3: 32–33.
15. See Dorer: docs. 312–320.
16. CDS-2: 26.
17. Ripa di Meana, F., *Roma clandestina*, Turin: Vincenzo Ramella Editore, 1946: 79.
18. EFM: 235.
19. Foà-Almansi reports.
20. *Kappler sentenza.*
21. They also suggest a reason why they were kept secret so long, providing answers to long-standing, embarrassing questions of how much the Allied governments knew about the Holocaust and what they might have done with that knowledge.
22. OSS RG 226, CIA, Doc. 7244, Kappler to Berlin, October 6, 1943.
23. Hilberg, R., *The Destruction of the European Jews*, rev. ed., Chicago: Quadrangle Books, 1967: 412; EFMi.
24. EFMi.
25. Foà-Almansi reports.
26. Ibid.
27. Montezemolo had been working with General Calvi di Bergolo in the Open City Command when on September 23—the day of the formal establishment of Mussolini's neo-Fascist regime at Salò—Stadtkommandant Stahel had summoned both men to swear allegiance to the new government. They refused and were immediately arrested, with Montezemolo escaping before being taken into custody. Count Calvi, rescued from deportation to Germany by Dollmann, would be held under house arrest at his Piedmont estate and eventually manage to join Princess Yolanda in Switzerland; Count Montezemolo, as will be seen, would die in the Ardeatine Caves Massacre.
28. Onofri, F., "GAP di zona: Roma, settembre '43–giugno' 44," in *Rinascita*, April 1945: 117–119.
29. AG: 177.
30. Ibid.

31. Telegram to Berlin, October 14, 1943, in Friedländer: 178.

32. JS: 35, diary entry of October 10, 1943.

33. See OSS RG 226, CIA, doc. 7185, Kappler to Berlin, October 5, 1943.

34. RL; cf. AG: 171.

35. After the war, Pius's early defenders would adopt and promulgate this latter version in spite of the evidence available at the time. The controversy would end, however, with the Vatican's 1975 release of some occupation-period documents clarifying that the offer was indeed a loan and not needed. (ADSS 9: 494, doc. 353, Nogara to Maglione, September 29, 1943.)

36. *BS*: 93; cf. De Felice, R., *Storia degli ebrei italiani sotto il Fascismo*, Turin: Einaudi, 1961: 527.

37. *BS*: 95.

38. GDB: 80.

39. KT.

40. AKi.

41. OSS RG 226, CIA, Box 4, doc. 7184, Kappler to Berlin, October 5, 1943.

42. The fate of the Rome Carabinieri and how a large number of those who escaped the raid, most with their weapons, joined and distinguished themselves in the Resistance have long been known, but not Kappler's role and its connection to the Jews of Rome. See especially F. Caruso, *L'Arma dei Reali Carabinieri in Roma durante l'occupazione tedesca*, Rome: Istituto Poli-Grafico Dello Stato, 1949.

43. KT.

44. Letter from Kappler to Kaltenbrunner, quoted in *Kappler sentenza*.

45. OSS RG 226, CIA, doc. 7244, Kappler to Berlin, October 6, 1943.

46. OSS RG 226, CIA, doc. 7459, Kaltenbrunner to Kappler, October 11, 1943.

47. *Kappler sentenza*.

FIVE: THE MÖLLHAUSEN TELEGRAM

1. AKi.

2. EFM: 111.

3. Ibid.: 112–113

4. AKi.

5. EFMi.

6. Fortunately for Möllhausen, the perils of his Rome fever were offset by Kappler's. The Gestapo Chief and great detective knew of Möllhausen's *liaison dangereuse* and told no one (KT, *BS*: 59).

7. Bertoldi, S., *I tedeschi in Italia*, Milan: Rizzoli, 1964: 222.

8. EFM: 112–113.

9. *BS*: 54.

10. NARA, *Inland II Geheim*, Documents of the German Foreign Ministry, 1920–45, Microcopy T-120, Roll 4353, doc. E421525.

11. RK ARC, Letter from Möllhausen to me, dated January 16, 1968; cf. *BS*: 136.

12. NARA, *Inland II Geheim*, Documents of the German Foreign Ministry, 1920–45, Microcopy T-120, Roll 4353, doc. E421524.

13. EFMi.

14. EFM: 117.
15. Telegrams from Thadden to Möllhausen, October 9, 1943, NARA, *Inland II Geheim*, Documents of the German Foreign Ministry, 1920–45, Microcopy T-120, Roll 4353, doc. E421521.
16. For an up-to-date, authoritative telling of the Kolbe story, see the ongoing series of articles by Greg Bradsher, in NARA's quarterly online publication, *Prologue*: "A Time to Act: The Beginning of the Fritz Kolbe Story, 1900–1943."
17. The phrase "on the basis of the Führer's instructions" is a direct quote from the telegram and until now had seemed nothing more than a synonym for the highest level of command, since no other document linked Hitler directly to the orders to deport the Jews of Rome. In Kappa Cable 19, however, Kolbe emphasizes the marking on Möllhausen's October 6 telegram as addressed not only to von Ribbentrop but first of all "For the Führer . . . personally" (OSS RG 226, Entry 210, Box 534, Kappa message 1494–95). Since the microfilmed original from the German Foreign Ministry reads "For Herr Reichsminister personally," the Kappa cable suggests that the marking was added in Berlin after receipt from Rome. Whether Hitler knew of the extermination of Jews is, unfortunately, still being asked. See the FAQs *www.nizkor.org*, which specializes in combating Holocaust denial.
18. The President did not receive these copies until January, nearly three months after the roundup, and there is no record of the date Kolbe's information reached the OSS. Nevertheless, the full extent of the threat to the Jews was clear from the Kappler decodes. The transmissions to and from Berlin were intercepted in real time, quickly deciphered and translated by Ultra and made available immediately. (See F. H. Hinsley et al., *British Intelligence in the Second World War: Its Influence on Strategy and Operations*, vol. 3, New York: Cambridge University Press, 1984: 487. Thus Washington and London, aside from having advance knowledge of the roundup, were aware of the number of arrests, where the prisoners were being held, the date and time of their departure, the train markings and its route, and the inadequate size of the escort.
19. *BS:* 113–118.
20. Dorer: doc. 497. The words were shouted as a warning by the mother in law of Angelo Di Veroli, thirty, who was escaping with his son. Like many families, they believed that the Germans wanted only males. Di Veroli's mother-in-law and wife were seized.
21. KT.
22. THK (*BS:* 127): This was not idle boasting. During his time in Rome, Kappler tried five times to be transferred to the front, earning a reprimand for insubordination when he finally went above his SS superiors and appealed directly to the Wehrmacht.
23. ADSS 9: 501, doc. 363, notes of the Secretariat of State.
24. MdW: 144.
25. JS: 31.
26. *BS:* 105–109.
27. Foà-Almansi reports.
28. *BS:* 147–151.
29. Emphasis in original. The article was published in a short-lived literary magazine called *Mercurio*, December 1944, and subsequently in book form in many editions

and translated into many languages. An electronic version can be found in Dorer: doc. 430.

SIX: PAOLO MEETS ELENA

1. Quoted in RPC 2: 179.
2. *Il giornale d'Italia*, October 16, 1943.
3. Quoted in Portelli: 153.
4. Quoted in *DIR:* 9.
5. Quoted in CDS-2: 38.
6. Quoted ibid.: 36–37.
7. Dorer: doc. 1026.
8. RB-1: 57–58, RB-2: 180.
9. CC: 125–126.
10. Quoted in CD'E: 46–47.
11. Montgomery in a letter to Lord Mountbatten, quoted in CD'E: 68.
12. Blumenson, M., *Salerno to Cassino*, Washington, D.C.: Government Printing Office, 1969: 180.
13. On the German side of the Winter Line, Kesselring had now turned the ratio of his forces to those of the Allies on its head, with more than twenty first-rate divisions opposing the Allies' eleven. Moreover, Allied planners were moving combat-hardened troops out of Italy to serve in Overlord and replacing them with inexperienced men.
14. WSC 5: 356.
15. On the "soft underbelly" see, e.g., A&W-2: 98; also CD'E: 32–33.
16. MC: 1–2.
17. Telegram from Roosevelt to Churchill, March 13, 1944, text in WSC 5: 504.
18. WSC 5: 188.
19. OSS RG 226, Entry 210, Box 436, "Report Covering the Activities of OSS Special Detachment G-2 Fifth Army in Italy."
20. PT-3: 42–43.
21. Tompkins to Chief, SI, "Report on Field Conditions," December 1, 1944: 12. *Tompkins papers.*
22. PT-3: 45.
23. RB-1: 64–66.
24. CC: 135.
25. Ibid.: 136; cf. RB-1: 67.

SEVEN: UNDER HIS VERY EYES

1. AP: 104.
2. Ibid.: 16.
3. *BS:* 293, SS.
4. A certain irony haunted the whole broken-down old building. Arrested on a lower floor were the jeweler, Angelo Anticoli, his wife, and two young children. Anticoli

had the weighing job in the gold collection. To the misfortune of many Jews who would survive the roundup, the dark-eyed eighteen-year-old girl in the apartment directly below Settimia's, one Celeste Di Porto, would escape. She would wax into the occupation's infamous *Pantera Nera*, "Black Panther," a treacherous spy for the Fascists against her fellow Jews.

5. Dorer: doc. 495.
6. Kurzman, D., *The Race for Rome*, New York: Doubleday, 1975: xxx–xxxi. Pignatelli's dialogue is from the Kurzman interview. Graham's account is in Graham, R., "La strana condotta di E. von Weizsäcker ambasciatore del Reich in Vatican," *La civiltà cattolica*, June 6, 1970: 455–471.
7. Ibid. (emphasis in Kurzman).
8. This is the approximate distance to Viale Giulio Cesare, 223, the address of sixty-nine-year-old Augusto Piperno, the victim who appears to have lived nearest to the enclave.
9. Debenedetti in Dorer: doc. 430.
10. ADSS 9: 505–506, doc. 368, notes of Cardinal Maglione, October 16, 1943. A copy of the original document reveals that the Cardinal uses ellipsis marks to separate some thoughts, but I have replaced these with dashes to avoid confusion. The punctuation is otherwise unchanged.
11. Weizsäcker may have known of what he spoke. The newly released OSS documents contain a 1942 assessment of the political leanings of the Vatican's College of Cardinals; it rates Maglione as "extremely sympathetic to America," but his influence is considered in decline because "he and Pope Pius XII do not see to an 'eye' with one another politically." Nearly all of the other leading prelates, moreover, including cardinals said to be very close to the Pope, are characterized as "pro-Fascist" and "reactionaries" (OSS RG 226, Entry 217, Box 2).
12. Ibid.
13. *BS:* 198–203.
14. GG: (*BS:* 202).
15. GG: cf. SZ: 162.
16. The Vatican's copy is in ADSS 11: 509–510, doc. 373.
17. Telegram from Gumpert to Berlin, October 16, 1943, NARA, *Inland II Geheim*, Documents of the German Foreign Ministry, 1920–45, Microcopy T-120, Roll 4353, doc. E421514.
18. The reference is to the strong protest issued by several bishops and archbishops in August 1942, when foreign Jews in the French unoccupied zone were handed over to the Germans in Paris for deportation.
19. Telegram from Weizsäcker to Berlin, October 17, 1943, NARA, *Inland II Geheim*, Documents of the German Foreign Ministry, 1920–45, Microcopy T-120, Roll 4353, doc. E421512.
20. For reasons unknown, Foà, whose address was in the hands of the Gestapo, was one of several Jewish leaders not sought in the roundup. Nevertheless, a representative number of prominent Jews would be among the captives, including two close relatives of two Nobel Prize physicists: Amelia Segrè Treves, mother of future Nobelist Emilio Segrè, and Admiral Augusto Capon, father-in-law of Enrico Fermi.
21. *Foà report, BS:* 188–189, 238.

22. This too was wrong. A painstaking labor of many years by the Jewish documentation center in Milan (Centro di Documentazione Ebraica Contemporanea) has identified 1,023 people actually deported (published in L. Picciotto, *Il libro della memoria*, rev. ed., Milan: Mursia, 2002), though that figure may also be too low. In a related matter, Picciotto, in a conversation with me in October 2002, concluded after consulting her own work that the number of survivors of the October 16 deportation was sixteen, thus revising both her long-maintained published figure of seventeen and the fifteen I had reported in *BS* ("Appendix II"); the untenable higher number was first pointed out by Fausto Coen in his 1993 book *16 ottobre 1943: La grande razzia degli ebrei di Roma*, Florence: La Giuntina.

23. The meaning of this sentence was lost in either the decoding or the translation. The original is clear: "In one case, for example, the police came upon the home of a Fascist in Blackshirt and with identity papers, which without doubt had already been used one hour earlier in a Jewish home by someone claiming them as his own" (quoted in *BS*: 223).

24. OSS RG 226, CIA, Box 4, doc. 7668. Cf., my translation of the original in *BS*: 222–223.

25. *L'Italia libera*, October 17, 1943, quoted in RPC 2: 134–135.

26. OSS RG 226, CIA, Box 4, doc. 7672. The interrupted intercept breaks off before the signature, but is uniquely attributable to Kappler.

27. SS.

28. ADSS 9: docs. 370 & 374, notes of the Secretariat of State, October 17, 1943 (doc. 370 is dated only October 1943 but refers to the events of the 17th).

29. JS: 39.

30. Notes by Thadden, October 19, 1943, in NARA, *Inland II Geheim*, Documents of the German Foreign Ministry, 1920–45, Microscopy T-120, Roll 4353, docs. E421511 and E421513.

31. FO, 371/3725/19; cf. ADSS 9: 506fn.

32. OSS RG 226, Entry 210, Box 534, #1576-9 Kappa (#152, from Weizsäcker to Grand, October 18, 1943).

33. OC: 288–89.

34. Osborne to London (via Bern), October 18, 1944; FO, 371/37571/R10995; quoted in OC: 289.

35. Telegram from Tittmann to Secretary of State Hull, October 19, 1943, in *FRUS*: 950. Pius's most outspoken present-day defender and the man in charge of making the case for that pope's sainthood, Jesuit Father Peter Gumpel, disputes the date of Tittmann's audience. Although Tittmann specifically stated that it took place "today," i.e., the 19th, Gumpel cites the Vatican's "very accurate" records in moving it back to the 14th, two days prior to the roundup of the Roman Jews. Thus, he says, any suggestion that the Pope had so little concern for the Jews that he didn't even mention them is inappropriate. Gumpel, however, has no difficulty with the date of the Osborne audience of the 18th, in which the Jews received no mention either.

36. Memorandum from Thadden to Eichmann October 23, 1943, in NARA, *Inland II Geheim*, Documents of the German Foreign Ministry, 1920–45, Microcopy T-120, Roll 4353, docs. E421509-E421510.

37. Eichmann's testimony at his war crimes trial, July 3, 1961, quoted in *BS*: 279.

38. His name was Lazzaro Sonnino. His fate is unknown. See *BS*: 255.

39. See ADSS 9: 511–525.

40. A final paragraph written in the grandiloquent language de rigueur in Vatican-speak endings is as a consequence usually ignored when cited, but a careful reading brings up the contours of the papal strategy for a separate peace in the West. It characterizes Pius's work as a "blessed activity" that can "hasten the day on which the shining glow of peace will return to the earth; and men, laying down their arms, will put aside their differences and bitterness, and, becoming brothers once more, will finally labor, in all good faith, for the common weal" (*L'osservatore romano*, October 25–26, 1943). Such words had meaning only to the initiated, to whom they sent the clearest signal that the crisis in the Vatican's relations with the Reich had passed, sent on hard rails far away from Rome.

41. Weizsäcker to Foreign Ministry, October 28, 1943 in NARA, *Inland II Geheim*, Documents of the German Foreign Ministry, 1920–45, Microcopy T-120, Roll 4353, docs. E421515-17.

42. Ibid. The underlined doc. is E421515.

43. ADSS 9: 538–539, doc. 405, notes of Montini, November 1, 1943.

EIGHT: FIRST BLOOD

1. Quoted in *DIR*: 59.

2. RDF 6: 123.

3. RB-2: 174.

4. Ibid.: 175; cf. RB-1: 24–25.

5. Giorgio Amendola, *Lettere a Milano, 1939–1945*, Rome: Editori Riuniti, 1976: 293–294.

6. Ernie Pyle, *Brave Men*, New York: Holt, 1943: 98.

7. A&W-1.

8. Ibid.: 118.

9. Quoted ibid.: 131–132.

10. Quoted ibid.: 134.

11. Quoted ibid.: 18.

12. RB-1: 81–83. The shooting is recorded in a police report in Dorer: doc. 1035; the victim, a member of the Palazzo Braschi Guardia Armata, or Armed Guard, was named Renato Cesaroni.

13. CC: 133.

14. For a discussion of the debate, usually led by Gesmundo at meetings in Carla's apartment, see RB-1: 92–93 and CC: 134.

15. CC: 143–144.

16. A recently discovered open-city police command report provides unmistakable identification of the dead man, who was in fact an NCO, not an officer. He was thirty-two-year-old Georg Von Iohasen Schmidt, a sergeant in the Wehrmacht, in the Ordnungspolizei. He was dead on arrival at 6:15 P.M., December 17, 1943, at the Italian Red Cross hospital in Piazza dell' Independenza. Schmidt had been shot twice on the southwest side of Via XXIII Marzo and the corner of the second inter-

section (Via San Nicola da Tolentino), where police found three 9-caliber shells and an unspent 9-caliber bullet. Adding a tinge of mystery is the figure of Wehrmacht officer Major Paul Empelmann, lodged at the Hotel Bernini (at the bottom of Via Veneto), who rushed to Schmidt just after he was shot and was still alive. At that moment, 6 P.M., Empelmann was walking on the northeast side of Via XXIII Marzo (Dorer: doc. 1047, dated December 18, 1943).

17. RB-1: 104–105, CC: 152.
18. RB-1: 98–99, CC: 149.
19. The prisoners were not the only ones to cheer. Diarist de Wyss records a visit that day with an eyewitness to the attack, a church official whom she identifies only as Monsignor T., who saw three Germans killed. She writes: " . . . lifting his eyes piously to heaven, [he] said, 'Three Germans less, that is a pleasure . . .' "
20. CDS-2: 52.

NINE: CHRISTMAS IN CAPTIVITY

1. On Koch and his special unit, see MG. This original study, the first of its kind in terms of documentation, renders almost all of the voluminous, largely hearsay-based literature on Koch virtually obsolete. See also the author's web site, *www.fabula.it/mgriner.*
2. In harboring this anti-Fascist, non-Communist elite, the Vatican risked incurring German wrath, but that was more than offset as insurance against the dreaded "Communist takeover." The men being sheltered were clearly going to play a major leadership role in postwar Italy, and in the government's relations with the Church.
3. ADDS 9: 617, doc. 482.
4. SZ: 220–222; cf. MG: 92–95.
5. His *Diario* in ALS is quoted in SZ: 221.
6. SZ: 221.
7. The actual number is of course incalculable, though far less than the million hiders required for half-and-half. Informed estimates usually range from 200,000 to 400,000. With a peak between the October 16 roundup and the end of the year, hiding became increasingly difficult. An ordinance issued by new Commandant General Mälzer just before Christmas, for example, required that a list of the names of every person residing in any building be posted at the entrance; anyone caught sheltering someone not on the list faced severe punishment, including confiscation of his or her food-ration card.
8. ADSS 9: 612, doc. 474, notes of the Secretariat of State, December 20, 1943.
9. Alvarez and Graham: 86–87.
10. SZ, see especially chapters 13–15: 189–232.
11. Nevertheless, Zuccotti's work brings into question the most widely accepted statistics regarding the number of Jews sheltered in Rome by the Church: 4,447 fugitives hiding in 155 religious institutions (convents, monasteries, schools, hospitals, parish churches, and Vatican properties). The authority cited for these figures is almost always renowned historian Renzo De Felice's 1961 work *Storia degli ebrei italiani,* but Zuccotti shows them to have originated from Vatican sources close to Pius XII. From evidence of significant duplication, she concludes that the numbers are exaggerated, even when offset by known omissions (SZ: 199–201).

12. ADSS 9: 626, note of the Secretariat of State, December 22, 1943, attached to doc. 482.
13. ADSS 9: 626, note of Cardinal Maglione, December 23, 1943, attached to doc. 482.
14. OSS RG 226, Entry 210, Box 534, #1576-9 Kappa (#314, from Weizsäcker to Grand, December 13, 1943).
15. His still-debated 1942 Christmas, often cited by his defenders as proof that he protested the Nazi slaughter of Europe's Jews, had been understood as such by almost no one. The difficulty was that he never mentioned the Nazis, the slaughter, or the Jews. In a brief passage, he referred only to innocent lives lost in the war, including "hundreds of thousands who, without personal guilt, are doomed to death or to a progressive deterioration of their condition, sometimes for no other reason than their nationality or descent" (Quoted in SZ: 1).
16. JS: 77. The text of the Pope's message is in AG: 192.
17. Text in AG: 191–192.
18. Quoted in JS: 78.
19. CT: 137.
20. Churchill to Chiefs of Staff, December 19, 1943, quoted in CD'E: 75; Churchill to Roosevelt, December 26, 1943, quoted in CD'E: 77.
21. Churchill to British Chiefs of Staff, December 26, 1943, quoted in CD'E: 77.
22. There were simply not enough available landing craft, all of which were in the process of being transferred to Overlord.
23. Churchill to Roosevelt, quoted in CD'E: 78.
24. Clark diary, quoted in CD'E: 97.
25. Cable, Churchill to Alexander, December 26, 1943, quoted in CD'E: 95.
26. Cable, Churchill to Wilson, January 18, 1944, quoted in CD'E: 96.
27. Clark to Adleman and Walton, November 1966, in A&W-2: 205–206 (emphasis in the original).
28. ACB: 485.
29. In his official mission report to the OSS, he wrote that Donovan had assigned him "to proceed on a mission to Rome to act as intelligence officer for the Fifth Army and coordinate sabotage and countersabotage activities with the Resistance movements" (Tompkins to Major Frank L. Ball, "Report on Mission to Rome," March 1, 1945: 1, Tompkins papers).
30. PT.
31. Tompkins diary.
32. Lombardi, G., Montezemolo e il fronte militare clandestino di Roma, Rome: Le Edizioni del Lavoro, 1947: 35, 43.
33. PT.
34. Dorer: Cronologia.
35. MdW: 185, diary entry for January 21, 1944.
36. Bourgoin wrote that he was in fact informed by his superior that Tompkins had been appointed by Donovan as Chief of OSS in occupied Italy, and in a complete fabrication he further claimed that they were indeed met at the beach, where he gave orders that the Rome agents were to be told of Tompkins' status as their superior and that a car was waiting for him to be transported to Rome by an OSS agent. RG 226 Entry 210, Box 80, Bourgoin report: 53.
37. PT-1: 43.

38. *Tompkins report:* 2, in *Tompkins papers*.
39. PT-2: 298. Menicante's version of the same meeting makes the false claim that "all leaders of political parties" were present (mission report of Menicante, in *Tompkins papers*).
40. MdW: 186, diary entry for January 22, 1944.
41. Dorer: doc. 1256.
42. PT-1: 66.
43. *Tompkins report:* 7, in *Tompkins papers*.
44. Ibid.

TEN: CHURCHILL'S CAT

1. WSC 5: 488.
2. Woodruff, W., *Vessel of Sadness*, Carbondale, Ill., 1978: 44–45, quoted in CD'E: 120.
3. Fitzgerald, *A History of the Irish Guards in the Second World War*: 217, quoted in CD'E: 120.
4. Lucas diary, January 22, 1943, quoted in CD'E: 119.
5. Quoted in A&W-2: 120.
6. Lucas diary, January 22, 1943, quoted in CD'E: 119.
7. The story of the American in his jeep reaching Rome has been known and embellished since such a rumor began to circulate on the beachhead the very first day. Lieutenant Cummings's letter to D'Este of June 20, 1988, appears to be its first documentation. More important is the indisputable truth that the road was undefended and that Rome itself at that moment was indefensible.
8. PT-1: 65.
9. BBC correspondent Wynford Vaughn-Thomas, quoted in RT: 47.
10. AK: 233.
11. Lucas diary, quoted in A&W-2: 129.
12. Lucas diary, January 22, 1943, quoted in CD'E: 133.
13. Lucas interview, May 24, 1948, quoted in CD'E: 113.
14. RB; cf. RB-1: 116, RB-2: 195; CC: 161.
15. Carroll-Abbing, J. P., *But for the Grace of God*, New York: Delacorte, 1965: 52.
16. RB-1: 117.
17. RB; cf., RB-1: 97.
18. AG: 196.
19. Dorer: doc. 1260.
20. Dorer: doc. 1263.
21. Testimony of May 10, 1996, in TEP, quoted in *DP:* 113.
22. *L'Arma dei Reali Carabinieri in Roma:* 26, quoted in AP: 179.
23. AP: 178.
24. Ibid.
25. Maria Teresa Regard (Piera), showing up at Gesmundo's apartment, had fallen into a Gestapo trap. Gesmundo, arrested in his apartment, was kept there to see who would call on him. Regard claimed she had knocked on the wrong door. She had just been preceded by another woman, who had no way to explain why she was delivering a bag filled with four-pointed nails. Both were taken to Via Tasso and held for trial. The first woman was sentenced to fifteen years, to be served in Germany. Regard

somehow made her story stick, winning a rare acquittal. Released after eight days, she returned to fight again, one of the earliest to bear witness to the torture undergone by Montezemolo, Gesmundo, and others.

26. JS: 95, diary entry for January 24, 1944.
27. CD'E: 135.

ELEVEN: MY CURIOUS HIDEOUT

1. *Tompkins report:* 13–14, in *Tompkins papers.*
2. Ibid.: 14.
3. Tompkins Anzio monograph: 21, in *Tompkins papers;* see also "Memo to Chief of Staff [of VI Corps, from head of G-2], January 29, 1944, in *Tompkins papers.* Signed by "J. L. L.," this memo vouches for the reliability of another Radio Vittoria transmission, of a day earlier, "obtained from an American officer working behind the lines." The information, regarding German troop movements to the front, proved accurate.
4. Tompkins Anzio monograph: 21, in *Tompkins papers.*
5. See CDS-2: 81–83.
6. *La nazione del popolo* (Florence), January 31, 1945.
7. *Lettere dei condannati a morte della Resistenza Italiana*, Milan: Mondadori, 1968: 192.
8. Kappler's calling Priebke a lieutenant, if such was the case, is not surprising. Priebke had only recently received his promotion to captain, and throughout the occupation he was known in the Via Tasso prison as "the Lieutenant."
9. When the family learned of the suicide, the Gestapo refused to release his body. His remains were recovered in 1945, in a common grave just north of Rome. Three nails had been torn from the fingers of his right hand (*DP:* 117).
10. Report by Koch to General Mälzer, undated, quoted in MG: 102.
11. Argentino interrogation of November 15, 1944, quoted in MG: 74.
12. Koch interrogation of May 23, 1945, quoted in MG: 97.
13. Only five are accounted for, Roman Jews who were subsequently deported to Auschwitz and did not return (see SZ: 224).
14. Algardi, Z., *Processo ai fascisti*, Florence: Parenti, 1968: 30–33.
15. *La civiltà cattolica*, March 4, 1944: 324.
16. Bonomi, I., *Diario di un anno: 1 giugno 1943–10 giugno 1944*, Milan: Garzanti: 146–147, entry of February 5, 1944
17. Ibid.: 147, entry of February 9, 1944.
18. ASL, *Diario*, "Appendice": 17–18, quoted in SZ: 225.
19. ADSS 10: 127–129, doc. 53, Anichini to Pius XII, February 13, 1944. The letter was in Italian but the final "invocation" was in Latin, *"salva nos, perimus!"*—a reference to Matthew 8:25.
20. ADSS 10: 129, Tardini note attached to doc. 53.
21. Cardinal Pizzardo's position relative to this case is unknown, but Cardinal Canali, the commission chairman, was an outspoken, long-time pro-Fascist, eager to avoid any conflict with the occupation authorities. He was said to be disliked by many of his colleagues, including Montini, but had the confidence of and easy access to the Pope (see SZ: 229).
22. As for the fugitive elite in the San Giovanni enclave, the Zuccotti study found no ev-

idence that anyone was actually expelled, even when "advised" to leave, and some who left voluntarily were later readmitted, though with more rigorous restrictions imposed in the meantime. On the other hand, more than fifty hiders, many of them Jews, at the Pontificio Collegio dei Sacerdoti, underwent what the director of the collegio, Monsignor Erminio Viganò, called in a lament to the Vatican a "forced departure" (SZ: 226–228).

23. *Tompkins report:* 23–24, in *Tompkins papers.*

24. Quoted in Tompkins Anzio monograph: 32, in *Tompkins papers.* Donovan sent a similar message to the U.S. Joint Chiefs of Staff.

25. CD'E: 251.

26. Truscott's advice to his young son; quoted in CD'E: 271.

27. A&W-2: 138.

TWELVE: HUPF, MEIN MÄDEL

1. CC: 184.

2. Dorer: doc. 1263. Not all the Gappisti concurred. Interviewed at the same late date as Musu, Bentivegna said, "If the Americans had marched on Rome they'd have taken it in twelve hours, but they had to start immediately. . . . The Allies made lots of mistakes like this, because the way they fight a war is not to lose men. That's why I don't agree that they did what they did on purpose to the leave the Resistance stranded" (Dorer: doc. 1261).

3. As a symbol of the plight of Rome's women under the occupation, she would become the first martyr of a movement about to be born. Her cold-blooded slaying is a piece of Resistance lore widely known from Rossellini's classic neorealistic film *Open City,* with the great actor Anna Magnani as Teresa. As for Elena, it was not until 2000 that she recounted her part in the incident that would galvanize the women of Rome in a heroic role they would play in the last and most trying days of the occupation.

4. *DIR:* 219.

5. *L'osservatore romano,* March 3, 1944, quoted in AG: 229.

6. EFM: 152–153. Möllhausen describes Kesselring as "enraged" and Hitler dismissing Farinacci's gesture as "idiotic"—both reactions underscoring the importance the Germans attributed to their guarantees of protecting Vatican sovereignty.

7. The bombing was the perverse triumph of will of a single general, the flamboyant New Zealander Sir Bernard Freyberg. Although Mark Clark was his nominal superior, Freyberg was responsible only to his own government. Clark's opposition to the bombing is well established, and his claim of being forced to yield to Freyberg's demands because of the politics of the New Zealander's special status has been received with both sympathy and scorn, but it does not alter the validity of his conviction that the abbey was not a legitimate target.

8. Tittmann in a 1966 interview with the authors of A&W-2: 149.

9. Code-named Operation Strangle, it was aimed at forcing German withdrawal from Rome and all of central Italy. It was to be the most relentless air offensive of the Mediterranean war, with nearly 10,000 sorties targeting supply lines throughout occupied Italy, from south of the Apennines to the Alps.

10. AG: 230. Spellman's remark is apparently paraphrased, with emphasis added by Giovannetti.

11. Ibid.: 236.
12. Text in ibid.
13. The *New York Times*, April 2, 1944: 19.
14. ADSS 10: 167, doc. 89, Notes of Monsignor Montini, March 4, 1944.
15. Estimates ranged from 50,000 to 300,000, with Mother Mary's 200,000 figure, as she saw it from inside the piazza, the most convincing: "Its capacity is 300,000, and it was undoubtedly two-thirds full" (JS: 133).
16. Text in AG: 240–241.
17. JS: 132–133.
18. CC: 212–214.
19. PT-1: 158–159.
20. MG: 105.
21. Text in PT-3: 149.
22. This was only a minor aspect of his real business as a power broker. The inquest found that most of the OSS funds in Rome were used by Menicanti "in a manner in no way connected with our activities." This made him "a powerful political figure because of the millions he had at his disposal with which he could support, in the name of OSS, either one group or the other, or one against the other, as he saw fit" ("2nd Interim Report of Activities of SIC," July 14, 1944 [Crockett Report], in ACB: 491).
23. *Tompkins report:* 29, in *Tompkins papers.*
24. "Relazione sul rintraccio di una radio clandestina," undated but probably May 1944, in MG: 105.
25. Ibid.
26. PT-1: 170.
27. OSS RG 226, E210, Box 436: Pacatte report: 26.
28. One such audience had been accorded to the wife and daughters of General Simoni, Montezemolo's fellow prisoner from the Military Front Resistance group. The papal intervention resulted in Simoni's being granted the rare privilege of periodic visits from his family. The old General was enduring the same tortures as Montezemolo as stoically as he. On one visit to Via Tasso, his daughter had embraced him lovingly, and he screamed in pain (RT: 116).
29. The audience is recounted in her memoir *Roma clandestina*: 228–231.
30. Ibid.
31. ADSS 10: 183, doc. 106, Notes by Monsignor Montini, March 19–20, 1944.
32. Ibid.: 190, doc. 116, note by the Secretariat of State, March 25, 1944.
33. Ibid.: 3.
34. Franceschini, C., "Il trauma di Roma," in *Südtirol Profil*, March 14, 1994: 8.
35. Dorer: doc. 627 (PRO: WO 311/359, interrogation of September 17, 1946).
36. Franz Bertagnoll interviewed in Gandini, U., "Quelli di via Rasella," in *Alto Adige*, 1979, I: 10.
37. Josef Prader interviewed ibid.: 11.

THIRTEEN: VIA RASELLA

1. DIR: 29–30.
2. Ibid.: 23–24.

3. Ibid.: 29.
4. Ibid.: 25–28, EFM: 213–15.
5. Bonomi.: 161.
6. MdW: 204.
7. FO 371/43869/21; quoted in OC: 290. According to Father Peter Gumpel, the Jesuit in charge of the long-standing sainthood proceedings for Pius XII, the Pope believed that black troops were more likely than white troops to commit rape (Gumpel to Cornwell in a 1998 interview, JC: 320).
8. PT; cf. PT-1: 182–185. An abbreviated and slightly different version is told in PT-3: 154, though he never names the actress.
9. None of those writers, including English-language authors such as Tompkins, Trevelyan, Cave Brown, and myself, took note of a 1946 challenge to Scottu's testimony by the chief judge in Koch's trial as a war criminal. That court, questioning whether the witness was suffering from a psychiatric illness, ordered a medical examination, which proved inconclusive. But the 2000 Griner study of Koch's Special Police Unit uncovered sealed documents showing that Scottu, although taken into custody, was never placed under arrest. Koch himself, when interrogated, declared that Scottu physically attacked and denounced Giglio for having gotten him into trouble over something he knew nothing about, and Giglio, he said, confirmed this. In any case, Koch found Scottu to have had no role in Giglio's OSS activities and released him. Griner's references to the original version of Scottu's deposition further show that all of the earlier writers had worked from an altered copy from which certain improbable erotic passages had been removed (MG: 218–220, 320–321).
10. Quoted ibid.: 225–226.
11. CC: 222–223.
12. Ibid.: 229–230.

FOURTEEN: THE ROAR OF THE WOLF

1. Gandini: 12.
2. Ibid.: 13.
3. The boy was Pietro Zuccheretti. Although he was identified immediately by his family and two telltale death notices appeared in *Il messaggero*, the incident remained unknown for fifty years. In the 1996 Priebke trial, it became a rallying cry for the Nazis' supporters, when two right-wing newspapers published a recently discovered photograph, of dubious authenticity, of a severed head said to be that of the Zuccheretti boy, "seen to be rolling down the street" after the explosion in Via Rasella. (See *DP*: 98–99.) Almost as bizarre was the case of the dead adult, a Partisan of Bandiera Rossa named Antonio Chiaretti. He too remained unidentified for decades, and when his identity was revealed was said to have been in Via Rasella with two other Bandiera Rossa Partisans about to carry out their own attack on the Germans (see MG: 133).
4. The shooters also caused Caruso to stumble worse than when he had been arrested in the German roundup on his first day as Questore. After getting out of his car with his driver, a twenty-year-old police officer named Erminio Rosetti, Caruso allowed him to move about freely with his gun drawn, and the young plainclothesman was

promptly shot and killed by a German, apparently in the belief that he had nabbed one of the Partisans.

5. Mureddu, M., "23 marzo 1944": 9. This unpublished vivid account was written by a captain in the Carabinieri who, during the occupation, was a member of Montezemolo's FMCR. The twenty-two-page manuscript is in RK ARC.

6. This shooting spree added eleven civilian casualties, including two dead: a male passerby and the apparently lifeless woman at the window of Palazzo Tittoni, who died days later. See CDS-2: 113, fn. 7.

7. Quoted in EMF: 229.

8. Quoted in ED-1: 245. Hitler's afternoon roar from his Wolf's Lair would become the basis for every legal defense thereafter. The Führer, however, never mentioned the matter again, and all the references to higher orders made in the postwar trials of Nazis and Fascists would prove unverifiable.

9. TAK in UNWCC 8: 9.

10. AG: 256fn.

11. Dollmann did not reveal his self-appointed mission to alert the Pope about the impending reprisal until twenty years later. When his account of his urgent call on Father Pfeiffer became known with the publication of my book *Death in Rome*, it raised considerable skepticism, in spite of independent corroboration by two other sources—a Vatican prelate, the outspoken Monsignor Ludwig Kaas, and Max Husmann, Allen Dulles's Swiss representative, who had extensive dealings with Dollmann in the secret surrender negotiations between the German forces in Italy and the OSS. Dollmann's own explanation of why he had made no mention of it in his 1949 memoir *Roma nazista* was that he had in fact told part of the story, but had omitted his visit with Father Pfeiffer to spare the Pope's liaison any embarrassment. At the time he had been unaware that Pfeiffer was no longer alive, he said. This doubt about Dollmann's credibility, nurtured for years by those who maintained that neither the Pope nor anyone else in the Vatican had prior knowledge that a reprisal was imminent, has since been overtaken by events definitively dispelled by the Vatican's own documentation released in 1980 (see pp. 241–243 and the section "Pacelli v. Katz et al."). Thus there can no longer be any reason to question Dollmann's unpublished 1975 sworn testimony subsequent to the earlier recounting, particularly since he had been called as a witness in an attempt to refute the original material's accuracy (see also *DIR*: 288).

12. Dollmann's references to the Hague Convention relate to the 1907 international agreement on the rules of land warfare. The pact makes no mention of reprisals or executing hostages, but gives the occupying power a free hand to restore and preserve public order. The only restraint is on punishing anyone but those guilty of the illegal act—unless other parties are shown to somehow share in responsibility. Thus it is a question of interpretation with the occupier, at least while in power, as judge and jury. In hostile territory such as Rome it was a license to kill.

13. Dollmann testimony: 6–7, in TRK.

14. Dollmann testimony: 13, ibid.

15. DIR: 104.

16. Ibid. The circumstances of this understanding to speak again would result in a controversy within the controversy. See p. 383, n. 19.

17. The *New York Times*, January 14, 1966: 9.
18. Voluntary Statement of General Harster to Lieutenant Colonel A. P. Scotland, February 22, 1946, in PRO: WO 311/350. Harster was a prisoner of war at the time.
19. Kappler testimony, June 4, 1948, in THK, see *DIR*: 109.
20. Dorer: doc. 629 (PRO: WO 311/359, interrogation of November 1, 1946).
21. Dorer: doc. 633 (PRO: WO 310/137, EP Afragola).
22. *DIR*: 112.
23. MdW: 294.
24. PT-1: 187.
25. CC: 236.
26. Calamandrei, F., *La vita indivisible*, Rome: Editori Riuniti, 1998: 195.
27. Interviewed in AP: 224.
28. Vittorio Gabrieli interviewed ibid.: 224.
29. Mario Menichetti interviewed ibid.: 223.
30. Silvio Gigliozzi interviewed ibid.: 225.
31. CT: 191.
32. JS: 143.

FIFTEEN: IL GRAN RIFIUTO

1. Kappler testimony, June 7, 1948, in THK, quoted in *DIR*: 120.
2. He had teamed up with another Jewish Partisan, a Genoese named Pino Levi Caviglione, whose memoir of their exploits is a classic of Italian Resistance literature: *Guerriglia nei Castelli Romani*, Rome: Einaudi, 1945. For how Moscati fell into Kappler's hands see below n. 25.
3. Dorer: doc. 633 (PRO: WO 310/137, EP Afragola).
4. *DIR*: 120.
5. TPC: 136; Caruso's testimony of September 20, 1944.
6. Koch interrogation, May 16, 1945, in MG: 139.
7. The Governatorato was the municipal administration of Rome, established in 1871 when the city became the capital of unified Italy, but during the German occupation it was in the hands of the neo-Fascist regime. Ferrero has never been further identified, but his superior was Mussolini appointee Giovanni Orgera, the Governatore, a kind of mayor. Orgera had close ties to both General Mälzer and the Vatican, as well as to the Fascist police and the SS. He was an honored guest at the March 23 Fascist event in the Ministry of Corporations (see RPC 2:35; Dorer: doc. 918). My own search of the ASC *Rubrica Gabinetto*, a diary of daily activities of the Governatorato, recorded Orgera sending a personal message of condolences to Mälzer on the day of the Via Rasella attack (n. protocollo 1209).
8. ADSS 10, doc. 115: 189–190. What follows is the Italian original: "*Vaticano, 24 marzo 1944, ore 10,15 L'Ing. Ferrero, del Governatorato di Roma dà i seguenti particolari circa l'incidente di ieri: il numero delle vittime tedesche è di 26 militari; tra i civili italiani si lamentano tre o quattro morti; non è facile ricostruire la scena dato che tutti si sono dati alla fuga; alcuni appartamenti sono stati saccheggiati e la polizia tedesca ha preso l'assoluto controllo della zona senza permettere ingerenza di altre autorità; sembra ad ogni modo che una colonna di automezzi tedeschi attraversando via Rasella abbia la responsabilità di aver*

provocato gli italiani che poi avrebbero lanciato delle bombe dall'edificio di fianco al Palazzo Tittoni; finora sono sconosciute le contromisure: si prevede però che per ogni tedesco ucciso saranno passati per le armi 10 italiani. L'Ing. Ferrero spera di dare più tardi maggiori particolari." "L'Ing." is "L'ingegnere," a professional title.

9. The Vatican itself, until the document's release in August 1980, steadfastly denied any prior knowledge whatsoever of an impending reprisal. See Pacelli v. Katz et al., p. 353.

10. They are Fathers Pierre Blet, Robert A. Graham, Angelo Martini, and Burkhart Schneider; all but Blet are deceased.

11. Testimony of Vatican historian Father Robert Graham in TRK (*RK appeal*: 53).

12. Testimony of Ottone Vinatzer in TRK (*RK appeal*: 35). Vinatzer was one of the most prominent lawyers allowed to represent political prisoners at the German Military Tribunal in Rome. On the evening of the 23rd, after a conversation with Padre Pancrazio about Via Rasella, he teamed up with Montezemolo's lawyer, Bruno Cassinelli, both of them fearing for the lives of their clients; they drew up a memo in which they presented the consensus view of the Partisans' strategy to the German High Command.

13. Ibid.

14. Testimony of Cesidio Lolli in TRK (*RK appeal*: 48).

15. ADSS 10: 12.

16. The complaint went no further than Wolff's desk. Dobbrick remained in his post, later taking the two remaining companies of his 3rd Battalion to northern Italy, where the anti-Partisan activities continued, with civilian atrocities added to the operations.

17. *Kappler sentenza*: 127, *DIR*: 127.

18. *DIR*: 127.

19. Ibid.

20. Ibid.

21. Dorer: doc. 633 (PRO: WO 310/137, EP Afragola).

22. Kappler testimony in THK, June 7, 1948: *DIR*: 128.

23. Ibid.

24. RT: 251. A drawing of Schütz's eyes by the prisoner, Michele Multedo, is reproduced therein.

25. In one of the more sordid acts of this day of endless horrors, one Jew whose name was already on the list was quietly *released* by someone in the Gestapo. He was replaced by the Roman Jewish prizefighter Lazzaro Anticoli, twenty-six, who before the racial laws had fought under the name "Bucefalo" (Bucephalus). Anticoli had been among those arrested that morning and was now added with the others to the list. His hiding place had been revealed by the notorious "Black Panther," the young woman named Celeste Di Porto, herself a Jew. She had turned in more than one-third of the seventy-five Jews on Kappler's list—including Partisan Marco Moscati—for the reward money, 5,000 lire per person. The ex-fighter would leave the following note in his cell: "I am Lazzaro Anticoli, called 'Bucefalo' the prize-fighter. If I never see my family again, it's the fault of that sellout by Celeste Di Porto. Avenge me." The man who was freed in the diabolical exchange was Angelo Di Porto, the Black Panther's brother (BS: 296–297fn).

26. There are two minor exceptions: a note to the Pope's brother Prince Carlo Pacelli

dated April 19, enclosing an unofficial partial list of victims (ADSS 10, doc. 154), and a formal request by the Secretariat on April 22 that the Germans provide the complete list (doc. 160).

27. Nevertheless, they speculated that Pius may have acted in some unknown manner, leaving no trace behind him. On the other hand, he may not have intervened, they said, because the Governatorato official "had not given the essential detail that the execution of the hostages had to take place within 24 hours" (ADSS 10: 12).

28. ADSS 10: 12.

29. AG: 255.

30. A vaguely worded final paragraph, apparently addressed to the occupiers to exercise restraint, added that anyone who really cared about the fate of Rome and Romans should trust in the wisdom and responsibility of the citizenry. *L'osservatore romano*, March 25, 1944: 1. The afternoon newspaper customarily was dated the following day.

SIXTEEN: VIA ARDEATINA

1. *DIR:* 135.

2. Kappler, on the eve of his 1948 trial, told one of his five codefendants that he would back them up if they testified that they, too, had been threatened with summary execution in case of disobedience, but in 1974 he admitted that it was a ruse to exonerate them. They were in fact acquitted.

3. *Raider statement:* 295.

4. It is unlikely that Raider's name was on Kappler's list, but neither was his unlisted presence at the caves surprising. As will be seen, there were others.

5. Dorer: doc. 631 (PRO: WO 310/137, D'Annibale's interrogation of September 9, 1945).

6. *Kappler sentenza*, quoted in *DIR:* 153.

7. Dorer: doc. 633 (PRO: WO 310/137, EP Afragola).

8. Understandably, Kappler and the other Germans present at the slaughter contributed little of the gruesome details, but the reconstruction of what took place, on which the above is based, is indisputable. It is the work of a team of specialists in forensic medicine headed by Dr. Attilio Ascarelli, who exhumed and identified the bodies after the Germans withdrew from Rome. See Attilio Ascarelli, *Le Fosse Ardeatine*, Rome, 2001, sixth ANFIM ed., originally published 1945.

9. *DIR:* 155.

10. Dorer: doc. 633 (PRO: WO 310/137, EP Afragola).

11. PRO: WO 310/137, Amonn's statement of October 13, 1945; cf. *DIR:* 165–166.

12. Nine men, numbers 41–49 on the list, had typically Italian Jewish names ; they were among those spared because the prison official who replaced them believed, correctly, that they had been chosen solely as Jews, tacked on to fill the quota (see *DIR:* 161–162; cf. Crawley report: 3, PRO: WO 310/137).

13. Crawley report: 7, PRO: WO 310/137.

14. ED-1: 249.

15. Another item discussed at the Excelsior meeting was Himmler's demand, a further countermeasure more monstrous than the reprisal. Wolff was under orders from Himmler to assign Kappler with the roundup and deportation of practically the en-

tire male population of Rome. Not only Kappler, but nearly all the ranking occupation officials, including Kesselring, openly opposed it. Machinations, based in part on a pretext of sparing Pope Pius XII further insult, were designed to win a "temporary" postponement. Led by Dollmann and Möllhausen, they succeeded, and once the wrath aroused by the Via Rasella attack subsided, the notion of a forced exodus from Rome was simply forgotten (see *DIR:* 176–178).

16. See p. 342.
17. CC: 238.
18. JS: 144.
19. *DIR:* 173. Dollmann, for reasons he never disclosed, later repeatedly denied this single aspect of our 1965 interview, i.e., the March 24 telephone call to Pfeiffer. The interview was not taped, but I have always felt confident in the accuracy of my notes, particularly since Dollmann, in his own handwriting, marked a copy of a manuscript of his, which he gave me, to indicate the point in the narrative when he made the call (both the notes and the manuscript—*Dollmann ms.* —are in RK ARC). Whether the Vatican first learned of a looming reprisal from Pfeiffer on the night of the 23rd or from Ferrero, the official of the Governatorato, the following morning seems only marginally relevant now, but, as already noted, until the 1980 release of the Vatican document by which it was informed that a ten-for-one reprisal was foreseen, it had maintained having no knowledge whatsoever of a German retaliation plan. In that context, Dollmann's phone call appeared more damaging to the Vatican's position than did his earlier contact with Pfeiffer alone. Dollmann, incidentally, never denied the phone call until it became an issue.
20. *Il messaggero*, March 25, 1944: 1.
21. Nasalli Rocca revealed this in vivid testimony taken in Vatican City in 1975. By then a cardinal, he had been called as a witness to substantiate the pre-1980 position that no one in the Vatican knew anything about the imminent reprisal, not even, he went on, in the Secretariat of State, which in fact had drafted the extraordinary Governatorato document. Nevertheless his description of the Pope's animated reaction appears to be the first news Pius personally received of the reprisal as a fait accompli. As for that reaction, I was present at Nasalli Rocca's testimony, taken in the comfort of his extraterritorial home, and the official transcript does not fully convey the witness's reenactment of that event. He demonstrated how the Pope threw his hands first above, then upon his head, crying out loudly, in anguish, the phrase quoted here, not once but several times in Italian. I therefore translated the transcript passage a bit loosely. The original reads: *"Il Santo Padre si portò le mani al capo, in atteggiamento di stupore e dolore, e disse: 'Cosa mi dice mai,' dandomi chiaramente a manifestare di nulla sapere di quanto era avvenuto."* (Testimony of May 6, 1975, in TRK, *RK sentenza tribunale:* 174.)
22. Pius XII played an unusually active role in the editorial decisions of the *Osservatore*, which was founded by his grandfather Marcantonio Pacelli. Only the Pope and the highest officials of the Secretariat could alter dalla Torre's writings, and indeed Pius would often make corrections to the galleys before press time, phoning them in to dalla Torre or sometimes his deputy Lolli (the latter, when receiving such a call, would kneel on the floor, receiver in hand, while the Pope dictated his instructions; see Hofmann, P., *Anatomy of the Vatican*, London: Hale, 1985: 19).
23. Dalla Torre, G., *Memorie*, Milan: Mondadori, 1967, quoted in *RK appeal:* 44–45.

24. The father of one victim would later compile the following albeit never to be completed statistics: Ages 15 to 75. Catholics 257; Jews 75. Accountants, lawyers 14; actors 2; administrators, businessmen, industrialists 7; architects, engineers, surveyors 5; Armed Forces 38; artists, designers 5; banker 1; butchers 5; carpenters 11; civil servants 4; domestics and waiters 2; electricians 5; farm owners, farm laborers 10; film technicians 2; insurance 1; mechanics 13; merchants, shopkeepers 42; musician 1; office workers 40; peddlers 16; pharmacists, physicians 4; police officer 1; postal-telegraph, telephone company 6; priest 1; printers, typographers 2; professors, teachers 6; railway personnel 3; shoemakers 5; store clerks 7; students 9; workers in various trades 28 (see *DIR:* 168).
25. *L'osservatore romano*, March 26, 1944.
26. Westphal testimony, March 26, 1947, in TAK: 237, 310. The affair of the Germans protesting the *Osservatore* article occupied thirteen days of testimony by Westphal, Beelitz, and Zolling. A copy of the transcript was introduced as an exhibit in THK and later TRK.
27. PT-1: 198.
28. *L'unità*, March 30, 1944.
29. Some individual parties spoke out on their own in the underground press. The Action Party's *Italia Libera* renewed a call to arms under the headline "We Shall Not Bow to the Nazi Terror," and the Communist *L'unità* vowed a war against the Germans "to the death," saying that the Romans would be "neither deceived, nor blackmailed, nor intimidated" by the Germans (quoted in *DIR:* 202–203).
30. Lepre, A., *Via Rasella: Leggenda e realtà della Resistenza a Roma*, Bari: Laterza, 1996: 64–68.
31. *Il messaggero*, March 26, 1944: 1.
32. The occupiers would continually identify the general population as an extension of the Resistance. At a press conference held some days later, Kappler reported on his investigation of the Via Rasella attack and insisted on the complicity of the residents of the neighborhood. On the day of the incident, he said, women hanging out clothes in the afternoon sun that passed overhead prior to the attack had to have noticed the Partisans preparing themselves on the street below, but reported nothing. "It is this attitude," Kappler said, "that authorizes the taking of hostages" (see *DIR:* 207).
33. The *New York Times*, March 29, 1944.
34. CT: 192.
35. JS: 146.

SEVENTEEN: THE SMILE

1. Irving Berlin, quoted in MC: 335.
2. Quoted in MSD: 462.
3. MC: 334.
4. Ibid.: 337.
5. Clark in his 1948 interviews with Sidney T. Matthews, but denied by Alexander; quoted in CD'E: 338.
6. CD'E: 299.
7. Quoted in CD'E: 300.

8. *Dale P. Harper in World War II* mag. Nov. 1995; online at *womenshistory.about.com/ library/prm/blaxissally1.htm*

9. A&W-2: 142.

10. Quoted in RT: 193.

11. 5th Mountain Division Report: German doc. quoted in A&W-2: 157.

12. AK: 271–75.

13. "Combatings of Partisans," Führer order signed by Keitel, text in "Report of British War Crimes Section of Allied Force Headquarters on German Reprisals for Partisan Activities in Italy," Annex "A": *www.ess.uwe.ac.uk/genocide.htm*.

14. "Concerning: New Measures in Connection with Operations Against Partisans," Order 4968/44 signed by Kesselring, dated May 10, 1944 (emphasis in original), text in "Report of British War Crimes Section" (see preceding note): Annex B.

EIGHTEEN: ROME MUST STARVE . . .

1. *Il tempo*, October 28, 1975.

2. A small controversy, and an intramural feud, developed many years later over when the Pope learned of the location of the massacre. Was it as early as the first day after the killings, by way of the sighting reported by don Fagioli and his party, or the seventh day, as claimed by their fellow Silesian don Michele Valentini? Valentini, whose 1944 detailed statement had been regarded the most authentic document on the Silesians' role (see *DIR*: 293–4), was contradicted by don Fagioli's account published in 1975 (in the Rome daily *Il tempo*, October 28). Much to Valentini's displeasure, Fagioli's version was corroborated by other eyewitnesses and still other Silesians, who said they had been cited less than accurately by Valentini. Church historian don Francesco Motto, while reserving final judgment until the Vatican opens its archives, found Valentini's claim of withholding news of Fagioli's discovery from the Vatican for all those days "unthinkable" (Motto, "Gli sfollati e i rifugiati nelle catacombe di S. Callisto durante l'occupazione nazifascista di Roma," in *Ricerche storiche salesiane*, no. 1, 1984: 122–133).

3. Pretrial interrogation of Caruso, August 9, 1944, quoted in *DIR*: 204.

4. CT: 211.

5. Ibid.

6. *L'unità*, April 13, 1944. The statement, dated March 28, was written in early April.

7. Morante, E., *La Storia*, Turin: Einaudi, 1974: 324–26.

8. OSS RG 226, Entry 210, Box 534, Folder 8, Kappa #722, To Grand from Rahn, March 28, 1944.

9. Ibid.

10. See CDS-2: 141–148.

11. ADSS 10, Secretariat of State to the Germany Embassy, April 22, 1944, doc. 160:234.

12. *Tompkins report:* 41, in *Tompkins papers*.

13. Menicanti report, June 14, 1944: 1, in OSS Agents in Rome, CIA Release, *Tompkins papers*.

14. "Summary of Information: Raimondo Lanza di Trabia," Report of Captain Mario E. Brod, Case no. 553–4, March 12, 1944, in *Tompkins papers*.

15. *Tompkins report:* 42, in *Tompkins papers.*
16. A survey of wartime clinical records of four of Rome's largest hospitals for the early spring of 1944 found a surprisingly large number of dead-on-arrival cases in which autopsies revealed denutrition as a cause of death. The victims, as would be expected at this stage, were among the very young—infants between eighteen months and less than one month old—and the elderly, people in their seventies, but there was also an unusual increase in the general population of poisoning from eating spoiled food (see CDS-2: 132–133).
17. OSS RG 226, Entry 210, Box 444, Boston Series 1054.
18. The latest open-city promises by the Germans to truly demilitarize Rome were brushed off as well. Allied bombers would go where the enemy went, Washington and London insisted. If the German supply routes to the front excluded the city, so would their pursuers. In any event, as it appeared more and more likely that the Allies would replace the Germans in Rome, it grew increasingly disingenuous for any of the parties involved to speak of an open city, since the new occupants would want to use Rome militarily too.
19. Quoted RT: 250.
20. Quoted ibid.: 264.
21. Quoted ibid.: 265.
22. Ibid.

NINETEEN: SHIMMERING CITY

1. MC: 346.
2. ES: 317.
3. Quoted in CD'E: 349.
4. For one of the exceptions see RT: 277.
5. Interior Ministry, Director General of Civil Administration to Cabinet Chief, February 8, 1945; Dorer: doc. 1317.
6. Dissertation interview by C. Venditti, University of Rome, 1976–1977, in Dorer: doc. 1307.
7. Dorer: doc. 1306.
8. MC: 348.
9. Ibid.: 357.
10. Churchill to Alexander, telegram of May 11, 1944, quoted in RT: 265.
11. Clark diary, quoted in CD'E: 338.
12. Fisher, E. F., Jr., *Cassino to the Alps,* Washington, D.C.: CMH Publication, 1977: 104.
13. MC: 352.
14. Ibid.: 357.
15. Unbeknownst to the Vatican, its own daily, *L'osservatore romano,* was harboring like-minded typographers who were secretly working with the extreme-left armed Resistance formation Bandiera Rossa, using the *Osservatore*'s printing plant to publish Bandiera Rossa's clandestine newspaper (unpublished research of Professor Antonio Parisella, University of Parma, interview with RK, May 2001).
16. The deposition, dated March 24, 1972, was made available by Vatican sources to Giorgio Angelozzi Gariboldi, the lawyer who represented Pius XII's niece in the case

against *Death in Rome* (TRK). He later published it in his *Pio XII, Hitler e Mussolini,* Milan: Mursia, 1995: 251–253.

17. The link to the Pope, as Wolff stated in his testimony, was maintained through Cardinal Ildefonso Schuster, archbishop of Milan, who had a hand in the negotiations.

18. These six intercepts are among many more in ACS: RSI, *Segretaria del capo della polizia, 1943–1944, busta* 39, *fascicolo* 14.

19. Carroll-Abbing: 94.

20. *Memoriale di autodifesa di Koch,* in MG: 239.

21. Quoted in *DP*: 38.

22. Testimony of Elvira Sabatini Paladini, in TEP; quoted in *DP*: 111.

23. CC: 269; cf. RB-1: 203.

24. MC: 211.

25. Ibid.: 351.

26. *Fifth Army* history (privately published), quoted in CD'E: 364.

27. CD'E: 365.

28. Ibid.: 366.

29. Even for Alexander the lure never slept. Toward the very end, when the race for Rome had begun in earnest and Clark's forces were blocked in the Alban Hills, he made a bid for the prize, telling Clark, whom he always called by his middle name, "Wayne, If you can't do it, or if you feel that you're going to be tied down here, I'll direct the Eighth Army into Rome." To which Clark replied, "Well, you wait until I holler, because we're going to take it!" (Quoted in A&W-2: 194.)

30. II Corps intelligence officer Colonel Robert van de Velde, quoted ibid.: 185.

31. JS: 191.

32. 36th Division website: *www.kwanah.com/txmilmus/texas.htm.*

33. CD'E: 389.

TWENTY: ROME ETERNAL

1. Quoted from Bede (673–735) in Edward Gibbon, *The Decline and Fall of the Roman Empire,* 1781, Chapter 71.

2. Morante: 344.

3. Angelozzi Gariboldi: 253; according to the author, Dollmann, quoting what Wolff had confided after the audience, told him, Angelozzi Gariboldi, that Pius had made this remark when they were discussing the German withdrawal from Rome—a subject, however, not mentioned in Wolff's sainthood testimony.

4. Pius XII on Vatican Radio, June 2, 1944; text in AG: 287–288.

5. Text (and emphasis) in AG: 282.

6. Ibid.: 285–286.

7. *Newsweek,* June 12, 1944: 70.

8. MC: 361.

9. Quoted in A&W-2: 200.

10. Quoted in CD'E: 392.

11. The code-phrase in Italian would be—*La neve è caduta sui monti*—just as London some days earlier had broadcast, *Anna Maria è stata promossa,* "Anna Maria has been promoted," to signal the Partisans to assist in opening the way through the Alban

Hills. A single code-word would signal the Allied entry into Rome itself: *Elefante*, "Elephant."

12. RB-1: 218–223.

13. AK: 204.

14. AG: 291–292.

15. JS: 193–194 (emphasis in original).

16. CT: 268.

17. MdW: 215.

18. AG: 295.

19. Morante: 344.

20. MdW: 215.

21. JS: 195.

22. Nucci was the woman at the curfew party referred to by Tompkins as being off in a corner with Priebke. The American, learning Priebke's identity after the party had ended, felt lucky that Nucci's charms had so absorbed the Gestapo man's attention and felt still luckier fifty-eight years later, when he first heard of the Mauser in Priebke's boot. See *DP*: 63.

23. ADSS 10, Note of the Secretariat, June 1, 1944, doc. 218.

24. Vassalli, quoted in Angelozzi-Gariboldi: 248–250.

25. A monument at La Storta commemorates all fourteen victims, among whom is a never-identified British prisoner of war. The OSS documents regarding the betrayal of Sorrentino and Bonocore (whose surname is recorded at La Storta as Conversi) would, however, seem to be beyond dispute.

26. ES: 410.

27. General John Sloan, commander, 88th Division quoted in A&W-2: 210.

28. A&W-2: 219. Cf. Mark Clark's version in MC: 365.

29. The anecdote has numerous versions. Adleman and Walton (A&W-2: 211) heard it directly from Frederick; Clark (MC: 364) relates a quite similar account, but replacing the "golly" dialogue with "I must say that sign had a great appeal for me" (cf. CD'E: 396).

30. A&W-2: 211.

31. The article appeared in the first number of *Stars and Stripes* to be published in Rome. This "Rome Extra" of the U.S. Army newspaper, dated June 5, 1944, was printed by *Il messaggero*, the daily controlled by the Fascists until the June 4 flight of its director, Bruno Spampanato. The typographers, who had seized the presses, worked with the Americans "with as much enthusiasm . . . as the people of Rome have in welcoming the Fifth Army," said the paper, adding, "They are proud and so are we."

32. JS: 200.

33. ES: 412.

34. MC: 365–366. An expanded version of the getting-lost incident appears in A&W-2: 226.

35. MC: 366.

36. Quoted in ES: 414; however, as with most of Clark's critics, the second part of the final sentence, beginning with "and for the French" is lopped off. The complete sentence is in A&W-2: 226; also in RT: 319–320.

37. ES: 414.

38. Tompkins's allegations would be substantiated in the post-liberation internal investigation, but not until the CIA release in 2000 would he be completely vindicated.

39. The matter did not end there. The dead man, Giorgio Barbarisi, was an officer in the Finanza, a Fascist police organization, but as of that morning incorporated in the Allied Military Government. Sasà would thus be tried by an Allied Military Court that summer and ultimately acquitted precisely for having acted in self-defense, but the case would go on to haunt him for decades. The sequence of events described here is drawn from the trial record at NARA: AMG/ACC Italy. Region IV. Lazio. Case No. 7762, Legal Section.

40. AG: 298 fn.

41. JS: 202.

42. CT: 274.

43. Text of Pius XII's speech in AG: 297.

44. ES: 415.

45. RB-1: 230.

46. CC: 306.

47. Giulio Farnesi, 1975, in AP: 303.

I: JUSTICE POSTPONED

1. Moscow Declaration on German Atrocities, November 1, 1943, online text at *www.yale.edu/lawweb/avalon/wwii/moscow.htm.*

2. INQ: 17; see also Ascarelli's affidavit to the Office of Special Investigations, British Military Police, September 26, 1945, in PRO; WO 310/137 (Dorer: doc. 625).

3. INQ: 40–41.

4. One of these would prove to be an error when, years later, the person named, a Russian arrested in occupied Rome, turned up alive. Two others, however, would join the list of positive identifications bringing it to 323, and of the remaining 12, the names of 9 would become known, leaving 3 victims about whom nothing is known.

5. Ascarelli's evidence that the hideous procedure of the killings took place on the death pile swept aside, though it did not prevent, any denial: the spent shells were found *between* the layers of corpses, indicating where the bullets had been fired, and the bodies were found in the pile with their knees bent—the kneeling position of execution that would not have been maintained if the victim had been dragged to the pile from another place.

6. The eyewitness was the renowed *New York Times* correspondent Herbert Matthews (*The Education of a Correspondent*, New York: Harcourt, Brace, 1946: 476). Another distinguished American writer then with the Fifth Army in Rome, Alfred Hayes, wrote of Caruso's vaunted remorse as being a "trifle tardy . . . these sketches of his humble spirit leave me singularly unmoved. Still, still, on the warm wind, where the road forks on the Street of the Seven Churches, I smell that terrible odor" (*All Thy Conquests*, New York: Howell, Soskin, 1946: 109).

7. MG: 305. Visconti was also at the trial, making a film for the U.S. Army's Psychological Warfare Branch. The footage, with additional scenes shot at the Caruso trial and execution as well as the Carretta lynching, was never shown in its entirety,

though some of it appears in the 1947 documentary *Giorni di gloria* (see MG: 312–313).

8. Verdict in Dorer: doc. 1365.

9. Quoted in MG: 308.

10. Mario Nasalli Rocca, *Accanto ai condannati a morte:* 63, in MG: 310–312.

11. Nasalli Rocca: 65–66, in ME: 310–312.

12. See *BS:* 302–303.

13. EZ: 182; cf. *BS:* 304.

14. Mackensen statement of June 27, 1946, PRO: WO 310/137, in Dorer: doc. 634.

15. Mälzer statement of October 9, 1946, PRO: WO 310/137, in Dorer: doc. 635.

16. UNWCC 8: 1–8.

17. The *New York Times*, December 1, 1946: 1.

18. Quoted in CD'E: 427.

19. UNWCC 8: 9.

20. Ibid.: 13.

21. Ibid.: 12.

22. "Concerning: New Measures in Connection with Operations Against Partisans," Order 4968/44 signed by Kesselring, May 10, 1944 (emphasis in original), text in "Report of British War Crimes Section of Allied Force Headquarters on German Reprisals for Partisan Activities in Italy," Annex B: *www.ess.uwe.ac.uk/genocide.html.*

23. AK: 276.

24. Barnett, C., ed., *Hitler's Generals*, New York: Grove Weidenfeld, 1989: 265–289.

25. CD'E: 426.

26. AK: 376.

27. Dannecker file, in Counter Intelligence Corps Collection Investigative Repository Records, RG 319, XE 009228.

28. *Kappler sentenza:* 154–155.

29. See *DIR:* 236.

30. *Kappler sentenza:* 155–56.

31. Ibid: 138–142. The judgment of the military tribunal that the attack was illegitimate was overturned in several higher courts, including the Military Supreme Court in its 1952 denial of Kappler's appeal. Ruling in a 1957 civil action, the Supreme Court of Cassation concluded that the assault was an "act of war," but it was not until 1999, when a Roman prosecutor tried to bring the surviving Via Rasella Partisans to trial for the death of the Zuccheretti boy, that the case was brought to the penal section of the highest court in Italy. That panel issued the final verdict in the matter, declaring the immunity of the Partisans, who were engaged in a "legitimate act of war." (Text of verdict: *Corte Supreme di Cassazione—Sezione I Penale sent. n. 1560/99* at *www. romacivica.net/anpiroma/resistenza3c.htm.*)

32. Carla and Sasà had married in the fall of 1944. At war's end, Sasà had gone on to complete his medical studies and is a practicing physician to this day. Carla was elected to Parliament and later served on the city council of Rome. Calamandrei, incidentally, married GAP Central Partisan Maria Teresa Regard.

33. Transcript, ABC News, *PrimeTime Live*, telecast of May 5, 1994. Priebke was discovered by an ABC News *PrimeTime Live* producer, Harry Phillips. Researching the fugitive-Nazi phenomenon in Argentina, he had received vague information from a

Picciotto Fargion, L., *Il libro della memoria: Gli ebrei deportati dall'Italia 1942–1945*, rev. ed. Milan: Mursia, 2002.

Sarfatti, Michele, *Gli ebrei nell'Italia fascista*, Turin: Einaudi, 2000.

THE GERMANS IN RETREAT

Battini, M., and Pezzino, P., *Guerra ai civili: Occupazione tedesca e politica del massacro: Toscana 1944*, Venice: Marsilio, 1997.

Klinkhammer, L., *Stragi naziste in Italia: La guerra contro i civili*, Rome: Donzelli, 1997.

Pezzino, P., *Anatomia di un massacro. Controversia sopra una strage nazista*, Bologna: Il Mulino, 1997.

———, *Storie di guerra civile. Il massacro di Niccioleta*, Bologna: Il Mulino, 2001.

———, "Sui mancati processi in Italia ai criminali di guerra tedeschi," in *Storia e memoria*, 2002, no. 1.

Pavone, C., "Note sulla Resistenza armata, la rappresaglia nazista e alcune attuali confusioni," in "Priebke e il massacro delle Ardeatine," supplement, *L'unità*, Rome, 1996.

Schreiber, G., *La vendetta tedesca*, Milan: Mondadori, 2000.

Breitman, R., *Official Secrets: What the Nazis Planned, What the British and Americans Knew*. New York: Hill & Wang, 1998. Understanding Ultra.

PIUS XII: THE CRITICS

Miccoli, G., *I dilemmi e i silenzi di Pio XII: Vaticano, Seconda Guerra Mondiale e Shoah*, Milan: Rizzoli, 2000.

Phayer, M., *The Catholic Church and the Holocaust, 1930–1965*, Bloomington: Indiana University Press, 2000. Phayer moves beyond the liberation into postwar Rome, touching on the rarely probed "Rat Line"; Pius XII, Phayer writes, allowed the Vatican "to become engaged in providing refuge for Holocaust perpetrators."

Wills, G., *Papal Sin: Structures of Deceit*, New York: Doubleday, 2000. An ex-seminarian finds the Church's own admission of a moral failure in the Holocaust lacking in candor.

Carroll, J., *Constantine's Sword: The Church and the Jews*, Boston: Houghton Mifflin, 2001. Carroll, a former priest, cites the primacy of the quest for papal power as blinding.

Kertzer, D. I., *The Popes Against the Jews: The Vatican's Role in the Rise of Modern Anti-Semitism*, New York: Knopf, 2001.

Goldhagen, D. J., *A Moral Reckoning: The Role of the Catholic Church During the Holocaust and Its Unfulfilled Duty of Repair*, New York: Knopf, 2002. The author of *Hitler's Willing Executioners* emerges as Pius's severest critic, and a critic of his fellow critics as well.

PIUS XII: THE DEFENDERS

Blet, P., *Pius XII and the Second World War* (trans. L. J. Johnson), New York: Paulist Press, 1999. The only survivor of the four Vatican historians who edited the eleven volumes of wartime documents of the Holy See (ADSS) summarizes their contents.

Forcella, E., *La Resistenza in convento*, Turin: Einaudi, 1999.

Marchione, M., *Yours Is a Precious Witness: Memoirs of Jews and Catholics in Wartime Italy*, Mahwah, New Jersey: Paulist Press, 1997.

———, *Pope Pius XII: Architect for Peace*. Mahwah, New Jersey: Paulist Press, 2000. The author, an American nun, picks up the baton carried by Fatima's Mother Pascalina.

McInerny, R., *The Defamation of Pius XII*, South Bend, Indiana: St. Augustine's Press, 2001.

Rychlak, R. J., *Hitler, the War, and the Pope*, Columbus, Mississippi: Genesis Press, 2000. A non-Catholic lawyer and professor at the University of Mississippi School of Law, now Pius's staunchest supporter, appends a twenty-seven-page attack on Cornwell's book to his own, adopting courtroom-style advocacy in treating the critics who followed.

Sánchez, J. M., *Pius XII and the Holocaust: Understanding the Controversy*, Washington, D.C.: Catholic University of America Press, 2002.

ARTICLES

Gumpel, P., "Pius XII As He Really Was," in *The Tablet*, February 13, 1999. This pre-Cornwell defense of Pius XII by the German Jesuit appointed by Pope John Paul II as the "independent judge"—the so-called relator—to assess the evidence for Pius's sainthood, and who issued an unequivocal yes, became the handbook for later defenders.

Dalin, D., "Pius XII and the Jews," in *The Weekly Standard*, February 26, 2001. A rabbi joins the defense, attempting to dismantle the critics' best evidence with the arguments of the Gumpel manual.

Madigan, K. "What the Vatican Knew About the Holocaust, and When," in *Commentary*, October 2001. The Harvard Divinity School professor tries to turn Dalin's demolition approach on the defenders—provoking the wrath of an overflow of letter-writers.

Katz, R., "Pius XII Protests the Holocaust," in *What If? 2: Eminent Historians Imagine What Might Have Been*, New York: Putnam, 2001 (anthology edited by Robert Cowley).

Goldhagen, D. J., "What Would Jesus Have Done? Pius XII, the Catholic Church, and the Holocaust," in *The New Republic*, January 21, 2002. A long review of the recent Pius XII books, and at the time a preview of his own.

INDEX

U.S. Navy Intelligence source about a still-wanted "2-i-C" (second-in-command) at the Gestapo interrogation center in Via Tasso. While in Bariloche tracking another ex-Nazi, Phillips followed a hunch that led to Priebke. The story of the scoop, in which I had a consultant role, is told in *DP*: 20–24.

34. Discretion being one of his weaknesses, however, he admitted to a Bariloche reporter visiting him during his 1996 trial that he had been "oriented" by none other than Rat Line chief Bishop Hudal. The journalist was Italo Pisani, of the *Río Negro* (see *DP*: 100).

35. Father Draganovic's CIA file, released in May 2002, shows him to have been employed by U.S. Army intelligence in the early Cold War years, operating against Yugoslavia. A Croatian and a Nazi sympathizer, he ran a dedicated line from the Slovenian Church of St. Jerome in Rome to Buenos Aires for escaped Croatian war criminals. As an American spy, however, he was found unreliable and dropped (see NARA news release 02-52 on RG 263 CIA Name Files, *www.archives.gov/iwg*).

36. Loftus, J., and Aarons, M., *The Secret War Against the Jews: How Western Espionage Betrayed the Jewish People*, New York: St. Martin's, 1994.

37. *DP*: 78.

38. Ibid.: 8–9.

39. Ibid.: 17; for the evidence see ibid.: 145–146

40. Priebke trial transcript, June 12, 1996, quoted *ibid.*: 136; see also 173, fn. 17.

41. *Priebke-Hass sentenza*: 51.

42. *Corriere della Sera*, July 23, 1997: 5.

II. *DEFENSOR CIVITATIS*, THE UNFINISHED STORY

1. Tardini, D., *Pio XII*, Rome, 1959: 79.

2. Quoted in SZ: 301.

3. Leiber, R., "Pio XII e gli ebrei di Roma, 1943–44," *La civiltà cattolica*, March 4, 1961: 449–458.

4. Lapide's famous computation, enshrined in the literature of Pius's defenders, but thoroughly discredited, repudiated by Catholic scholars, and used only by the most zealous advocates, was reached by sheer guesswork. From the approximately 8.3 million Jews in prewar Europe who fell under German control, he explained, he subtracted 6 million Jews who died in the Holocaust and another million who fled on their own, and split the balance not quite in half, giving the short end to a combination of Protestants and a catch-all category of non-Christians who saved Jews. This left him with 700,000 to assign to Catholics, but, he said, the number was probably higher, hence the 860,000. Lapide, Israel's representative to the Holy See with a mission to gain diplomatic recognition for the Jewish state, attributed the rescue credit to Catholics in general, but the number—when hurled back at the Pope's critics, along with the source and his religious affiliation—is usually expressed exclusively as the result of Pius's direct or indirect intervention (see Pinchas Lapide, *The Last Three Popes and the Jews*, London: Souvenir, 1967).

5. Presented in Rome as *Il Vicario*, the play was immediately shut down by Vatican intervention. It branded the performance in the city of its savior as egregiously offen-

sive, redolent of "ingratitude toward [Pius XII], to whom many of today's denigrators . . . owe their safety" (*The New York Times*, February 15, 1964: 14).

6. Text in Bentley (with a response from Hochhuth): 66–71.

7. Father Peter Gumpel, quoted in *Zenit*, September 16, 1999.

8. JC: 384 and 296–297.

9. International Catholic-Jewish Historical Commission: *The Vatican and the Holocaust: A Preliminary Report*, October 2000, at *www.bnaibrith.org/cpp/randa/vatican.html*.

10. Apparently stung, the Vatican early in 2003 opened the floodgates to millions of documents in its secret archives. But it stopped short of the outbreak of World War II, 1939, the year that coincides with Pius's election to the papacy. A coordinator of the commission of scholars called it "a step in the right direction," noting that four of the forty-seven questions dealt with then Cardinal Pacelli's prewar career as a Vatican diplomat in Hitler's Germany. The Vatican's chief archivist, however, cautioned not to expect "shocking revelations." (See *The New York Times*, Feb. 13, 2003.)

11. Nevertheless, the word *silence* when used by the defenders is invariably placed in quotation marks, in deference to Pius's generic lamentations about the horrors of war. Pius himself, however, showed a keen awareness of the qualitative difference between the vague and the specific. After an October 1942 audience given by Pius to Monsignor Angelo Giuseppe Roncalli, the future John XXIII wrote in his diary, "He asked me if his silence regarding Nazism was not judged badly." This recent disclosure prompted the Catholic-Jewish Historical Commission to ask in its forty-seventh and final question whether the Pope had doubts about the "wisdom or correctness" of this silence and whether there were documents in the Vatican archives that might illuminate this issue. (See *The Vatican and the Holocaust*, question 47 and fns. 57 and 58.

PACELLI V. KATZ ET AL.

1. One was entirely new at the time: the account related to me by Dollmann of his meeting with Padre Pancrazio to warn the Pope of an impending bloodbath. Soon afterward, I found corroboration for this disclosure. See *DIR:* 250–252.

2. Ibid.: 252, 258. The reader, referring to these pages, may want to know that the Vatican official with whom I met, Carlo Croce, testified at the trial that I had "never asked him for clarification and information on the position assumed by the Holy See with regard to the events of March 23 and 24, 1944" (*RK sentenza tribunale:* 185).

3. See *The New York Times*, January 22, 1967; see also January 24, 25, and 29, 1967.

4. *The New York Times*, January 23, 1967.

5. Ibid.: 127.

6. *RK sentenza appello:* 22–28.

7. Ibid.: 31–32.

8. *RK sentenza corte suprema:* 20.

9. Ibid.: 9, 21.

10. Ibid.: 21.

BIBLIOGRAPHY

The first bibliography dedicated to the year in which Rome was occupied appeared in 1994. Part of a larger study, a guidebook densely titled *Roma e Lazio 1930–1950, Guida per le ricerche: Fascismo, antifascismo, guerra, Resistenza, dopoguerra* (Milan: Franco Angeli), it listed some 500 works and where in and around Rome even the rarest among them could be consulted. It remains a powerful tool for studying the German occupation of Rome. The product of a collaborative effort of fifteen archivists and librarians, led by historian Antonio Parisella,* the *Guida* provides information about every archive and library in the region with holdings relevant to the period, even those still inaccessible. Nearly ten years have passed since publication, more than enough time to send any guidebook into oblivion, but a long essay written by Parisella for the Dürer CD-ROM (see the Sources and Notes section) brings his Rome bibliography a good deal closer to the present.

Anyone in possession of these two publications would have an incomparable overview of the literature of the occupation, seen from every side, in book form, periodicals, and, to a lesser degree, films.

Although the Parisella update appeared in 2001, it was written a year earlier, predating the CIA's release of wartime OSS documents and the flare-up of the Pius XII controversy stirred by the publication of John Cornwell's *Hitler's Pope*, which was followed by a new round of studies. Some of these later works are among important publications that have appeared since the Priebke affair, which unloosed the lowest forms of revisionism and produced a strong backlash. Several have already been cited, a few of them frequently, such as Carla Capponi's long-awaited memoir, Massimiliano Griner's myth-shattering research on the Koch Gang, Susan Zuccotti's equally original *Under His Very Windows*, and Alessandro Portelli's innovative oral history of the Ardeatine Caves massacre. Other works, though uncited, have been helpful as well. What follows is a list of these newer works, dating back to the mid-90s. Where necessary, I have added a brief explanation.

MEMOIRS AND DIARIES

Musu, M., *La ragazza di Via Orazio. Vita di una comunista irrequieta*, Milan: Mursia, 1997.
  The youngest Gappista adds her part of the tale.
Ossicini, A., *Un'isola sul Tevere: Il Fascismo al di là del ponte*, Rome: Editori Riuniti, 1999.
  Another late-reporting Partisan.
Sabatini Paladini, E., *Arrigo Paladini: Il lungo cammino della libertà*, rev. ed., Rome: Edi-

---

* Currently professor of contemporary history at the University of Parma and president of the Museo Storico della Liberazione di Roma (formerly Kappler's Gestapo headquarters in Via Tasso).

zioni FIVL, 2001. The wife of an OSS operative in Tompkins's network, today director of the Via Tasso museum, recalls life on the run until Paladini's capture and tenure
as Kappler's prisoner.

Carandini Albertini, E., *Dal terrazzo, diario 1943–1944*, Bologna: Il Mulino, 1997. The
diary of a woman of the Roman aristocracy in the circle of CLN President Bonomi.

Chilanti, G., *Bandiera rossa e borsa nera. La Resistenza di una adolescente*, Milan: Mursia,
1998. Adventures of a fourteen-year-old girl running errands for the Partisans.

Caputo, G., *La speranza ardente. Storia e memoria del movimento studentesco antifascista romano. Il diario di Orlando (Lallo) Orlandi dal carcere di via Tasso*, Rome: n.p., 1998.

Raganella, L., *Senza sapere da che parte stanno. Ricordi dell'infanzia e "diario" di Roma in
guerra (1943–44)*, Rome: Bulzoni, 1999. A priest of the San Lorenzo district recon-
structs the period in the form of a diary many years later, with episodes that have a
Zelig-like quality.

PARTISANS AND THE ROMAN RESISTANCE

Avagliano, M., *Il partigiano Tevere: Il generale Sabato Martelli Castaldi dalle vie dell'aria alle
Fosse Ardeatine*, Cava de' Tirreni: Avagliano Editore, 1996.

———, ed., *Roma alla macchia: Personaggi e vicende della Resistenza*, Cava de' Tirreni:
Avagliano Editore, 1997. Contributions to an anti-revisionist conference; includes a
fact-filled tribute to the women of the Roman Resistance by Carla Capponi.

———, and Le Moli, G., eds., *Muoio innocente. Lettere di caduti della Resistenza a Roma*,
Milan: Mursia, 1999. Last words, some newly discovered, from the anti-Fascists on
occupation's "death row"; an addition to the 1954 collection edited by P. Malvezzi and
G. Pirelli.

Gremmo, R., *I partigiani di Bandiera Rossa: il Movimento comunista d'Italia nella Resistenza
romana*, Biella: Edizioni Elf, 1996. A report from the extreme left, taking aim at the
Gappisti, finds many unsolved mysteries in the Via Rasella attack.

Grimaldi, F., Soda, L., and Garasi, S., eds., *Partigiani a Roma*, Rome: Manifesto Libri,
1996.

Parisella, A., *Sopravvivere liberi: riflessioni sulla della Resistenza a cinquant'anni dalla liberazione*, Rome: Gangemi, 1997.

Tompkins, P., *Una spia a Roma*, rev. ed., Milan: Il Saggiatore, 2002. An updated version of
the author's 1962 *A Spy in Rome* (with the real names for those earlier withheld).

THE HOLOCAUST IN ITALY

Breitman, R., "New Sources on the Holocaust in Italy," in *Holocaust and Genocide Studies*,
Winter 2002.

Katz, R., "The Möllhausen Telegram, The Kappler Decodes, and The Deportation of
Roman Jewry: The New CIA-OSS Documents, 2000–2002," *The Jews of Italy Under
Fascist and Nazi Rule, 1922–1945: The Proceedings of an International Holocaust Confer-
ence, October 6–8, 2002, Yeshiva University*, New York.

Impagliazzo, M., ed., *La Resistenza silenziosa: Leggi razziali e occupazione nazista nella
memoria degli ebrei di Roma*, Milan: Guerini, 1997.

Loy, R., *First Words: A Childhood in Italy* (trans. G. Conti), New York: Metropolitan
Books/Henry Holt, 2000. A memoir of the childhood of a Jewish girl in occupied
Rome.

Picciotto Fargion, L., *Il libro della memoria: Gli ebrei deportati dall'Italia 1942–1945*, rev. ed. Milan: Mursia, 2002.

Sarfatti, Michele, *Gli ebrei nell'Italia fascista*, Turin: Einaudi, 2000.

The Germans in Retreat

Battini, M., and Pezzino, P., *Guerra ai civili: Occupazione tedesca e politica del massacro: Toscana 1944*, Venice: Marsilio, 1997.

Klinkhammer, L., *Stragi naziste in Italia: La guerra contro i civili*, Rome: Donzelli, 1997.

Pezzino, P., *Anatomia di un massacro. Controversia sopra una strage nazista*, Bologna: Il Mulino, 1997.

———, *Storie di guerra civile. Il massacro di Niccioleta*, Bologna: Il Mulino, 2001.

———, "Sui mancati processi in Italia ai criminali di guerra tedeschi," in *Storia e memoria*, 2002, no. 1.

Pavone, C., "Note sulla Resistenza armata, la rappresaglia nazista e alcune attuali confusioni," in "Priebke e il massacro delle Ardeatine," supplement, *L'unità*, Rome, 1996.

Schreiber, G., *La vendetta tedesca*, Milan: Mondadori, 2000.

Breitman, R., *Official Secrets: What the Nazis Planned, What the British and Americans Knew*, New York: Hill & Wang, 1998. Understanding Ultra.

Pius XII: The Critics

Miccoli, G., *I dilemmi e i silenzi di Pio XII: Vaticano, Seconda Guerra Mondiale e Shoah*, Milan: Rizzoli, 2000.

Phayer, M., *The Catholic Church and the Holocaust, 1930–1965*, Bloomington: Indiana University Press, 2000. Phayer moves beyond the liberation into postwar Rome, touching on the rarely probed "Rat Line"; Pius XII, Phayer writes, allowed the Vatican "to become engaged in providing refuge for Holocaust perpetrators."

Wills, G., *Papal Sin: Structures of Deceit*, New York: Doubleday, 2000. An ex-seminarian finds the Church's own admission of a moral failure in the Holocaust lacking in candor.

Carroll, J., *Constantine's Sword: The Church and the Jews*, Boston: Houghton Mifflin, 2001. Carroll, a former priest, cites the primacy of the quest for papal power as blinding.

Kertzer, D. I., *The Popes Against the Jews: The Vatican's Role in the Rise of Modern Anti-Semitism*, New York: Knopf, 2001.

Goldhagen, D. J., *A Moral Reckoning: The Role of the Catholic Church During the Holocaust and Its Unfulfilled Duty of Repair*, New York: Knopf, 2002. The author of *Hitler's Willing Executioners* emerges as Pius's severest critic, and a critic of his fellow critics as well.

Pius XII: The Defenders

Blet, P., *Pius XII and the Second World War* (trans. L. J. Johnson), New York: Paulist Press, 1999. The only survivor of the four Vatican historians who edited the eleven volumes of wartime documents of the Holy See (ADSS) summarizes their contents.

Forcella, E., *La Resistenza in convento*, Turin: Einaudi, 1999.

Marchione, M., *Yours Is a Precious Witness: Memoirs of Jews and Catholics in Wartime Italy*, Mahwah, New Jersey: Paulist Press, 1997.

————, *Pope Pius XII: Architect for Peace*. Mahwah, New Jersey: Paulist Press, 2000. The author, an American nun, picks up the baton carried by Fatima's Mother Pascalina.

McInerny, R., *The Defamation of Pius XII*, South Bend, Indiana: St. Augustine's Press, 2001.

Rychlak, R. J., *Hitler, the War, and the Pope*, Columbus, Mississippi: Genesis Press, 2000. A non-Catholic lawyer and professor at the University of Mississippi School of Law, now Pius's staunchest supporter, appends a twenty-seven-page attack on Cornwell's book to his own, adopting courtroom-style advocacy in treating the critics who followed.

Sánchez, J. M., *Pius XII and the Holocaust: Understanding the Controversy*, Washington, D.C.: Catholic University of America Press, 2002.

ARTICLES

Gumpel, P., "Pius XII As He Really Was," in *The Tablet*, February 13, 1999. This pre-Cornwell defense of Pius XII by the German Jesuit appointed by Pope John Paul II as the "independent judge"—the so-called relator—to assess the evidence for Pius's sainthood, and who issued an unequivocal yes, became the handbook for later defenders.

Dalin, D., "Pius XII and the Jews," in *The Weekly Standard*, February 26, 2001. A rabbi joins the defense, attempting to dismantle the critics' best evidence with the arguments of the Gumpel manual.

Madigan, K. "What the Vatican Knew About the Holocaust, and When," in *Commentary*, October 2001. The Harvard Divinity School professor tries to turn Dalin's demolition approach on the defenders—provoking the wrath of an overflow of letter-writers.

Katz, R., "Pius XII Protests the Holocaust," in *What If? 2: Eminent Historians Imagine What Might Have Been*, New York: Putnam, 2001 (anthology edited by Robert Cowley).

Goldhagen, D. J., "What Would Jesus Have Done? Pius XII, the Catholic Church, and the Holocaust," in *The New Republic*, January 21, 2002. A long review of the recent Pius XII books, and at the time a preview of his own.

INDEX

Weizsäcker, Ernst von (*cont.*)
  and response to Vatican editorial
    on deportation of Jews,
    115–16
  telegram of, 107, 108
Westphal, Siegfried, 151, 179, 230,
    231, 261
Wetjen, Lieutenant, 252
Wilhelmstrasse, *see* Foreign
    Ministry, German
Wilson, Henry Maitland, 140
Winter Line, 92, 95, 120–21
Wolff, Karl, 203, 231, 243, 255, 271
  papal audience with, 290–92, 305
Wolfsschanze, 229
Wolgast, Lieutenant, 204, 223
Wolkonsky, Princess, 50
Wollenweber, Karl Gustav, 103

women, as urban guerrillas, 90–91
"Women of Rome" leaflets, 184
women's demonstration, 194–95
Wood, George, *see* Kolbe, Fritz
World Jewish Congress, 343,
    344

Y

Yolanda of Savoy, 37
Yom Kippur, 84

Z

Zolli, Israel, 63, 333
Zuccotti, Susan, 136